Traveler's Guide to
Wildlife in Minnesota

Minnesota Department of Natural Resources
Division of Fish and Wildlife
Nongame Wildlife Program

Carrol L. Henderson
Andrea Lee Lambrecht
Joel Anderson
Bonnie Erpelding
Joan Galli
Katie Haws
Jeff Hines
Jack Mooty
Pam Perry
John Schladweiler
Jamie Schulz

11-24-98
To Gary,
Best wishes for success on your wildlife outings.
Carrol Henderson

Acknowledgments

As you may have guessed from the number of authors and volume of material included in this book, this project represents several years of cumulative team effort by the staff of the DNR's Nongame Wildlife Program and other cooperating wildlife enthusiasts who were determined to make this the best wildlife viewing guide in the nation.

Senior authors Henderson and Lambrecht wrote and edited major portions of text, but depended on the talents of the DNR Regional Nongame Specialists as co-authors to select the top 20 sites in their six DNR regions and to contribute a narrative for each site and featured species information. Since most of these specialists have worked in their regions since 1982, they are among the top experts in the state for selection of wildlife viewing areas. They deserve special acknowledgment and appreciation for their contributions to this book:

Northwest Minnesota:	Katie Haws
Northeast Minnesota:	Jack Mooty and Jeff Hines
Central Minnesota:	Pam Perry
Southwest Minnesota:	John Schladweiler and Joel Anderson
Southeast Minnesota:	Bonnie Erpelding and Jamie Schulz
Twin Cities Metro:	Joan Galli

Tracy Guthmiller, Jane Norris, Sue Wieseler, Scott Mehus and Matt Sprenger assisted with production of the regional accounts. Guest writers Kim Eckert and Dr. Harrison B. Tordoff contributed featured species sections on Hawk Ridge and peregrine falcons, respectively. Additional editing talent and support were provided by Holly Welch, Margaret Dexter, Chris Drassal, Steve Stucker, Bill Penning and Jan Welsh.

One of the greatest assets in this book is the extensive set of maps that help readers find areas easily and explore the sites with a minimum of confusion. Graphic designer Tom Klein of the DNR Natural Heritage Program provided monumental service in producing the 120 directional maps. The companion set of 120 site maps were prepared by Jean Miller of the graphics unit in the DNR Bureau of Information and Education with assistance from Debbie Sroka. Adele Smith, DNR graphics unit supervisor, directed the graphics work and coordinated map production with Tom Klein. Jean Miller also did the graphic design and layout for the book. Tom Baumann managed publication arrangements with Minnesota's Bookstore.

Carrol Henderson contributed most of the photos. Other photographers include Robert Dana, Jim Gerholdt, Katie Haws, Dave E. Heffernan (USFWS), John and Karen Hollingsworth, Andrea Lee Lambrecht, Stephen Maxson, Ron Morreim, Dr. Gary Nuechterlein, Jane Norris, Barney Oldfield, W. L. Penning, William Redig of the International Wolf Center, Lynn and Donna Rogers, Carl R. Sams II, A. B. Sheldon, Gary Tisher (USFWS) and Dr. Merlin Tuttle. All photos are the property of the respective photographers and may not be reproduced without permission.

Many DNR wildlife managers, state park managers, park resource specialists and naturalists, area foresters and conservation officers reviewed text and maps for their respective areas. Biologists and wildlife refuge managers of the United States Fish and Wildlife Service also helped review text and maps for their refuge lands.

This book has been developed and produced with funding from the Nongame Wildlife Checkoff on state income tax and property tax forms, the Reinvest in Minnesota Critical Habitat Matching Fund administered by the Legislative Commission on Minnesota Resources (environmental trust fund receipts from the state lottery), the National Fish and Wildlife Foundation, Wildlife Forever and the U. S. Fish and Wildlife Service.

About the Senior Authors...

Carrol L. Henderson, a native of Zearing, Iowa, has a bachelor of science degree in zoology from Iowa State University (1968) and a master of forest resources degree from the University of Georgia (1970). He did his graduate studies on the fish and wildlife of Costa Rica.

Henderson joined the Minnesota DNR in 1974 as the assistant manager for the Lac qui Parle Wildlife Management Area near Milan. In 1977 he became supervisor of the DNR's new Nongame Wildlife Program and has continued in that role to the present. During the past 21 years, Henderson has developed a statewide program for the conservation of the state's nongame wildlife and has had responsibility for planning and developing projects to help bring back bluebirds, bald eagles, peregrine falcons, river otters and trumpeter swans.

Henderson received the national Chevron Conservation Award in 1990, the 1992 Chuck Yaeger Conservation Award from the National Fish and Wildlife Foundation, the 1993 Minnesota Award from the Minnesota Chapter of The Wildlife Society, and the 1994 Thomas Sadler Roberts Memorial Award from the Minnesota Ornithologist's Union.

He has served as president of the Nongame Wildlife Association of North America, the Minnesota Chapter of The Wildlife Society, and the Minnesota Fish and Wildlife Employee's Association. His writings include *Woodworking for Wildlife, Landscaping for Wildlife, and Wild About Birds: the DNR Bird Feeding Guide.* He is a regular contributor of feature stories for *Birder's World* magazine. An avid wildlife photographer, Henderson has taken most of the photos used in his books and is the primary photographer for the 1995 book *Galapagos Islands-Wonders of the World.* His bird photography has received five national awards from *Wild Bird* magazine from 1995-1997. Experience in nature tourism helped provide Henderson with a valuable perspective for writing this book. He and his wife Ethelle have led over 20 nature tours to Latin America since 1987.

Naturalist and writer Andrea Lee Lambrecht has made wildlife watching a lifelong pursuit. From the grizzlies and belugas of Alaska, sharks and manatees of Florida, pronghorns and wapiti of Montana, bay-winged hawks and gray whales of the Baja to the wolves and bears of Minnesota, Lambrecht combines travel with her love of wildlife and the outdoors.

Further reflecting her professional career and personal lifestyle, Lambrecht has penned "Nature's Notebook", her weekly newspaper column, since 1986. It is a blend of educational, environmental and experiential concepts and events. Her column, feature stories and photographs appear in newspapers across the state, as well as in magazines and on public radio.

She is the recipient of an American Association of University Women professional advancement grant to publish a "Nature's Notebook" anthology. For her outstanding accomplishments in promoting environmental awareness via her column, she was an Environmental Quality Award nominee (professional category). Lambrecht also received the Richard Doerr Ecology Salute for exceptional contributions in conservation and ecology and been awarded three Audubon Society scholarships.

Since 1990 she has coordinated monthly DNR nongame wildlife segments for *Venture North*, a PBS television program. Additional work experience includes that of DNR nongame outreach liaison, fire information officer and park naturalist.

Lambrecht has been a judge for the Minnesota Conservation License Plate and the Migratory Waterfowl Stamp Competition.

As a University of Minnesota graduate Lambrecht holds a Bachelor of Science degree in Environmental Biology with an emphasis in interpretation.

Table of Contents

Carl R. Sams II

Introduction

Minnesota! The "Land of 10,000 lakes." "A great place to fish for walleyes." But there is much more to Minnesota than traditional travel brochures would have you believe. It is home to some of the most exciting wildlife species and stunning wildlife spectacles in North America.

On the edge of a northern lake, a cow moose stands belly deep in the water as her calf feeds on succulent lily pads. Overhead a bald eagle soars, chirping in defense of its nest in a white pine.

In Minnesota's northwest, great flocks of sandhill cranes trumpet as they lock their outstretched wings and float gracefully to earth. On the nearby grassland, male prairie chickens inflate bright orange air sacs on their necks, lower their heads, and "boom" with the classic ventriloqual sound that epitomizes the wildness of northern prairies.

Marshes and woodland swamps are home to muskrats, beavers, otters and mink; to wood ducks, northern pintails, canvasback, American white pelicans and western grebes. These wetlands are great travel destinations in the spring and fall. Springtime forests are alive with a rainbow assemblage of migrating warblers, scarlet tanagers, indigo buntings and rose-breasted grosbeaks.

C. Henderson

Minnesota's natural beauty is not limited to birds and mammals. There is a living collage of butterflies, moths, dragonflies, frogs, toads, turtles, and other hopping, flying, crawling and swimming creatures that offer the potential for endless hours of observation, photography and enjoyment.

Each species of native wildlife creates its own "spectacles" throughout the year during rituals of migration and courtship, feeding and rearing young. Some wildlife adventures are as close as your own backyard. Others might be at a DNR Wildlife Management Area, County or State Park or National Wildlife Refuge. Whether your quarry is a monarch or a moose, Minnesota's wildlands offer dozens of opportunities for wildlife viewing that can be matched to your budget, time and travel requirements.

Wildlife can provide exciting experiences and a sense of discovery that is fun to share with your family and friends. Whether you are looking at wildlife, photographing or sketching it or listening to the sounds of unseen creatures, wildlife tourism has become an increasingly popular hobby. It is a growth industry for resorts and chambers of commerce looking for business beyond the fishing season.

In 1991, the U. S. Fish and Wildlife Service estimated that 738,000 Minnesotans took trips for the primary purpose of seeing wildlife, and they spent about $182 million while on those outings. That does not include expenditures for binoculars, spotting scopes, field guides, cameras and film. In other words, this is a $200 million per year industry as well as a wonderful hobby. It is an industry that benefits from the protection and management of natural habitats without degrading or using up our natural resources. Public wildlife viewing areas can provide major economic benefits for local communities that wish to expand their appeal and the length of their tourism seasons.

The *Traveler's Guide to Wildlife in Minnesota* is for people who enjoy nature and all forms of wildlife. Bird guides have been written previously, but this book goes beyond birds. It is for birders, nature lovers, youth group leaders, teachers, conservationists, photographers and families who wish to experience a variety of wildlife and plant communities throughout the year.

This book identifies 120 "hotspots" where you have a reasonably good chance to see, photograph and enjoy some of the best wildlife concentrations in our state. It will give you some great new reasons to "Explore Minnesota". These locations have been selected by some of the state's best wildlife biologists—the Department of Natural Resources' Regional Nongame Specialists. Each specialist picked 20 sites within their work area. Since each biologist has worked in their work respective region for up to 14 years, they are very familiar with locations that are outstanding for their observation potential. This book is a chance for those biologists—Katie Haws, Jack Mooty (retired), Jeff Hines, Pam Perry, John Schladweiler, Joel Anderson, Bonnie Erpelding, Jamie Schulz and Joan Galli—to share their collective knowledge so you can see and enjoy the best of Minnesota's rich wildlife heritage.

How to Use This Book

We've tried to keep the book easy to use, yet comprehensive enough to enhance your wildlife watching experience. So to start with, see "Wildlife Lands Defined", then check out "Just a Little Respect", "Improving Your Chances", "For Your Comfort... Be Prepared" and "Binocular Basics". Since habitat in our state is ecologically diverse, we've also included a section entitled "Minnesota's Landscape Regions".

Wonder what wildlife watching opportunities exist in the dead of December? You'll be surprised—just read through "Wildlife in a Theater of Seasons" to get a feel for the delights available year-round.

Eagles, loons, moose and wolves often come to mind when people think of Minnesota wildlife, so these and a few other "popular" species are highlighted as "Featured Species". They're the appetizers on the book's menu.

Next, is the hearty main course—the wildlife watching sites. Because Minnesota is geographically large we've divided the state into six regions. In each region we focused on 20 sites.

The statewide map and listing on page 38, with regional division lines and site numbers, is a good place to get a preview of our selections. Sites are numbered starting in the northwestern Pines to Prairie corner and ending with site 120 in the Blufflands and Big Woods of the southeast.

A regional map and introduction precede the individual site accounts. Each site entry describes why the area is special, what wildlife you might see, the general terrain, best viewing time and field notes about the site and/or surrounding vicinity.

In addition, a directional map, Minnesota Highway Map coordinates, PRIM Area map reference, DeLorme *Minnesota Atlas & Gazetteer* grid numbers and supplemental written directions are included to help you find your way. Data regarding the maps are listed in "References and Resources" on page 317.

Since sites vary from a few acres to thousands of acres, the amount of detail we are able to provide on the site map varies. The idea is to show the entrance, parking and location of information, as well as some of the features, but not every trail, campground and amenity. Detailed maps are often available at the site or upon request.

Symbols are used to let you know what facilities and recreational opportunities each location offers. Keep in mind that changes, additions or restrictions may have occurred since we compiled the information, so verify beforehand any aspect critical to your visit. If you need more information, a contact address and phone number are provided.

There are a variety of public lands available for wildlife observation in Minnesota. Different patterns of land ownership give rise to different "acronyms" that we use to describe these areas like WMA, NWR and SNA. In the section entitled "Wildlife Lands Defined" you will become acquainted with the various types of wildlife lands, the kinds of facilities and activities associated with these areas and the abbreviations we use to describe them.

For those familiar with Minnesota, there is an "Alphabetical Site Listing" *following* site 120 on page 310.

In case you're looking for a particular bird, mammal, amphibian or reptile, browse the "Species List" on page 313. Minnesota animals classified as endangered, threatened or species of special concern were identified based on the July 1996 listing, which is subject to future revisions.

"References and Resources" include supplemental information on maps, bird check-lists, books, publications, computer connections, birding hotlines, organizations, other places to see Minnesota wildlife and the Minnesota Birding Network.

And now for dessert, you'll have to visit the great assortment of wildlife watching sites. We can't guarantee you'll see everything we've written about, but we hope you enjoy each adventure and find something special about each spot. Have fun! Bon appetit!

Wildlife Lands Defined

Understanding the abbreviations that deal with public and private wildlife lands in Minnesota.

Minnesota has had the benefit of land protection initiatives from a variety of state, federal and private agencies. This has resulted in thousands of acres of protected wildlife habitat that are generally open for wildlife observation and photography. However, the abbreviations often associated with these different kinds of areas may be confusing, and the rules pertaining to each type of area will differ.

State Areas

WMA. A Wildlife Management Area is purchased with funds from a surcharge on small game hunting licenses or donated to the Department of Natural Resources by private citizens. It is managed by the Section of Wildlife in the Department of Natural Resources. Hunting is allowed in season and special regulations may apply to specific WMAs. There are usually parking spots but no toilet facilities, camp sites or asphalt trails. There may be informal walking paths or field roads. See regulation signs at entry points. Eight large wildlife management areas like Lac qui Parle and Thief Lake have a headquarters building and a resident manager.

C. Henderson

Carlos Avery WMA

At most of these larger areas you can usually obtain a detailed unit map and a bird list during business hours. All are included in this guide. There are 23 smaller WMAs included in this book, but don't limit your exploration to those. There are over 1200 WMAs throughout Minnesota totaling more than 726,000 acres!

SNA. A Scientific and Natural Area is land donated to the Department of Natural Resources or purchased with funds appropriated from the Minnesota Legislature from bonding money or the Environmental Trust Fund. Many activities are restricted to maintain ecological integrity. Permits may be required to visit these areas. SNAs usually have a parking area but few other developments. There may be informal walking trails, but no resident manager or headquarters building. There are accounts for 16 SNAs in this book.

Natural plant and animal communities protected in SNAs require utmost care. To minimize human impact and facilitate preservation and research activities, do not remove any stakes, signs or other objects. They may be part of a research project. Don't make new trails and avoid walking in boggy, wet areas that are sensitive to the effects of foot traffic. Please do not remove any plants, animals or their parts. Thank you!

Federal Areas

WPA. A Waterfowl Production Area has been purchased by the U.S. Fish and Wildlife Service (USFWS) with funds derived from the sale of migratory waterfowl hunting stamps. They are open to the public but some portions may closed as sanctuaries. WPAs typically contain both wetlands and adjacent grassy nesting cover to benefit waterfowl. There are usually parking lots and boundary roads, but few other improvements like trails or toilet facilities, and no resident managers or headquarter buildings. There are 805 WPAs in Minnesota totaling 168,053 acres. Although none of these areas are included in the 120 sites described in this book, some of them offer some excellent wildlife viewing opportunities.

NWR. A National Wildlife Refuge is a large area of public land that has been purchased with federal funds generally for the benefit of migratory waterfowl and other wildlife. There are 11 national wildlife refuges in Minnesota totaling 268,185 acres. Some parts may be closed to hunting and public access to provide waterfowl sanctuaries. National wildlife refuges usually have a headquarters building and a resident manager and staff, including naturalists who conduct educational activities about wildlife. Seven NWRs are featured in this book.

Private Areas

TNC. This refers to The Nature Conservancy, which owns and manages a variety of natural reserves across Minnesota ranging from native prairies to unique habitats of the northern forests. These areas have been either donated to The Nature Conservancy or purchased with funds donated from private citizens and often matched from other sources. Uses on these areas are often restricted as they are on Scientific and Natural Areas. Read the signs at the entrance to TNC lands to learn of any special regulations that apply.

Just a Little Respect

Respect Private Property Ask First

While almost all sites are on public lands, a few are on property owned by individuals or organizations. It is imperative to respect all locations, but please pay particular heed to the generosity of those parties who allowed us to share their property with you.

In addition, private property abuts public sites, so searching for wildlife could cause you to unwittingly trespass. If you're wandering through an area, be alert for boundary markers and pay attention to the map to avoid trespassing. If for some reason you must tread on private property, ask permission ***first***. Trespassing without permission is not only unethical, in most cases it is also illegal.

It may be obvious, but please follow signs and obey the rules. This is especially true when it comes to animal-human encounters. Don't harass, pursue, touch or feed animals or remove them or their young from their habitat. Capturing that once-in-a-lifetime photo at all costs is certainly not worth trampling and tearing up the surroundings and disrupting or traumatizing the subject. Should you run across an animal truly in trouble, contact the nearest person in authority.

Disturbing nature may be harmful to the resource and usually is against the law. Leave feathers, eggs, nests or animals where you find them, and please do not pull or dig up plants or harvest firewood from any site.

Pets and wildlife don't mix. While we all love our pets, it's best to leave them at home when you're wildlife watching. If you're traveling with a pet, keep it safe in your vehicle, and be mindful of the time you are away and watchful of weather, such as increasing heat or cold, that may be harmful to your animal.

And lastly, be courteous to others you meet during your wildlife watching forays. *Remember...just a little respect goes a long way.*

Improving Your Chances

Bring binoculars, spotting scope or camera with a telephoto lens to get a better view of wildlife. It's best to avoid moving in for a closer look, which might flush an animal from a favorite perch, feeding area, den or nest.

Remember, you're not the only person out there looking for wildlife. Repeated human disturbance near nests or feeding sites causes animals to flee, leaving their young vulnerable to weather, predators or starvation. Even if you scare an animal only once, you add to the cumulative effect of repeated disturbances that may result in nesting failure or site abandonment.

Choose the right place to find the species you desire to spot. We picked sites across the state for their variety of wildlife watching opportunities, but some are known for particular species. For example, if sandhill cranes rank high on your list, check out Crane Meadows or Sherburne NWRs or the Mille Lacs WMA; if raptors will make your day, visit Hawk Ridge in the fall.

C. Henderson

Seasons are also a factor in successful wildlife watching. Owls are easier to spot during the winter, warblers are at their highest concentration in spring and seeing them is easier before the trees leaf out. Butterflies and black bears are best sighted in summer and waterfowl are wonderfully abundant during spring and fall migration. The "Wildlife in a Theater of Seasons" section on page 10, will give you a feel for year-round delights.

The hours around dawn and dusk are often the most visually productive. Look for mammals and birds then. Mid-day in spring, summer and fall will bring out many reptiles, amphibians and insects, so that's when you're more likely to see turtles basking on a pond log or butterflies pollinating flowers.

Once you're on site be alert, move slowly and quietly or find a place to sit. Be patient. Look near the edges of forests and fields for bluebirds, fox and deer; pond margins for raccoons, shorebirds and waterfowl; and treetops for orioles and cardinals.

Search for tracks in the mud or snow, gnawed saplings, freshly dug soil, den holes, scat, rub marks, nests, chiseled excavations in snags and other signs of wildlife. Watch all around you—look up for eagles and osprey, down for skinks and salamanders, under leaves for butterfly caterpillars and chrysalises and on tree bark for well-camouflaged tree frogs. Get the idea?

Setting your heart on spotting a particular species may lessen your overall experience if it does not cooperate. Broaden your hopes and you won't be disappointed. Invariably you will find something special, and perhaps even very unexpected, at each site. *Enjoy!*

Binocular Basics

"Look!", "Wow!" and exclamations of "Cool!", followed by cheers and grins are wonderful if you can share in the joy. However, if you can't see what others are seeing, you'll be disappointed. Looking at an otter, osprey or ovenbird is certainly delightful, but peering at their detail close-up is clearly better.

To enhance your wildlife watching, we recommend investing in a pair of good binoculars. There are too many models and manufacturers, as well as constantly changing technology, to provide a comprehensive commentary here.

Stephen Ingraham's "Better View Desired", a birding optics newsletter, and the National Camera Exchange's "Binocular & Spotting Scope Buying Guide" are two of the many resources to review before purchasing equipment. In addition, check out wildlife, birding and trade publications, outdoor recreation stores, optical retailers, the library, and one of the best up-to-the-minute references, the Internet, for excellent evaluations on binoculars to meet your needs.

Do not be fooled into buying "cheap" binoculars. You'll soon be discouraged by the relatively poor image quality and constant repair problems. Inexpensive binoculars may need to be replaced every couple years, so you will be much better off investing in a high-quality pair. After "sticker shock" wears off, keep in mind that a good pair of waterproof binoculars, well-taken care of, may easily last a lifetime.

For Your Comfort...Be Prepared

Weather

Minnesota's renowned ice box winters are just that—long and cold. Some Minnesotans refer to themselves as "the chosen, frozen people." Snow usually covers the ground from December through March. Despite the snow and cold, wildlife viewing for resident birds and mammals is very good. Snowshoes or cross-country skis will get you out in the woods. Even drives on rural roads offer wildlife watching opportunities, particularly at dawn and dusk.

Springtime conditions in April and May, before the trees and shrubs leaf out, are prime months for viewing birds and many other wildlife species.

Summer weather is pleasant with moderate daytime temperatures and cool nights. Rain is common with extended periods of cloudy, wet weather in June. Thunderstorms are typical in July and August, with temperatures generally in the 70–90 degree range.

Visibility is reduced during summer due to dense foliage. Some wildlife you'll be sure to experience at this time of year are insects. Mosquito, fly and tick season is June through August. Take adequate precaution with appropriate clothing and repellents.

September and October are the golden months of autumn. Leaf colors are spectacular from mid-September to early October. Weather is variable with everything from cold, wet days to sunny, warm Indian summer conditions. Wildlife viewing improves as the leaves color and drop. Leaf fall is usually complete by mid-October. November is our cloudiest month and the weather turns cold.

The "layered" clothing approach, wearing a combination of light, moderate and heavy weight clothes, works well here year-round. However, winter excursions should be undertaken using utmost planning and safety. If you're still unsure of how to dress for our environment, get tips from outdoor recreation specialists or outfitters.

Bacteria, Bug Bites, Berries, Black Bears and More....

Deer ticks, found throughout the state, may carry bacteria that cause Lyme and other diseases. Learn to identify the tiny deer tick. From spring through late fall, check your body and clothing for these miniature pests and follow proper methods for removing ticks adhering to your skin.

Be prepared to swat and spray in summer. However, some years are definitely better than others. If you're not bothered by bugs or their bites, a T-shirt and shorts with a touch of repellent may be all you'll need. In worst-case scenarios the uniform of the day may consist of a hat, long-sleeved shirt, pants and head net as well as insect repellent.

Only one plant—poison ivy—poses a potential problem for those individuals susceptible to its irritating oil. From spring until snowfall, avoid the woody stems, pale green berries and variable leaves of *Rhus /Toxicodendron radicans*. Here's a quick identification tip: "Leaves of three, let it be."

Lastly, a few words regarding possible dangerous encounters with wildlife. While many species are capable of inflicting injury to humans, only a handful may be life-threatening. To avoid an incident keep your distance from all wildlife. Do not approach moose, black bears, rattlesnakes or animals acting strangely (they may be rabid). The careless urge to take a close-up photo of a potentially dangerous animal like a moose or bear could threaten you or a family member. Use common sense.

Personal Safety

When going afield, whether in an urban park or in a remote northern wilderness, it is always best to explore the outdoors with a friend. This is a good way to avoid or reduce any significant health or safety problems that may arise.

Minnesota's Landscape Regions

Minnesota lies at the crossroads of four major landscapes—prairie grasslands, deciduous woods, coniferous forest and aspen parkland. Each region provides distinctive habitats for plants and animals and offers unique opportunities for seeing wildlife. As you explore Minnesota, be sure to include all four landscapes in your travels.

Prairie Grasslands

Remaining prairies and wetlands of western and southern Minnesota provide a historic view of the landscape as it appeared to pioneers—a vast sea of grass dotted with marshes that teemed with wildlife. Only 150,000 acres of native prairies remain out of an original 18 million acres. These habitats are vital to grassland and wetland species, which do not thrive in areas of intensive row-crop agriculture. While prairie grasslands may look monotonous at a distance, they are ecologically diverse, with as many as 200 plant species in a natural prairie. There is also a rich assortment of butterflies, birds and mammals.

Among the grassland birdlife is the prairie chicken, marbled godwit, upland sandpiper, dickcissel, bobolink, short-eared owl, northern harrier, red-tailed and Swainson's hawks and western meadowlark. Wetlands, also referred to as "prairie potholes", provide habitat for canvasback, northern pintail, blue-winged teal, northern shoveler, ruddy duck, Canada goose, sora and Virginia rails, marsh and sedge wrens, yellow-headed and red-winged blackbirds, American bittern, eared, western and pied-billed grebes and the magnificent trumpeter swan.

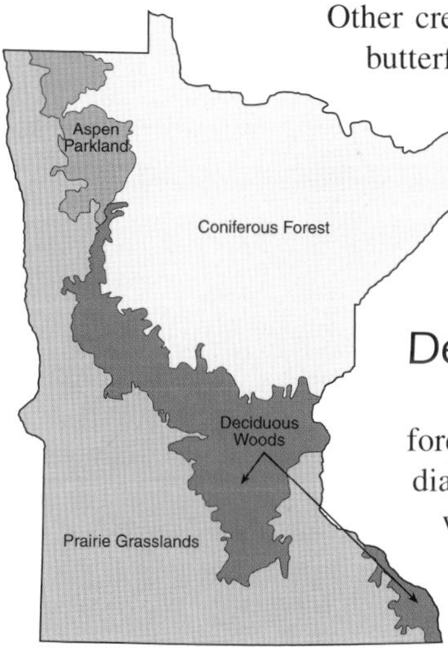

Other creatures of the grassland ecosystem are the regal fritillary butterfly, Richardson's ground squirrel, Dakota toad, coyote, red fox, badger, northern prairie skink, and red-sided garter snake. Hundreds of less conspicuous invertebrates like earthworms and ants help process organic materials of the prairie into the rich topsoil that characterizes this landscape.

Deciduous Woods

The deciduous woods landscape, also called the hardwood forest transition zone, extends from southeastern Minnesota diagonally to Becker County and Itasca State Park in northwestern Minnesota. "Deciduous" refers to trees that lose their leaves in winter. This ecosystem includes maple-basswood forest (sometimes called "Big Woods"), oak-hickory forest, aspen and birch forest, northern hardwood forest, lowland hardwood forest, and oak savanna. An excellent discussion of the ecology of these forest types is contained in the book *Minnesota's Natural Heritage* (Tester 1995).

While the prairie ecosystem is structurally simple with a layer of grass and flowering plants at ground level, the deciduous forest has more habitat niches for wildlife because of a more complex structure including an overstory of trees and an understory of smaller trees and shrubs. The ground-level, mid-canopy and upper-canopy plants all fulfill habitat needs for wildlife.

Birds of the hardwood forest are the tufted titmouse, scarlet tanager, eastern screech-owl, broad-winged hawk, barred owl, red-eyed vireo, wood thrush, black-capped chickadee, great crested flycatcher, ovenbird, northern cardinal, red-headed, downy, hairy and pileated woodpeckers, indigo bunting, brown thrasher and gray catbird. Northern forests with mixed conifers, as well as birch and aspen forest, also provide habitat for ruffed grouse, chestnut-sided warbler, white-throated sparrow, mourning warbler, song sparrow and yellowthroat.

Other wildlife includes gray and red fox, striped skunk and southern flying squirrel, opossum, white-tailed deer, cottontail rabbit, woodchuck, several species of bats, gray treefrog, spring peeper, wood frog, fox, bull, garter and hog-nosed snakes, and in a few places, the eastern timber rattlesnake. Distinctive insects are the luna, cecropia and polyphemus moths and monarch and tiger swallowtail butterflies.

Deciduous forests are also well-known for the wildflowers that bloom in early spring before the trees leaf out. These "spring ephemerals" include trillium, hepatica, Jack-in-the-pulpit, skunk cabbage, bloodroot, mayapple, wild ginger, trout lily, Dutchman's breeches, shooting star and spring beauty.

Aspen Parkland

A second type of deciduous woodland is actually a separate major landscape area generally associated with Canadian habitats—aspen parkland. It is characterized by open terrain that has wet prairie, sedge meadow, thickets of willow, alder and hazel, and scattered groves of aspen.

Big bluestem, Indian grass, prairie cordgrass, chokecherry, serviceberry and hazel shrubs are typical plants in aspen parkland. Distinctive wildflowers are northern gentian and prairie-fringed orchid. Moose, sandhill crane, sharp-tailed grouse, sharp-tailed sparrow, black-billed magpie and yellow rail all characterize this habitat.

Coniferous Forest

Coniferous forests cover roughly the northeastern 40 per cent of Minnesota. It is the largest of these four landscape areas. "Coniferous" refers to trees like pine, spruce and cedar that do not lose their needles in winter. As with aspen parkland, coniferous forests are more typically associated with Canadian flora and fauna. Much of the distinctive landscape of Minnesota's outdoors is provided by the northern coniferous forests. Types of coniferous forests include balsam-fir-white spruce, black spruce-feathermoss, white cedar, white and red pine, and jack pine. An excellent discussion of the ecology of northern coniferous forests is contained in *Minnesota's Natural Heritage* (Tester 1995).

There is a rich diversity of migratory warblers, flycatchers, vireos, woodpeckers and northern owls in these forests that draw nature lovers from throughout the country. Northern Minnesota provides some of the best habitats in the United States for many neotropical migrant warblers. Birds of this landscape are the magnolia, black-throated green, bay-breasted, blackburnian and Tennessee warblers, ovenbird, boreal chickadee, gray jay, black-backed woodpecker, golden-crowned kinglet, pine grosbeak and red-breasted nuthatch.

Peatlands in these forests provide a prehistoric natural habitat occupied by great gray and northern hawk-owls, spruce grouse, moose, timber wolf and bog lemming. Songbirds of the peatlands are the alder and yellow-bellied flycatchers, Lincoln's, clay-colored, LeConte's and swamp sparrows and Connecticut, yellow, yellow-rumped and palm warblers.

Each of the coniferous forest types has a distinctive assemblage of wildlife and plants that provide rich opportunities for nature study and wildlife photography.

Wildlife In a Theater of Seasons

Many people enjoy complaining about Minnesota's variable weather, especially the long, cold winters. However, the seasonal changes associated with the coming of spring, the warmth of pleasant summer days, the cool colorful days of fall and the frosty white beauty of the winter all provide a continuing reason to explore Minnesota's outdoors. Each season has unique opportunities for seeing, enjoying, and photographing the state's wildlife. Following is a sampler of what to expect as you plan a year of outdoor adventures in the "Land of 10,000 Lakes."

C. Henderson

Trumpeter swans

January–February

This is a great time to get out and enjoy the state parks where you can see wildlife near the nature centers and along the trails. You can enjoy the sight of creatures ranging from coyotes and ravens to downy woodpeckers and northern cardinals. Try "reading" the mammal tracks in the snow to decipher what animals are present—perhaps white-tailed deer, red fox, coyotes, or even bobcats, fishers and timber wolves.

Owls provide special opportunities for a winter outing, but the best locations for viewing them vary from year to year. It is best to call the Minnesota Ornithologist's Union "birding hotline" to get the current locations of snowy, boreal, great gray and northern hawk-owls. Open water sites along rivers and near power plants provide habitat for Canada geese, trumpeter swans and mallards. Look closely among them for common goldeneyes, American mergansers and American black ducks. Bald eagles provide great opportunities for viewing near Red Wing and Wabasha.

C. Henderson

Eastern bluebird

March–April

Lengthening daylight and gradually warming temperatures in March make it fun to seek out the first signs of spring. Early returning migrants include Canada geese, bald eagles and American kestrels. The first eastern bluebirds and wood ducks return in March to explore for nest boxes. Check out the major state and federal wildlife refuges for returning waterfowl. Some of the best waterfowl migration activity occurs from mid-March through mid-April. In wetland areas also look for river otters, beavers and muskrats. Wild turkeys can be seen courting in woodlands of southern and central Minnesota and the resonant call of sandhill cranes can be heard in larger wetlands of east central, northern and southeastern Minnesota. Make reservations for an April visit to an observation blind to experience the excitement of a prairie chicken or sharp-tailed grouse booming ground. Great horned owls are already nesting and raising their young and Canada geese and bald eagles begin incubating eggs by early April. Northern Minnesota visitors may also be treated to the sight of moose, deer, fishers or pine martens.

Spring weather in southern Minnesota arrives about two to three weeks earlier than along the Canadian border, so if you are anxious to experience signs of spring after a long winter, check out the prairie wetlands of the southwest and the hardwood forests and river valleys of the southeast. Mid to late April is a great time to look for the migration of shorebirds. Yellowlegs, willets, dunlins and other sandpipers can be seen on shallow wetlands and mudflats throughout the state. The last week of April should also bring in the first wave of early migrant songbirds like the yellow-rumped warbler, ruby-crowned kinglet and palm warbler.

May–June

The first half of May is the best time to enjoy the passage of warblers in their full breeding plumage. The spectacular colors add a dramatic highlight to spring in the forest—especially if you are lucky enough to see an indigo bunting, scarlet tanager or rose-breasted grosbeak. If you need an introduction to the migrating songbirds, check out the annual birding festival in

Detroit Lakes in mid-May. There are field trips and great opportunities to learn about wildlife from experienced guides. Contact the Tamarac NWR (site 15) for details.

Prairies are also memorable places to enjoy the sight of upland sandpipers, marbled godwits, bobolinks, dickcissels and many prairie butterflies and wildflowers.

Trumpeter swans may be seen nesting in an increasing number of marshes in central and northern Minnesota. The young, called cygnets, hatch by mid-June. If you visit northern regions in early June it is possible to continue to enjoy the drumming of ruffed grouse and spring birdsongs of the woodland because spring arrives later in northern Minnesota. Along the Gunflint Trail near the Canadian border in the northeast you can experience the beauty and variety of warblers in the last weekend of May in case you missed them earlier in the month in southerly locations.

Early to mid-June is an excellent time for canoe trips in the shallow prairie marshes to see abundant waterfowl and waterbirds. Grebes, coots, ducks, geese, swans, blackbirds, wrens, rails, minks, raccoons and an occasional otter can be seen on these wetlands. Many sites may be viewed from adjacent roads, but a canoe can provide access to even more memorable wildlife experiences.

C. Henderson

Common loon and chick

July–August

With summer in full swing, head for northern lakes where you can hear the haunting call of the loon at sunset and watch bald eagles and ospreys. Many popular lakes have wildlife that is accustomed to the presence of people, so they provide great viewing and photography opportunities. A quiet walk along a lakeshore or an early morning canoe trip might reveal a family of otters, great blue heron, eastern phoebe or kingfisher along the water's edge, as well as wood ducks, common goldeneyes, hooded mergansers, beavers, muskrats and black terns.

At Blue Mounds State Park (site 77) a July visit will be rewarded by the sparring of bull bison as they fight for mating dominance in the park's herd. The sparring is accompanied by grunting, bellowing and clouds of dust as the shaggy beasts collide, head to head. Don't limit your attention to the larger creatures. Prairies abound with native butterflies like the regal fritillary. Summer is also a good time to visit the Minnesota River dam in Granite Falls, the dam near Watson or the spillway on Marsh Lake near Appleton to see American white pelicans. They put on a great show as they fish and are incredibly graceful in flight.

By July, shorebirds are migrating through Minnesota en route to wintering grounds in Central and South America. Look for them on shallow wetlands and mudflats. The best areas will vary from year to year, so call the local DNR wildlife manager to learn which marshes might provide the best viewing. Sandhill crane families also begin coming out of their nesting marshes and into adjacent hayfields and grasslands in August. A late summer visit to St. Croix State Park (site 50) might yield a sighting of black bears feeding on berries along the trails.

September–October

The passage of summer is met with much enthusiasm by many Minnesotans. There are fewer mosquitoes! And there are some great destinations to enjoy the rainbow of fall colors and the wildlife. Perhaps the best-known attraction is the migration of birds of prey along Hawk Ridge in Duluth (site 36). Sharp-shinned and broad-winged hawks, peregrine falcons and other raptors can be seen from early September through mid-November, with the peak of migration in mid-September. Fall woodlands are also active in early September with migrating songbirds heading for wintering sites ranging from the southeastern states to Peru and Brazil.

The aspen parklands of northwestern Minnesota in September provide the opportunity to see staging areas of sandhill cranes, watch for moose and deer, listen for bugling elk, see the golden colors of fall tamarack trees and enjoy the migration of thousands of waterfowl at the major state and federal wildlife refuges. The waterfowl migration is not limited just to northwest Minnesota, however. Ducks, geese and swans may be seen at hundreds of state and federal wetlands and wildlife refuges throughout the state.
Late October is an excellent time for a journey down Highway 61 to see waterfowl in the Weaver Bottoms (site 110) in the Upper Mississippi River National Wildlife Refuge.

C. Henderson

November–December

Don't quit your wildlife excursions as the weather gets colder. The first couple weeks of November are best for again visiting Weaver Bottoms along the Mississippi River to see thousands of migrating tundra swans en route from arctic nesting sites to wintering grounds in North Carolina and Virginia. Stop by the city park at Red Wing (site 106), Read's Landing (site 107) south of Lake City and Wabasha to check for bald eagles. By early December it is also time to be dropping serious hints for the perfect Christmas gift-a new set of binoculars, spotting scope or camera with a telephoto lens so you can enjoy the wildlife next year even more.

Minnesota's Featured Species

Loons

The common loon is more than a bird in Minnesota—and it is more than the official "state bird." It is a symbol of pristine northern lakes, sparkling blue waters and forested Northwoods environments that provide us with both solitude and inspiration. With an estimated adult population of 12,000 loons, Minnesota has the largest number of these birds in the contiguous 48 states.

The common loon regularly nests in the state, but on rare occasions red-throated, Pacific and yellow-billed loons have all been seen. If you see one of these rare loons you are encouraged to report them to the Minnesota Ornithologist's Union (MOU) rare bird alert.

Loons are found in the northern two-thirds of the state, excluding the agricultural Red River Valley. Some loons nest south to lakes in the Twin Cities metropolitan area (sites 82 and 96) and west to Willmar.

Some larger lakes and chains of lakes have exceptional loon numbers. The Sportsmen's Club of Lake Vermilion does a count of loons on their lake every summer. In 1997 they counted 234 loons! To enjoy loons in a northern wilderness setting, consider a trip to the Boundary Waters Canoe Area.

Loons prefer clear lakes with plenty of small fish and a quiet bay with undeveloped shoreline for nesting. Lakes with high use of motorboats and personal watercraft can cause too much disturbance for loons to nest successfully. Adults or their chicks are sometimes run over by careless or irresponsible operators of boats or personal watercraft.

C. Henderson

Common loon

Loons may nest on lakes as small as 15 acres, but they usually nest on larger lakes. While nesting, they are territorial and will chase away other loons. A pair will defend an area up to 100 acres on larger lakes. Loons without chicks may visit lakes as small groups in mid to late summer.

Loons return from their wintering grounds in late March to late April, depending on when the lake ice breaks up. While some winter in the Gulf of Mexico along the Florida panhandle, others winter off the coast of North Carolina. Upon arriving in Minnesota, loons may stay in the open water of rivers until the lakes open up.

Nesting begins in May and most chicks hatch in early June. Loon nests are usually located at the water's edge on an island or point of land in a fairly wind-sheltered location. One or two eggs are usually laid. Late clutches and renesting efforts may cause some chicks to hatch in July. One of the most enjoyable sights on northern lakes is watching a pair of adult loons fishing and passing small minnows to their chicks. The chick frequently rides on the back of a parent—apparently to conserve body heat and to avoid being eaten by large pike or bass.

As loons migrate in fall, they frequently gather in great numbers on Mille Lacs Lake (sites 45 and 47). Several hundred loons may sometimes be seen from the western and southern shores during October. Parents migrate first and young loons leave later in the fall.

Minnesota's loon population appears stable, but there are several threats to loon survival. They include increasing harassment on nesting lakes by motorboats and personal watercraft, potential mercury contamination, poisoning from swallowing lead fishing sinkers that have been lost and loss of aquatic shoreline habitat that provides habitat for the fish that they eat. The Minnesota DNR Nongame Wildlife Program helps protect loons by doing annual surveys that involve more than 800 volunteers, through promotion of loon nesting platforms, promoting lakeshore restoration, banding projects and circulation of "loon learning trunks" in schools.

The best way to see loons is to explore a lake by canoe, boat or pontoon. Staying at a lakeshore campground or resort may provide opportunities to see loons during the day and hear their haunting calls at night.

When viewing loons, don't approach nests too closely. The adult may leave the nest and expose the eggs to predators like crows or gulls. If you approach a loon too closely on the water, especially if it is caring for a chick, it will rise up out of the water and patter across the surface with its feet in what is called the "penguin dance." If you cause a loon to do a penguin dance, you are disturbing it and should leave the area immediately. You could also cause parent loons to become separated from their chicks, exposing them to extended chilling in cold water and an increased chance of predation by large fish. By keeping your distance and using binoculars, you can enjoy loons without disturbing them.

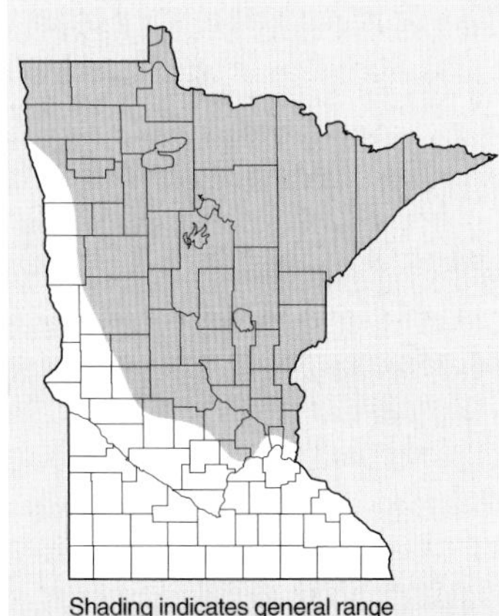
Shading indicates general range of loons within Minnesota

Sites to see loons

Northwest	1-6, 10-12, 15 and 17
Northeast	21-23, 26, 28-31 and 40
Central	45-47
Metro	82, 84, 85, 90, 92 and 96

Bald Eagles

Seeing a bald eagle may have been a once in a lifetime experience thirty years ago, but today seeing an eagle can occur while driving to work in Minneapolis or while standing by an office window in downtown St. Paul.

Eagles in Summer

Minnesotans enjoy the largest population of bald eagles in the 48 contiguous states except for Florida. There are more than 650 nesting pairs, and the numbers continue to climb by about 30 to 40 pairs per year. This is in contrast to only about 40 pairs in 1963.

One of the most dramatic changes now occurring with eagles is that they are pioneering from the Northwoods lake country and spreading to the Minnesota River in southwest Minnesota and the Mississippi River and its tributaries in the southeast. There are about 20 pairs nesting in the Twin Cities metropolitan area—some even in backyards!

C. Henderson

Bald eagle

If you wish to see eagles in summer it involves viewing them during the nesting season when they are more sensitive to disturbance. Eagles typically build their nests at the top of tall white or red pines or in tall aspen or cottonwood trees along the shorelines of lakes and rivers. On lakes heavily used by boats, it is usually acceptable to view the eagles from a boat at a distance because the eagles are accustomed to boating activity. Do not go ashore near the nesting tree. Such visits can disturb the eagles while they are incubating eggs or caring for young.

Eagles have become increasingly visible in summer during recent years. A pair of eagles nests by a parking lot in Bearhead State Park in northeast Minnesota. Lakeshore nests are fairly common at many of the larger lakes in northern portions of the state. If you check with resort owners, they will probably know if there are nests that can be viewed from a boat without disturbing the eagles. Good places to explore for eagles are along the Mississippi, Minnesota and St. Croix Rivers and in the Boundary Waters Canoe Area or on any of the larger northern lakes like Vermilion. The best way to enjoy eagles is at a distance is with binoculars or a spotting scope.

Eagles in Winter

The best time to look for bald eagles is from October through March. As winter approaches, eagles concentrate along the few remaining places where the lakes or rivers stay open during winter. As eagles migrate south from Canada and northern Minnesota they travel along the shore of Lake Superior and follow either the St. Croix or Mississippi Rivers south to southeastern Minnesota, Iowa and Illinois. In mild winters about 200 eagles winter along the Mississippi River near Red Wing, Read's Landing and Wabasha south to the Iowa border. During cold spells many eagles move farther south to open water along the Mississippi River between Iowa and Illinois.

More than 50 eagles congregate at Read's Landing on the Mississippi River along Highway 61 between Lake Pepin and Wabasha. This is directly across from where the Chippewa River in Wisconsin flows into the Mississippi River. The eagles gather there in early November. The best viewing is from mid-December through March. Use the pullout spots along the highway that are provided as scenic overlooks by the Department of Transportation. There is a lot of traffic along Highway 61 and it can be dangerous to stop along the highway shoulders. Best viewing times in winter are from about 9:00 a.m. through mid-afternoon.

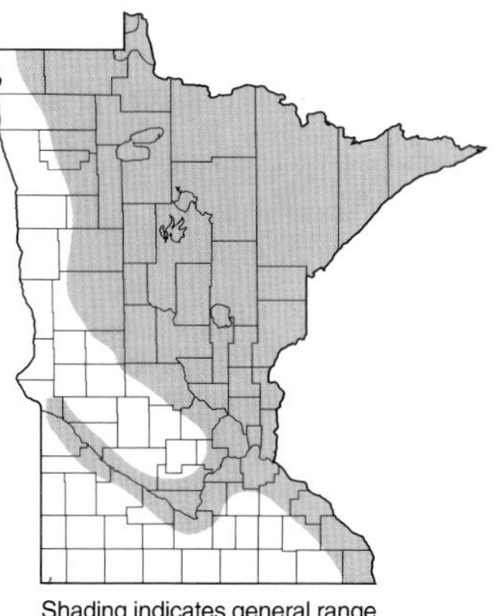

Shading indicates general range of eagles within Minnesota

Watch for eagles perched in trees on either side of the river. You will need binoculars or a spotting scope. Some will be all brown and quite hard to see without a spotting scope. Those are immature eagles that lack white heads and tails. Eagles do not get their white heads and tails until their fourth year. Look closely, however. Sometimes there are a few golden eagles wintering in the southeast.

Adult bald eagles are easier to see because their white heads stand out against the brown background of the trees. By mid morning the eagles make frequent flights over the water to catch fish or to attempt to catch the mallards, goldeneyes and common mergansers that are wintering there.

If you are a novice eagle watcher, you may wish to join a field trip. Following is a list of groups that may lead eagle-watching trips during the winter.

Sites to see summer eagles

Northwest	1, 3-6, 10-12, 15, 17 and 19
Northeast	21-23, 26, 27, 30-33, 36 and 40
Central	41, 42, 45-50, 53, 55, 58 and 60
Southwest	62 and 64
Metro	81, 82, 85, 91 and 98
Southeast	105,107, 115 and 120

Sites to see winter eagles

Southwest	62, 64
Metro	82, 91
Southeast	104, 105, 107, 110, 115, 117 and 120

Contact:

James Ford Bell Museum
10 Church St. SE
Minneapolis MN 55455
(612) 624-9050

The Raptor Center
1920 Fitch Avenue
St. Paul MN 55108
(612) 624-4745

Upper Mississippi River National Wildlife Refuge
51 Fourth St. E. Room 101
Winona MN 55987
(507) 452-4232

Eagle Watch Weekend
(first weekend in March)
Winona Convention and Visitors Bureau
P. O. Box 870
Winona MN 55987-0870
(507) 452-2272
(800) 657-4972

Eagle Watch, Inc.
P. O. Box 242
Wabasha MN 55981
(612) 565-4989
A viewing platform along the riverfront in Wabasha is open all winter, but there is a naturalist present from November through March each Sunday from 1:00-3:00 p.m. They sponsor the Soar With the Eagles event on the third Sunday in March.

Wabasha Chamber of Commerce
P. O. Box 105
Wabasha MN 55981
(612) 565-4158
(800) 565-4158

Whitewater State Park
RR 1 Box 256
Altura MN 55910
(507) 932-3007

Peregrine Falcons

The peregrine falcon offers the prospect of breathtaking encounters to wildlife enthusiasts who seek out this spectacular bird. The peregrine has been called "the ultimate bird" by those who are awed by its mastery of high speed flight and aerial maneuverability. It also represents a stunning conservation success story because of its return to Midwestern skies after being completely wiped out by pesticides in the 1950s and 1960s.

We can all take pride in the return of the peregrine because the state's citizens made it happen through their support of The Raptor Center, The Nature Conservancy, Bell Museum of Natural History, Minnesota Falconer's Association, Raptor Research Project and the Nongame Wildlife Checkoff on state tax forms.

The peregrine has demonstrated a dramatic ability to adapt from life on cliffs to high-rise "cliffs" of urban skyscrapers, power company smokestacks and the girders of bridges over large rivers. The cliffs along the Mississippi River in southeast Minnesota were the primary habitat of peregrines in presettlement days, but those now remain largely vacant because of predation by great horned owls.

C. Henderson

Peregrine falcon

Peregrine falcon restoration began in Minnesota in 1982. A total of 182 falcon chicks were released through 1994. The first nesting occurred in Minneapolis in 1987. The state population has grown to 19 pairs in 1997 and now equals or exceeds the historic population levels that occurred in the state. A total of 49 young were fledged in 1997—a modern era record!

The peregrine is a crow-sized raptor with a steel-gray back, buff-colored breast and black helmet-shaped head marking that extends down the side of the face and chin area. The female is slightly larger than the male. Prey consists of birds taken in flight and includes species ranging in size from nighthawks and blackbirds to pigeons and blue-winged teal.

A few peregrines may winter in Minnesota. Most return to their nesting sites in March to early April and are especially visible in the vicinity of their nesting locations from April through July when the young fledge. They are especially active and vocal in the early morning. For the best peregrine viewing, you will need binoculars and preferably a spotting scope. When viewed at a distance, your presence at a nesting area should not disturb the peregrines. Look for peregrines in the following places:

Northern Minnesota

1. **Grand Rapids/Cohasset.** A pair has nested on a tall smokestack at the Minnesota Power and Light Company plant in Cohasset, near Grand Rapids, for the past several years. Ask at the gate for permission to get a closer look.

2. **North Shore of Lake Superior.** Illgen City/Palisade Head. Reachable by car, this beautiful spot near Silver Bay is the place to see cliff-nesting falcons. Spend a hour or two around the cliff-top parking lot. Best times are early April during courtship and again in July when the young are flying. Ask Tettegouche State Park personnel at their headquarters a mile to the north for an update on the peregrines' status.

3. **Duluth.** Two pairs live in the Duluth Harbor—one on the Bong Bridge and the other on the Blatnik High Bridge. The Blatnik pair is most readily seen. Go to the Port Terminal and check the bridge structure beneath the roadway and the cement silo nearby.

Central Minnesota

4. **St. Cloud.** A pair of falcons nest on the water tower at the St. Cloud Correctional Facility along Highway 10 on the south side of St. Cloud.

Twin Cities Metropolitan Area

5. **St. Louis Park.** The nest box is on the 15th floor of the northeast corner of the 16-story Colonnade Building at the intersection of Highway 100 and I-394. The building is on the north side of I-394. The birds usually are easily seen on the high ledges of the Colonnade building or on the letters of the Park Sheraton Hotel sign across the highway.

6. **Minneapolis-Downtown.** The International Multifoods Tower has a nest box in the uppermost set of openings that overlook the Nicollet Mall. Good places to watch the falcons are the top floors of the IDS Tower and any upper floors of the Norwest Center, directly across the street from the nest. Nesting activity is sometimes displayed on closed-circuit video in the City Center main lobby.

7. **Minneapolis/St. Paul-Ford Bridge.** A pair of falcons nests on the west end of the Ford Bridge and may be seen frequenting both the north and south sides. To get to the Ford Bridge, take I-94 to St. Paul, and go south on Snelling Avenue to the Ford Parkway. Go west on the Ford Parkway and you will encounter the Ford Bridge where it crosses to Minneapolis.

8. **St. Paul-Mendota Bridge.** A pair of falcons began nesting here in 1996. Best viewing is from under the west end of the bridge in Fort Snelling State Park. The Mendota Bridge is the Mississippi River crossing for Highway 149 in St. Paul. From downtown St. Paul take West 7th Street west to the intersection where Highway 149 goes south to cross the river.

9. **St. Paul-Downtown.** The North Central Life Building's name is displayed in big letters on the east side of the building. The nest box is just under the letter "L" and is easily seen from the east.

10. **Bayport.** A nest box is on the middle catwalk on the southeast side of the NSP King Plant smokestack. It is best seen along Highway 95 along on the St. Croix River south of the plant or from the plant parking lot. Be sure to ask the gate guard for permission.

Southern Minnesota

11. **Rochester.** The Mayo Clinic nest box is on the east side of the Plummer Building in downtown Rochester. A television monitor is set up inside the building to view the nesting activity.

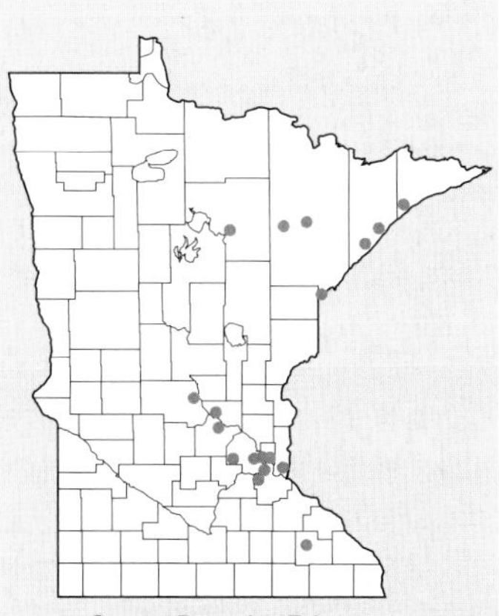

Current Peregrine Falcon Nesting Sites

Fall Hawk Migration

One of the great migratory spectacles in all of North America is the fall migration of birds of prey at Hawk Ridge in Duluth! If you visit Hawk Ridge on a good day you can see thousands of raptors passing the bluffs overlooking Lake Superior. Migrating birds are reluctant to cross large bodies of water, so they are "funneled" southward along the north shore of Lake Superior and then catch rising thermals of air as they pass Hawk Ridge. Large flocks of broad-winged hawks, or other species, may form great circling formations called "kettles" as they move southward. When weather conditions are favorable, the hawks pass by at eye level and provide exceptional opportunities to identify more than a dozen kinds of raptors.

Fourteen species of hawks are regularly seen on the ridge. Six others, including the Mississippi kite and gyrfalcon, are less common. Turkey vultures, bald and golden eagles and numerous owls also use this flyway corridor which serves a broad region of Canada and northern arctic regions.

The fall migration begins in mid-August as kestrels, sharp-shinned and broad-winged hawks head south. Migration is fairly slow in August but picks up in September. There is usually a peak of hawk movement between the 15th and 25th of September, but substantial movements of raptors continue through late October. Migration continues into December with the last of the eagles, northern goshawks and red-tailed and rough-legged hawks.

C. Henderson

Raptor biologist Kim Eckert, right, and friends at Hawk Ridge.

October is an excellent time to visit Hawk Ridge because that month is highlighted by good numbers of northern goshawks, impressive "kettles" of soaring red-tailed hawks as well as bald and golden eagles. There is also an intriguing variety of other unusual birds in the vicinity—boreal chickadees, Bohemian waxwings, northern shrikes, snow buntings, rusty blackbirds, Lapland longspurs, snow geese and sandhill cranes.

The best days for impressive hawk flights are characterized by cold fronts with winds from the northwest or west. On most days, hawks begin to fly a couple hours after sunrise and the activity slows by mid-afternoon. Because of the unpredictability of weather patterns, only a few days yield massive movements of raptors. Don't expect to see the sky filled with hawks on every visit, but you can always look forward to an interesting variety of birds.

Fun and festive, Hawk Watch Weekend takes place in mid-September. It is intentionally scheduled to coincide with the peak migration of broad-winged hawks. The three-day annual event features educational programs, field trips, nature hikes and guest speakers. It is also possible to see raptors in hand being briefly displayed by biologists who operate the Hawk Ridge banding station. The banding station itself is normally off-limits to the public without prior arrangements.

If you visit Hawk Ridge on weekends during September and early October there will be a naturalist on hand to answer questions and help in identifying raptors.

You may wish to join the "Friends of Hawk Ridge" to receive their very interesting newsletter and migration summaries for annual dues of $15. Use the contact address to correspond.

To reach Hawk Ridge: From Highway 61/London Road, turn up 45th Avenue East (43rd or 47th will also work) to its end at Glenwood Street. Turn left on Glenwood and go 0.5 mile to Skyline Parkway at the top of the hill. Then go one mile on Skyline Parkway to the Main Overlook. See the map for site 36 on page 120.

Sites to see hawks

Northeast	29
Central	50 and 60
Southwest	62 and 64
Southeast	105

American kestrel

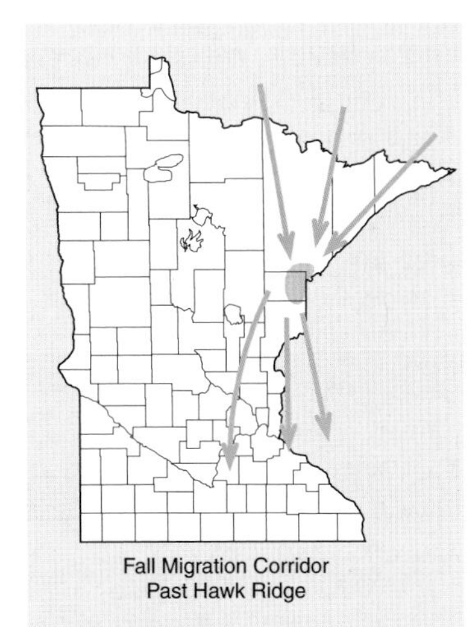

Fall Migration Corridor
Past Hawk Ridge

Contact:

Hawk Ridge Nature Reserve
Duluth Audubon Society
c/o Biology Department
University of Minnesota
Duluth MN 55812

Northern Winter Owls

Among Minnesota's most sought-after birds are owls of the boreal forests and tundra that sometimes winter in the state. The great gray, boreal and northern hawk-owl nest across boreal regions of Canada, the Northwest Territories and Alaska. A few even nest in northern Minnesota. Snowy owls nest in treeless tundra of northern Canada, Alaska and the Northwest Territories. These birds depend on prey whose numbers fluctuate greatly from one year to the next. The populations of voles, lemmings, snowshoe hares and other rodents fluctuate according to a general ten-year wildlife cycle, which may also have three-year population peaks within the ten-year cycle. When prey is abundant, the owls stay in northern regions and few are seen in Minnesota during the winter.

When prey is scarce, the owls move south to Minnesota. Dozens of these owls may be seen in the state during some winters—even south to the Twin Cities and southern Minnesota. Snowy owls disperse widely and may be encountered throughout the state including agricultural areas of southwestern Minnesota. The other three owls are more closely tied to forested habitats.

C. Henderson

Snowy owl

At a time that the snowy landscape may seem devoid of life, the quest to see and photograph these owls heats up and draws persons from throughout the United States. One appealing characteristic of great gray, boreal and northern hawk-owls is that they can often be approached very closely because boreal wildlife species typically show no fear of humans.

Boreal owls are usually encountered in the northeastern counties of St. Louis, Lake and Cook, and in coniferous forests of Roseau County in the northwest. Great gray owls are similarly found in Roseau County. They nest there in the summer and are frequently seen in the winter in the Lost River State Forest along State Highway 310 just south of the Canadian border. Great grays are also encountered in St. Louis, Lake and Cook Counties south to Aitkin County. They are particularly well-known from Pietz's Road in Aitkin County and the Sax-Zim tamarack bog of St. Louis County (site 34). The northern hawk-owl is a diurnal species. It is found in coniferous forests, tamarack bogs and peatland habitats of northwestern Minnesota like those in the Red Lake Wildlife Management Area (Site 4) and the Red Lake Peatland SNA (Site 7). They are encountered east to the Sax-Zim bog of St. Louis County and to northern Aitkin County. Snowy owls winter regularly in the Duluth harbor, but are very erratic in their occurrences elsewhere.

In some years, like early 1997, many owls moved south of their usual northern wintering sites and were even found in woodlots and parklands of the Twin Cities. A boreal owl stayed for weeks at the Springbrook Nature Center in Fridley and was seen by over a thousand visitors from as far away as California. A northern hawk-owl spent over a month in trees overlooking a meadow and residential area in nearby Blaine. Three great gray owls wintered in open fields and scattered trees and woodlots near Stillwater. In other words, they were totally unpredictable. The best way to keep up with their movements and current wintering sites is to call or e-mail the numbers under the contact information.

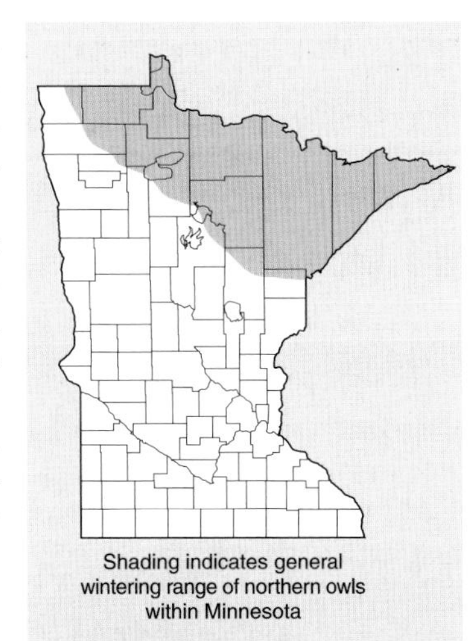
Shading indicates general wintering range of northern owls within Minnesota

Sites to see northern owls

Northwest 1, 4 and 7
Northwest 29 and 34

Contact:

Duluth and North Shore Birding Hotline
(218) 525-5952

Statewide Birding Hotline
(612) 780-8890

Minnesota Birding Network
http//:www.skypoint.com/members/dac/mnbird.html

C. Henderson

Great gray owl

Sharp-tailed Grouse

The sharp-tailed grouse is a member of the grouse family and is characteristic of "brushland" habitats of northern Minnesota. At one time a common bird of the state's prairies, sharp-tailed grouse have declined significantly due to changing habitat conditions. Reasons for their decline include large scale land conversion, succession of brushlands into forest, reforestation of brushland habitats and an absence of fires that tend to maintain brushland.

Over 200 of their ritual-type dancing grounds are still known in 13 counties of northern Minnesota. They are surveyed by DNR wildlife managers every year. As a game bird they are popular among hunters who use pointing dogs to locate them during the fall hunting season. The annual harvest of sharp-tailed grouse has declined from over 100,000 in the 1940s to about 5000 in recent years.

The range of sharp-tailed grouse extends from Kittson County in the northwest to St. Louis and Aitkin Counties in eastern portions of the state. This range includes two distinct populations which are shown on the accompanying map. Scattered populations are found south to Sherburne County. The range in the United States includes the prairies and plains of Montana, the Dakotas, Nebraska and Colorado, as well as Minnesota and Wisconsin.

These grouse are about the size of a hen pheasant, with a sandy-brown mottled body that is lightly speckled with brown on the belly. In contrast, a prairie chicken has a heavily-barred breast and it is darker brown above. The males have purplish neck sacs that are inflated during the courtship displays. Their tailfeathers all end as a pointed tip and this is the feature that gives them their name. In contrast, a prairie chicken has a squared-off tip to its tail.

The vegetarian diet of this grouse is comprised of items like bearberry, rose hips, wild buckwheat, labrador tea, blueberry and leatherleaf.

Although it is possible to see sharp-tailed grouse in brushlands as they fly from night roosting sites to daytime feeding areas, the most memorable way to experience them is to watch at close range from a blind on one of their spring dancing grounds, called "leks." Leks are on open grassland or old field sites that are usually slightly higher than the surrounding countryside. Males fly to the lek before sunrise and begin their elaborate dancing displays to attract the hens. The dancing continues until about 7:00 or 8:00 in the morning. It can be observed from March through May, with a peak of activity in April. The birds are most active on days with little wind.

C. Henderson

Mounted specimens of a prairie chicken (left) and sharp-tailed grouse (right) showing differences in breast barring.

The courtship dance includes cackling and cooing by the male, a rapid pattering of feet as it rotates its body and a rattling of wing quill feathers on its outspread wings. The neck sacs are inflated, the head is extended forward, the tail is pointed skyward. The dance is highlighted by leaps into the air among fighting males as they compete for prime territory in the lek. Hens wander throughout the lek and eventually select a mate. After mating, they nest in the nearby grasslands. The nest contains about 12 olive, buffy or brownish eggs, which hatch after 23 to 24 days. The precocial young leave the nest shortly after hatching.

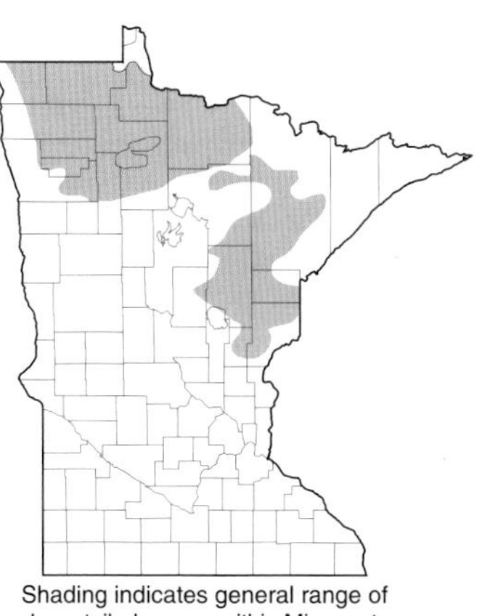
Shading indicates general range of sharp-tailed grouse within Minnesota

Sharp-tailed dancing grounds should be visited cautiously to make sure they are not disturbed during the dancing process. The best way to watch sharptails is from a "blind" that has been previously placed on the lek. Schedule your visit so you are in the blind by 4:00 am.

Several blinds are available at no charge to the public at various locations. The contact wildlife managers and their phone numbers are shown here. Reservations are mandatory and issued on a first-come, first-served basis, so book your reservations well before the dancing season begins in March.

For more information about Minnesota's sharp-tailed grouse, you can join the Minnesota Sharp-tailed Grouse Society at P. O. Box 16074, St. Paul, MN 55116 (phone 612-698-9358). Membership fees are $5 per year.

Sites to see sharp-tailed grouse

Northwest	1, 4, 5 and 7
Northeast	25, 34 and 39
Central	45 and 46

Contacts:

Red Lake WMA
Box 100
Roosevelt MN 56673
(218) 783-6861

Thief Lake WMA
HCR Box 17
Middle River MN 56701
(218) 222-3747

DNR Area Wildlife Office
123 Main Ave. N.
Thief River Falls MN 56701
(218) 681-0946

DNR
Wildlife Research Office
1201 E. Hwy 2
Grand Rapids MN 55744
(218) 327-4432

DNR Area Wildlife Office
P. O. Box 138
Aitkin MN 56431
(218) 927-6915

DNR Area Wildlife Office
2005 Hwy 37
Eveleth MN 55734
(218) 744-7448

DNR Area Wildlife Office
1604 Hwy 33 S.
Cloquet MN 55720
(218) 879-0883

DNR Area Wildlife Office
P. O. Box 398
Hinckley MN 55037
(320) 384-6148

Greater Prairie Chickens

The greater prairie chicken is a member of the grouse family found in Minnesota's tallgrass prairie and northern grasslands. The prairie chicken has a rich history associated with our state's original fauna, with native American traditions and with our pioneer settlement era. The prairie chicken has survived dramatic changes in the landscape and is a distinctive symbol for conservationists working to preserve remaining prairies.

The original grouse of the state's prairies was the sharp-tailed grouse. It was referred to by pioneers as the "prairie chicken" in the accounts of early explorers. As the vast prairies were plowed up to create cropland, the new mixture of grassland and scattered fields became ideal habitat for the greater prairie chicken. Sharp-tailed grouse declined as prairie chicken numbers exploded throughout the Midwest during the late 1800s and early 1900s. As the percentage of remaining grassland declined, the habitat eventually became unsuitable for greater prairie chickens as well. Today, only about one-tenth of one percent of the original prairies remain. Northwest Minnesota harbors some of the largest remaining tracts of tallgrass prairie in the Upper Midwest, and those grasslands support some of the best remaining populations of prairie chickens.

Stephen J. Maxson

Greater prairie chicken

Populations once ranged from the Dakotas east to Michigan, with additional subspecies ranging east to Massachusetts and south to Texas. The eastern subspecies, known as the heath hen, is now extinct, and the subspecies found on the Texas coast called the Attwater's prairie chicken is on the verge of extinction.

Minnesota's prime prairie chicken range is along the eastern margin of the Red River Valley in northwest Minnesota. Some remaining prairies are found on the beach ridge habitats of Glacial Lake Agassiz. Gravelly and sandy soils of the old beach ridges were too poor for farmers to raise crops, so many native plants and wildlife species were preserved there as the remainder of the countryside was converted to croplands. Prairie chickens are now found primarily in Polk, Mahnomen, Norman, Clay, Ottertail, and Wilkin Counties. A second remnant population continues to hold out in Hubbard, Cass and Wadena Counties.

Prairie chickens are pheasant-sized birds with heavily barred markings of brown, cinnamon and pale buff. The tail is short and more squared-off than that of the sharp-tailed grouse. In flight they alternate between a rapid wing-beat and a gliding pattern. Males have a fleshy orange eye comb, dark tail, and elongated neck feathers referred to as "pinnae." This is the source of one of their nicknames—pinnated grouse. These long neck feathers are raised during the courtship display. They also inflate large orange neck sacs during the display. There is one on each side of the neck—slightly larger than a hen's egg. Females are similar but have more barring on the tails and lack the neck sacs.

Annual counts are made on prairie chicken booming grounds to determine population trends. In 1988 a total of 492 males were counted on 66 booming grounds and in 1996 the count had increased to 1447 males on 142 booming grounds. The state population is estimated to be over 3000 birds. Prairie protection and management efforts by The Nature Conservancy, the U. S. Fish and Wildlife Service, Minnesota Prairie Chicken Society and the Department of Natural Resources, as well as the restoration of grasslands through the federal Conservation

Reserve Program, have all helped restore prairie chicken numbers.

The best way to experience prairie chickens is to watch them from a blind on their booming grounds. Most displaying occurs from late March through April. Each courtship area, called a "lek," covers several acres of bare ground on a prairie or cropland site adjacent to a prairie. From eight to 11 males occupy a typical booming ground. The first males fly to the lek about 30 minutes before sunrise and display for two to three hours. Each male vies for the best "territory" within the lek, with each territory covering about 300 square yards.

Males lower their heads, slightly spread their wings, erect their pinnae and inflate their air sacs. Amid much strutting, cackling, sparring and cooing, they emit an enormous ventriloqual sound that has been likened to the name "Old Muldoon." The sound can be heard up to two miles away. As males display, females enter the grounds and wander among the males to pick their mate. After mating, hens nest in nearby grasslands. They lay about 15 eggs in a typical nest and the eggs hatch after about 25 days.

It is no accident that the state's best prairie chicken populations occur north of the range of ring-necked pheasants. Pheasants are nest parasites, like cowbirds, and lay their eggs in the nests of prairie chickens. Pheasant eggs frequently hatch before the prairie chicken eggs, so the hen raises pheasants instead of her own chicks. Prairie chicken populations tend to die out where they compete with pheasants in the same habitat.

You can learn more about prairie chickens by joining the Minnesota Prairie Chicken Society at P. O. Box 823, Detroit Lakes, MN 56501. The annual dues are $10. They have a newsletter and an annual meeting each spring.

Several public observation blinds are maintained during the spring on booming grounds. There is no fee, but reservations are mandatory and are filled on a first-come, first-served basis. Reservations need to be made with one of the contact persons listed here. Each person maintains different blinds. (You will need to be in your blind at least an hour before sunrise to avoid scaring the prairie chickens off the area.)

Sites to see prairie chickens

Northwest 1-9, 13 and 14

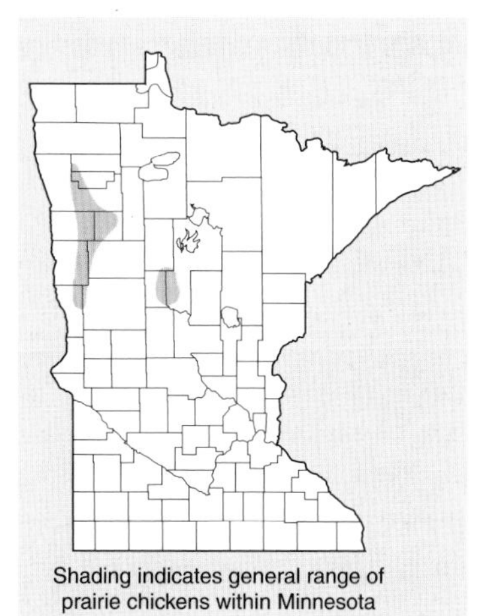

Shading indicates general range of prairie chickens within Minnesota

Contact:

DNR Area Wildlife Office
203 W. Fletcher St.
Crookston MN 56716
(218) 281-6063

DNR Area Wildlife Office
1221 Fir Ave. E.
Fergus Falls MN 56537
(218) 739-7576

DNR Area Wildlife Office
301 Grove St.
Park Rapids MN 56470
(218) 732-8452

Wildlife Manager
Cass County
Pine Mountain Professional Building
Backus MN 56435
(218) 947-3338

Director of Stewardship
The Nature Conservancy
RR 2 Box 240
Glyndon MN 56547
(218) 498-2679

Tundra Swans

Each fall the Mississippi River near Winona features one of the greatest waterfowl spectacles in the Midwest—the staging of tundra swans en route to wintering areas on the East Coast. These huge white swans are among the most impressive of all native waterfowl. Adults are pure white and have a six-foot wingspread. Immatures are light grayish to brownish. The swans usually migrate in large flocks of up to 50 or 60 birds.

Large concentrations of swans start arriving at the Weaver Bottoms (site 110) along Highway 61 in mid-October and stay until late November or when an early blizzard forces them out. Tundra swans begin migration from nesting grounds on the Alaskan and Canadian coasts near the Arctic Circle. They cross the Canadian prairie provinces, North Dakota and northern Minnesota, and turn east in southern Minnesota. Many swans may be seen flying high over the Twin Cities in November. They stop to rest and feed in shallow wetlands and bays of the Mississippi River before flying eastward to the coasts of Virginia and North Carolina.

The wetlands where tundra swans stop in the Weaver Bottoms are protected as part of the Upper Mississippi National Wildlife and Fish Refuge. You can see thousands of swans on a late fall trip to the Weaver Bottoms and surrounding area, including Rieck's Lake Park on the Wisconsin side of the River. The Weaver Bottoms area is a traditional waterfowl resting spot that has been rich in aquatic plants for ducks, geese and swans to feed on.

From mid-October through mid-November the Weaver Bottoms are also an excellent place to see Canada geese, northern shovelers, canvasbacks, gadwalls, northern pintails, mallards, American black ducks, blue-winged and green-winged teal, redheads, American wigeons, buffleheads, lesser scaup, wood ducks and a few snow geese. Bald eagles frequent the area as they search for dead or injured waterfowl.

The Weaver Bottoms marshes are approximately 120 miles south of the Twin Cities on Highway 61. The main bay where swans are visible is immediately south of where the Whitewater River crosses under the highway and empties into the Mississippi River. Stopping along Highway 61 can be dangerous because of high volumes of traffic and narrow shoulders.

C. Henderson

Tundra swans

For a safe view of the bay, go 1.75 miles south of the intersection where Highway 74 intersects with Highway 61. There is a rather inconspicuous gravel road on the west side of Highway 61 that turns abruptly right and turns back to the north, up a short hill, to a small parking area. For current information on the swan migration, contact the U. S. Fish and Wildlife Service.

Each fall the Winona Convention and Visitor's Bureau sponsors a Swan Watch Weekend at the Weaver Bottoms in early to mid-November. Naturalists with spotting scopes are present to enhance your viewing experience during this special weekend.

A second spot to check for swans is at Prairie Island in Winona. Take Huff Street toward the river where it becomes Riverview Drive. Stay on Riverview Drive, following the river for 1.5 miles. At the junction with Prairie Island Road turn right. Viewing is best at the dam spillway by the edge of Latsch Prairie Island Park. Further down Prairie Island Road you may view swans at the U. S. Fish and Wildlife Service Verchjota Landing Public Water Access.

Another great spot to see tundra swans at close range is across the river at Rieck's Lake Park which is two miles north of Alma, Wisconsin on Highway 35. A viewing platform is staffed by volunteers who provide viewing scopes and binoculars during peak periods of the migration. For up-to-date information on this site, call the Reick's Lake Volunteers at 608-685-4249.

Sites to see tundra swans

Northwest	1, 3, 5 and 6
Central	45
Southwest	62 and 64
Metro	82 and 91
Southeast	110 and 111

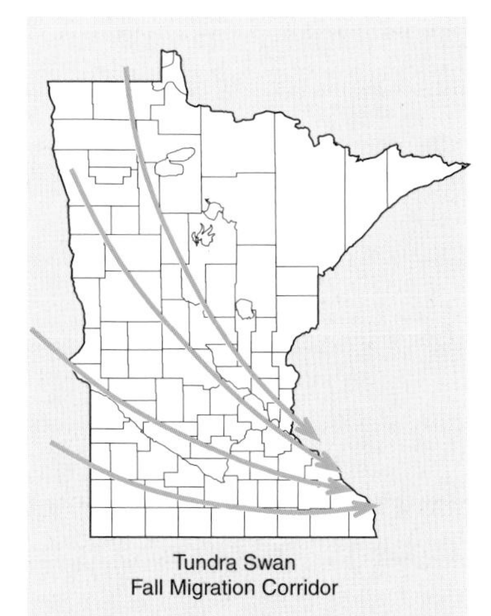

Tundra Swan
Fall Migration Corridor

Contact

U. S. Fish and Wildlife Service
51 East 4th St.
Winona MN 55987
(507) 452-4232

Winona Convention and Visitors Bureau
168 West 2nd St.
P. O. Box 870B
Winona MN 55987-0870
(507) 452-2272
(800) 657-4972

Trumpeter Swans

The magnificent trumpeter swan, North American's largest waterfowl species, is one of Minnesota's wildlife success stories. These huge white birds were totally extirpated from the state in the nineteenth century by pioneer settlers. Trumpeter swans represented a lot of fresh meat to a pioneer family. Unfortunately, the swans were so conspicuous that they were among the first wildlife species to be completely eliminated from Minnesota. They were all gone by 1890. By the 1930s, the swan population had declined to only 69 swans in the lower 48 states. Those birds were in remote lakes and wetlands of the Yellowstone National Park region.

Trumpeter swans stand about three-and-a-half feet tall and have a seven-foot wingspread. Adults are all white with black bills and feet. They have a characteristic red edging on their lower bill. Trumpeters weigh from 20 to 35 pounds. Tundra swans can be confused with trumpeter swans, but they are smaller and weigh from 12 to 20 pounds. They are also white with a black bill and feet but do not have the red edging on the lower bill, and about 80 percent of tundra swans have a yellow "teardrop" marking on the black skin in front of their eyes.

C. Henderson

Trumpeter swans

Tundra swans, formerly called whistling swans, do not nest in Minnesota. While tundra swans are usually seen migrating as large flocks, trumpeter swans tend to stay in family groups in their summer nesting areas until late fall. Then they move to wintering sites along the Ottertail River northeast of Fergus Falls, the Mississippi River below the power plant at Monticello and to scattered open water sites in Missouri, Kansas, Oklahoma and Arkansas.

Trumpeter swans begin nesting in May and lay from two to eight eggs. The nest may be on a large pile of vegetation that they build in a shallow marsh or it may be on top of a muskrat or beaver lodge. They defend a territory of up to 150 acres against other trumpeter swans, so most nesting marshes only support one pair.

The eggs take about 34 days to hatch and most hatching occurs in early June. The parents are very protective of their cygnets, and in Alaska they have even been observed chasing Alaskan brown bears from their nesting sites! The young migrate south with their parents, spend the winter with them, and return north with their parents in the spring. The cygnets are silvery gray in contrast to the white adults. Once the swans return in the spring, the young are chased off and the adults use the same nesting area as in previous years. Subadults begin pairing off in their third year and usually begin nesting at four years of age.

Hennepin Parks began a restoration project in the 1960s, and those were followed by expanded efforts of the Nongame Wildlife Program in 1982. The Nongame Wildlife Program obtained 50 trumpeter swan eggs each year from the nests of wild swans in the Minto Flats west of Fairbanks, Alaska from 1985–87. The eggs were transported in incubator suitcases back to Minnesota, hatched in incubators and reared in captivity to the age of two years.

Additional young swans were donated by the Minnesota Zoo in Apple Valley, and the Tulsa, Brookfield, Alaska and Topeka Zoos.

From 1987 through 1997, a total of 259 trumpeter swans have been released by the Department of Natural Resources. Most of the birds were released in the vicinity of the Tamarac National Wildlife Refuge northeast of Detroit Lakes. Supplemental releases have been made in northeast Minnesota and at Heron Lake in southwest Minnesota in cooperation with the North Heron Lake Game Producer's Association and the Red Rock Sportsmen's Club

Trumpeter swans have successfully adapted to the wild. There are now at least 35 nesting pairs in the state. The total statewide population is nearly 400 birds. Over 140 cygnets were hatched in the wild in 1997.

The Department of Natural Resources' swan restoration effort is funded by donations to the Nongame Wildlife Checkoff on state tax forms. When you see a trumpeter swan, it is a wild reminder of how important the Checkoff has been in helping Minnesota's wildlife. It provided the means and the hope that Nongame Wildlife Program biologists needed to carry out this innovative and ambitious project. Other midwestern states have followed Minnesota's lead and have initiated trumpeter swan restoration projects, including Michigan, Iowa, Wisconsin and Ohio.

Trumpeter swans are difficult to see in the nesting season. In northwest Minnesota they are most abundant at the Tamarac National Wildlife Refuge (site 15). Check with refuge personnel to learn where they can be seen without disturbing the swans. There is usually a pair of swans nesting near the refuge headquarters.

One of the most visible nesting pairs of swans can be seen in May and early June about six miles north of Park Rapids on the west side of Highway 371 on the marsh that is on the south side of the Summerhill Farms craft stores and restaurant. The swans nested in this marsh in 1996 and 1997. The swans hatched six young in 1997. The nesting mound can be viewed from the south end of the Summerhill Farms parking lot.

Check with personnel at Hennepin Parks to learn of the best summer and winter viewing opportunities at the Crow Hassan Park Reserve (site 84), Elm Creek Park Reserve (site 85) and Carver Park Reserve (92). They can also provide details on how to join the Trumpeter Swan Society. Most other wintering sites except on the St. Croix River at St. Croix State Park (site 50) and Wild River State Park (site 60) are on private land and are not accessible to the public .

Sites to see trumpeter swans

Northwest	2, 14, 15
Central	45, 48, 50, 58, 60
Southwest	72, 78
Metro	84, 85 and 92

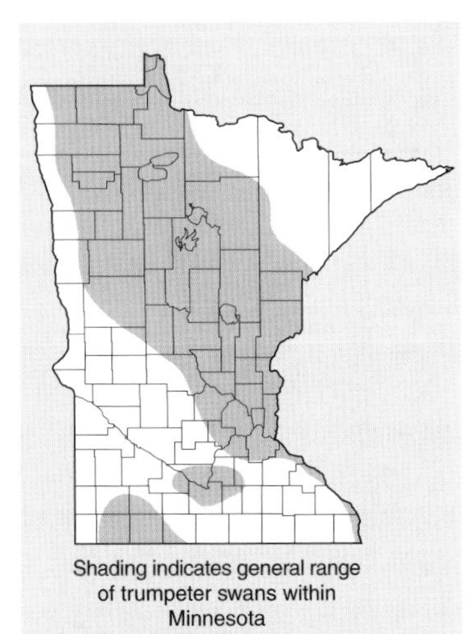

Shading indicates general range of trumpeter swans within Minnesota

Contact:

Wildlife Biologist
Hennepin Parks
3800 County Road 24
Maple Plain MN 55359
(612) 476-4663

Swan Biologist
Nongame Wildlife Program
DNR
500 Lafayette Road
St. Paul MN 55155
(888) MINNDNR

Warblers

When Minnesota's long, cold winters finally release their grip on the landscape, nature lovers crave every sign of spring. There are obvious signs like Canada geese returning north in V-shaped flocks and American robins hopping across the lawn in search of worms. Some signs, however, are more subtle but much more exciting to wildlife enthusiasts: the return of warblers to our woodlands. As forests take on the first hints of green, a diverse array of warblers return from wintering grounds that might have been anywhere from Georgia to Peru.

Springtime woodlands come to life beginning in mid-April with the arrival of orange-crowned, yellow-rumped and palm warblers in southern Minnesota. By early May the migration includes colorful warblers en route to northern nesting grounds. Most are not the common backyard species that we associate with bird feeders. These are insect-eating species that have wintered primarily in Central and South America. They include the northern parula, ovenbird, American redstart, and black-throated green, blackburnian, cerulean, Canada, chestnut-sided, bay-breasted, golden-winged, blue-winged, yellow, Tennessee, magnolia and prothonotary warblers.

Exploring springtime forests can be an enriching outdoor experience, and can occur in natural woodlands throughout the state—whether they are oak woods in the southeast or coniferous forests in the northeast. All are used in migration. The cold silence of winter is replaced by sensory overload from songs of warblers and a host of other springtime songbirds. And there are flashes of beautiful colors as flitting birds move through the forest in search of insect prey: orange of redstarts, glowing orange on the breasts of blackburnian

C. Henderson

Black-and-white warbler

warblers, bright yellow on yellow, magnolia and golden-winged warblers, and the deep chestnut color of bay-breasted warblers.

The best time to experience the spring warbler migration is from mid-April to mid-May. The peak migration days in any given year will vary depending on how early the warm temperatures bring on hatches of insects that provide food for these birds. In some years the birds move through in just a few days in early to mid-May. In other years the migration is extended over a couple week period through late May. There is about a two-week lapse from the first arrival of these birds in southern Minnesota until they arrive in more northerly portions of the state, including boreal forest nesting areas. Check with local bird club members and the Minnesota Birding Network (see page 323) for updates on the progress of the migration.

Enjoying the spring warbler migration requires a good set of binoculars and a field guide. It would help if you obtain a tape of bird calls and review them before going afield. Knowing the songs of some species will help you in identifying many birds even before you see them. Once you have tried "spring warbler-watching," you will likely find it becomes an annual tradition for enjoying the outdoors in springtime Minnesota.

Sites to see warblers

Northwest	7, 10-12 and 15-20
Northeast	22-24, 31-34, 37, 38 and 40
Central	41-44, 47-51, 53, 57-60
Southwest	64, 65, 69, 71 and 73
Metro	81-83, 85-89, 91-99
Southeast	102, 103, 105, 106, 108, 114, 115 and 117-119

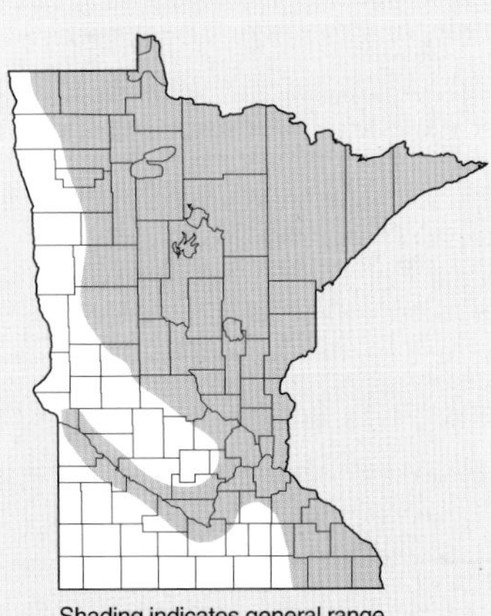

Shading indicates general range of warblers within Minnesota

Contact:

Minnesota Birding Network
http//:www.skypoint.com/members/dac/mnbird.html

Moose

The majestic-looking moose adds a distinctive character to the wildlands of northern Minnesota. Whether they are standing shoulder-deep among the lily pads of a lake in the Boundary Waters or standing quietly among the aspen parklands of the northwest, they are thrilling to see.

The moose is the largest member of the deer family. It can stand up to six feet high at the shoulder and weigh up to 1100 pounds. The hair is long and coarse and ranges from tan on the lower legs to blackish over most of the body. Mature moose have a slight hump over the shoulders and a unique flap of skin called a bell that hangs under the throat. Bulls, which are slightly larger than the cows, have large antlers with a distinctive palmated pattern. As with white-tailed deer, moose lose their antlers after the breeding season each year. The antlers usually drop in December.

Moose are vegetarians. Their name comes from an Algonquin Indian word meaning "twig eater." In summer they eat leaves and aquatic vegetation, and in late fall and winter they primarily eat twigs.

There are two populations of moose in the state—the northeast population and the northwest population. The northeast population is in lake country and mixed aspen and coniferous forests of St. Louis, Lake and Cook Counties. This area is what we typically consider good moose habitat. The northwest population is in the aspen parklands, prairies and brushlands of the Red River Valley from Karlstad south to Crookston. After seeing moose in the pristine lake country of northeast Minnesota, it sometimes comes as a surprise to see a moose standing in a farm grove of the northwest. The primary moose range encompasses 8500 square miles, with 15,000 square miles of secondary range.

In the 1800s moose were plentiful over most of northern Minnesota, but unlimited subsistence hunting by settlers caused the numbers to decline. The hunting season closed in 1922. After many years of protection, the population increased until the season was opened

C. Henderson

Moose

again in 1971. A system of random drawings, strict quotas and management of moose by hunting zones has been implemented to prevent overharvest. Seasons were held biennially until 1994 when annual seasons became possible.

Surveys conducted by the DNR reveal that the northeastern moose population is relatively stable at 6000 animals. Moose populations in the northwest have undergone recent declines that may be related to parasites, disease or changing land-use practices.

Moose are most active at dawn and dusk, but they also continue feeding throughout the day. In summer they spend much time in the water to avoid biting insects and to keep cool in hot weather. In early winter, moose move to more wooded habitat where their diet consists of twigs rather than green vegetation.

In northeast Minnesota, look for moose as they are partially submerged in boggy wetlands. In the northwest, moose can be more difficult to locate, but larger areas of public land like the Agassiz National Wildlife Refuge, as well as the Roseau River, Twin Lakes and Thief Lake Wildlife Management Areas (sites 1, 2, 5, 6) provide good habitat. Sometimes on hot summer days they can be seen lying in drainage ditches along roadsides in brushland habitats. Moose can be aggressive when approached too closely, so it is best to keep at a safe distance while viewing them.

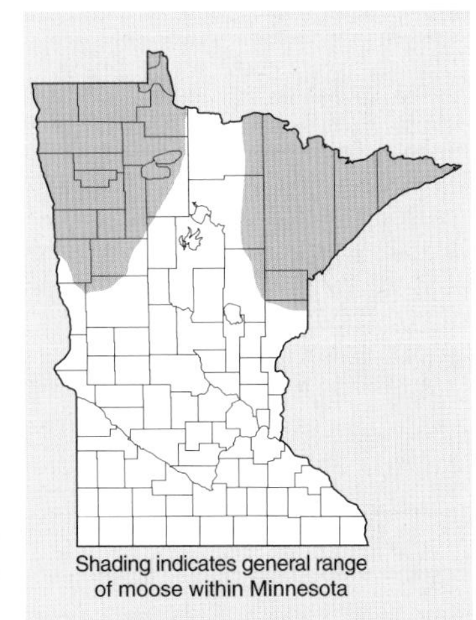

Shading indicates general range of moose within Minnesota

Sites to see moose

Northwest	1-9 and 15.
Northeast	21, 22, 26-28 and 35
Central	41

Timber Wolves

A howl in the night—listening to the sound of a howling pack of timber wolves at night in the wilds of northern Minnesota is one of the most moving and even mystical natural events you will ever experience. When two wolves hit a harmonic chord together while howling, the sound seems to penetrate right through your body! The howl of the wolf has been considered a symbol of wilderness ever since Aldo Leopold wrote. "In wildness is the salvation of the world. Perhaps this is the hidden meaning in the howl of the wolf, long known among mountains, but seldom perceived among men."

William Redig

Timber wolf

Here in Minnesota you have the best chance outside of Alaska for hearing or seeing a timber wolf. Although the prospects of actually seeing a timber wolf in the wild are very low, the continuing recovery of this federally threatened species has brought the wolf back as a widespread resident of the state's northern forests in addition to the wilderness areas that we usually associate with them.

Originally, the wolf played an important role in the legends, culture and customs of Indian tribes throughout much of the North American continent. They portrayed the wolf as a helper, teacher and beneficial contributor to their lives. Later, European colonists perceived the wolf as a nuisance and undesirable predator. As the country was settled and cleared, the timber wolf endured decades of persecution and bounty hunting. Control efforts eliminated them from all of the lower 48 states except the northeastern corner of Minnesota by the early 1960s.

In the 1960s, however, state bounties paid to kill wolves were discontinued, and federal endangered species legislation in 1973 provided complete protection for the wolf. Concurrently, the wolf began to enjoy unprecedented popularity as prominent wildlife biologists began long-term studies on timber wolf ecology. Durward Allen, Rolf Peterson, Victor Van Ballanberghe and Dave Mech are among the best known of those researchers.

During the past thirty years the timber wolf has staged a steady recovery and has expanded its range to include all of the northern third of Minnesota. The statewide population is now estimated at more than 2000 individuals. Their state status has improved from being a "threatened" species to one of "special concern."

Timber wolves are slightly larger than German shepherd dogs, and they have slightly more massive heads and a thicker muzzle than German shepherds or coyotes. Wolves may be from four to six-and-one-half feet long, including the tail, and they stand about 30 inches high at the shoulder. Adult females may weigh 65 to 75 pounds and males average about 80 pounds. Large individuals may weigh up to 115 pounds.

Wolves are easily confused with coyotes, but coyotes (often called "brush wolves") usually don't weigh over 35 to 40 pounds. A coyote has a proportionally smaller head and a more slender, pointed muzzle than a timber wolf. Both coyotes and wolves usually have grizzled gray coats, but wolves can vary in coloration from ebony black to pure white, and include intermediate shades of red, tan, brown and silver. Timber wolves will usually kill coyotes that they encounter in their pack territories. So within the prime range of wolves, the chances of seeing a coyote are low.

Timber wolves are a social species that live and hunt cooperatively as "packs." A pack is a family group consisting of a dominant "alpha" male and female and additional non-breeding adults, yearlings and young-of-the-year. Only the alpha female produces young. A pack may range in size from several up to 8 or 10 individuals. Wolves feed primarily on white-tailed deer and moose but they will also feed on beaver, hares or other mammals as the opportunity presents itself.

Most sightings of timber wolves occur along roadsides in northern forests. You may see a wolf crossing the road ahead or see a wolf standing in the ditch watching the traffic pass. Such sightings are fleeting and unexpected, but memorable. It is much more likely that if you hike in areas frequented by wolves—like along logging roads—you will encounter their tracks or find droppings that are almost entirely comprised of deer hair. While camping in such areas you may also hear them howling at night. The howling helps reinforce social bonds within the pack and provides a chilling and thrilling reminder to us that even though the wolf is a controversial species, it fills an essential role as a predator in the northern forest.

If you wish to observe captive timber wolves up close, you can see them at the International Wolf Center, Wildlife Science Center, Como Park Zoo, Minnesota Zoo and the Zollman Zoo. The Science Museum of Minnesota's famous "Wolves and Humans" exhibit is now on permanent loan to the International Wolf Center and provides excellent information about wolf ecology as well as their history in human culture.

Sites to see wolves

Northwest	1, 3-7, 11-12, 15 and 17
Northeast	23-24, 31, 34 and 35
Central	41 and 50

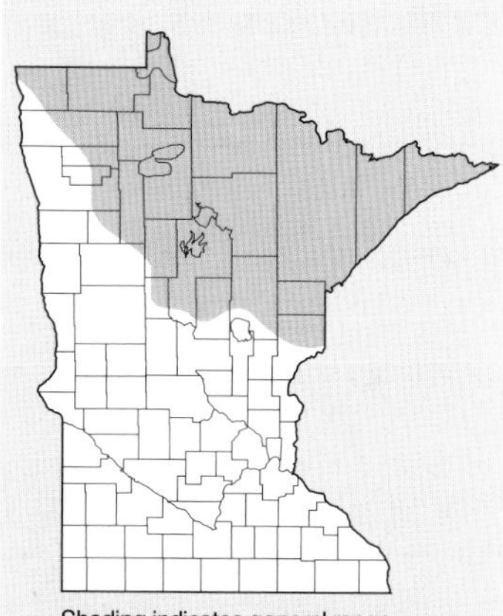

Shading indicates general range of wolves within Minnesota

Contact:

International Wolf Center
1369 Highway 169
Ely MN 55731-8129
(800) ELY-WOLF (359-9653)
http://www.wolf.org

Wildlife Science Center
5463 West Broadway
Forest Lake MN 55025
(612) 464-3993

Como Park Zoo
Midway Parkway and
Kaufman Drive
St. Paul MN 55103
(612) 487-8200

Oxbow Park/Zollman Zoo
5731 County Road 105
Byron MN 55920
(507) 775-2451

Statewide Site Map and Listing

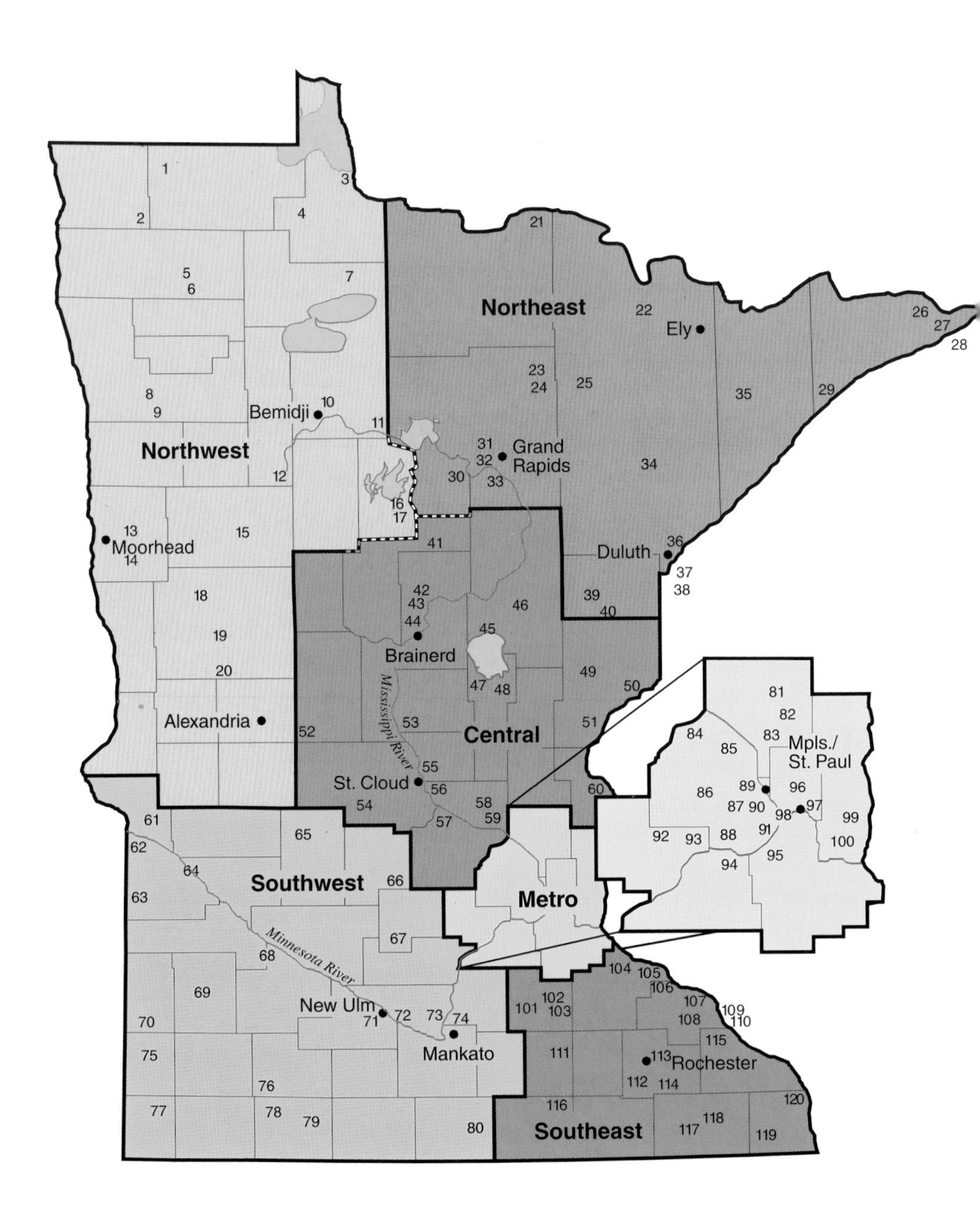

Northwest-Pines to Prairie

1. Roseau River WMA
2. Twin Lakes WMA
3. Lake of the Woods
4. Red Lake WMA
5. Thief Lake WMA
6. Agassiz NWR
7. Red Lake Peatland SNA
8. Pembina Trail Preserve SNA
9. Agassiz Dunes SNA/Prairie Smoke Dunes SNA/Agassiz Environmental Learning Center
10. Lake Bemidji State Park
11. Mississippi River/Cass Lake/Lake Winnibigoshish
12. Itasca State Park
13. Felton Prairie WMA/SNA
14. Buffalo River State Park/Bluestem Prairie SNA
15. Tamarac NWR
16. Pine Point Research Natural Area
17. Deep Portage Conservation Reserve
18. Maplewood State Park
19. Glendalough State Park
20. Inspiration Peak

Northeast-Arrowhead Country

21. Gold Portage WMA
22. Vermilion Lake
23. George Washington State Forest
24. Peloquin WMA
25. Sharp-tailed Grouse Dancing Grounds
26. Northern Light Lake
27. Portage Brook Overlook
28. Swamp River WMA
29. Beaver Bay to Grand Portage Bay
30. Mud-Goose WMA
31. Suomi Hills Recreation Area
32. Bass Brook WMA
33. Mississippi River
34. Sax-Zim Bog
35. Murphy City/Stoney River Grade
36. Hawk Ridge Nature Reserve
37. Snively and Magney City Parks
38. Park Point Recreation Area/ Minnesota Point Forest
39. Sharp-tailed Grouse Dancing Grounds
40. Moose Lake State Park

Central-Heartland Lakes Country

41. Washburn Lake Solitude Area
42. Big Island Natural & Recreation Area
43. Uppgaard WMA
44. Northland Arboretum/Paul Bunyan Jack Pine Savanna
45. Mille Lacs Lake-North Shore (Highway 18)
46. Rice Lake NWR/Kimberly WMA/ McGregor Marsh SNA
47. Mille Lacs Lake Area & Kathio State Park
48. Mille Lacs WMA
49. Banning State Park
50. St. Croix State Park
51. Chengwatana State Forest
52. Lake Osakis
53. Crane Meadows NWR/Rice-Skunk & Crane Meadows WMAs
54. Roscoe Prairie SNA
55. Graham's Island in the Mississippi River
56. Sand Prairie WMA
57. Lake Maria State Park
58. Sherburne NWR
59. Sand Dunes State Forest/ Uncas Dunes SNA
60. Wild River State Park

Southwest-Prairie & Wetland Country

61. Thielke Lake WMA
62. Big Stone NWR
63. Salt Lake WMA
64. Lac Qui Parle WMA/State Park
65. Sibley State Park
66. Pigeon Lake Rookery
67. Schaefer Prairie
68. Swede's Forest SNA
69. Camden State Park/ Prairie Marshes WMA

70. Hole-in-the-Mountain WMA/ TNC/Co. Park
71. Flandrau State Park
72. Swan Lake
73. Seven Mile Creek County Park
74. Kasota Prairie SNA
75. Pipestone National Monument/WMA
76. Talcot Lake WMA
77. Blue Mounds State Park
78. Heron Lake System
79. Kilen Woods State Park/ Prairie Bush Clover SNA
80. Walnut Lake WMA

Metro-Wildlife In & Around the Cities

81. Boot Lake SNA
82. Carlos Avery WMA
83. Springbrook Nature Center
84. Crow-Hassan Park Reserve
85. Elm Creek Park Reserve
86. Wolsfeld Woods SNA
87. T. S. Roberts Bird Sanctuary
88. Wood Lake Nature Center
89. Eloise Butler Wildflower Garden & Bird Sanctuary/the Quaking Bog
90. Lakes Calhoun & Harriet
91. Minnesota Valley NWR/Black Dog Preserve SNA
92. Carver Park Reserve
93. Minnesota Landscape Arboretum
94. Murphy Hanrehan Park Reserve
95. Lebanon Hills Regional Park
96. Lake Vadnais/Sucker Lake
97. Battle Creek Regional Park
98. Crosby Farm-Hidden Falls Parks
99. Afton State Park
100. Lost Valley Prairie SNA

Southeast-Blufflands & Big Woods

101. Boyd Sartell WMA
102. Cannon River Wilderness Area
103. Nerstrand Big Woods State Park
104. Colville Park
105. Frontenac State Park
106. Hok-si-la City Park
107. Read's Landing River Route
108. Zumbro Bottoms Forestry Unit
109. McCarthy Lake WMA/ Kellogg-Weaver Dunes SNA
110. Weaver Bottoms (Upper Miss. NWR)
111. Rice Lake State Park
112. Keller WMA
113. Silver Lake
114. Chester Woods County Park
115. Whitewater WMA/State Park
116. Geneva Lake WMA
117. Forestville State Park
118. Hvoslev WMA
119. Beaver Creek Valley State Park
120. Sheperd's Marsh (Upper Miss. NWR)

Wildlife Watching Sites by Region

Northwest–Pines to Prairie

Northwestern Minnesota is a rich mosaic of boreal and hardwood forests, aspen parklands, marshes, farmlands, brushlands, prairies, peatlands, and beautiful lakes.

Prairies once covered the western portion of this region and have been largely converted to croplands in the bed of what was once a great glacial lake—Lake Agassiz. The Red River of the North is in the heart of that former lakebed. There are high quality prairie remnants along the eastern edge where the sandy beach soils were less conducive to agriculture. There it is still possible to encounter greater prairie chickens, chestnut-collared longspurs, marbled godwits, and upland sandpipers.

Stephen Maxson

Sandhill cranes

Expansive brushlands and aspen parklands of Kittson County in the far northwest look like central Saskatchewan. On the Beaches Wildlife Management Area you can enjoy the sight of black-billed magpies, moose, sharp-tailed grouse and sandhill cranes.

Some of the largest and most impressive wetlands in the Midwest are found here in wild areas that have been preserved or restored by the Minnesota DNR or the U.S. Fish and Wildlife Service: Agassiz National Wildlife Refuge and Roseau River, Thief Lake, and Twin Lakes wildlife management areas. There are healthy breeding populations of Franklin's gulls, horned grebes, ring-necked ducks, redheads, canvasbacks and dozens of other waterbird and waterfowl species. These areas have moose, timber wolves, white-tailed deer, bobcat and fishers.

Farther east is the vast Red Lake bog and peatland complex that is one of the highest quality and most extensive in North America. Spruce, tamarack and cedar stands among the open heath bogs and peatlands provide habitat for great gray, short-eared and northern hawk-owls and Connecticut warblers.

Major lakes of the region, such as Lake of the Woods, Leech, Winnibigoshish, Upper and Lower Red Lake and Cass, provide habitat for American white pelicans, endangered piping plovers, common terns, bald eagles, ospreys, great blue herons, common loons, common goldeneyes, spotted sandpipers, beavers and river otters.

Itasca State Park has classic boreal forests of red pine, as well as stands of jack pine and mixed hardwoods. These forests are home to blackburnian, bay-breasted and black-throated green warblers, as well as scarlet tanagers and broad-winged hawks.

The hardwood forests of the southeastern United States reach their northwestern extension in the Detroit Lakes area, including Tamarac NWR. There it is possible to encounter eastern towhees, red-shouldered hawks and gray foxes.

Finally, the southern portion of this region in the Otter Tail and Douglas County vicinity has hundreds of excellent prairie wetlands.

All of these habitats make northwestern Minnesota a great place for outdoor enthusiasts to enjoy wildlife all year long.

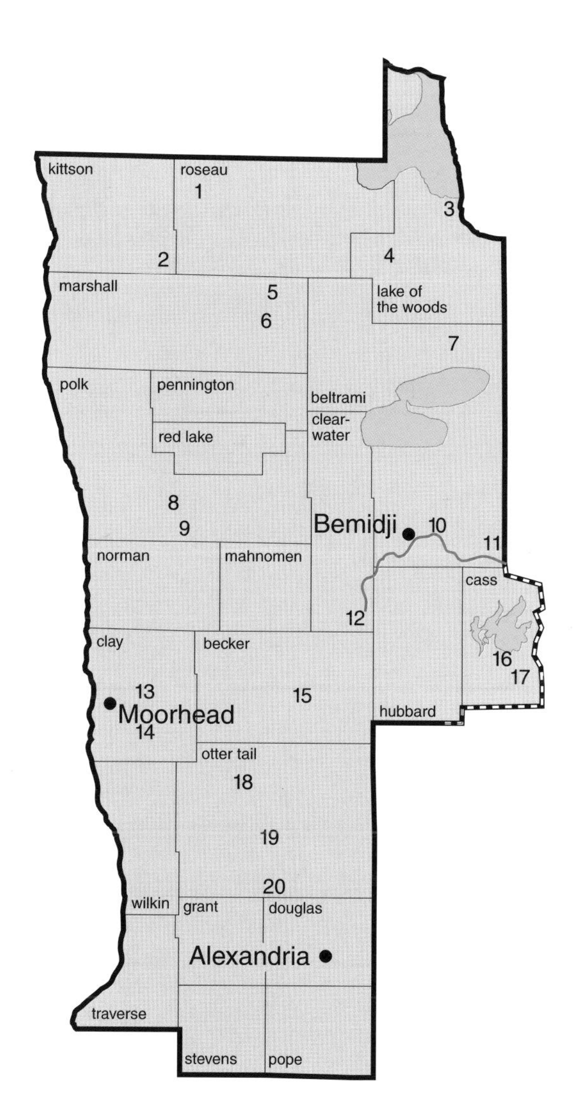

Sites

1. Roseau River WMA
2. Twin Lakes WMA
3. Lake of the Woods
4. Red Lake WMA
5. Thief Lake WMA
6. Agassiz NWR
7. Red Lake Peatland SNA
8. Pembina Trail Preserve SNA
9. Agassiz Dunes SNA/ Prairie Smoke Dunes SNA/ Agassiz Environmental Learning Center
10. Lake Bemidji State Park
11. Mississippi River/Cass Lake/Lake Winnibigoshish
12. Itasca State Park
13. Felton Prairie WMA/SNA
14. Buffalo River State Park/ Bluestem Prairie SNA
15. Tamarac NWR
16. Pine Point Research Natural Area
17. Deep Portage Conservation Reserve
18. Maplewood State Park
19. Glendalough State Park
20. Inspiration Peak

I–Roseau River WMA

Canada geese

Why is this area special?

The Roseau River Wildlife Management Area encompasses 62,025 acres of northwestern Minnesota's Roseau County. This large marshland is one of the most spectacular waterfowl breeding and migration sites in the state. It's also important for migrating sandhill cranes, swans and shorebirds. A total of 149 bird species breed in the vicinity, including horned and western grebes, American bitterns, northern harriers, sharp-tailed grouse, marbled godwits, black-billed magpies and boreal chickadees.

You can expect to see waterfowl in breeding plumage from late April to May and cranes in April, May and September. During some visits, you might even see Franklin's ground squirrels, black bears or moose. Visit during the winter to see great gray owls, gray jays and northern hawk-owls.

Near the WMA, but actually a part of the Lost River State Forest, is a tamarack forest noted for its high densities of great gray owls. Other forest types include aspen, bur oak, jack pine, black spruce, and white cedar.

This part of the Glacial Lake Agassiz plain is low and flat. Vegetation is primarily sedge meadow, shallow wetland pools and lowland brush. Some of the plants you might see here include swamp milkweed, blazing star, dogwood, hardstem bulrush, bearberry, fringed gentian, big bluestem, bladderwort, bracken fern, balsam willow, narrow-leaved cattail and water hemlock.

The Roseau River flows west for 14 miles through this site, and three marshes totaling 10,600 acres have been constructed along its banks. These wetlands are managed for resident and migratory waterfowl, wetland wildlife, hunting and other recreation.

Special note:

The headquarters is open Monday through Friday from 8 a.m. to 4:30 p.m. Refuge dike roads are open only in mid-April and as conditions allow during the fall. Information about bird concentrations and local conditions may be obtained from the area wildlife manager.

Hunting allowed. Call ahead for hunting season dates.

Best viewing time:

How do I get there?

Maps: MN Highway Coordinate: C/D-2
PRIM Area: Hallock/Roseau
DeLorme MN Atlas Grid #: 91 B-7/10

Additional directions:

The Roseau River WMA is located 20 miles northwest of Roseau. Drive six miles west of Roseau on Highway 11, then 11 miles north on Highway 89. Drive west for three miles on County Road 3 to the unit headquarters.

The tamarack/spruce forest, a part of the Lost River State Forest is located between six and 10 miles north of Roseau on either side of Highway 310.

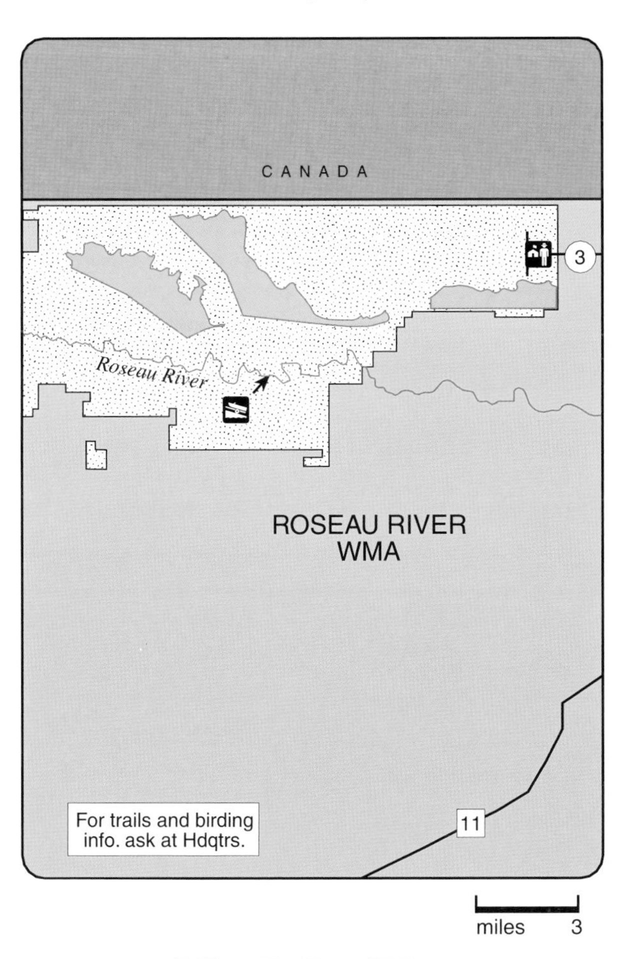

Facilities:

Recreational Opportunities:

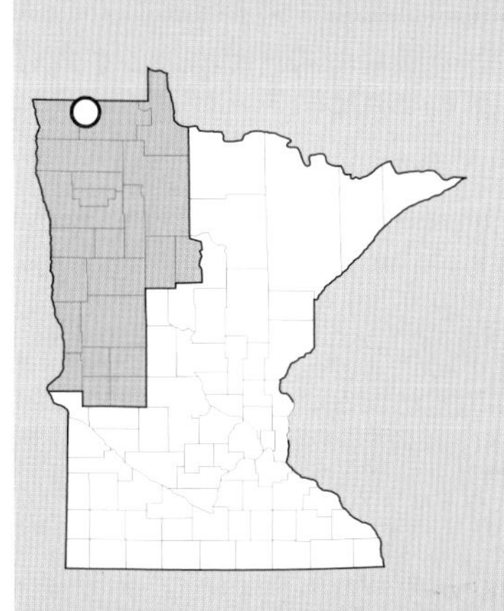

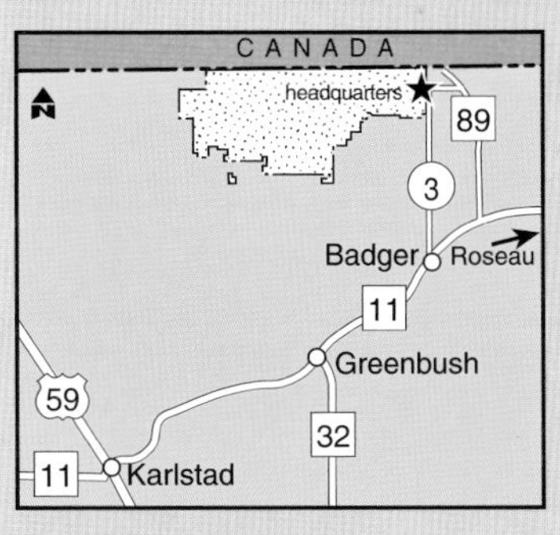

Contact:

DNR Wildlife Area Office
HCR 5 Box 103
Roseau MN 56751
(218) 463-1557

2–Twin Lakes WMA

Why is this area special?

Sandhill cranes flock to the Twin Lakes Wildlife Management Area during fall migration, roosting in the oak savanna. A beach ridge of Glacial Lake Agassiz that harbors oak savanna crosses through the Twin Lakes area and supports a wide range of wildlife, from moose to ruffed grouse. If you watch carefully, you could see white-tailed deer, yellow rails, river otters, beavers and muskrats. You might even see signs of black bears, timber wolves or coyotes.

Except for the beach ridges covered with bur oak, this 8,780-acre wildlife area is very flat. Three large marshes—Twistal Swamp, North Twin Lake and South Twin Lake—cover the 2,200 acres of lowland. Aspen stands, brushland, sedge meadow, prairie and 584 acres of agricultural fields are scattered across the remainder of the area.

Katie Haws

A 50-acre field along Highway 11 has been restored with native grasses and forbs. Some of the plants to look for in this area include balm of Gilead, American hazelnut, red osier dogwood, big bluestem, Indian grass, pasqueflower, prairie smoke, both purple and white prairie clover, lead plant and wood lily.

Two square miles of the Twin Lakes WMA is a sanctuary for migratory waterfowl from September through October each year. When you visit this area, you'll be able to see blue-winged teal, black terns, great blue herons, American bitterns, woodcocks and perhaps trumpeter swans.

Note:

There are several visitor access spots throughout the WMA, as well as primitive camping sites, parking areas and a boat access. There are no trails or facilities.

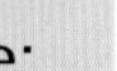

Hunting allowed. Call ahead for hunting season dates.

Best viewing time:

How do I get there?

Maps: MN Highway Coordinate: C-4
PRIM Area: Hallock
DeLorme MN Atlas Grid #: 91 E-7

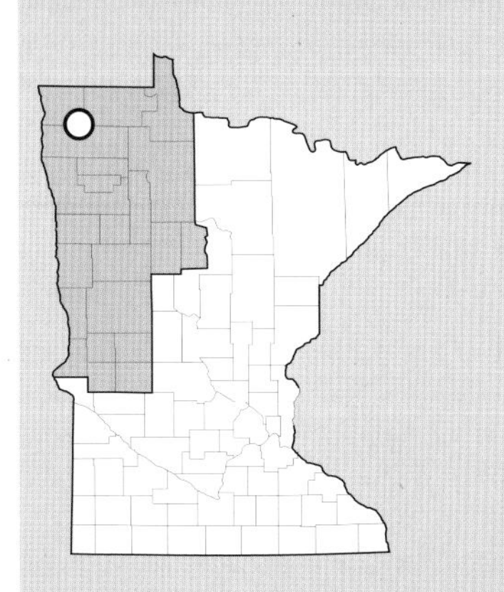

Additional Directions:

From Karlstad in Kittson County, drive east on Highway 11 for two miles. Highway 11 continues through the WMA for 6.5 miles to the town of Pelan.

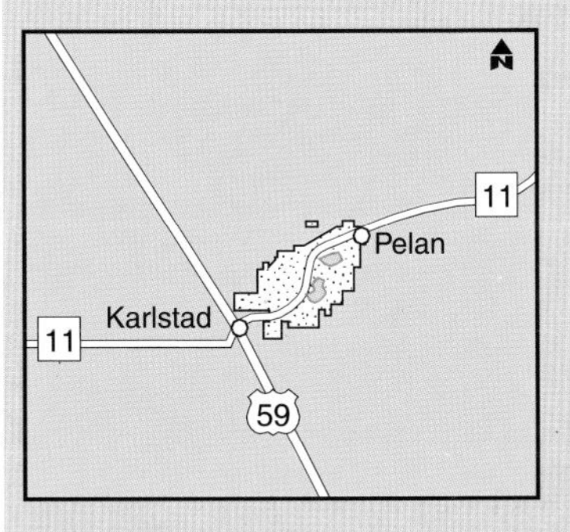

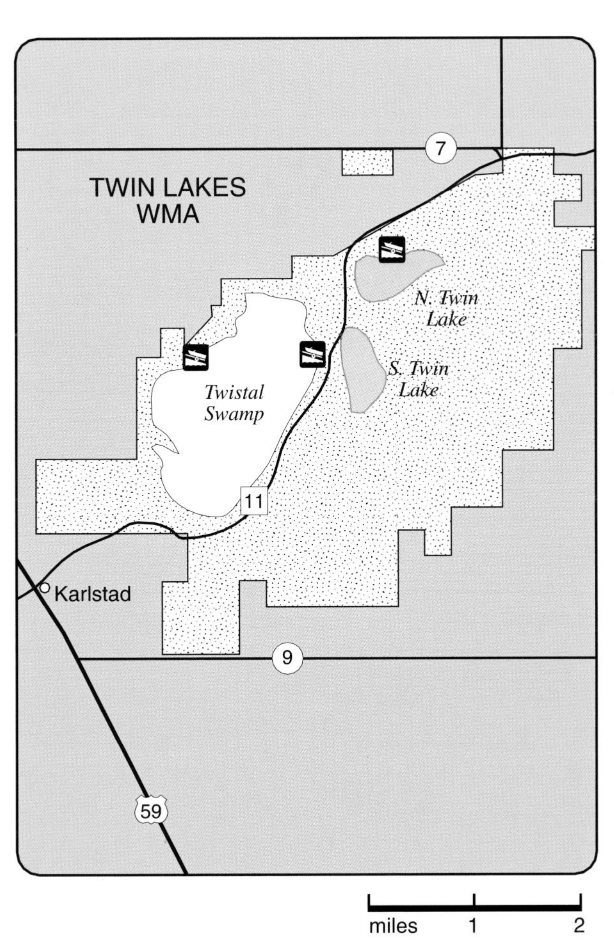

miles 1 2

Recreational Opportunities:

Contact:

DNR Area Wildlife Office
P.O. Box 154
Karlstad MN 56732
(218) 436-2427

3–Lake of the Woods

Why is this place special?

Lake of the Woods is one of Minnesota's relatively unexplored natural treasures. It is the 45th largest lake in the world. With 65,000 miles of shoreline, 485 square miles of water and 14,000 islands, this lake represents Minnesota and southern Canada at their best.

Lake of the Woods is renowned as a walleye and trout lake, but it is also a haven for other wildlife. Look for beavers, muskrats, black bears and river otters. Particularly impressive is the lake's high concentration of bird species. Come and see common loons, Wilson's phalaropes, Franklin's gulls, Forster's terns and short-eared owls. Bald eagles also nest on the islands.

Stephen Maxson

Pelican, cormorant, and gull colonies

If you're a bird lover, use a boat to watch the breeding colonies of ring-billed gulls, common terns, double-crested cormorants and American white pelicans. The cacophony of bird calls and the colorful activity of the birds feeding their young provides a noisy and exciting viewing experience.

Visit Lake of the Woods to see balsam poplar, spotted jewelweed, beach peas and Canada yew.

For common terns and white pelicans, **Northwest Angle** islands of Crowduck and Techout represent two of only a few nesting sites in Minnesota. Due to the fragile nature of the habitat and the importance of leaving the threatened species undisturbed, you may only see these nesting areas only by boat. Begin your adventure from one of the private boat landings on the Northwest Angle. Watch from a distance; don't go into any bird nesting colony.

A good place to visit in the Lake of the Woods area is **Zippel Bay State Park,** located just northwest of Baudette. Jack pine, aspen and birch forests cover much of this 3,000-acre state park, which also boasts three miles of beach along Lake of the Woods. The shoreline is used

Best viewing time:

by migrating shorebirds, such as semipalmated sandpipers and yellowlegs, as well as many species of gulls. Look for migrating shorebirds beginning in early July.

As you watch killdeers along the Zippel Bay beach, you might hear cranes calling from their nesting territories in the extensive marshland. Other birds include red-necked grebes, black terns and mallards. You might also encounter forest birds such as ovenbirds, scarlet tanagers and American redstarts.

You should also visit the **Pine and Curry Island Scientific and Natural Area.** This sandspit island at the mouth of the Rainy River is four miles long and, in some places, only a few feet wide. You can find open beach, sparsely vegetated dunes, marshland and patches of deciduous woods on the island, providing a home for white-tailed jackrabbits and the only remaining nesting population of piping plovers in Minnesota. Piping plovers are a state and federally listed species. In 1997, only one nested. Do not enter their nesting colonies in the marked sanctuaries.

Bald eagles, spotted sandpipers, common terns, common ravens and killdeer also nest here. In one field season, an observer counted 170 different bird species on the island. Highway 11 between Baudette and Warroad is a designated wildflower route and has many orchids blooming in June.

Stephen Maxson

Piping plover

Note:

Many of these viewing areas are ecologically fragile. Special measures must be taken to protect the birds seen here, especially during the nesting season. Even well-intentioned observers visiting in the nesting colony can cause chaos among the nesting birds. Adult birds may respond by harming or abandoning their young.

Zippel Bay is not home to nesting colonial birds, so there are no precautions other than the regular park rules. The Pine and Curry Island SNA, however, does have restrictions. People are not allowed in sanctuaries for nesting plovers and terns between April 15 and September 1. At least three miles of the island are not classified as a sanctuary and may be visited. The sanctuary areas are clearly marked by orange signs.

If you are looking for a place to stay, check out the resorts in Angle Inlet, on Flag and Oak Islands, in Baudette, and along the Rainy River between Baudette and Wheeler's Point.

continued...

How do I get there

Maps: MN Highway Coordinate: F-1, F-3, G-3
PRIM Area: Baudette
DeLorme MN Grid #: 89 inset, 93 A/B-9, 94 C-1

Additional directions:

Northwest Angle: From Warroad in Roseau County, take Highway 313 north for nine miles to the Canadian border. This becomes Canadian Highway 12. Continue west for 12 miles to the town of Sprague, Manitoba. From there turn north on Highway 308 and follow the signs to Highway 525, the Northwest Angle, and the small town of Angle Inlet.

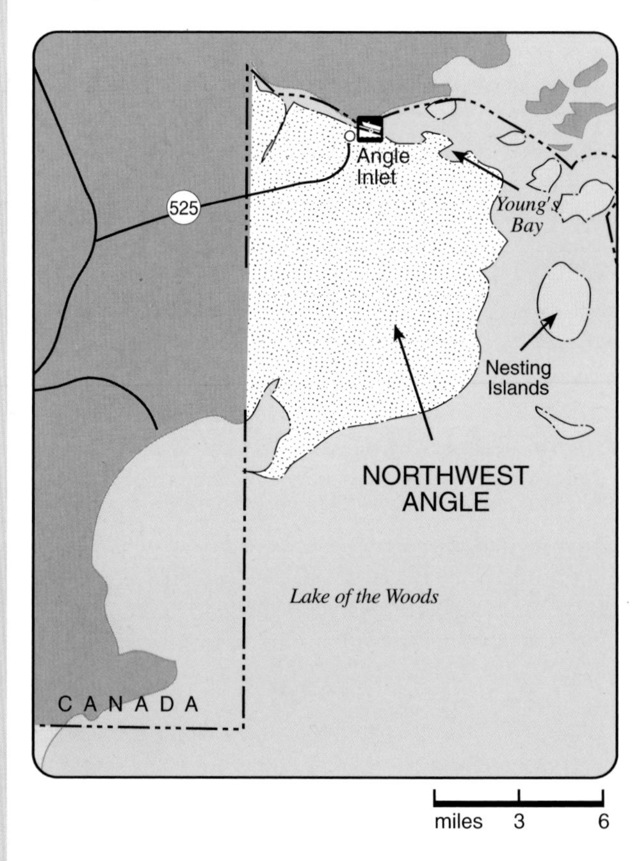

Facilities:

Recreational Opportunities:

Zippel Bay State Park: From Baudette in Lake of the Woods County, take Highway 172 north for 11 miles to the junction of Highway 8. Go west on Highway 8 for six miles to County Road 34. Turn right (north) and continue for one mile to the park headquarters.

Pine and Curry Island SNA: From Baudette, take Highway 172 north for 12 miles to Wheelers Point, where there is a public boat access. The island is located three miles north of the access across Fourmile Bay. The island can also be accessed by using private boat launching facilities at Bostick Creek. This decreases the distance from the launch site to the island.

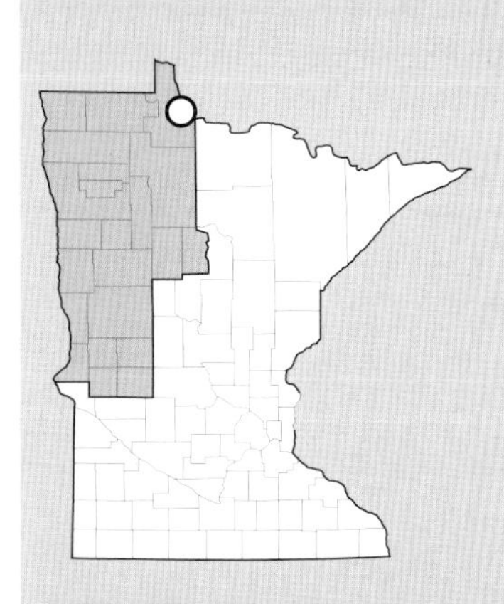

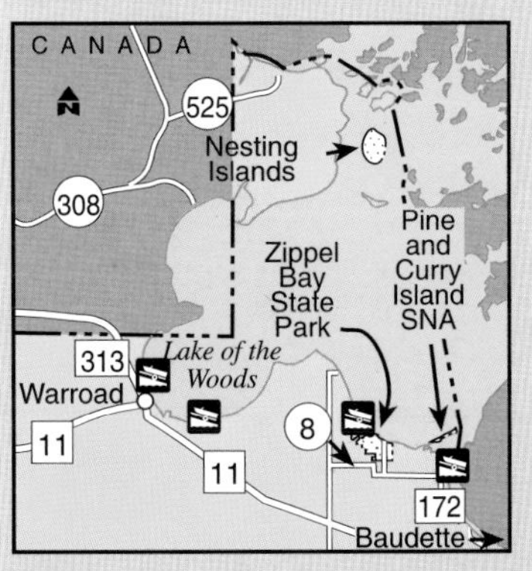

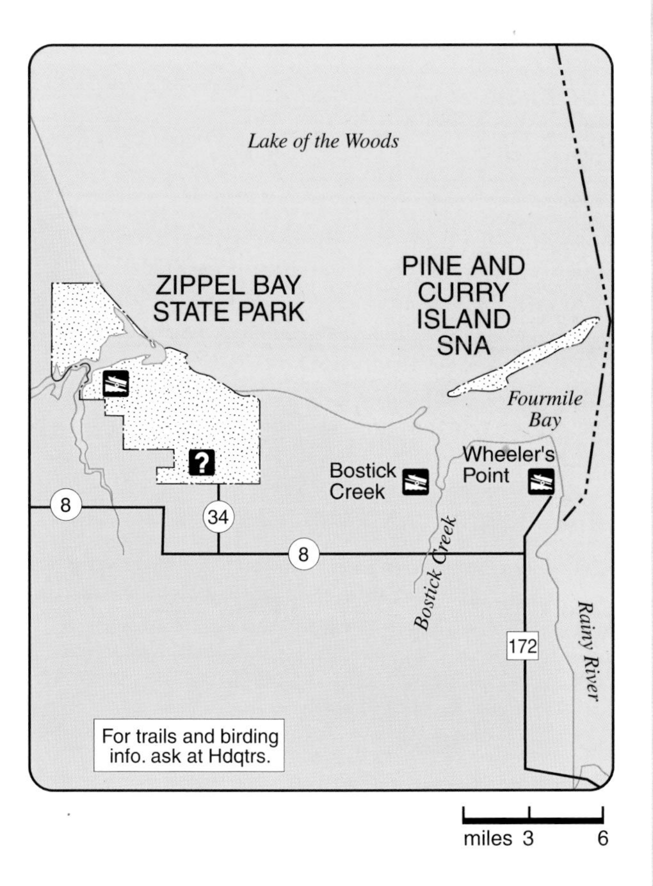

Facilities-both:

Recreational Opportunities

Zippel only:    

Contact:

Zipple Bay State Park
Williams MN 56686
(218) 783-6252

Scientific and Natural Areas Program
DNR
Box 25
500 Lafayette Road
St. Paul MN 55155
(612) 297-2357

Nongame Wildlife Program
DNR
2115 Birchmont Beach Road
Bemidji MN 56601
(218) 755-2976

Tourism Bureau
P.O. Box 578
Baudette MN 56623
(800) 382-3474

4–Red Lake WMA

Why is this area special?

An expanse of 417,456 acres in Lake of the Woods and Beltrami counties makes the Red Lake Wildlife Management Area the largest in the state. Here you can experience black spruce and tamarack habitats as well as hardwoods, lowland brush, open bog and fen. You can also enjoy upland forests of aspen, jack pine, birch, white spruce and balsam fir. As you explore these habitats, look for bog laurel, pitcher plants, sundew, Indian pipe, fringed gentian and yellow, showy and stemless lady's slippers.

Most of the forest roads in the WMA run along the beach ridges of Glacial Lake Agassiz, and this is where you can find sandy soils and the upland forests. Much of the WMA, however, is lowland bog, including several bog lakes and three impounded marshes. The bog is both open and forested, with limited access.

Ron Morreim

Spruce grouse

You will regularly see Connecticut warblers at this site, and you can occasionally get a glimpse of a rare great gray or boreal owl. Approximately 200 bird species frequent the WMA, with 144 of these species presumed nesting. Some of the birds you should expect at this site include turkey vultures, northern goshawks, spruce, ruffed and sharp-tailed grouse, great gray owls, black-backed woodpeckers, boreal chickadees, red-breasted nuthatches, hermit thrushes, red-eyed vireos, blackburnian warblers, ovenbirds, Canada warblers and Nelson's sharp-tailed sparrows.

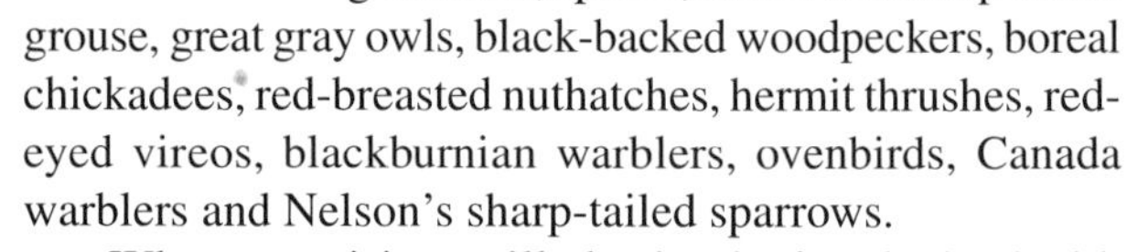

When you visit, you'll also be sharing the land with snowshoe hares, red squirrels, timber wolves, fishers, lynx, black bears and moose. This area is one of the most remote wildlife watching spots in the state. If you want to watch wildlife with minimal disturbance, this is the place.

Note:

The headquarters has bathrooms and telephones, but they are open only on weekdays. There are no groomed trails, but backcountry skiing, snowmobiling and mountain biking are permitted. A bird list is available.

Hunting allowed. Call ahead for hunting season dates.

Best viewing time:

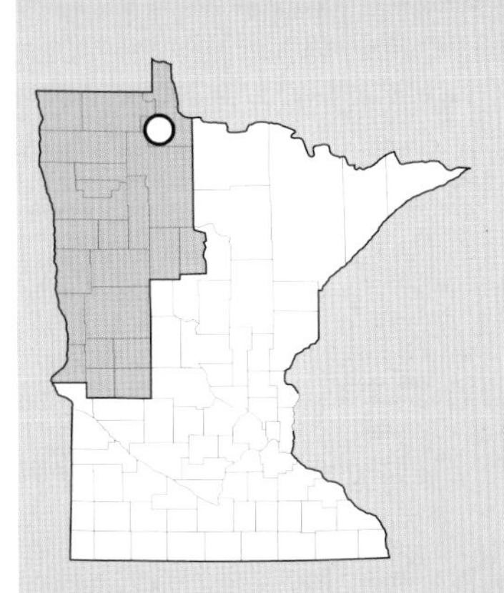

How do I get there?

Maps: MN Highway Coordinates: E-4, F-4, G-4, E-5, F-5, G-5

PRIM Area: Upper Red Lake

DeLorme MN Atlas Grid #: 83 A/B-5/6, 84 B-1, 93 E-5 to 9

Additional directions:

From Warroad, drive 12 miles south on County Road 5, then 10 miles south on Dick's Parkway, then seven miles east on the Faunce-Butterfield frontage road.

From Fourtown, go north on County Road 44, then north on Township Road 704. Continue north about 19 miles on Dick's Parkway frontage road. Turn east on the Faunce-Butterfield frontage road and drive for 7 miles.

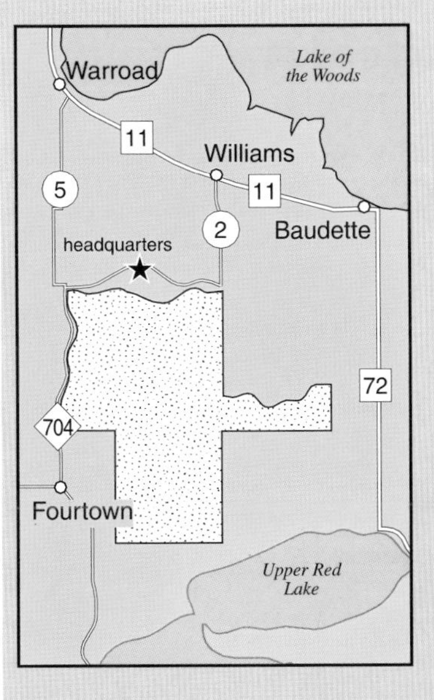

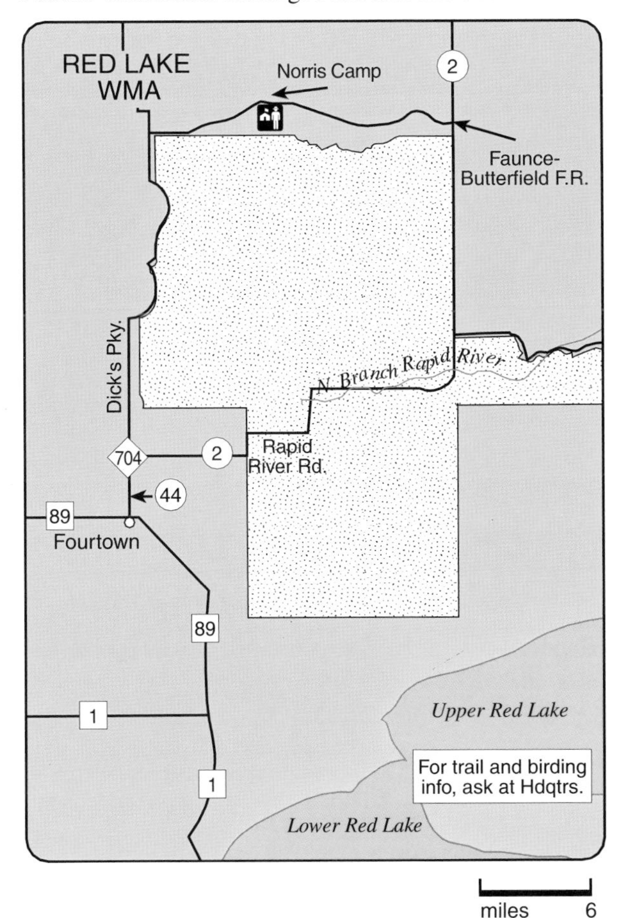

Facilities:

Recreational Opportunities:

Contact:

DNR Wildlife Area Office
Red Lake WMA
Box 100
Roosevelt MN 56673
(218) 783-6861

5–Thief Lake WMA

Why is this area special?

Expect a lot of activity, particularly in June, at this premier wetland wildlife spot. A colony of Franklin's gulls with counts of 5,000–10,000 pairs has been recorded, although there have been only 50 nests in recent seasons. Approximately 250 pairs of eared grebes nest on the lake, as do approximately 300 pairs of western grebes.

Thief Lake is an exciting location to view migratory waterfowl in the spring and fall, when thousands of ducks and geese gather. A total of 232 species of birds have been seen on Thief Lake, and 99 are known to nest there. Both Forster's and black terns nest on the lake, along with ring-necked and ruddy ducks. You might also see American bitterns, black-crowned night-herons, northern shovelers, canvasbacks, sandhill cranes, magnolia warblers, savannah sparrows, western meadowlarks or yellow-headed blackbirds.

C. Henderson

Elk

The Thief Lake WMA and adjacent lands are the home of Minnesota's only elk herd. The herd of about two dozen animals moves around the area, so contact the wildlife manager for current locations. The elk are especially interesting during their mating season in September when you can hear the bulls' bugling calls. In your search for the elk, you might run across a snowshoe hare, southern red-backed vole, short-tailed weasel, white-tailed deer or even a moose.

Plant species you'll want to watch for at the Thief Lake WMA include showy and yellow lady's slippers, blue flags, fringed and bottle gentians and large-flowered trilliums.

Note:

Thief Lake WMA has a special wildlife-viewing mound for watching birds on the lake. A bird list is available. There are several primitive boat launch sites and some gated roads that are occasionally open for wildlife viewing. There are no trails. The headquarters has bathrooms, telephones and information areas. These facilities are only open on weekdays. Facilities are handicapped accessible.

 Hunting allowed. Call ahead for hunting season dates.

Best viewing time:

How do I get there?

Maps: MN Highway Coordinate: D-4
PRIM Area: Grygla
DeLorme MN Atlas Grid #: 81, 82, 91, 92

Additional Directions:

From Thief River Falls, drive north on Highway 32 for 41 miles to Middle River. Turn right, or east, on County Road 6 and continue for 10 miles. A sign at County Road 49 will direct you to the WMA headquarters three miles north on the west shore of the lake.

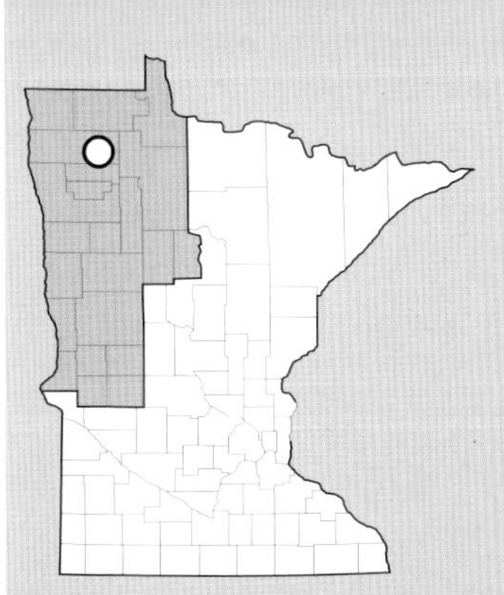

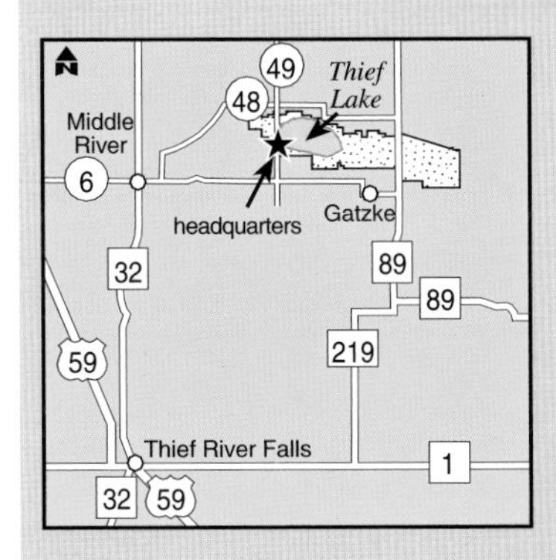

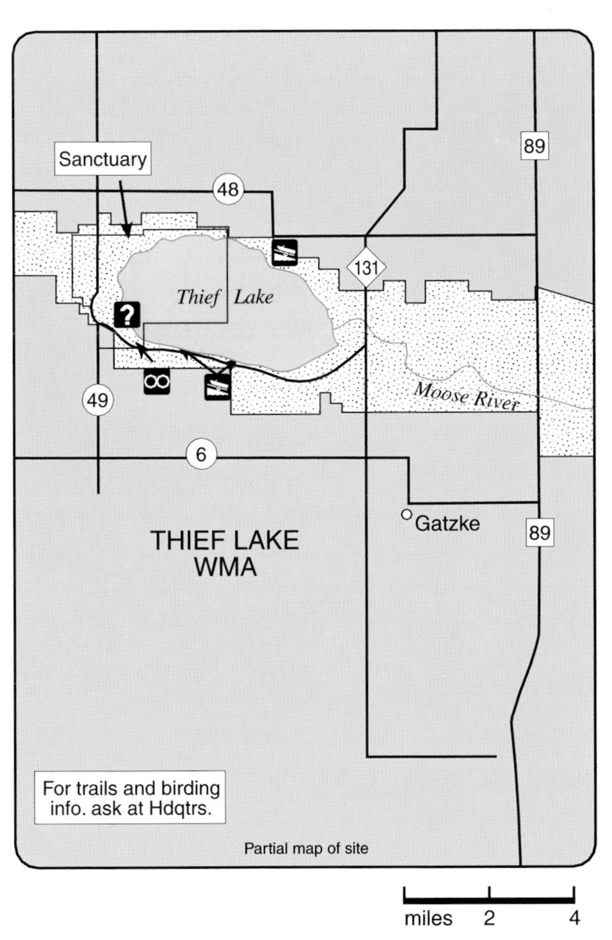

Facilities:       

Recreational Opportunities:

Contact:

DNR Wildlife Area Office
Thief Lake WMA
HCR Box 17
Middle River MN 56737
(218) 222-3747

6–Agassiz NWR

Why is this area special?

This 61,500-acre refuge was established in 1937 and managed by the U.S. Fish and Wildlife Service, the refuge occupies a portion of the former Glacial Lake Agassiz.

Thousands of migrating waterfowl bring this refuge to life in early April, and an impressive migration of songbirds fills the sky in May. Watch the courtship rituals of canvasbacks, redheads, ruddy ducks and mallards on the pools. As spring progresses, the "peenting" of woodcocks, winnowing of snipe, trumpeting of sandhill cranes, drumming of ruffed grouse, chorusing of wood frogs and squawking of Franklin's gulls will fill the air.

Gary Tischer, U.S. Fish and Wildlife Service

A total of 280 bird species have been observed here. The area's 132 nesting species includes 18 species of waterfowl. Agassiz Pool, an excellent area for viewing wetland birds, is accessible most of the year. Keep your eyes open for eared and red-necked grebes, black-crowned night herons, American bitterns, American white pelicans, northern shovelers, ring-necked ducks, black-billed magpies, northern harriers, yellow rails, Franklin's gulls, Forster's and black terns, LeConte's sparrows and Nelson's sharp-tailed sparrows.

In 1909, attempts were made to drain the area. The refuge is now a haven for both aquatic and terrestrial wildlife. Twenty shallow pools encompass 40,094 wetland acres between scattered stands of grassland and forestland.

Note:

Office hours are Monday through Friday from 7:30 a.m. to 4 p.m. There is information and an interpretive display area. Outdoor kiosks provide refuge information.

A four-mile drive and a short hiking trail are open from May through October in the Lansing Parker observation area. There is also a 100-foot observation tower; the key can be checked out during regular business hours.

There is no camping allowed in the refuge, but primitive camping is permitted in designated areas on adjacent state wildlife management areas. Lodging and eating establishments are available in Thief River Falls, Middle River and Grygla. Group tours can be arranged in advance.

Best viewing time:

How do I get there?

Maps: MN Highway Coordinate: D-4, D-5
PRIM area: Thief River Falls
DeLorme MN Atlas Grid #: 81, 82

Additional directions:

Drive north from Thief River Falls on Highway 32 for 12 miles to the town of Holt. Turn right on County Road 7 and continue east for 11 miles to the refuge headquarters.

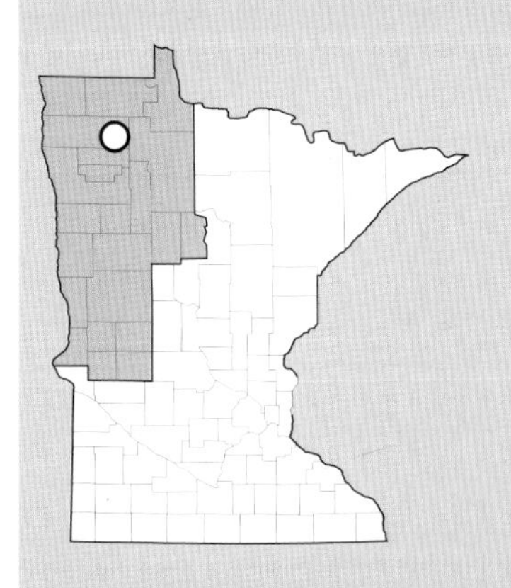

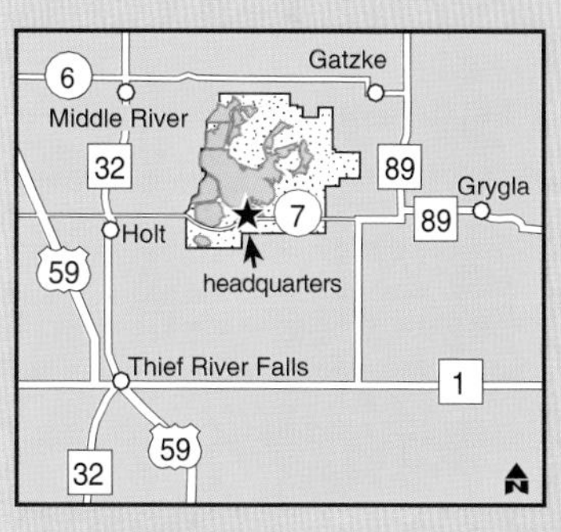

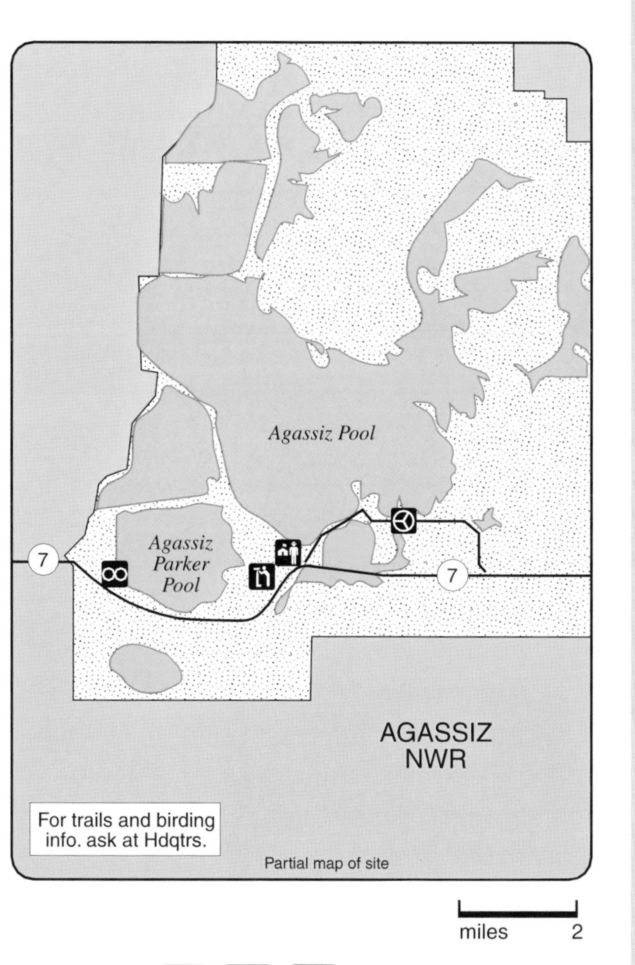

Facilities: 

Recreational Opportunities:

Contact:

Agassiz NWR
RR 1 Box 74
Middle River MN 56737
(218) 449-4115

7–Red Lake Peatland SNA

Why is this area special?

The Red Lake Peatland contains the largest, most diversely-patterned natural peat formations in the United States. Open sedge mats are interspersed with islands of lowland conifer tamarack and black spruce. Often referred to as the Big Bog, this peatland and its watershed protection areas measure more than 360 square miles.

This SNA features the largest, best-developed peatland water drainage patterns, called water tracks, in the United States. The peatland here is of worldwide significance and a portion of the area has been designated a national landmark. This is a prime spot to see rare plants such as sundews and orchids. Where there are nutrient-poor bogs, you can see stunted black spruce, heath shrubs and sphagnum mats. The fens develop more of a shrub and tree layer.

C. Henderson

Gray jay

Other plants you might find here include jack-in-the-pulpit, rosemary, leatherleaf, Labrador tea, stemless, showy and yellow lady's slippers, black spruce and tamarack.

Several rare bird species, such as great gray owls, Nelson's sharp-tailed sparrows and LeConte's sparrows, call this peatland home. Approximately 110 bird species use this peatland habitat, including Wilson's phalaropes, northern harriers, sharp-tailed grouse, yellow rails, marbled godwits, short-eared owls, gray jays, red-eyed vireos, ovenbirds, common yellowthroats, swamp and savannah sparrows, bobolinks, and Nashville, Connecticut and black-throated green warblers.

You can also see mammals here. Look for arctic and masked shrews, snowshoe hares, southern bog lemmings, fishers and bobcats.

Note:

This peatland preserve has been set aside to protect the natural plant and animal communities and requires utmost care. Snowmobiles are restricted to marked and maintained trails. Summer considerations include rubber boots and plenty of mosquito repellent.

Highway 72 passes through the center of this SNA. Cars may be parked at the side of the road, although traffic can be heavy at times.

Best viewing time:

How do I get there?

Maps: MN Highway Coordinate: G-5
PRIM Area: Upper Red Lake
DeLorme MN Atlas Grid #: 83, 84

Additional directions:

Drive 12 miles north of Waskish on Highway 72.

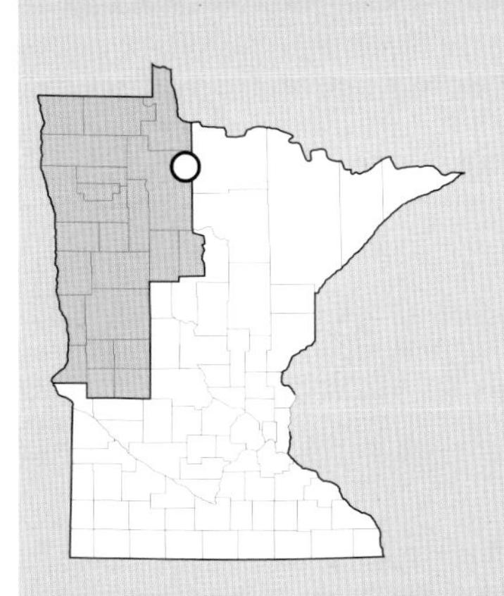

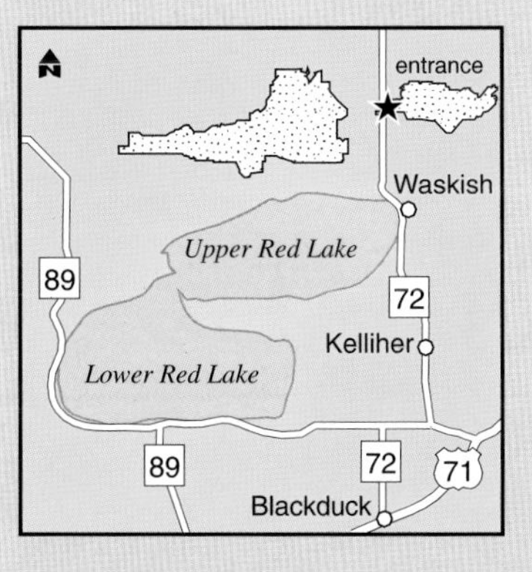

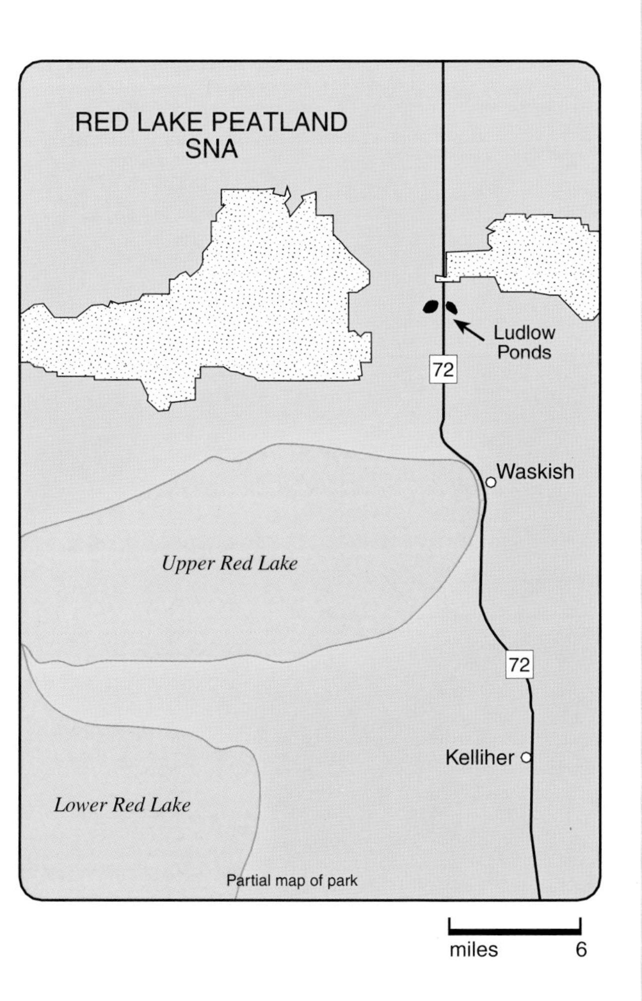

Facilities:

Recreational Opportunities:

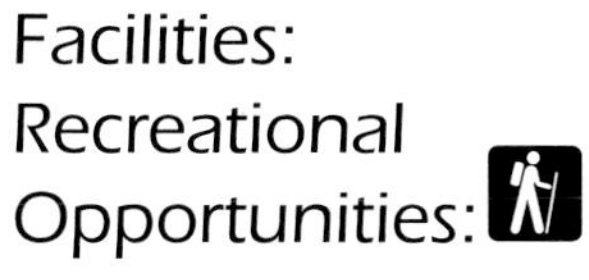

Contact:

Scientific and Natural Areas Program
DNR
2005 Highway 37
Eveleth MN 55734
(218) 744-7447

8–Pembina Trail Preserve SNA

Why is this area special?

Pembina Trail Preserve SNA is one of northwest Minnesota's finest native prairies. The nearby Pembina Trail, a major ox cart route once used to haul goods between St. Paul and Winnipeg, gives the area historical significance.

The SNA is an excellent example of tallgrass prairie with great vegetational diversity. Look for big bluestem, Indian grass, cord grass, large-headed blazing star, black-eyed Susan, Canada anemone and Culver's root. Meadows, marshes, shrub swamps and calcareous fens are interspersed throughout the area. The land here remains mostly flat, with slight elevation resulting in moisture differences.

C. Henderson

Greater prairie chicken

The prairie springs to life as the birds return north, and mallards, teal, prairie chickens, snipe and meadowlarks call loudly to announce their presence. Thousands of cranes congregate nearby during migration. This is also a good time to spot prairie chickens.

This area is a great place to watch for upland sandpipers, marbled godwits, Wilson's phalaropes, yellow rails, bobolinks and savannah, LeConte's and clay-colored sparrows. The frantic activity can be lulled only by a northern harrier cruising overhead.

While you're visiting the Pembina Trail Preserve, you might want to look for butterfly species such as Delaware and poweshiek skippers and regal fritillaries. Also keep an eye out for white-tailed jackrabbits, badgers, white-tailed deer and moose.

Note:

This prairie preserve was set up to protect its natural plant and animal communities and requires special care. Be on the lookout for plants and animals that are endangered, threatened or of special concern, such as Dakota skippers, yellow rails, prairie voles and white-fringed prairie orchids. Avoid disturbing them.

Summer is an excellent time to photograph blooming wildflowers. Different flowers will be in bloom throughout the season, so plan several trips.

Best viewing time:

How do I get there?

Maps: MN Highway Coordinate: C-7
PRIM Area: Crookston
DeLorme MN Atlas Grid #: 69 B-7

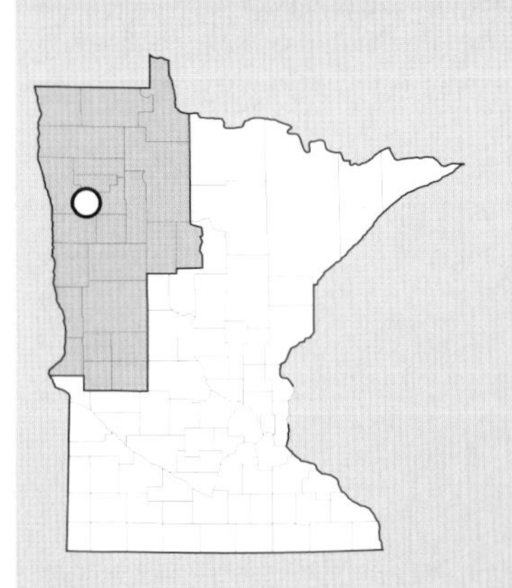

Additional directions:

Pembina Trail Preserve is located nine miles west of Mentor on Highway 45. From Highway 2, head east from Crookston to Highway 32. Turn south on Highway 32 and drive for four miles. Turn west on County Road 45 for 3 miles. There are three units of this SNA: the Foxboro Prairie, Crookston Prairie and the Pembina Trail Units. These units sit on either side of County Road 45 and east of County 44 south of the Pembina Trail Unit.

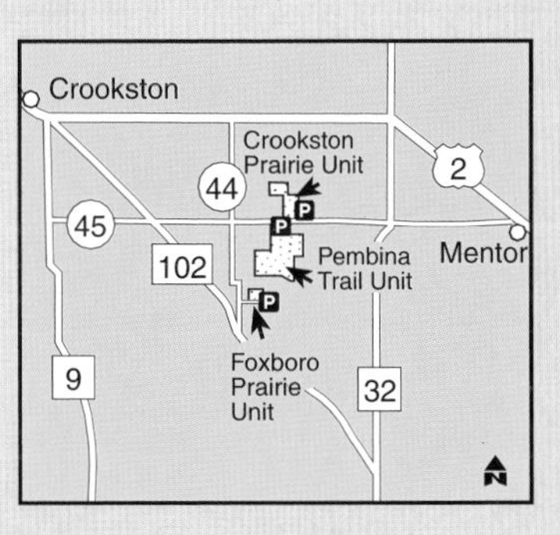

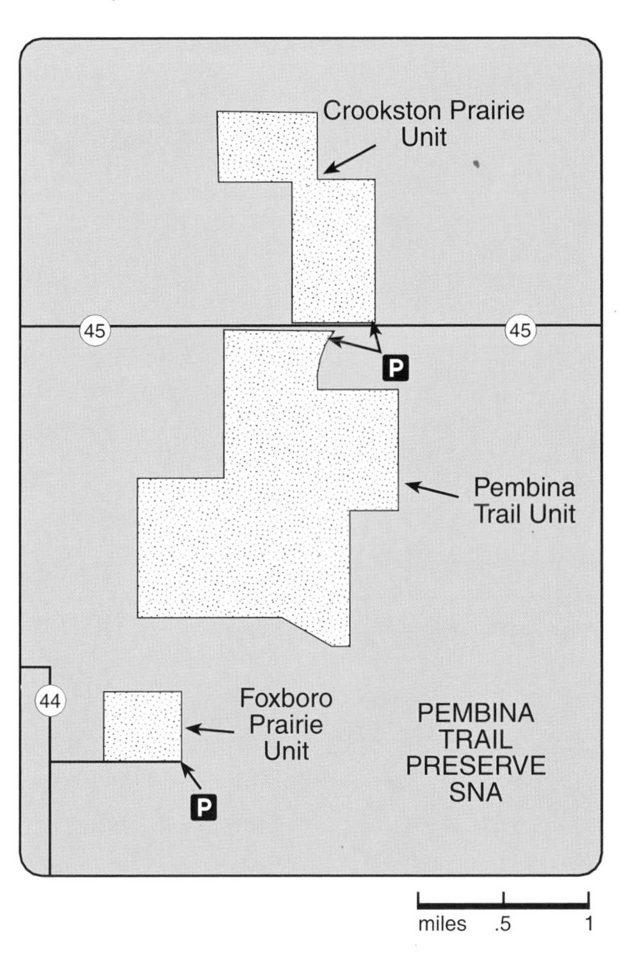

Facilities:

Recreational Opportunities:

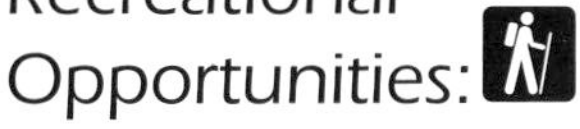

Contact:

DNR Area Wildlife Office
716 Pine Street
Crookston MN 56716
(218) 281-6063

Scientific and Natural Areas Program
DNR
Box 25
500 Lafayette Road
St. Paul MN 55155
(612) 297-2357

9–Agassiz Dunes SNA/ Prairie Smoke Dunes SNA/ Agassiz Environmental Learning Center

Why is this area special?

The sand dunes found in these three areas—Agassiz Dunes, Prairie Smoke Dunes and the Agassiz Environmental Learning Center—are associated with Glacial Lake Agassiz and combine to form the only dune field in Minnesota. Deposits from the Sand River formed a delta here between 9,000 and 12,000 years ago, and the wind sculpted it into a succession of dunes. You can still see some of the original dune formations, as well as the modern Sand Hill River and traces of the original Sand River.

Prior to European settlement, the area was comprised of oak openings and oak barrens maintained by fire. Ash and cottonwood-forested river bottoms, sedge meadow, aspen thickets, oak savanna and prairie now cover the land. Look for big and little bluestem, bur oak, prairie smoke, rough blazing star and purple prairie clover.

While you're here, watch for birds such as greater prairie chickens, bobolinks and western meadowlarks. Mammals such as white-tailed jack rabbits, red-backed voles, meadow jumping mice and moose abound here.

C. Henderson

Prairie smoke

Note:

The prairie preserves have been set aside to protect the natural plant and animal communities and are managed to resemble the land's pre-settlement condition. Do not disturb the plants or wildlife.

The Learning Center is managed for recreation. When you visit, watch for birds of the prairie like upland sandpipers and clay-colored sparrows. If you visit this site in late summer, you will be able to see colorful blazing stars, purple coneflowers and sunflowers in bloom.

The Learning Center has picnicking, bathrooms, telephones, information, camping, canoeing, interpretive trail and an interpretive center with nature programs.

Best viewing time:

How do I get there?

Maps: MN Highway Coordinates: C-7, C-8
PRIM AREA: Ada
DeLorme MN Atlas Grid #: 69 C/D-7

Additional directions:

Agassiz Dunes is located one mile south of Fertile on Highway 32 and a quarter of a mile west. Prairie Smoke Dunes is located five miles south of Fertile on Highway 32, then a quarter of a mile west on Highway 7. The AELC is located just west of Fertile.

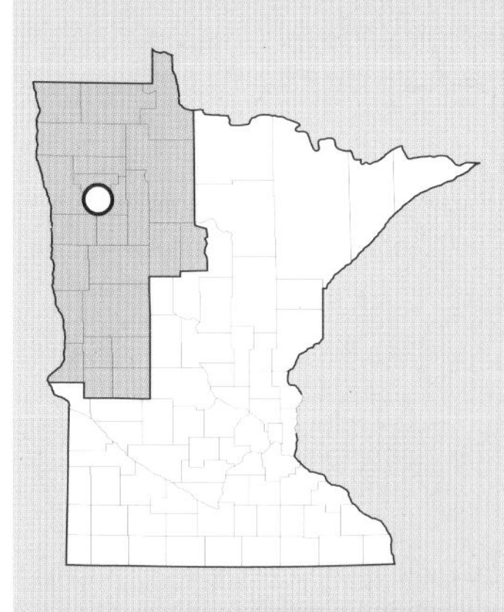

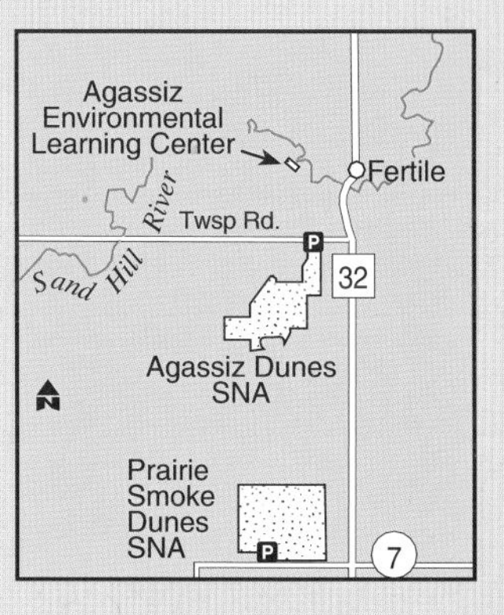

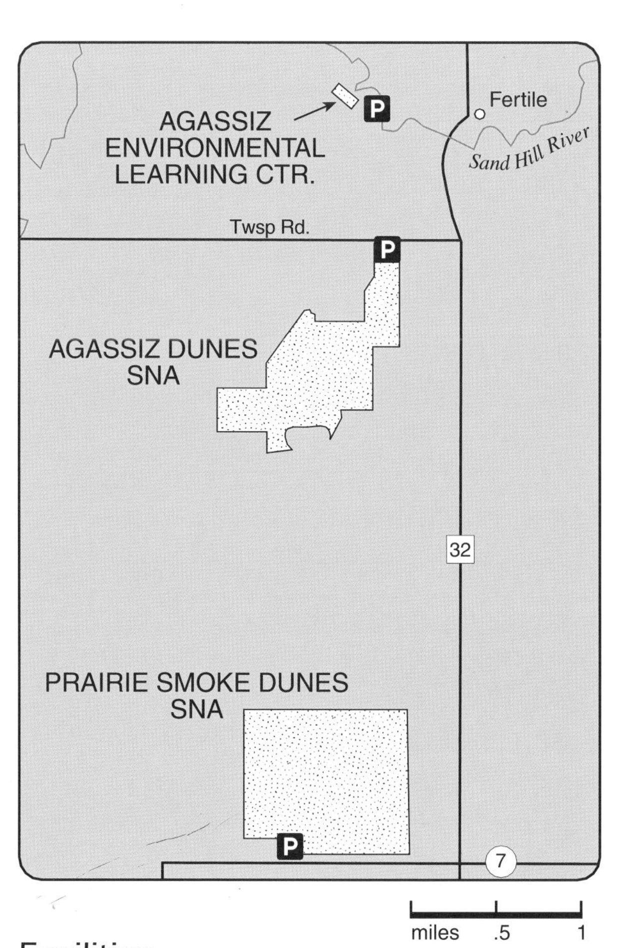

Facilities- Center only:

Recreational Opportunities:

Contact:

Scientific and Natural Areas Program
DNR
1221 Fir Avenue East
Fergus Falls MN 56537
(218) 739-7497

Agassiz Environmental Learning Center
P.O. Box 388
Fertile MN 56540
(218) 945-3129

Scientific and Natural Areas Program
DNR
Box 25
500 Lafayette Road
St. Paul MN 55155
(612) 297-2357

10–Lake Bemidji State Park

Katie Haws

Why is this area special?

This park is special for wildlife associated with old growth red pine, white pine and northern hardwoods.

The Minnesota state legislature first established this 1600-acre park in 1923. The park serves 112,000 visitors each year and contains many northern Minnesota plants and wildlife species. Black spruce and tamarack bog, basswood and sugar maple, birch, jack pine, lowland hardwood and wetland species can all be found here. Plant enthusiasts can look for alder, bog birch, Labrador tea and moccasin flower grass.

A recently-completed 1,200-foot boardwalk will take you through the tamarack spruce lowland forest. From the boardwalk you can view stemless, yellow and showy lady's slippers, dragon's mouth orchids and insectivorous plants such as pitcher plants and sun dews.

The park has three active bald eagle nests. You should also keep your eyes open for brown creepers, black-backed woodpeckers, scarlet tanagers, osprey, common loons, great blue and green herons, wood ducks, goldeneyes, ruffed grouse, belted kingfishers, pileated woodpeckers, eastern wood pewees, hermit thrushes, and Nashville and chestnut-sided warblers. Almost 200 different kinds of birds can be seen throughout the year in Lake Bemidji State Park.

There are more than 50 species of mammals known in the park. Among these are star-nosed moles, Franklin's ground squirrels, red foxes, long-tailed weasels, fishers, black bears and white-tailed deer.

Note:

Two spots in the park are particularly scenic: Rocky Point and Bass Creek. Rocky Point sits high on a bluff above the blue waters of Lake Bemidji and is an excellent duck-watching spot.

A new boardwalk along Bass Creek gives you a spectacular view of eagles, herons and grebes as well as an undisturbed view of a bog pond.

Lake Bemidji State Park has interpretive boardwalks and observation decks, which are located at Sundew Pond, Cass Creek and Rocky Point. The park has a full-time naturalist and a large pontoon boat for guided excursions.

The site also has a beach, a new paved bike trail, and over a mile of lakeshore. A boat launch/marina offers boats for rent. The area is handicapped accessible and the trail center is open all year.

Best viewing time:

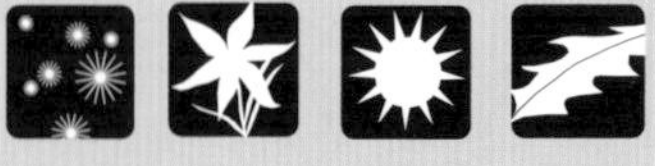

How do I get there?

Maps: MN Highway Coordinate: F-7
PRIM Area: Blackduck (Bemidji detached portion)
DeLorme MN Atlas Grid #: 71 C-9

Additional Directions:

From Bemidji, drive north on Highway 71 for six miles. Turn right onto Glidden Road and continue for one mile, then turn left on Highway 197/County Road 21 and continue for a quarter mile. The park is located 1.7 miles east on Highway 20. The park entrance is on the south side of this highway.

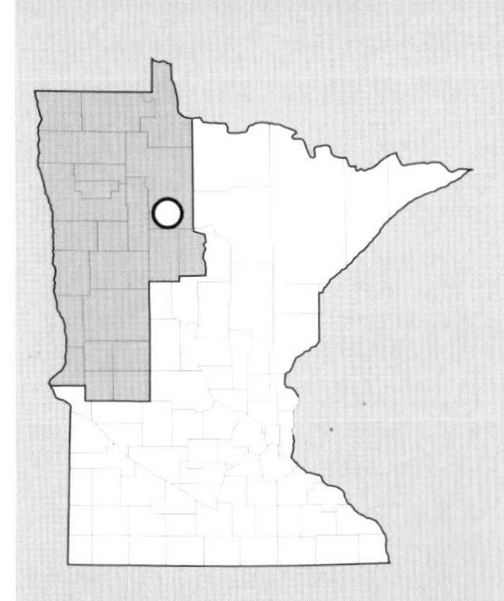

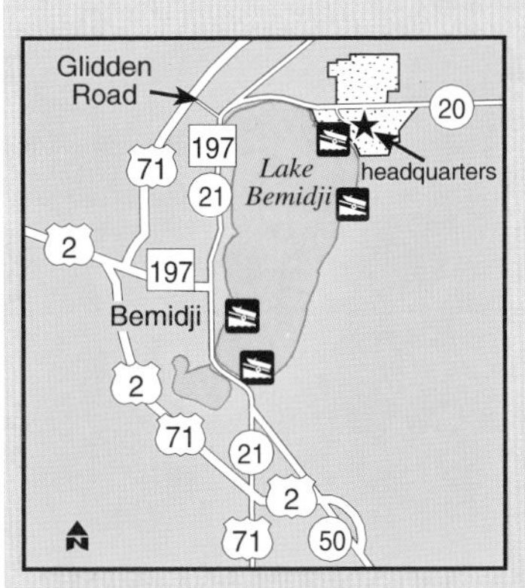

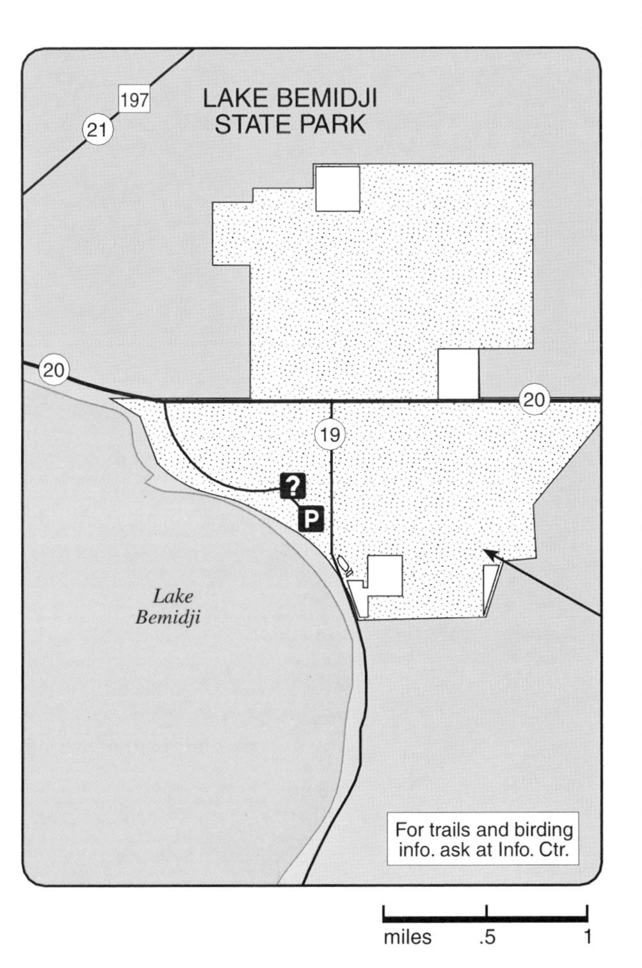

Facilities:    

Recreational Opportunities:

Contact:

Lake Bemidji State Park
3401 State Park Road NE
Bemidji MN 56601
(218) 755-3843

Division of Parks and Recreation
DNR
500 Lafayette Road
St. Paul MN 55155-4040
(612) 296-6157
(888) MINNDNR

11–Mississippi River/Cass Lake/ Lake Winnibigoshish

Why is this area special?

The Mississippi River flows leisurely between Cass Lake and Lake Winnibigoshish for 10 river miles. One of many established canoe and boating routes in Minnesota, this segment is home to many bald eagles.

You can also explore the maple, basswood and pine forests by car from the Great River Road. If you would rather canoe, you'll have access to the river at several spots, including the dam at Cass Lake, the Third River Bridge and Reese and West Winnibigoshish landings. Where the Mississippi River meanders through undeveloped marshland you have an excellent chance of spotting coots, herons and terns. The backwaters and oxbows are filled with wild rice and cattail, serving as a breeding and molting habitat for ducks. Look for common loons, wood ducks and ring-necked ducks. You might also spot an osprey, pileated woodpecker or Lincoln's sparrow.

C. Henderson

Mink on the Mississippi

Many songbirds inhabit the surrounding forests. Sixteen species of warblers breed here, as well as vireos, flycatchers and tanagers. Look for their colorful plumage and distinct vocalizations in late May and June.

The area is primarily under state and federal ownership and, due to the Indian burial mounds and relicts of native villages in the vicinity, it has archeological significance. The area falls within the Leech Lake Indian Reservation and Chippewa National Forest, and it is important to the Ojibwe Band of Indians because of the abundant water, wildlife and food resources.

Mammals that you might find in the area include arctic shrews, star-nosed moles, beavers, coyotes, timber wolves, black bears, river otters, wood frogs and spring peepers. Plant species include jack and red pine, bur oak, American hazel and blazing star.

Note:

There are several campgrounds in the vicinity, but no designated trails. Forest maps are available from the Cass Lake office of the Chippewa National Forest. Canoe route maps are available from the DNR office in Bemidji.

Best viewing time:

How do I get there?

Maps: MN Highway Coordinates: H-7, G-7
PRIM Area: Bemidji
DeLorme MN Atlas Grid #: 72 D-3

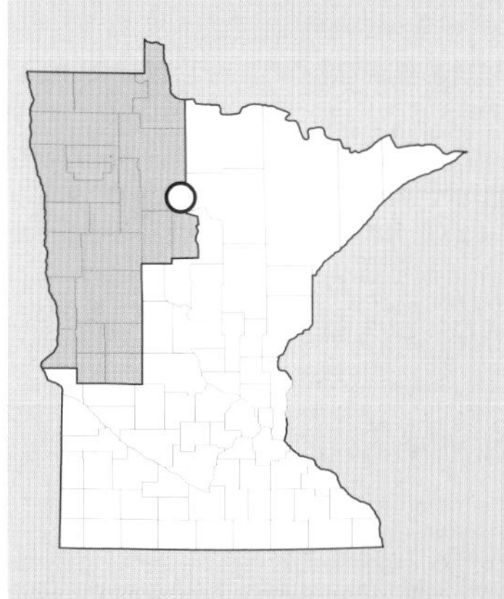

Additional directions:

Go east from Cass Lake on Highway 26 to Highway 10. Turn left, or north. The Great River Road is the first paved road heading east, approximately five miles north of Highway 2. This road continues to the east along the Mississippi River and Lake Winnibigoshish until it returns to Highway 2 just west of Bena.

There are access points for canoes along this stretch of the river, and campsites along both lakes and the river.

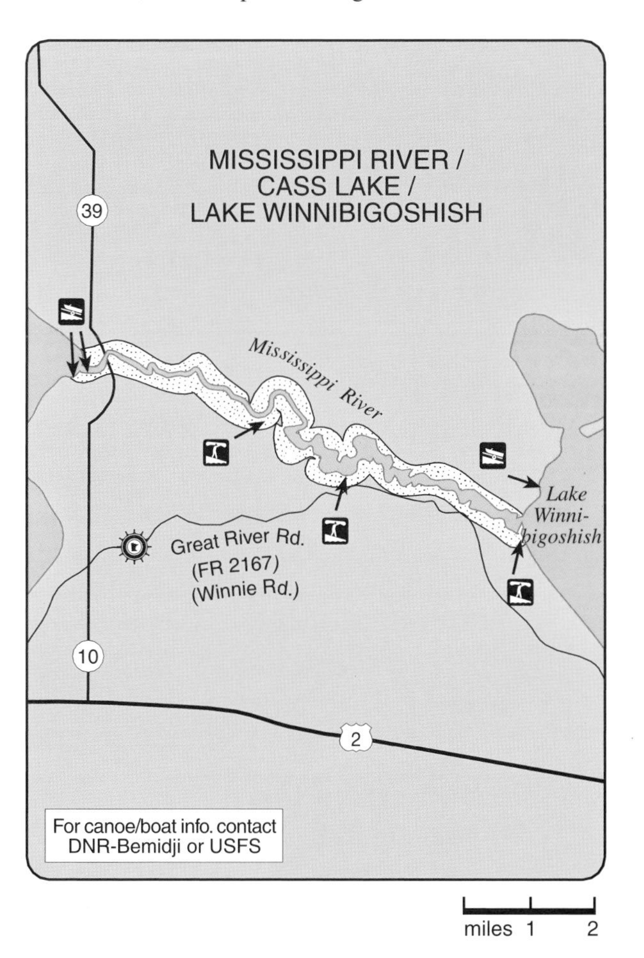

Facilities:   

Recreational Opportunities:

Contact:

Trails and Waterways Section
DNR
2115 Birchmont Beach Road
Bemidji MN 56601
(218) 755-3969

Cass Lake Ranger Station
Chippewa National Forest
RR 3 Box 219
Cass Lake MN 56633
(218) 335-2283

12–Itasca State Park

Why is this area special?

Itasca Park, with its 32,000 acres of stately red and white pines, countless undisturbed lakes and ponds, and miles of gently rolling hills, has become a famous natural and cultural landmark in North America. Here, at Lake Itasca, is where the mighty Mississippi begins its 2,552-mile journey to the sea.

Itasca State Park is a product of the last ice age, when huge glaciers scoured the land and left in their wake the moraines and kettle/bowl topography so easily appreciated at Itasca. The park contains the largest old growth white and red pine ecosystem in the state. Much of the forest is 100-300 years old, but the west side was logged in the 1800s and sports a newer forest of aspen and associated hardwoods.

In addition to Lake Itasca, the park has hundreds of small lakes, including several, like Lake Arco and Lake Deming, that are hydrologically unique. You can see numerous creeks, small lakes and wetlands when you visit this park.

C. Henderson

Common loon

Loons nest on many of the park's lakes, and there are two eagle territories within the park. Ospreys and turkey vultures often dot the skies and, in the spring, you'll be overwhelmed by the songs of warblers. More than 200 species of birds have been seen in the park and 139 species nest here.

Some of the birds you can watch for are great blue herons, wood ducks, hooded mergansers, red-tailed hawks, northern goshawks, ruffed grouse, black-backed and pileated woodpeckers, ruby-throated hummingbirds, scarlet tanagers, gray jays, brown creepers, red-eyed vireos, wood and hermit thrushes, northern parulas, ovenbirds and evening grosbeaks.

Best viewing time:

One of the best times to visit Itasca State Park is from May 10 through May 20 so you can experience the spring migration of forest songbirds. There is a wonderful variety of colorful birds that can be enjoyed in the woodlands at that time. Warblers are a special treat at that time of year.

While staying at the park, you may also wish to go out on the tour boat "Chester Charles." The tour guides are very good at pointing out the bald eagles and other wildlife that is easily viewed from the boat. The park is also home to 53 species of mammals. You might run across a deer, black bear, beaver, northern flying squirrel, porcupine, river otter, timber wolf or raccoon.

While at Lake Itasca, take a moment to search for reptiles and amphibians like smooth green snakes, blue-spotted salamanders, spring peepers and wood frogs. Plant species of note are large-flowered trillium, pitcher plants, high bush cranberries, and American mountain ash. You can also look for the park's 27 different species of orchids.

Note:

In 1996, straight-line winds felled many trees in the park. You can see a severely wind-damaged area west of Wilderness Drive. Use the interpretive trail running through the area to learn about the damaged spots.

There are a few specific areas at Itasca State Park that you'll want to visit:

Be sure to check out the Itasca Wilderness Sanctuary, which can be seen from the Bohall Wilderness Trail. Here

Andrea Lee Lambrecht

Showy ladyslipper

continued...

you will find rare plants such as bog adder's mouth and matricary grape fern.

Lake Alice bog, located two miles east of the park along County Road 3, is a spruce and tamarack bog where you'll see Connecticut warblers, gray jays and olive-sided, yellow-bellied and alder flycatchers.

Another excellent spot to watch birds is the Deer Park Trail, which runs along small lakes inhabited by kingfishers, yellow warblers and ospreys. Large maple, birch and basswood grow in this transitional area.

You'll also want to see an important archaeological area called the Itasca bison kill site, Lake Itasca's forestry demonstration station and the natural history museum.

If you're most interested in birding, visit the park between mid-May and July. Fall is also a treat, with both fall migration and the flaming red maples. Look for gray jays and black-backed woodpeckers in the winter.

This park has an excellent system of paved bicycle trails and 20 miles of groomed cross-country ski trails. Lodging can be reserved at cabins or at travel trailer or tent camping sites in the park and there are also rooms available at Douglas Lodge. Other lodging is available at private resorts in the Lake Itasca area.

C. Henderson

How do I get there?

Maps: MN Highway Coordinate: E-8, E-9
PRIM Area: Lake Itasca
DeLorme MN Atlas Grid #: 61 A-6

Additional Directions:

Drive 20 miles north of Park Rapids on Highway 71. There are several entrances into the park; the south entrance is only open during the summer. All entrances are clearly marked from the highway.

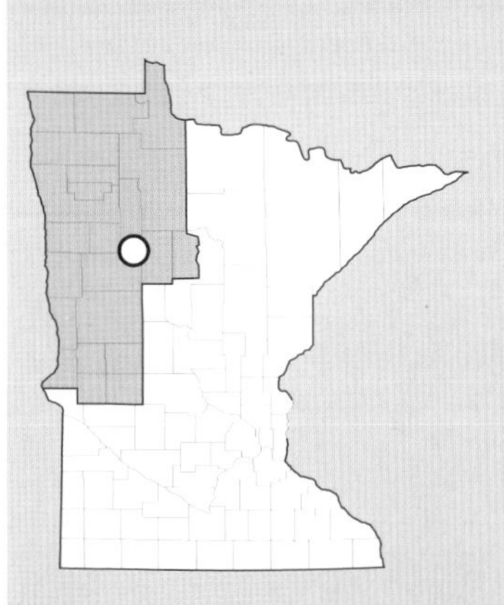

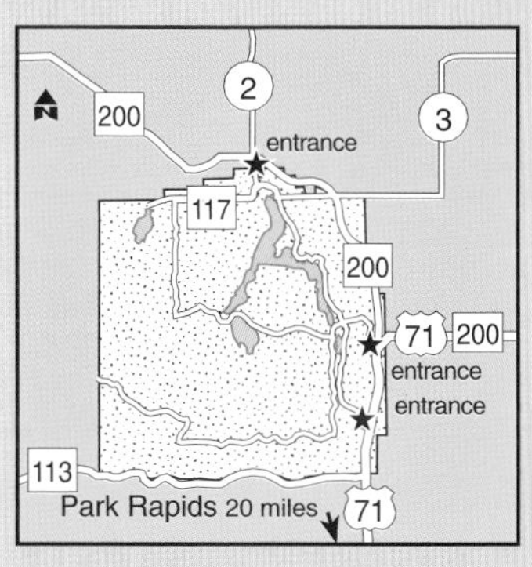

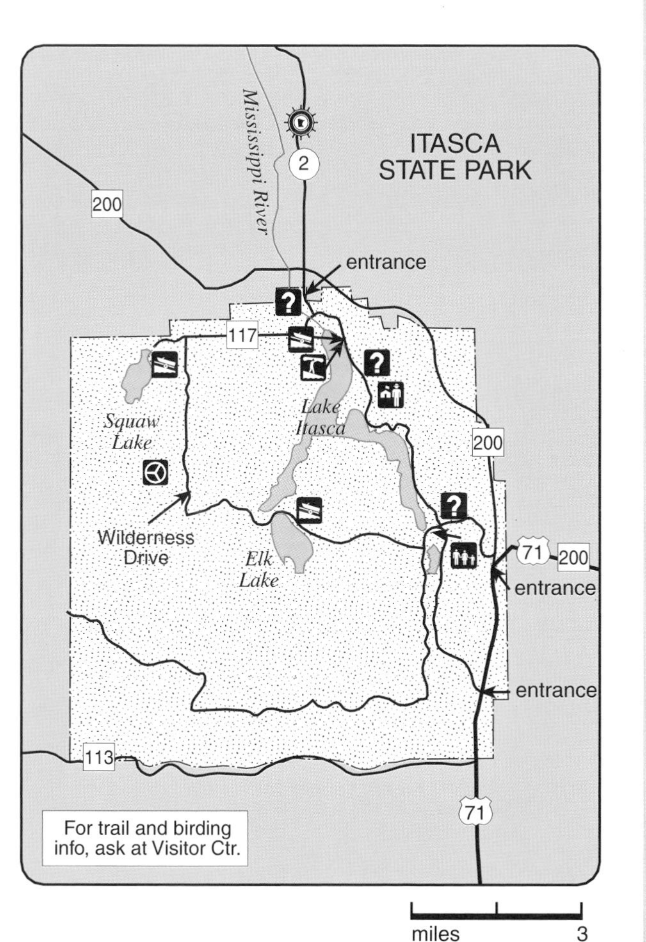

Facilities:      

Recreational Opportunities: 

Contact:

Itasca State Park
Lake Itasca MN 56460
(218) 266-2114

Division of Parks and Recreation
DNR
500 Lafayette Road
St. Paul MN 55155-4040
(612) 296-6157
(888) MINNDNR

13–Felton Prairie WMA/SNA

Why is this area special?

Felton Prairie has been renowned for a long time as a place to watch highly unusual prairie birds, but it's only recently that Felton Prairie's public land tracts have been recognized as vitally important habitat relics.

Much of the surrounding land, previously grazed as pasture, has now been converted to million-dollar gravel pits. But the Felton WMA and three units of the Felton Prairie SNA, over 700 acres in all, protect the remaining virgin shortgrass prairie in its pre-settlement condition. The area is managed by prescribed burning.

Robert Dana

Dakota skipper

When you visit the Felton Prairie Complex, you could see many different bird species, including Sprague's pipits, chestnut-collared longspurs, prairie chickens, LeConte's sparrows, upland sandpipers, northern pintails, marbled godwits, loggerhead shrikes, bobolinks, western meadowlarks, northern harriers and grasshopper, vesper, clay-colored and Baird's sparrows.

Come in June and July to see beautiful prairie plants such as prairie smoke, prairie dropseed, blazing star, wood lilies, purple coneflowers, prairie sunflowers and showy goldenrod in bloom. You can also watch the butterflies; you'll find Delaware and poweshiek skippers and regal fritillaries in the Felton Prairie Complex.

Mammals include white-tailed jack rabbits, prairie voles, long-tailed weasels, white-tailed deer and coyotes.

Note:

Glaciers left a huge rock in the Felton Prairie Complex. The soil at its base has been deeply eroded from thousands of buffalo using it as a rubbing rock. When you visit this site, you can sit on the rock, peer out over the horizon, and imagine the herds of buffalo.

You will need a permit to camp on the Felton Prairie Complex; these can be obtained from the prairie biologist in Fergus Falls. There are no maintained hiking trails at this site.

Best viewing time:

How do I get there?

Maps: MN Highway Coordinate: C-9
PRIM Area: Ada
DeLorme MN Atlas Grid #: 59 B-6

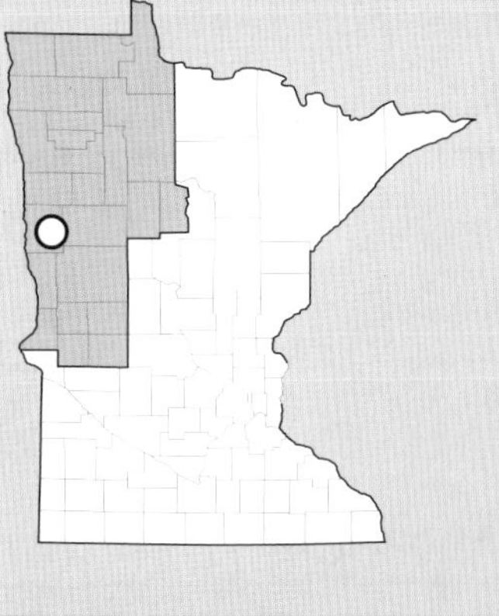

Additional directions:

The town of Glyndon is located nine miles east of Moorhead on Highway 10. From Glyndon, continue three miles east on Highway 10. Drive north on Highway 9 for 12 miles to County Road 108. Turn right, or east, onto 108 and continue for three miles to the end of the gravel road. The Shrike Unit and Felton WMA can be accessed from County Road 34, between two and three miles east of Felton.

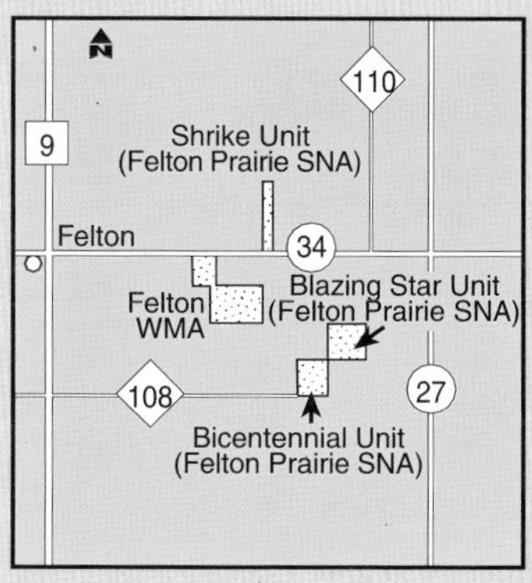

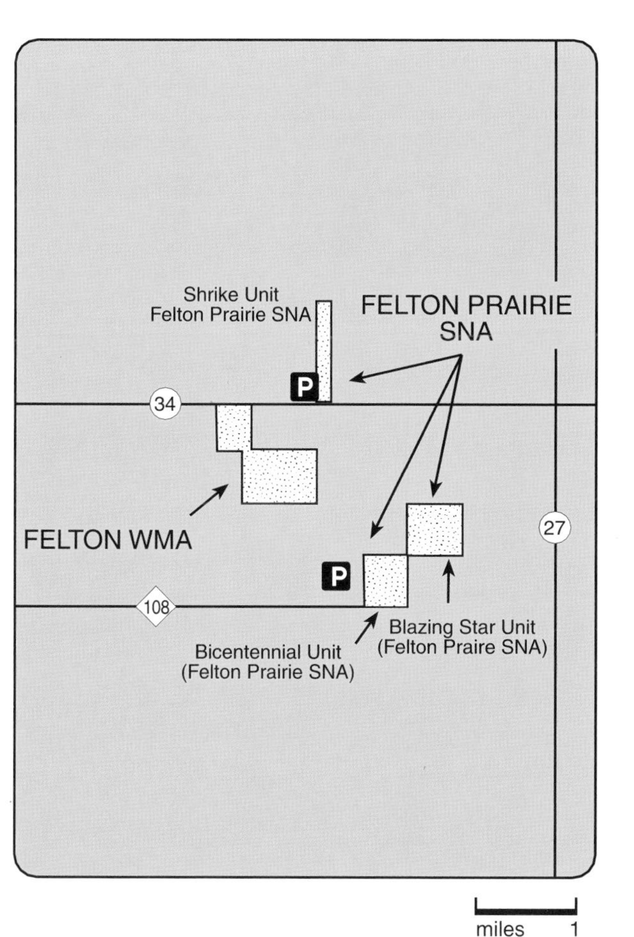

Contact:

Scientific and Natural Areas Program
DNR
Box 25
500 Lafayette Road
St. Paul MN 55155
(612) 297-2357

Prairie biologist
Wildlife manager
DNR
1221 Fir Avenue
Fergus Falls MN 56537
(218) 739-7576
(218) 739-7497

Facilities:

Recreational Opportunities:

14–Buffalo River State Park/ Bluestem Prairie SNA

Why is this area special?

The Bluestem Prairie, owned by The Nature Conservancy, is one of the highest-quality prairie sites in the United States. Its 1,296 acres include mesic, dry and wet prairie along with sedge meadows, aspen stands and willow brush. The Buffalo River State Park sits just north of the Bluestem Prairie and contains virgin prairie and river hardwoods associated with the Buffalo River.

Two old gravel pits near the entrance to the state park have been restored to prairie. Although the land will never again be native prairie, this restoration may bring some plant and animal species back to the area.

C. Henderson

Loggerhead shrike

You will be amazed at the variety of wildlife you can find here. The area contains more than 250 plant species, including pale purple coneflowers, silky asters, dotted blazing stars, Maximillian's sunflowers and prairie roses. Among these plants you'll see Delaware skippers, spring azures, regal fritillaries and Melissa blues.

Prairie chickens gather here to perform their elaborate spring courtship ritual, known as booming, and you can watch them closely through the blinds provided by The Nature Conservancy. Sandhill cranes, upland sandpipers, marbled godwits, bobolinks, western meadowlarks, dickcissels, loggerhead shrikes, and vesper, clay-colored and Henslow's sparrows are among the 200 bird species that you might see.

You may also encounter a few of the 40 different species of mammals, including mink, red foxes, northern grasshopper mice, coyotes and white-tailed deer.

Note:

A large new interpretive center, the **Moorhead State University Regional Science Center,** is located two miles east of the Buffalo River State Park headquarters. The Center, which provides environmental programs for school groups, is often open to the public.

A seasonal naturalist presents programs at the state park during the summer months. You may also use the prairie chicken blinds; reservations must be made with The Nature Conservancy's Glyndon office.

Facilities at the state park are handicapped accessible.

Best viewing time:

How do I get there:

Maps: MN Highway Coordinate: C-10
PRIM Area: Moorhead
DeLorme MN Atlas Grid #: 59 D-6

Additional directions:

To get to Bluestem Prairie, drive 11 miles east out of Moorhead on Highway 10. Go south for one mile on Highway 9, then east for one mile on County Road 79.

The state park is located in the same general area, 12 miles east of Moorhead. The state park road turns south from Highway 2.

The Moorhead Science Center, located two miles east of state park headquarters, is also accessible from the state park road.

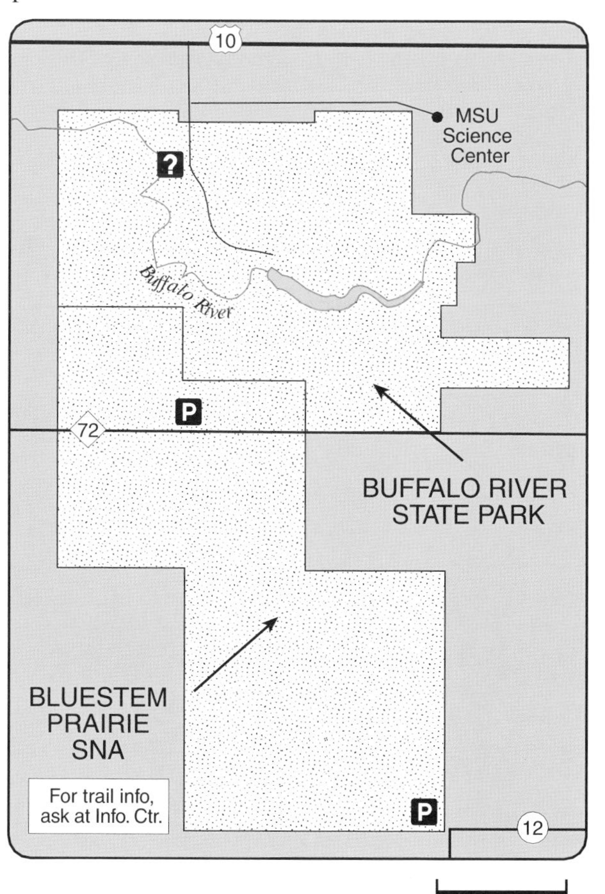

Facilities:     

Recreational Opportunities:

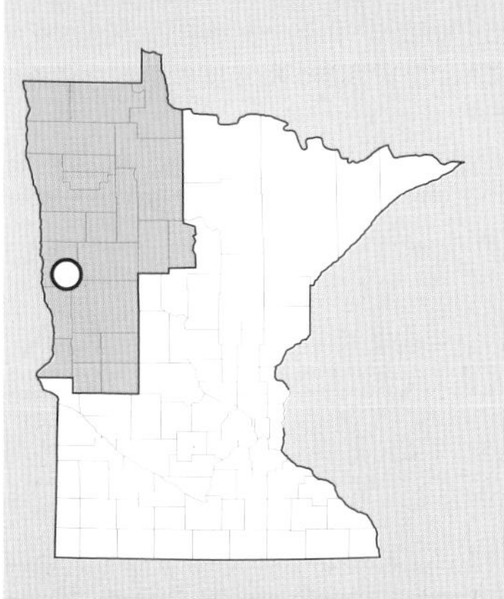

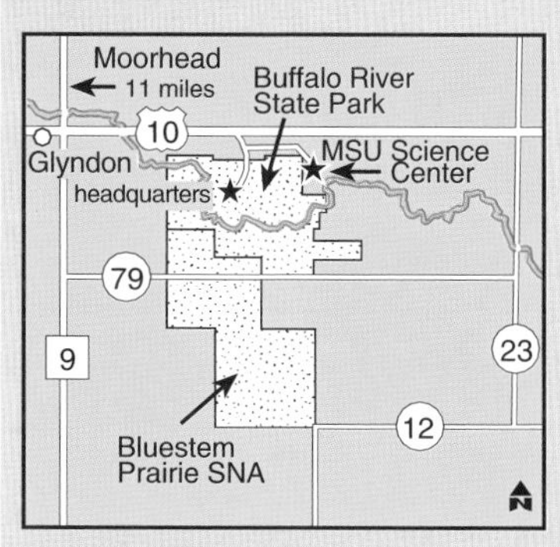

Contact:

Director Science and Stewardship
The Nature Conservancy
RR 2 Box 240
Glyndon MN 56547
(218) 498-2679

Buffalo River State Park
RR 2 Box 118
Glyndon MN 56545
(218) 498-2124

Regional Science Center
Buffalo River Site
Moorhead State University
Moorhead MN 56563
(218) 236-2904

Scientific and Natural Areas Program
DNR
Box 25
500 Lafayette Road
St. Paul MN 55155
(612) 297-2357

15–Tamarac NWR

What makes this area special?

The Tamarac National Wildlife Refuge lies in a place where tallgrass prairie, northern hardwood and coniferous forests meet. This transitional area is rich in American Indian and early pioneer settler history, and much of the refuge remains in nearly pristine condition.

At the top of a watershed, the refuge's numerous lakes, rivers and marshes are free from invasion by exotic species and pollution. You'll find a rich diversity of natural habitats from tamarack and black spruce to white pine. Stands of upland hardwoods, aspen, birch and lowland conifer as well as bogs and remnant grasslands are managed to meet the needs of native wildlife species. Look for wild rice, Indian paintbrush, blazing star and showy and yellow lady's slippers.

C. Henderson
Golden-winged warbler

Established in 1938 as a breeding ground and sanctuary for migratory birds, most of the refuge's early development was done by the Civilian Conservation Corps. The Corps made way for the area's present populations of common loons, red-necked grebes, trumpeter swans, wood ducks, bald eagles, red-shouldered hawks, ruffed grouse, Forster's terns, ovenbirds, scarlet tanagers, rose-breasted grosbeaks, and golden-winged, chestnut-sided and black-throated green warblers.

Mammals include porcupines, timber wolves, fishers, badgers, bobcats, river otter, mink and deer.

Note:

The visitor center and office are open Monday through Friday from 7:30 a.m. to 4 p.m. all year long. It's also open Saturday and Sunday from noon to 5 p.m. from Memorial Day weekend through Labor Day weekend. Both the office and the visitor center are closed on all federal holidays. The Visitor Center book store, auditorium, exhibits and bathrooms are handicapped accessible.

Arrange to have a group presentation at the site. The center offers presentations that have been arranged in advance as well as assistance with school field trip planning, annual teacher workshops and summer guided tours. There are hiking trails and a self-guided auto tour and opportunities to pick mushrooms and berries.

Hunting allowed. Call ahead for hunting season dates.

Best viewing time:

How do I get there:

Maps: MN Highway Coordinate: D-9
PRIM Area: Lake Itasca/Detroit Lakes
DeLorme MN Atlas Grid #: 60 C-2

Additional directions:

From Detroit Lakes, head east on Highway 34 for eight miles, then north on County Road 29 for nine miles. The visitor center and headquarters are located at the junction of County Roads 26 and 29.

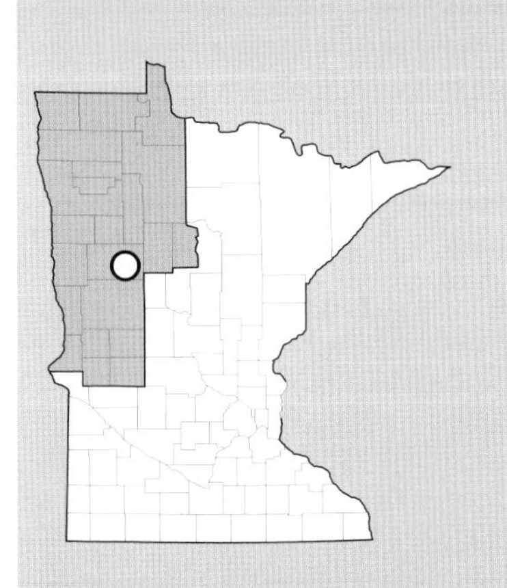

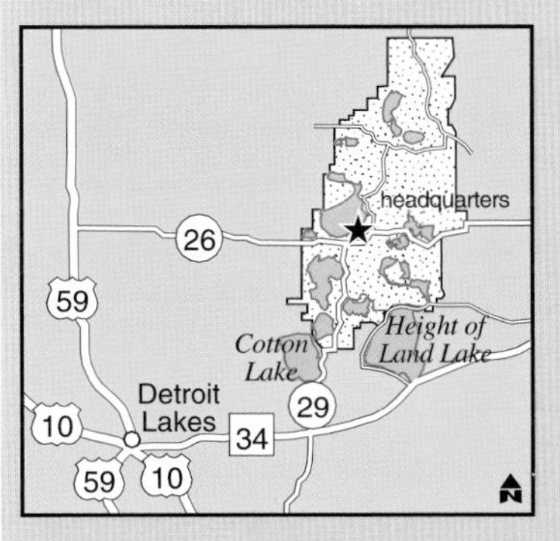

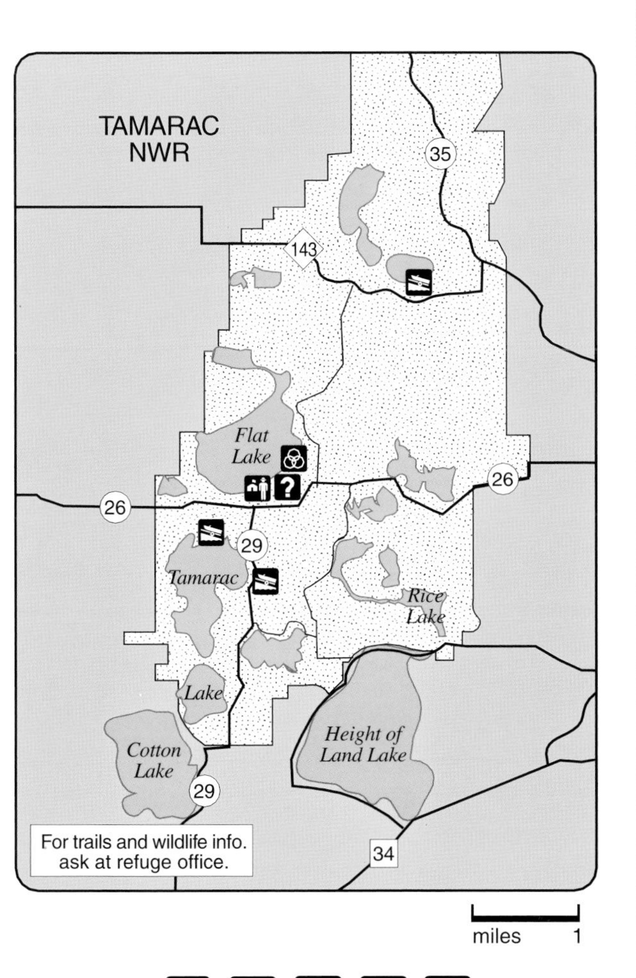

Facilities:   

Recreational Opportunities:

Contact:

Tamarac NWR
HC 10 Box 145
Rochert MN 56578-9735
(218) 847-2641

16–Pine Point Research Natural Area

Why is this area special?

This 800-acre research natural area is part of the Chippewa National Forest. Largely protected from logging in the 19th century, this area now consists primarily of old growth red pine forest, with some of the red pines dating back more than 300 years. American Indians once traveled through the area and collected wild rice from low areas along the shore.

The site was originally established in 1932 and it is one of 50 original research natural areas set up by the Forest Service. It is an excellent place to feel the tranquillity of the wind in the pines. Relax among the large-flowered bellwort, wild sarsaparilla, bunchberries, blueberries, snowberries and stemless lady's slippers.

Barney Oldfield

Wood frog

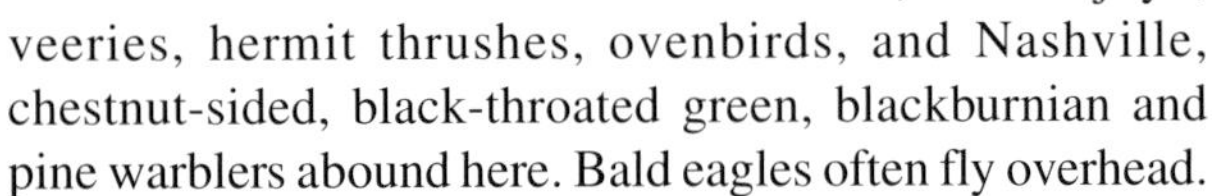

Black-backed woodpeckers tap on the old trees, and you will see an occasional brown creeper exploring tree bark. You might also see red-breasted nuthatches, blue jays, veeries, hermit thrushes, ovenbirds, and Nashville, chestnut-sided, black-throated green, blackburnian and pine warblers abound here. Bald eagles often fly overhead.

It's not unusual to spot a porcupine at Pine Point. Black bear can be found here, along with fishers and bobcats.

Note:

Parking is only available along the side of the road at the research natural area. There are several trails within the site, but you should use a compass or GPS unit to explore. No camping is allowed and there are no facilities.

The facilities and recreational opportunities listed for this site can be found at Stony Point Campground only. Stony Point has an interpretive trail and is an excellent spot to watch Leech Lake's water birds: black and common terns, American white pelicans and double crested cormorants.

Best viewing time:

How do I get there?

Maps: MN Highway Coordinate: G-9
PRIM Area: Bemidji
DeLorme MN Atlas Grid #: 62 A-2

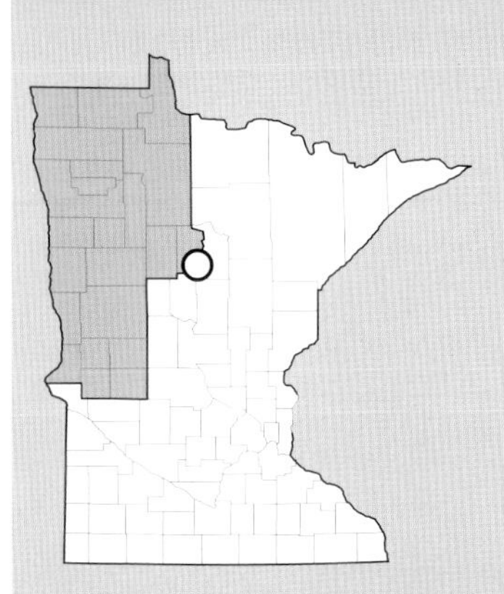

Additional directions:

Head south of Walker for 7.5 miles to the intersection of Highway 200 and County Road 13. Turn north on County Road 13 and continue for 6.5 miles to the junction of County Road 72. Head north on 72 for three miles. The research natural area is located to the west and there are several forest service roads that enter the site.

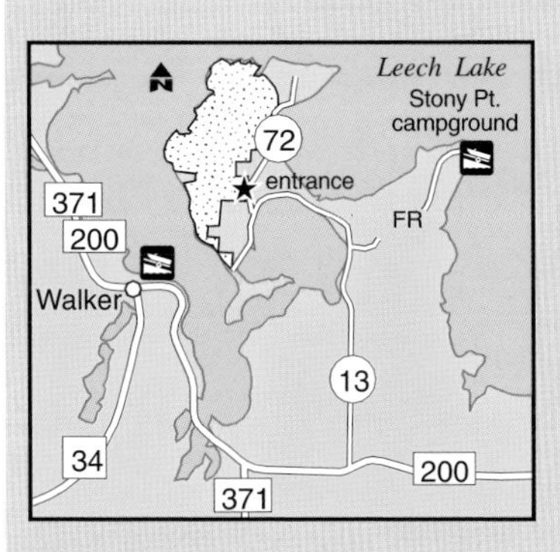

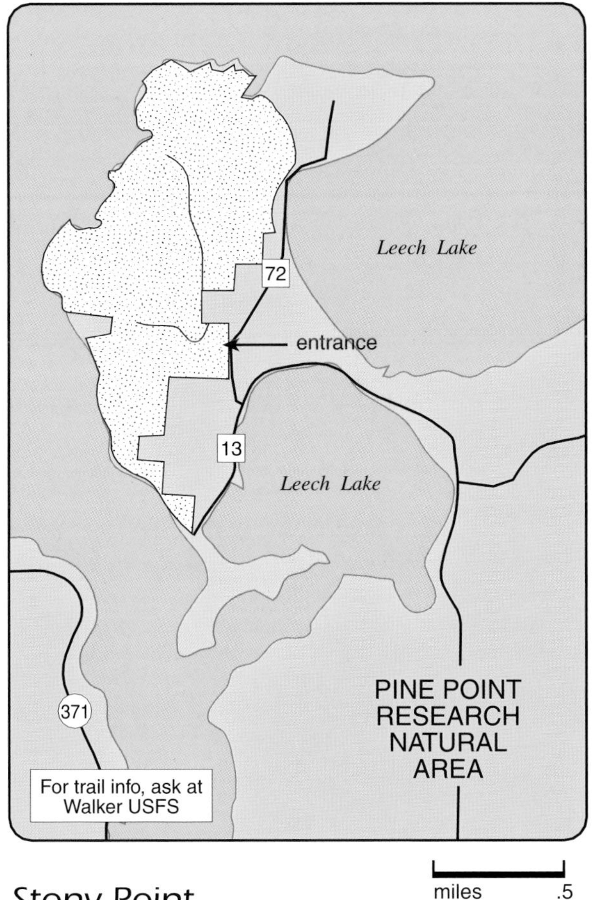

Stony Point only

Facilities: 

Recreational Opportunities:   

Contact:

District Ranger
Walker District
Chippewa National Forest
HC 73 Box 15
Walker MN 56484
(218) 547-1044

17–Deep Portage Conservation Reserve

Why is this area special?

The Deep Portage Conservation Reserve is a 6,000-acre research and recreation area dedicated to environmental education. Participate in programs here to learn about natural resources and resource management.

The five-mile by two-mile reserve contains five lakes and twelve miles of shoreline. Glaciers carved out its spectacular deep lakes and steep hills 12,000 years ago. Forests consist of aspen, birch, maple, oak and basswood with scattered red and white pine. You will see marsh marigolds, fireweed, wood lilies and clintonia when you visit.

Lynn and Donna Rogers

Porcupine

You might see loons, woodpeckers and Nashville, blackburnian and other woodland warblers. Look for green herons, wood ducks, common goldeneyes, osprey, bald eagles, broad-winged hawks, saw-whet owls, hermit thrushes, red-eyed vireos, ovenbirds and scarlet tanagers. In the springtime, listen for the "peenting" of woodcocks, the winnowing of snipe and the drumming of grouse.

The reserve is also home to a variety of mammals. Look carefully and you might see a snowshoe hare, northern flying squirrel, beaver, coyote, bobcat, white-tailed deer or even a black bear.

Note:

The reserve's year-round conference and education center is located near Hackensack. Groups may visit the center for overnight environmental education experiences. Outdoor classrooms include the wild flower garden, archery range, compass schoolyard, rifle range, sporting clays, bog boardwalk, orienteering course and forest management demonstration sites.

The reserve also has a visitor center, gift shop, interpretive trails and boardwalk.

 Hunting allowed. Call ahead for hunting season dates.

Best viewing time:

How do I get there?

Maps: MN Highway Coordinate: G-10
PRIM Area: Pine River
DeLorme MN Atlas Grid #: 62 C-3

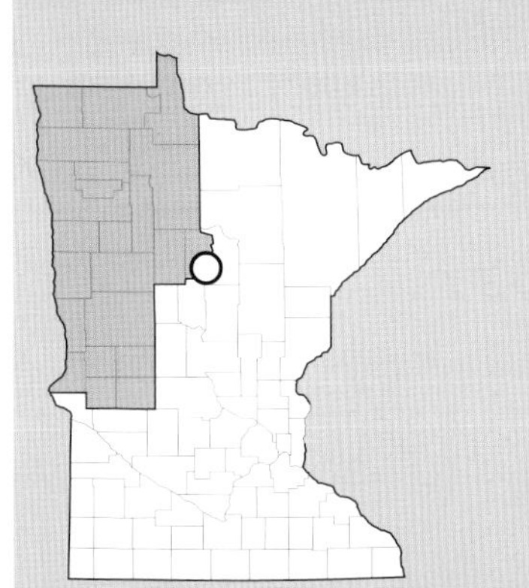

Additional directions:

From Hackensack, head east on County Road 5 for 5.5 miles to County Road 46. Turn south on 46 and continue for four miles to the entrance road. Turn right and continue up the hill to the headquarters.

From Pine River head north on County Road 44, which will turn into Highway 84. Drive north for 13.5 miles and turn left onto County Road 46. Continue on 46 for 3.5 miles to the entrance road.

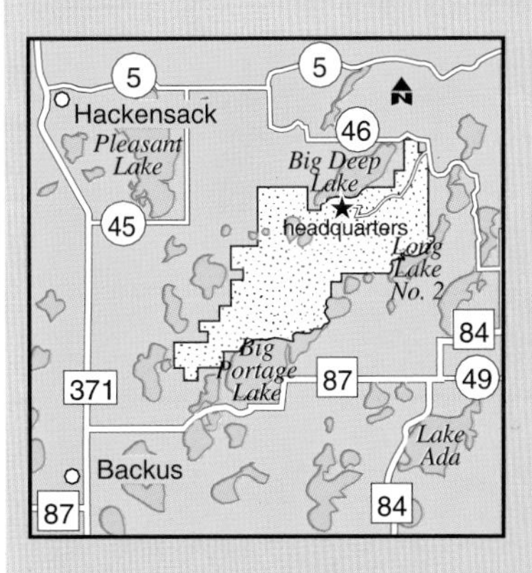

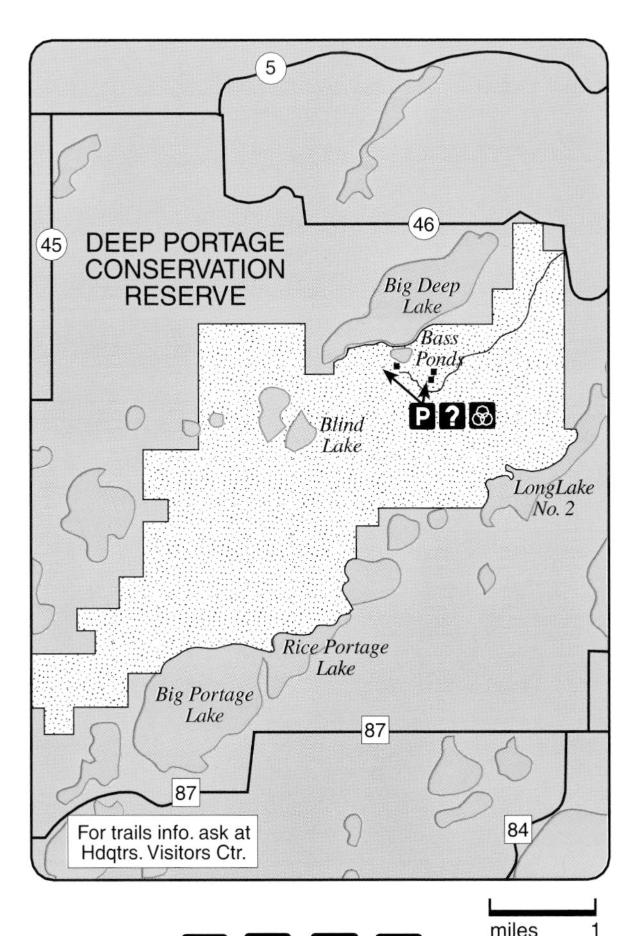

Facilities:    

Recreational Opportunities:  

Contact:

Deep Portage Conservation Reserve
RR 1 Box 129
Hackensack MN 56452
(218) 682-2325

18–Maplewood State Park

Why is this area special?

Established by the legislature in 1963, this 9,000-acre transitional zone park contains 13 different plant communities, and trees like sugar maple, basswood, bur oak, elm and aspen. Take the time to look for plants such as swamp milkweed, great lobelia, purple coneflower, purple prairie clover, nodding trillium, yellow lady's slipper and pasqueflower.

The area also contains steep hills, the highest approaching 1,600 feet. Nestled among the hills are 28 lakes, ranging from the 21-acre Lake Andrew to the 7,200-acre Lake Lida.

Great blue herons can be seen spearing fish in the shallow waters. Ospreys and turkey vultures fly overhead. The 150 species of breeding birds in Maplewood State Park include green herons, wood ducks, northern harriers, red-shouldered hawks, ruby-throated hummingbirds, red-headed woodpeckers, warbling vireos and golden-winged warblers. You will find a mixed heron, egret and cormorant colony in the park, and you may see scarlet tanagers and indigo buntings during the spring and summer.

You might also spot some of the 40 different species of mammals when you visit. Look for Franklin's ground squirrels, muskrats and red foxes. Deer and beavers are abundant.

C. Henderson

Great blue heron

Best viewing time:

How do I get there?

Maps: MN Highway Coordinate: C-11
PRIM AREA: Battle Lake, Detroit Lakes
DeLorme MN Atlas Grid #: 51 A-9, 52 A-1

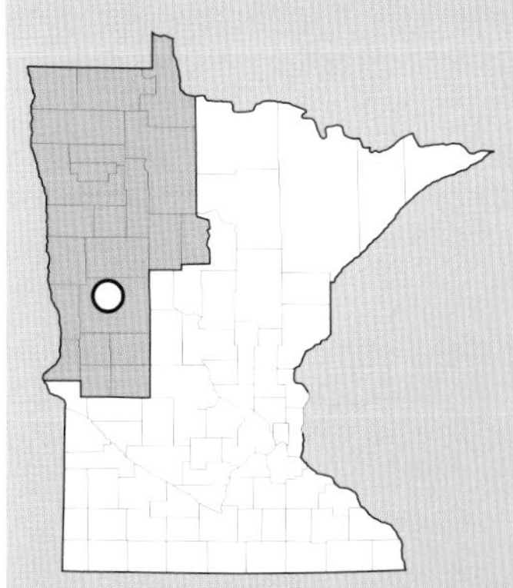

Additional directions:

Maplewood State Park is located seven miles east of Pelican Rapids on Highway 108 in Otter Tail County.

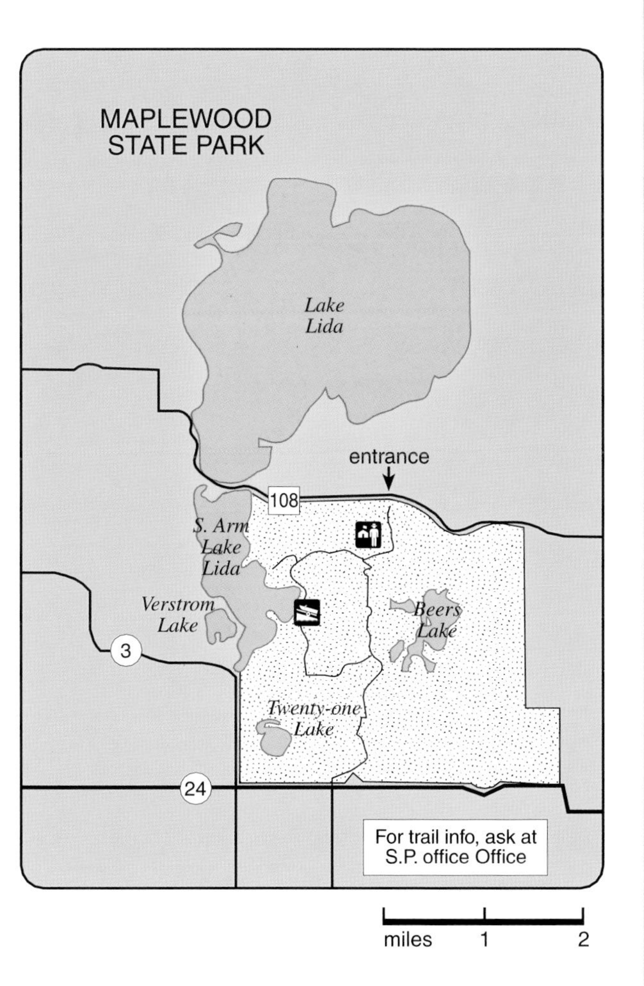

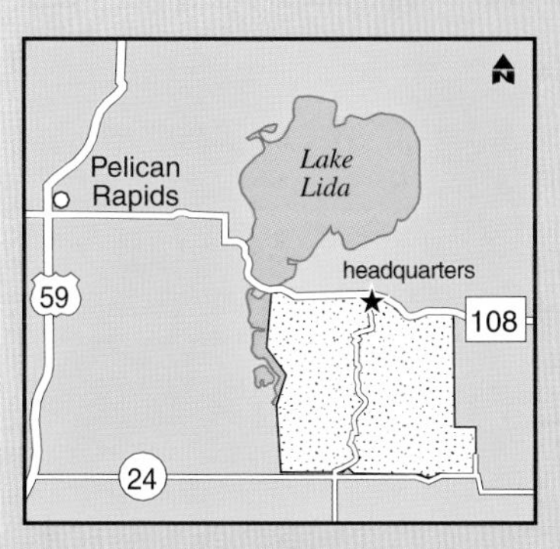

Facilities: 

Recreational Opportunities:    

Contact:

Maplewood State Park
RR 3 Box 422
Pelican Rapids MN 56572
(218) 863-8383

Parks and Recreation
DNR
500 Lafayette Road
St. Paul MN 55155-4040
(612) 296-6157
888-MINNDNR

19–Glendalough State Park

Why is this area special?

Located near Battle Lake in Ottertail County, Glendalough is Minnesota's newest state park. The park was known as the Glendalough Game Farm and Corporate Retreat when the Cowles family donated it to The Nature Conservancy in 1990. In 1992, the land was deeded to the state as parkland. This park contains 1,971 acres of land and has more than nine miles of shoreline on six lakes, including Lake Blanche, Annie Battle, Sunset and Molly Stark Lakes.

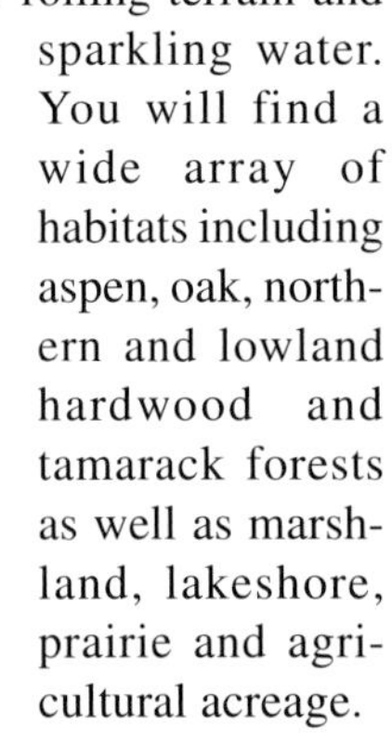

The park is noted for its steeply rolling terrain and sparkling water. You will find a wide array of habitats including aspen, oak, northern and lowland hardwood and tamarack forests as well as marshland, lakeshore, prairie and agricultural acreage.

C. Henderson

Western painted turtle

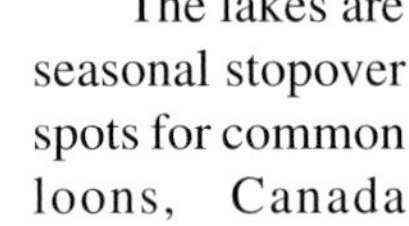

The lakes are seasonal stopover spots for common loons, Canada geese and wood ducks. Nesting bald eagles inhabit the area. Watch also for pied-billed grebes, blue-winged teal, northern harriers, American kestrels, eastern screech-owls, red-headed woodpeckers, eastern bluebirds, American redstarts, scarlet tanagers and savannah sparrows.

Mammals to watch for include beavers, muskrats, coyotes, red foxes and white-tailed deer. The park goals place specific emphasis on managing the site for wildlife.

Note:

The park is still undeveloped. There are few facilities. Cart-in camping is now available and plans are underway, for several wildlife photography and viewing blinds, including a treetop blind, a floating thatched blind and a walkway.

There is a boat launch on Molly Stark Lake. Annie Battle Lake is a non-motorized, non-electronic heritage fishing lake.

Best viewing time:

How do I get there?

Maps: MN Highway Coordinates: D-12
PRIM AREA: Battle Lake
DeLorme MN Atlas Grid #: 52 C-2

Additional directions:

From Battle Lake, drive north on Highway 78 three miles to County Road 16. Turn right on County Road 16 and go three miles to the park entrance.

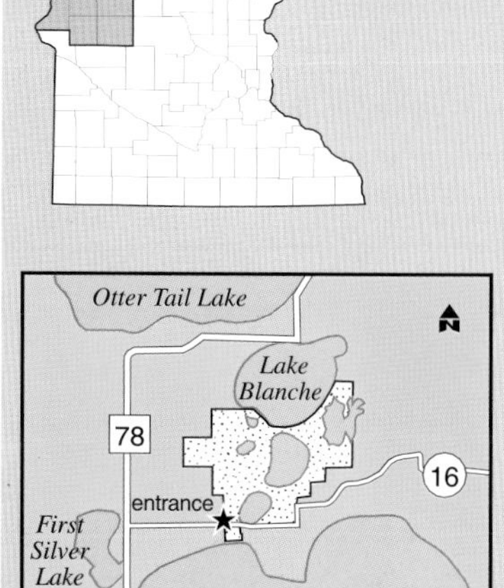

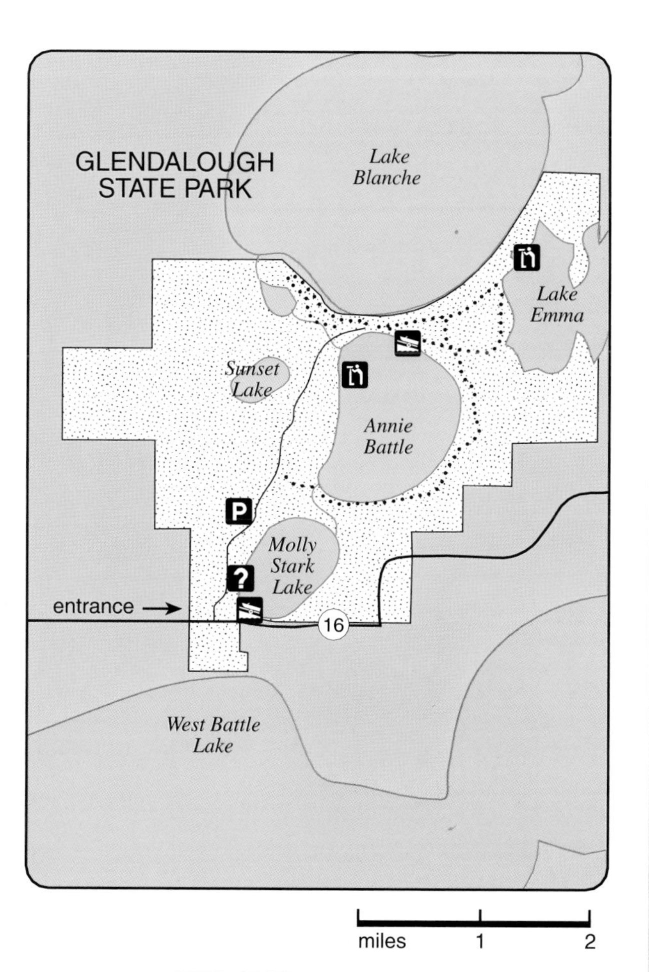

miles 1 2

Facilities:

Recreational Opportunities:   

Contact:

Glendalough State Park
P.O. Box 358
Battle Lake MN 56515
(218) 864-0110

20–Inspiration Peak

Why is this area special?

Inspiration Peak is a high point in the landscape where you can get a spectacular view of the surrounding fields, woodlands and lakes. The 80-acre site is located on the prairie/forest transition zone that once stretched the length of the state. To the west, conditions favored prairies, and to the east conditions favored forests.

C. Henderson

Turkey vulture

Inspiration Peak itself is an example of a gravel prairie. You will find this type of prairie on well-drained soils, and the vegetation is dominated by drought-tolerant grasses and forbs. Some of the plant life that grows here is grama grass, little bluestem, Indian grass, prairie smoke and purple prairie clover.

The native prairie on the top of Inspiration Peak has not changed significantly since pre-settlement times. Prescribed burning helps the prairie's pristine condition by simulating wild fires that occurred in pre-settlement times. These fires keep smooth sumac and prickly ash from encroaching.

The actual prairie is confined to 10 hilltop acres, while the rest of the site is forested with bur and red oak and birch trees.

Wildlife you can see in this area includes the rare Swainson's hawk, northern harriers, eastern screech-owls, bobolinks, bluebirds, western meadowlarks and grassland sparrows. You may also see open land inhabitants such as pocket gophers, white-tailed jack rabbits, and northern grasshopper and meadow jumping mice.

C. Henderson

Eastern bluebird

Best viewing time:

How do I get there?

Maps: MN Highway Coordinates: D-12
PRIM AREA: Battle Lake
DeLorme MN Atlas Grid #: 52 D-3

Additional directions:

From Alexandria, head north on Highway 29 for 19 miles to Parker's Prairie. Continue west on Highway 235 for 10 miles to Urbank. From Urbank, the highway becomes Highway 38. Continue west for approximately three miles to the parking lot, picnic area and trailhead.

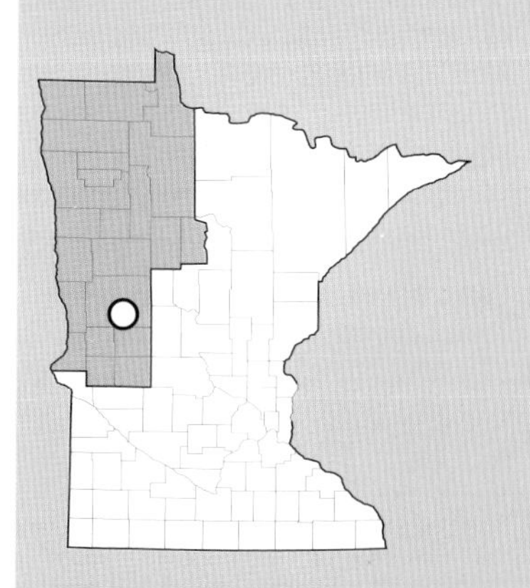

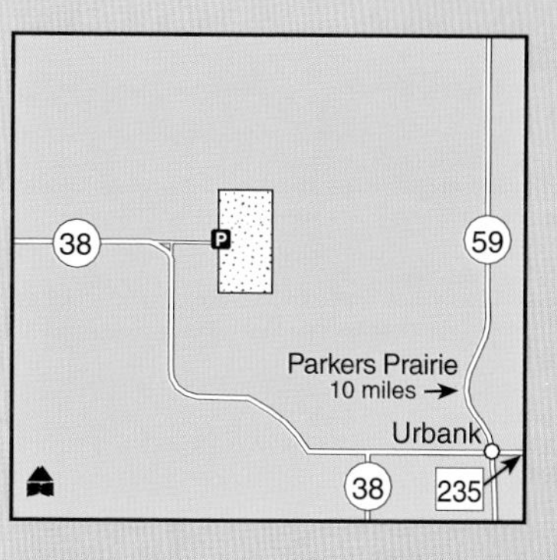

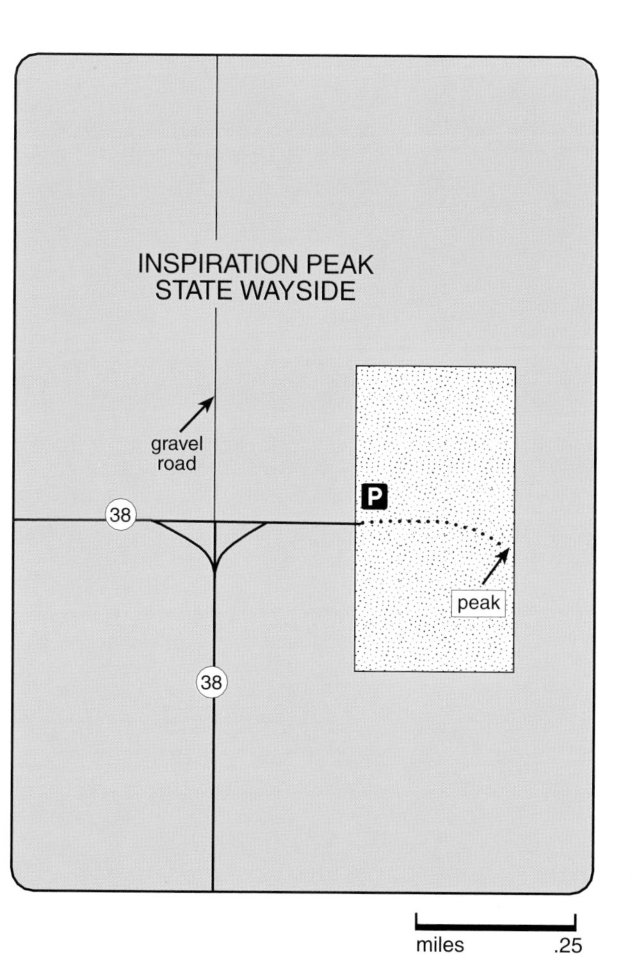

Facilities:   

Recreational Opportunities:

Contact:

Lake Carlos State Park
2601 County Road 38 NE
Carlos MN 56319
(320) 852-7200

Northeast-Arrowhead Country

The extensive forests and pristine lakes of the northeast epitomize the rustic northland setting that many people associate with Minnesota. The land, lakes and rivers made famous by French voyageurs still offer wonderful adventures for viewing wildlife in natural settings that have remained largely unchanged since presettlement times.

Minnesota's northeastern "Arrowhead Country" is the most heavily forested part of the state. More than 3,500 lakes and numerous rivers and streams are found here. The woodlands include forests of aspen, birch and maple in the western counties of Itasca and Koochiching. There is a transition to boreal coniferous forests of pine, spruce, fir and cedar in the northeastern counties of St. Louis, Lake and Cook. Large open bogs and forested swamps are common.

William Redig, International Wolf Center

Timber wolf

In Arrowhead Country you can experience nature on county, state and national forest lands, wildlife management areas, state parks and Scientific and Natural Areas, as well as in the Boundary Waters Canoe Area Wilderness (BWCAW) and Voyageurs National Park. The International Wolf Center in Ely offers the opportunity for seeing captive wolves and learning about the ecology and lore associated with timber wolves. Hawk Ridge in Duluth is famous nationwide for its role as a major migratory pathway for birds of prey in the fall.

Prominent wildlife species of this region are eagerly sought by wildlife enthusiasts because many are associated with boreal forests and can only be seen in a few places in the United States. There are nesting boreal and great gray owls, spruce grouse and many warblers of coniferous habitats like the black-throated blue, Tennessee, Nashville, northern parula, magnolia, Cape May, black-throated green, blackburnian and bay-breasted. Gray jays, boreal chickadees, common mergansers, common goldeneyes, bald eagles, common loons, ruffed grouse, moose, fisher, pine martens, river otters, black bears and timber wolves all inhabit this region. Minnesota has the largest population of common loons, moose, and timber wolves in the lower 48 states.

Good all-weather roads serve the entire region. Many roads are gravel but are well maintained. Even so, a few may be impassable during spring (late March through early April). Forest trails and logging roads are poorly maintained and should be checked out on foot first. Logging trucks are common on rural roads. Visitors should be careful when encountering these vehicles. Limit your speed to a moderate level and keep to the right as you encounter logging trucks. Watch out for oncoming traffic on blind curves in the woods. When in doubt, walk. It's the best way to see the northwoods anyway.

There are a few other things to keep in mind while exploring northeastern Minnesota. Black bears can become a nuisance at campsites because they are continually in search of campers' food. They are not typically a threat to people. Don't leave exposed food or garbage around camp or in your tent. Insect repellent is extremely important from late spring through early fall. Don't leave home without it. In some situations a head net is necessary to alleviate mosquito or blackfly problems.

Minnesota's hunting seasons are from September through December. During this time you may encounter bear, duck, grouse, moose or deer hunters. Consider wearing fluorescent orange jackets, vests and caps when afield in that season to alert hunters to your presence.

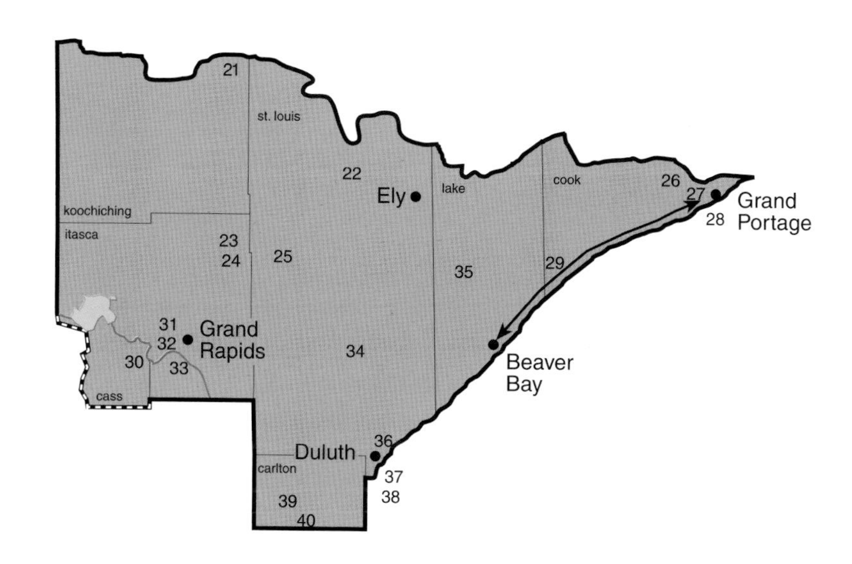

Sites

21. Gold Portage WMA
22. Vermilion Lake
23. George Washington State Forest
24. Peloquin WMA
25. Sharp-tailed Grouse Dancing Grounds
26. Northern Light Lake
27. Portage Brook Overlook
28. Swamp River WMA
29. Beaver Bay to Grand Portage Bay
30. Mud-Goose WMA
31. Suomi Hills Recreation Area
32. Bass Brook WMA
33. Mississippi River
34. Sax-Zim Bog
35. Murphy City/ Stoney River Grade
36. Hawk Ridge Nature Reserve
37. Snively and Magney City Parks
38. Park Point Recreation Area/ Minnesota Point Forest
39. Sharp-tailed Grouse Dancing Grounds
40. Moose Lake State Park

21–Gold Portage WMA

Why is this area special?

This wildlife management area has 24 acres of northern boreal forest and 776 acres of wetland. The remaining acres are water with emergent vegetation, such as cattails, wild rice and bulrushes. The area is not heavily used during the summer, so this is a good place to get a primitive wilderness experience without a great deal of travel.

This site is inhabited by migrating waterfowl each spring and fall. The mud flats are good spots to see migrating shorebirds. Keep your eyes open for bald eagles, ospreys, double-crested cormorants, American white pelicans, great blue herons, common goldeneyes, American black ducks, wood ducks, American wigeons and common mergansers. You might also see mammals such as moose, deer, black bears, river otters, beavers, muskrats or mink.

Note:

You will need a boat or canoe to experience this area. It should provide some exceptional photo opportunities for nesting and migrant waterbirds. You can gain access to this site by water on Rainy Lake, only four miles from the Rainy Lake Visitor Center.

Hunting allowed. Call ahead for hunting season dates.

C. Henderson

American black duck

Best viewing time:

How do I get there?

Maps: MN Highway Coordinate: K-4
PRIM Area: International Falls
DeLorme MN Atlas Grid #: 95 A-6

Additional directions:

From International Falls, take Highway 11 east for 10 miles. Turn right on County Road 96. Follow this road for two miles to the Rainy Lake Visitor Center.

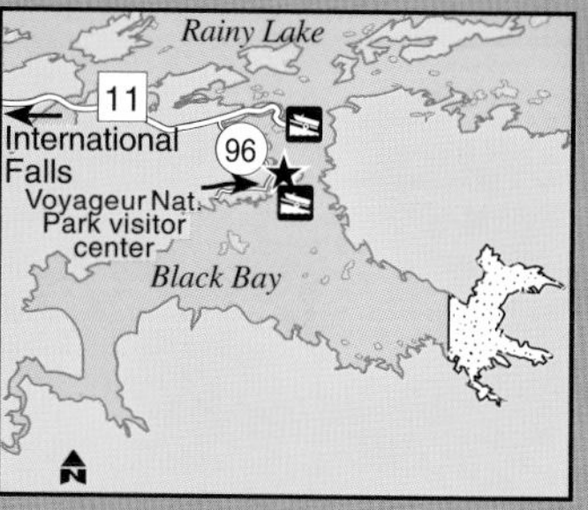

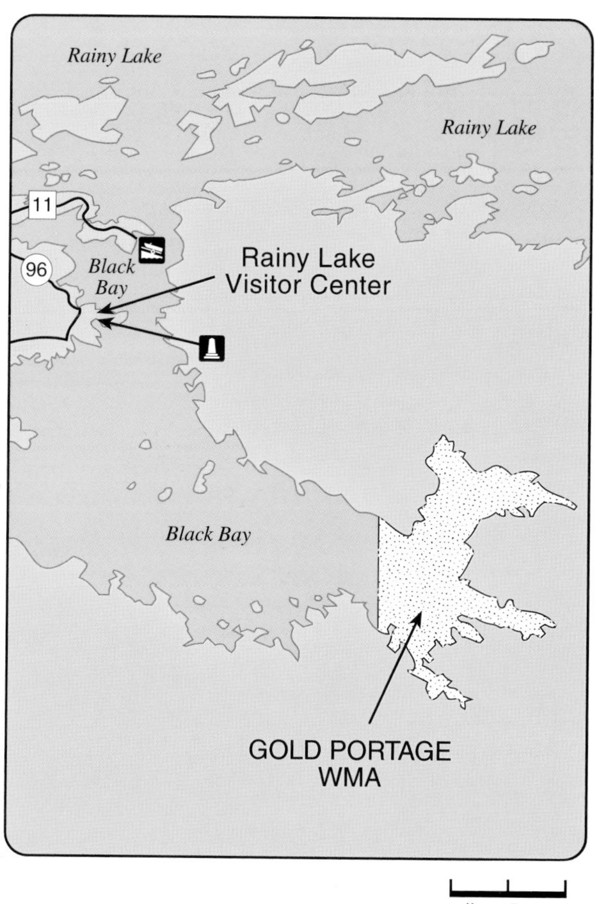

Facilities:  

Recreational Opportunities:

Contact:

DNR Area Wildlife Office
RR 8 Box 8
International Falls MN 56649
(218) 286-5434

Rainy Lake Visitor Center
International Falls MN 56649
(218) 286-5258

22–Vermilion Lake

Why is this area special?

Vermilion Lake is one of those exceptionally beautiful north country lakes where you can experience the beauty of the northern forest and associated wildlife. For the best outing, camp or stay at a nearby resort. Get out on the lake early on a spring or summer day to enjoy the solitude, the call of common loons and the sight of eagles fishing. You might even spot the large stick nest of a bald eagle in a tall, white pine along the lakeshore.

C. Henderson

Vermilion Lake will offer many photo opportunities. The best light for photography will be early and late in the day.

This 49,000-acre clear, deep lake is marked with many bays and islands, with geology and boreal forest vegetation similar to that of the adjacent Boundary Waters Canoe Area Wilderness. It is the essence of northern Minnesota lake country. The shoreline and island vegetation are primarily aspen-birch and pine-spruce. Look for abundant blueberry plants in the understory.

Bald eagles and common loons are very abundant here. You might also see black bears, moose, white-tailed deer, ospreys, herring gulls, American white pelicans and great blue herons.

Visit the Soudan Underground Mine State Park, located along the south shore of the lake, to see what it was like to mine iron half a mile underground.

Note:

Some of Vermilion Lake's shoreline and islands remain undeveloped, but there are also resorts and some public and private campgrounds located on the south shore. The lake is open for motorized boats.

This is a big water lake, which means that bad weather can create dangerous boating conditions. The weather is important, so keep an eye out. Bays and narrows may have rocks near the water surface, so go slow and observe navigation markers in these areas.

C. Henderson

Common loon

Best viewing time:

How do I get there?

Maps: MN Highway Coordinate: L-6
PRIM Area: Crane Lake
DeLorme MN Atlas Grid #: 87 E-7/9,
88 E-1

Additional directions:

From Duluth, take Highway 53 north for 56 miles to Virginia. From Virginia, follow Highway 169 north for 30 miles to Tower.

From Grand Rapids, take Highway 169 north for 80 miles to Tower.

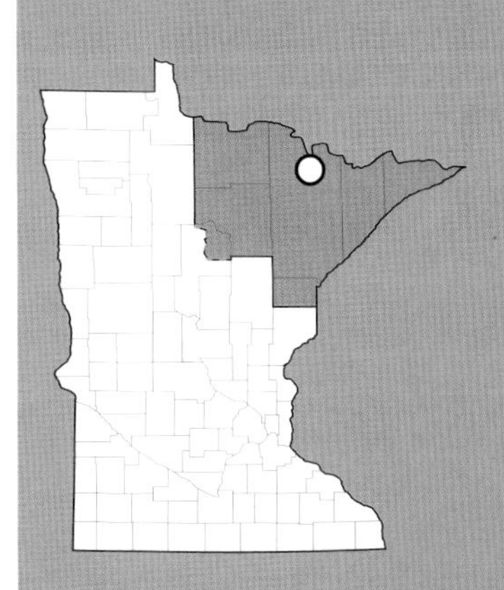

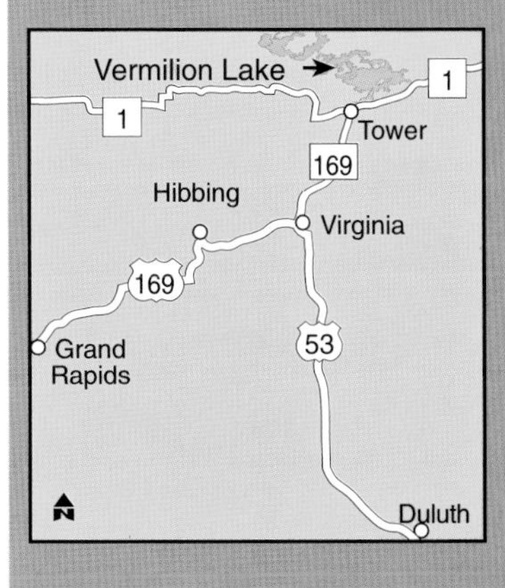

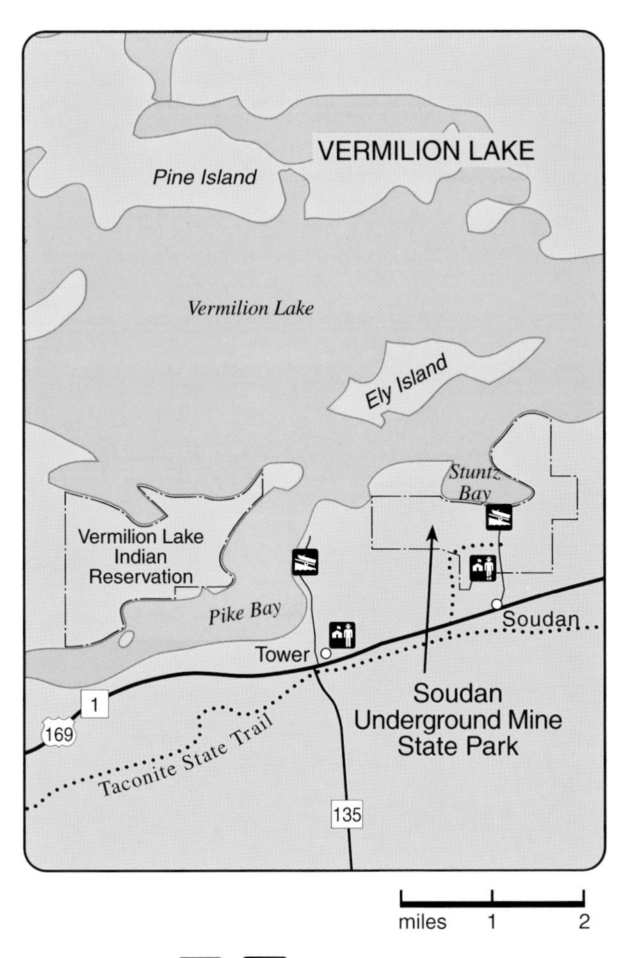

Facilities:

Recreational Opportunities:  

Contact:

DNR Area Wildlife Office
1429 Grant McMahon Blvd.
Ely MN 55731
(218) 365-7280

23–George Washington State Forest

Why is this area special?

At the George Washington State Forest you'll find northern coniferous forests including scenic stands of red and white pine, fir, spruce and tamarack, as well as mixed hardwood forests of aspen and birch. The woodlands are home to white-tailed deer, black bears, fishers, pine martens, snowshoe hare, bald eagles and a multitude of songbirds like black-throated green, black-and-white, chestnut-sided and bay-breasted warblers. Watch for northern specialties like red-breasted nuthatches, pine siskins, gray jays and evening grosbeaks.

Maintained gravel forest roads here are the Holstrom, Link Lake, O'Leary and Roller Coaster Trails. Watch for the tracks and scats of timber wolves along gravel roads and forest logging trails. The scats, or droppings, are typically identified by their composition of deer hair. Try howling on nighttime excursions; wolf howl imitations or recordings may bring a response from a nearby pack.

Lynn and Donna Rogers

Snowshoe hare

Boat or canoe outings on Deer, Thistledew, Bear, Bass, Coon, Larson, Stingy and Round Lakes can provide photo opportunities for river otters, deer, bald eagles, ospreys, great blue herons and belted kingfishers, as well as common loons, common mergansers and common goldeneyes.

Note:

The best time of day here is just after dark. Wolves will respond to a taped or human-produced wolf call.

Camp at Bear, Buttonbox, Larson, Lost, Bass, and Thistledew Lakes. There is a small fee to stay at the campgrounds and no advanced reservation is needed.

 Hunting allowed. Call ahead for hunting season dates.

Best viewing time:

How do I get there?

Maps: MN Highway Coordinate: J-6/7, K-6/7
PRIM Area: Bigfork and Vermilion Lake
DeLorme MN Atlas Grid #: 74 A/B-1/2

Additional directions:

Drive north on Highway 65 from Nashwauk to Highway 1 West. Take Highway 38 north from Grand Rapids to Highway 1 East.

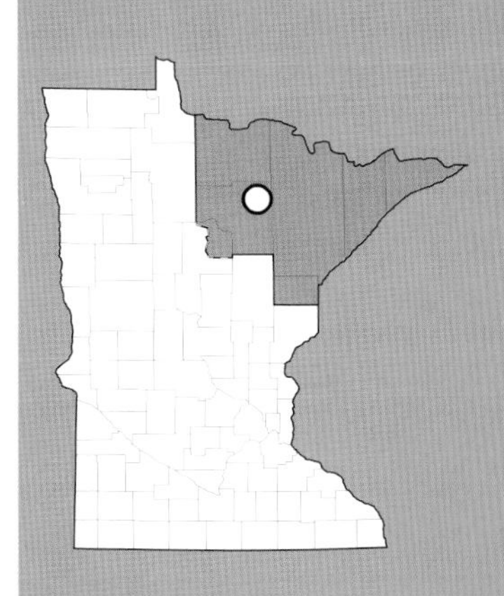

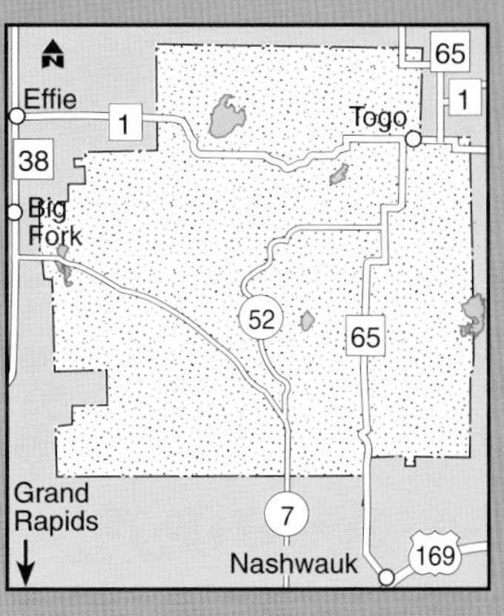

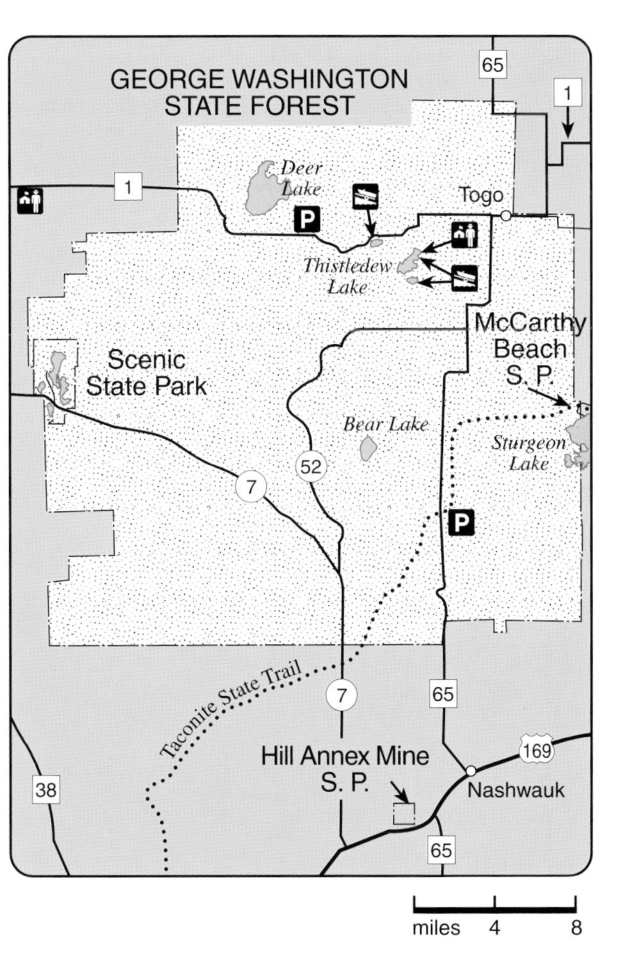

Facilities: 

Recreational Opportunities:    

Contact:

Nongame Wildlife Program
DNR
1201 East Hwy 2
Grand Rapids MN 55744
(218) 327-4267

24–Peloquin WMA

Why is this area special?

Visit this site for a chance to explore a young aspen-birch forest. There is also some balsam fir and white spruce. White-tailed deer and ruffed grouse are common here, and you could also see ducks, black bears, great blue herons, timber wolves, fishers and woodpeckers. Forest songbirds include the chestnut-sided, black-and-white, Tennessee and yellow warblers, as well as wood thrushes and veeries.

There are two small impoundments, one with an observation platform, where you can watch the beavers and other aquatic animals. The impoundments provide habitat for muskrats, beavers, river otters, ring-necked ducks, mallards and wood ducks. The observation platform can provide some excellent viewing in late April and early May during the waterfowl migration.

Stephen Maxson

Ruffed grouse

Note:

You can camp at Beatrice Lake and Bear Lake State Forest Campgrounds, as well as at McCarthy Beach State Park. You will need to make advanced reservations and pay a small fee to stay at the campgrounds.

There are many insects here during the summer, so bring bug repellent.

Hunting allowed. Call ahead for hunting season dates. Hunters use this area mostly on weekends in October and early November.

James E. Gerholdt

Blue-spotted salamander

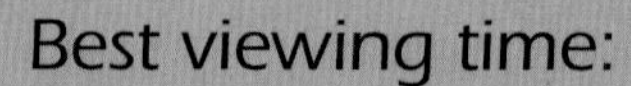

Best viewing time:

How do I get there?

Maps: MN Highway Coordinate: J-7
PRIM Area: Bigfork
DeLorme MN Atlas Grid #: 74 B-3

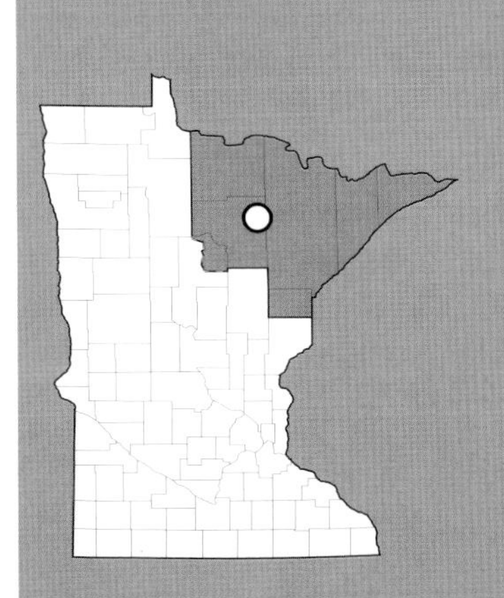

Additional directions:

Take Highway 65 north from Nashwauk for 23 miles. Drive 2.2 miles east on the Link Lake State Forest Road to the WMA sign.

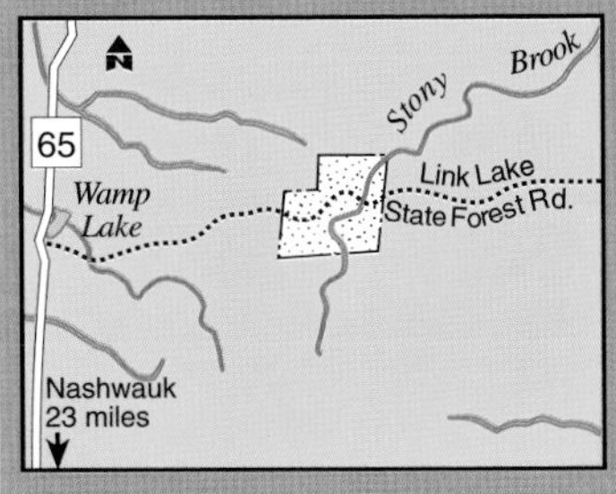

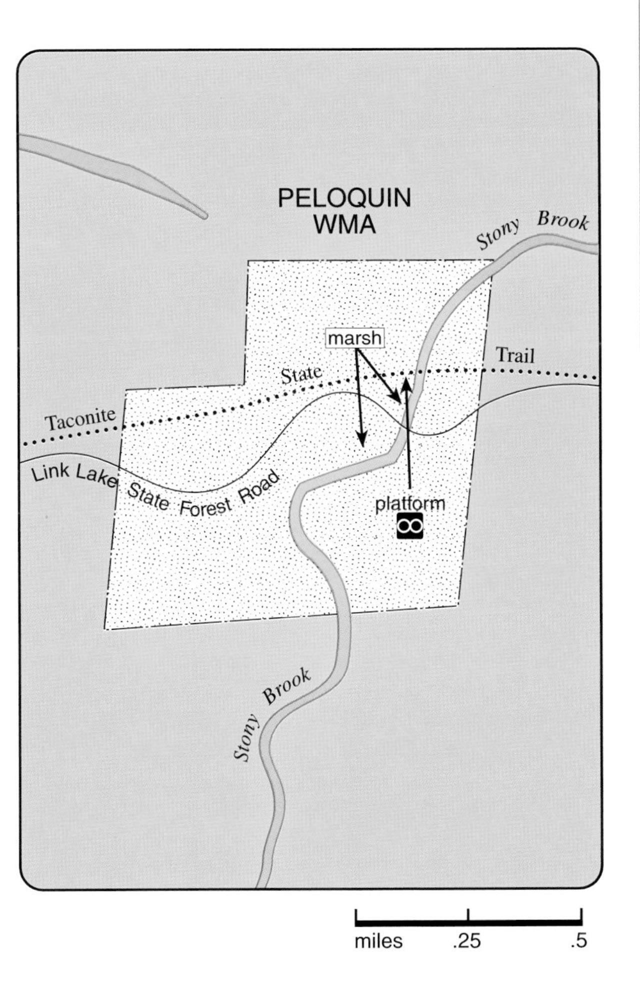

Facilities:

Recreational Opportunities:

Contact:

DNR Area Wildlife Office
1201 East Highway 2
Grand Rapids MN 55744
(218) 327-4428

25–Sharp-tailed Grouse Dancing Grounds

Why is this area special?

Sharp-tailed grouse figure prominently in early accounts of Minnesota settlement because they were distributed statewide at that time. Prairie chickens reported along the Minnesota River by English geologist Featherstonhaugh in 1835 were actually sharp-tailed grouse.

As grassland areas were cultivated, prairie chickens became more abundant and the range of sharp-tailed grouse shrank to brushland areas of northern Minnesota. Declining amounts of the brushland needed by sharptails has caused great declines in their numbers. It is increasingly difficult to find areas where they can be observed.

Stephen Maxson

Sharp-tailed grouse

Observation blinds maintained by the DNR Section of Wildlife provide the best viewing opportunities. Displaying begins each morning in April between 4:15 and 4:30 a.m. You need to be in the blind before the birds arrive on the site. The many sights and sounds associated with a springtime morning makes getting up this early an even more memorable experience. Watching the males' primitive ritual of ventriloqual cooing, chuckling, cackling and rapid pattering of feet on an early spring morning is one of the most stirring natural events that you can witness in Minnesota.

Note:

These sites are on private land and you need a reservation to use the blinds. Contact the DNR Area Wildlife Manager in Eveleth at (218) 744-7448. The Area Wildlife Manager will provide directions to the site, so details are not provided here. See the Featured Species section on page 24 for more information on sharp-tailed grouse.

If you wish to learn more about sharp-tailed grouse and their management, join the Minnesota Sharp-tailed Grouse Society, P. O. Box 16074, St. Paul, MN 55116. Annual dues are $5.

See site 39 for another opportunity to reserve a blind.

Best viewing time:

How do I get there?

Maps: MN Highway Coordinate: L-6, L-8
PRIM Area: Hibbing, Vermilion Lake
DeLorme MN Atlas Grid #: 75, 76

Additional directions:

The two St. Louis County sites are near Cook and Palo.

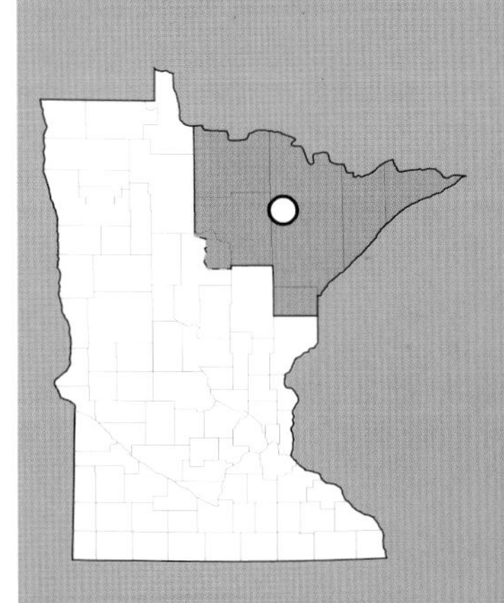

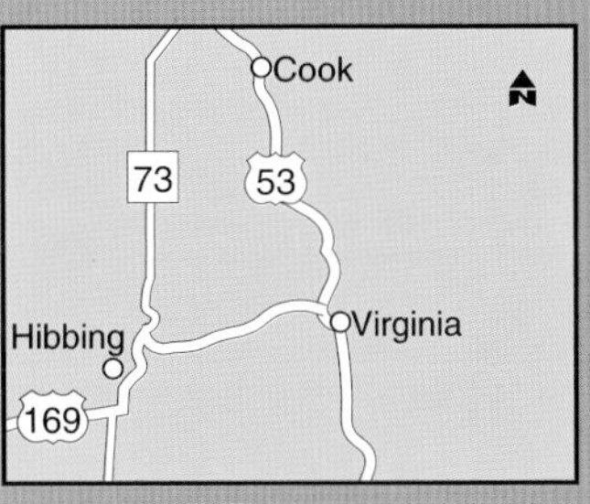

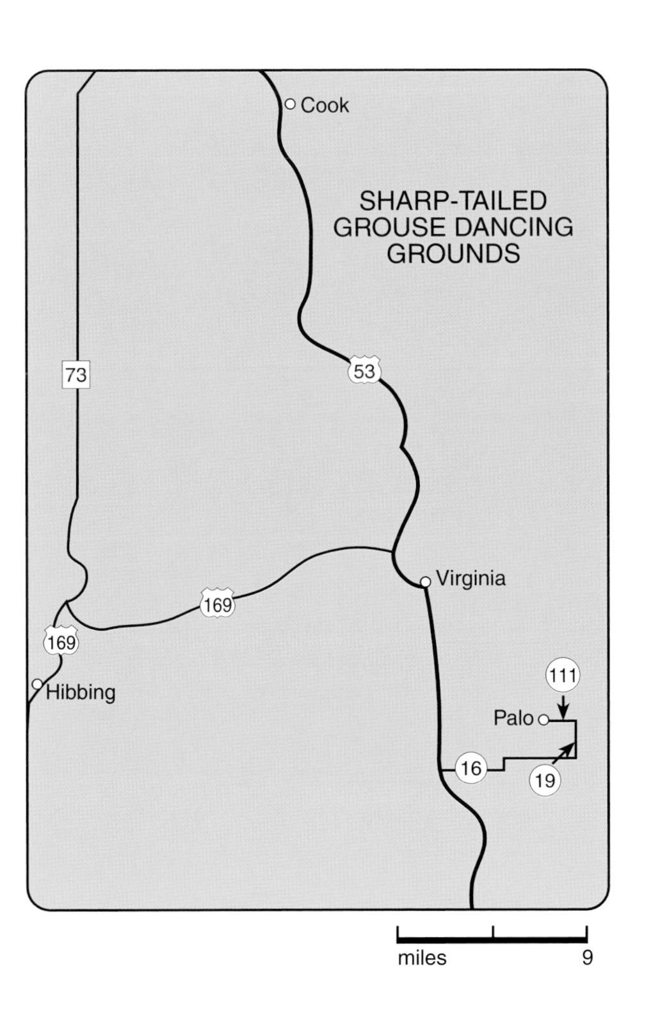

Facilities:

Recreational Opportunities:

Contact:

DNR Area Wildlife Office
2005 Highway 37
Eveleth MN 55734
(218) 744-7448

26–Northern Light Lake

Why is this area special?

Northern Light Lake provides a classic northwoods experience on a very shallow marshy lake where your chances of seeing a moose feeding in the water are very good. Here is a place where you can try for that ultimate photo of a bull in velvet as it raises its head out of the lake with water dripping from the palms of its fuzzy antlers. The lake is especially appealing to moose in spring and summer as they seek out succulent water plants after a long winter of eating twigs. The northwest portion of the lake has the most emergent marsh vegetation that serves as fodder for this huge member of the deer family, but you can see them anywhere along the shoreline. Late afternoon is a good time to look.

With a boat, you can work the edge of the lake and watch for moose as well as river otters, common loons, common mergansers, common goldeneyes, bald eagles, osprey, great blue herons, belted kingfishers, common snipes, red-winged blackbirds, yellow warblers and eastern kingbirds.

Note:

You can access this area from the water, one mile downstream on the Brule River. A small boat with motor works the best. There are a lot of weeds growing there, so by late summer they may get in the way of your prop. See the Featured Species section on page 38 for more information on these magnificent mammals.

Lynn and Donna Rogers

Moose

Best viewing time:

How do I get there?

Maps: MN Highway Coordinate: Q-6
PRIM Area: Grand Marais
DeLorme MN Atlas Grid #: 79 C-8

Additional directions:

Drive 12 miles north of Grand Marais on the Gunflint Trail (Cook Co. 12) to the intersection with the Brule River.

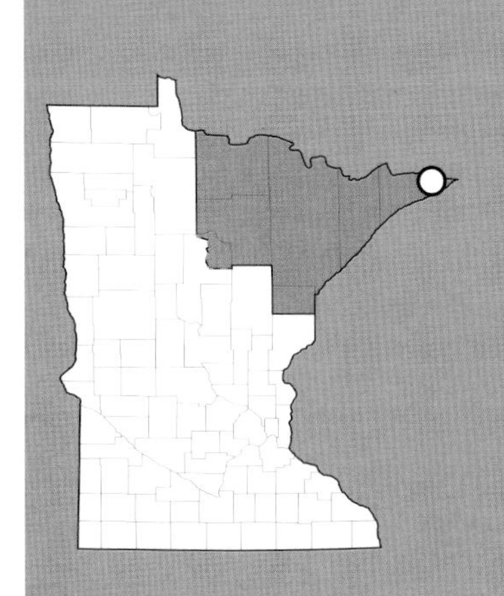

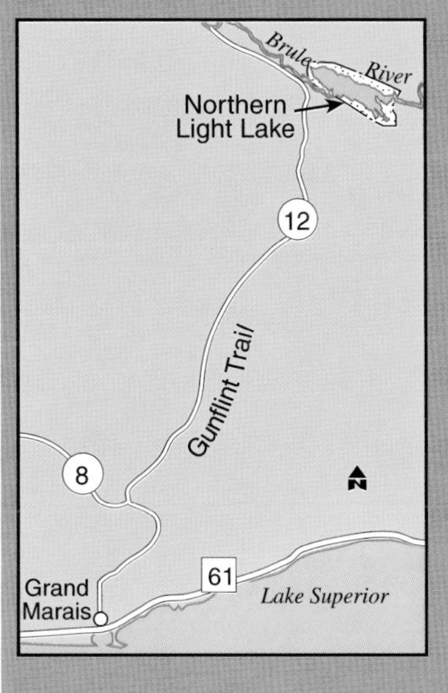

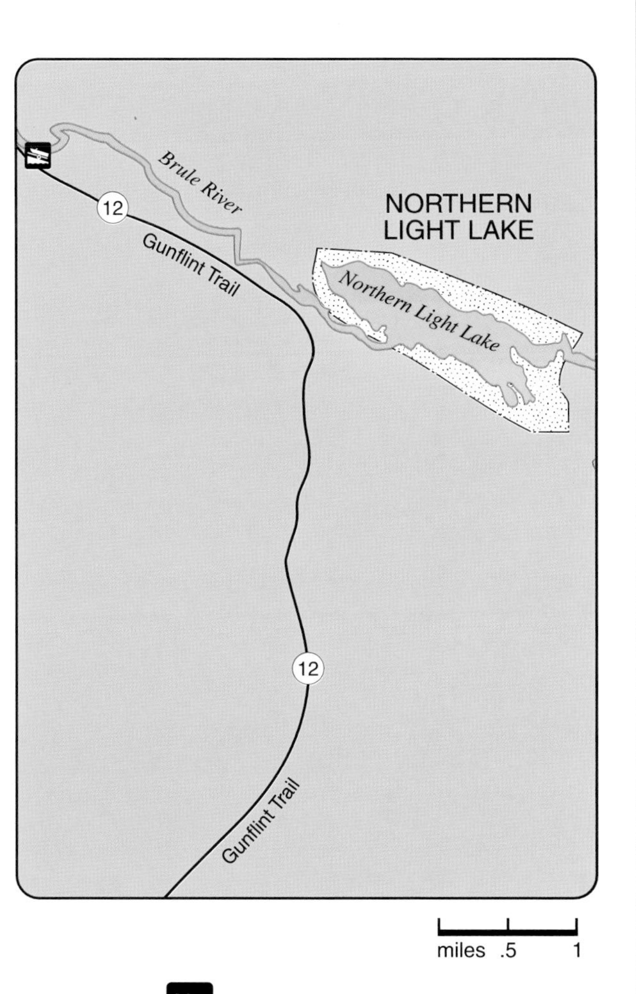

Facilities:

Recreational Opportunities:

Contact:

DNR Area Wildlife Office
PO Box 156
Grand Marais MN 55604
(218) 387-3034

27–Portage Brook Overlook

Why is this area special?

Come to Portage Brook Overlook to experience the northern boreal forest and northern hardwood forest during the fall and winter. The scenic overlook is a great place to watch for moose.

You can see several recent timber cuts from this spot that have stimulated the growth of nutritious young trees and shrubs. Moose eat these trees and shrubs in the fall as their diets change from the succulent marsh plants they eat during the summer months. December offers the best chance to see moose from the Overlook. They may also be seen in October and November, after the leaves fall. Birds in the area at that time include common ravens, boreal chickadees, gray jays and red-breasted nuthatches.

James E. Gerholdt

Western chorus frog

Note:

You will need binoculars or a spotting scope because moose may be as far as a half-mile from the Overlook. Drive or hike the nearby state forest roads for additional wildlife watching opportunities. Canoeing the Swamp River (site 28) will bring you in closer proximity to local marshland birds and mammals.

See the Featured Species section on page 34 for more information on moose.

Lynn and Donna Rogers

Moose

Best viewing time:

Hunting allowed. Call ahead for hunting season dates.

How do I get there?

Maps: MN Highway Coordinate: R-6
PRIM Area: Grand Marais
DeLorme MN Atlas Grid #: 79 B-9

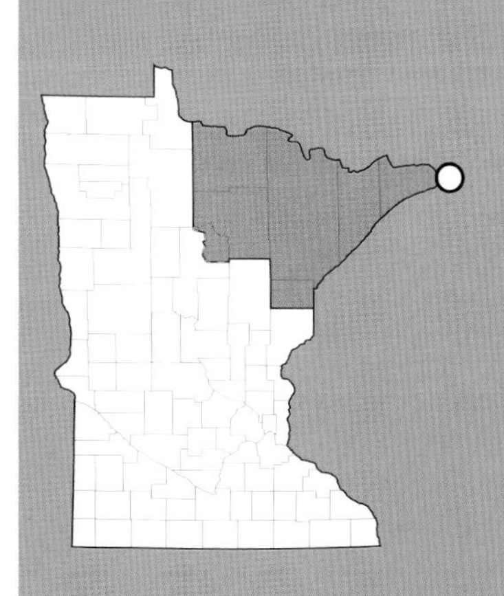

Additional directions:

Take Highway 61 to Hovland. From Hovland, go north on Cook County Road 16 (Arrowhead Trail) for 12.5 miles to Portage Brook.

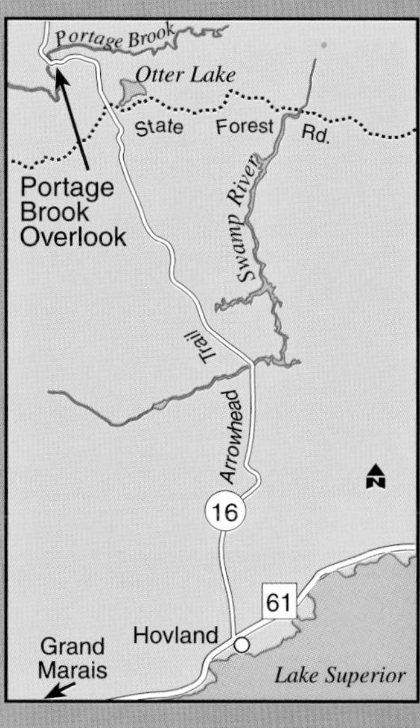

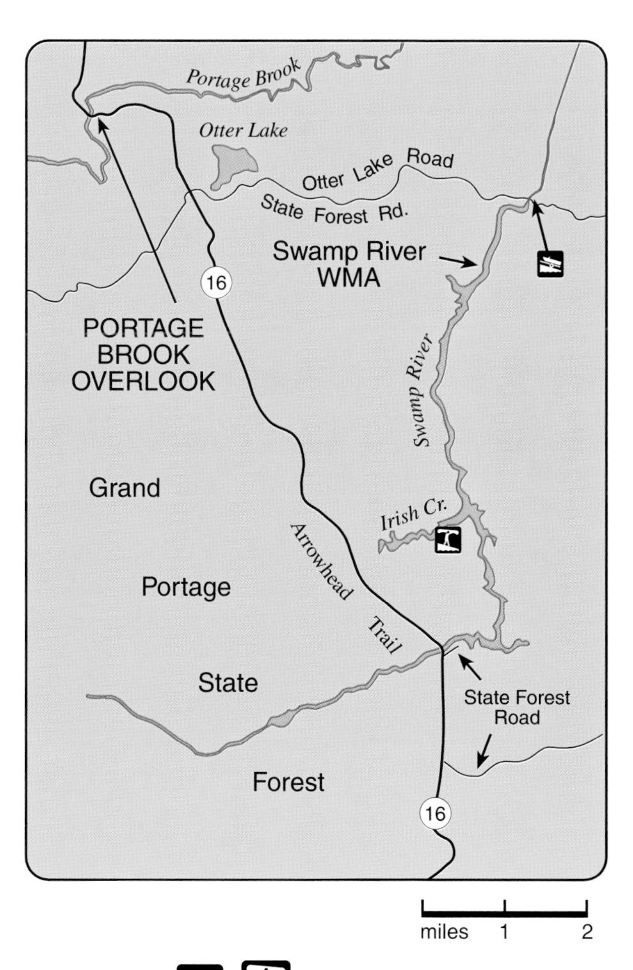

Facilities:

Recreational Opportunities:

Contact:

DNR Area Wildlife Office
PO Box 156
Grand Marais MN 55604
(218) 387-3034

28–Swamp River WMA

Why is this area special?

Swamp River is one of the best wetland wildlife viewing sites in northeast Minnesota because it is probably the largest marsh complex in this otherwise-forested region. The 760-acre Swamp River Wildlife Management Area is part of this wetland system. The background setting for the marsh is boreal forest, black spruce swamp, muskeg and northern hardwood forest. The marsh vegetation includes wild rice as well as bulrush, blue flag, marsh marigold and a small white water lily that is especially common near the junction of Swamp River and Irish Creek.

This is an excellent spot to see moose, beavers and river otters in the lake. Ospreys nest in the vicinity and may be seen fishing. Look for common loons as well as common mergansers, common goldeneyes, great blue herons, belted kingfishers, yellow warblers, common yellowthroats, red-necked grebes and eastern kingbirds as you work your way through the marsh.

Gary Nuechterlein

Red-necked grebe

The adjacent woodlands provide a northern habitat that features the croaking sounds of common ravens and occasional views of gray jays, red-breasted nuthatches and boreal chickadees.

Note:

The area north of the marsh is accessible by small boats with motors. The area south of the marsh is only accessible by canoe. Once you move away from the landing, there is no solid ground along the shore. All wildlife watching must be done from the water.

You can camp at Magney State Park at sites on Esther, Chester, Devil Fish or McFarland Lakes.

Check out Portage Brook Overlook (site 27) for a chance to spot a moose and take in a panoramic view of the area.

 Hunting allowed. Call ahead for hunting season dates.

Best viewing time:

How do I get there?

Maps: MN Highway Coordinate: R-6
PRIM Area: Grand Marais
DeLorme MN Atlas Grid #: 79 C-10

Additional directions:

Drive north from Hovland for 12 miles on Cook County Road 16 (Arrowhead Trail) to Otter Lake Road. Travel east for 4 miles on Otter Lake Road to Swamp River.

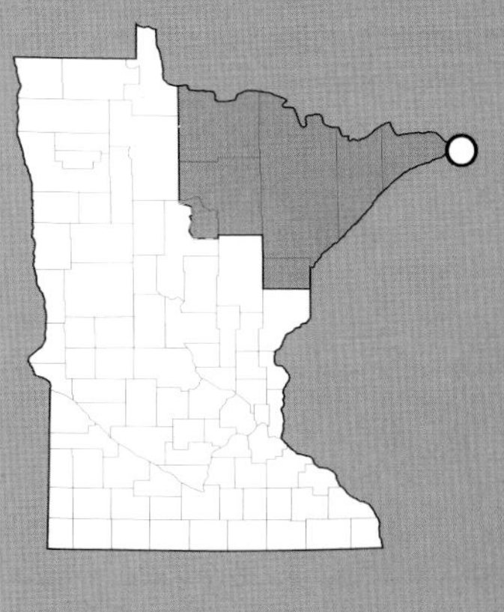

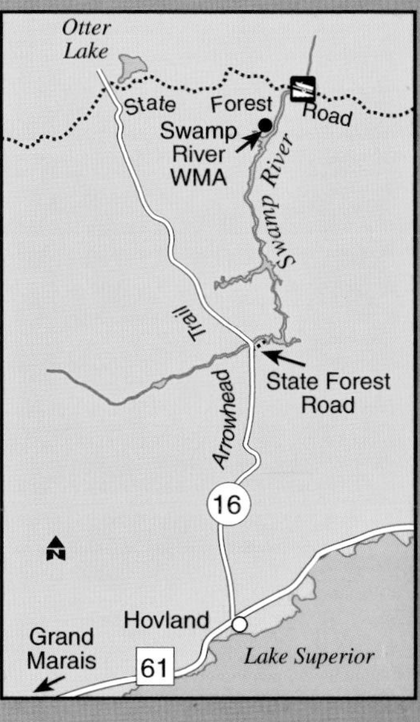

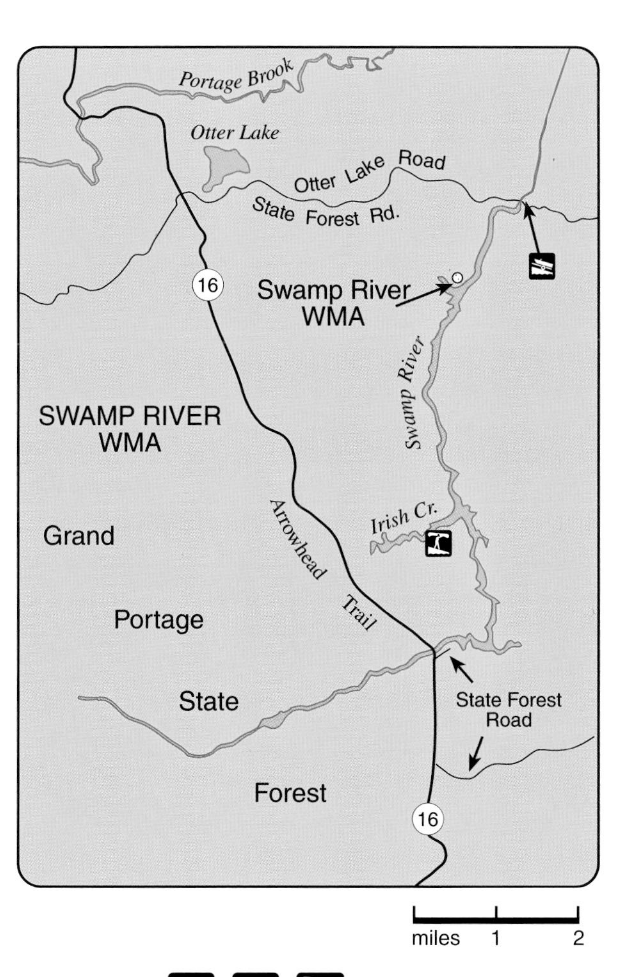

Facilities:

Recreational Opportunities:

Contact:

DNR Area Wildlife Office
PO Box 156
Grand Marais MN 55604
(218) 387-3034

29–Beaver Bay to Grand Portage Bay

Lynn and Donna Rogers

Pine marten

Why is this area special?

One of the most intriguing features of the landscape along Lake Superior is that a variety of boreal forest and Canadian wetland wildlife species frequently show up along the North Shore. Cyclic northern species such as snowy, great gray and boreal owls often appear in winter along Highway 61. Black bears and even lynx occasionally roam the roadsides of the lake's edge. Caribou and ptarmigan have been recorded, as well as more common species like white-tailed deer, pine martens and common ravens. Most of these sightings take place during the late fall and winter.

Cold-water rivers and open water along Lake Superior also have harbored such rare species as oldsquaw, harlequin ducks and dippers. You can find other rare birds here occasionally throughout the year.

Note:

There are good observation points between Beaver Bay and East Beaver Bay, as well as at Taconite Harbor, Silver Bay Marina, Grand Marais Harbor, Cutface Creek, Grand Portage Bay and Shovel Point at Tettegouche State Park.

Camping and cross-county skiing are available at various state parks and at state and federal forest campgrounds.

Check with the Duluth area birding hotline for the latest in bird sightings along the North Shore. Their phone number is (218) 525-5952.

 Hunting allowed. Call ahead for hunting season dates.

C. Henderson

Red-breasted nuthatch

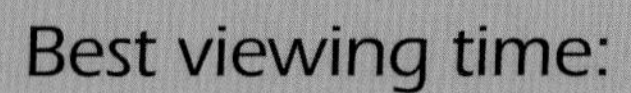
Best viewing time:

How do I get there?

Maps: MN Highway Coordinate: O-8 to S-6
PRIM Area: Two Harbors & Grand Marais
DeLorme MN Atlas Grid #: 77 E-9, 78 E-4, 79 E-9

Additional directions:

All sites are near or along Highway 61 from Duluth to Grand Portage.

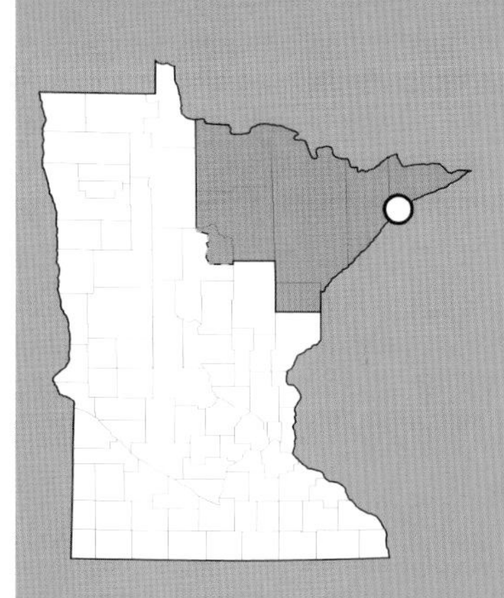

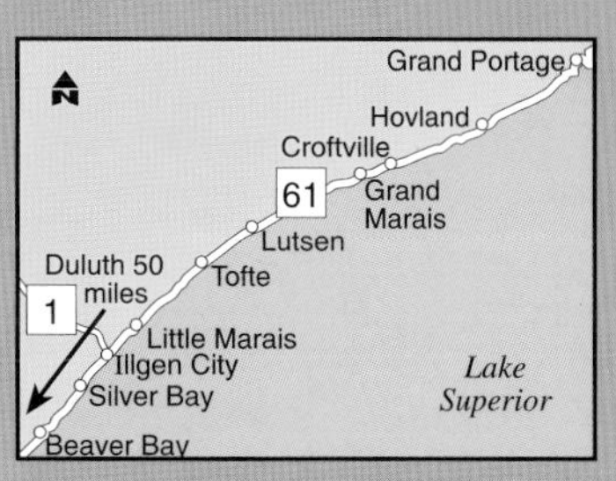

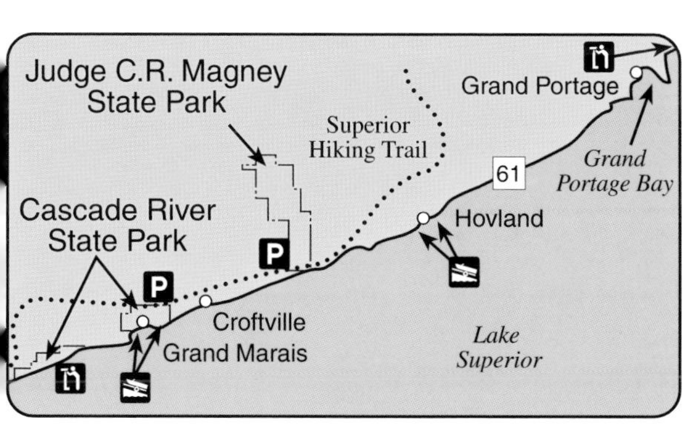

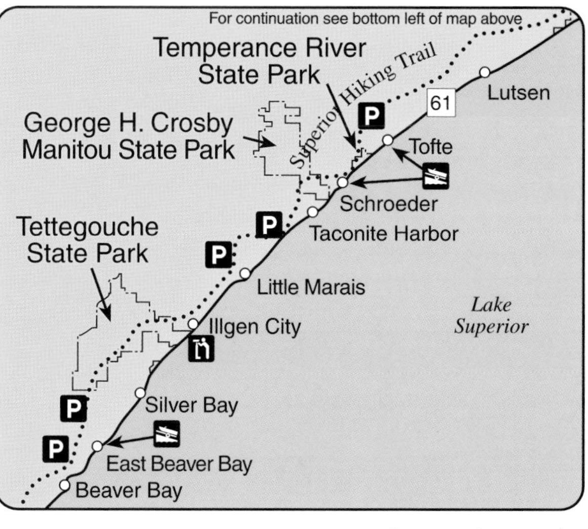

miles 4 8

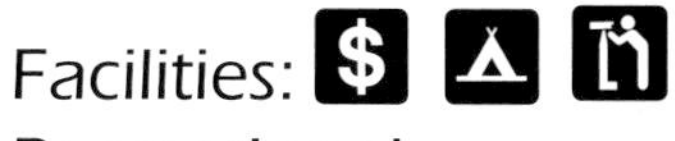

Facilities:

Recreational Opportunities:   

Contact:

DNR Area Wildlife Office
PO Box 156
Grand Marais MN 55604
(218) 387-3034

30–Mud-Goose WMA

C. Henderson

Common goldeneye

Why is this area special?

The Mud-Goose Wildlife Management Area is a 14,000-acre complex of forest, marsh and lakes. This area features a 5,000-acre sedge meadow that surrounds 1,700-acre Mud Lake and 850-acre Goose Lake. The water levels of this wetland complex are managed by a dam on the Leech Lake River to benefit wildlife and the production of wild rice. These wetlands feature vegetation ranging from sedges and grasses to marsh marigold, blue flag, cattail, arrowhead, phragmites, bulrush and wild rice.

This is an excellent place to watch and photograph migratory waterbirds in the spring and fall. Species include mallards, common goldeneyes and American black, wood and ring-necked ducks. There are Canada geese, common loons, great blue herons, American bitterns, bald eagles, ospreys, black terns, belted kingfishers and red-necked and pied-billed grebes. Mammals of the area include white-tailed deer, black bears, bobcats, fishers, river otters, beavers, mink and muskrats.

Note:

You'll need a boat or canoe to access Goose Lake. Mud Lake can be seen from County Road 139. This road parallels the Leech Lake River and the east shore of Mud Lake. Motorized watercraft are permitted except during the waterfowl hunting season, which runs from October through November. The scenic and historic Great River Road runs near this site.

Hunting allowed. Call ahead for hunting season dates.

Lynn and Donna Rogers

Pine grosbeak

Best viewing time:

How do I get there?

Maps: MN Highway Coordinate: H-8, I-8
PRIM Area: Grand Rapids
DeLorme MN Atlas Grid #: 73 E-7, 63 A-7

Additional directions:

To Mud Lake take Highway 2 to Itasca County 18 (4 miles west of Deer River). Drive south on County Road 18 for three miles to Itasca County 139. Drive west for three miles on County Road 139 to the Mud Lake access.

From Remer, take Highway 6 north to Itasca County Road 18. Turn west on County Road 18 and continue to Mud Lake.

To Goose Lake take County Road 52 to the southeast corner boat access.

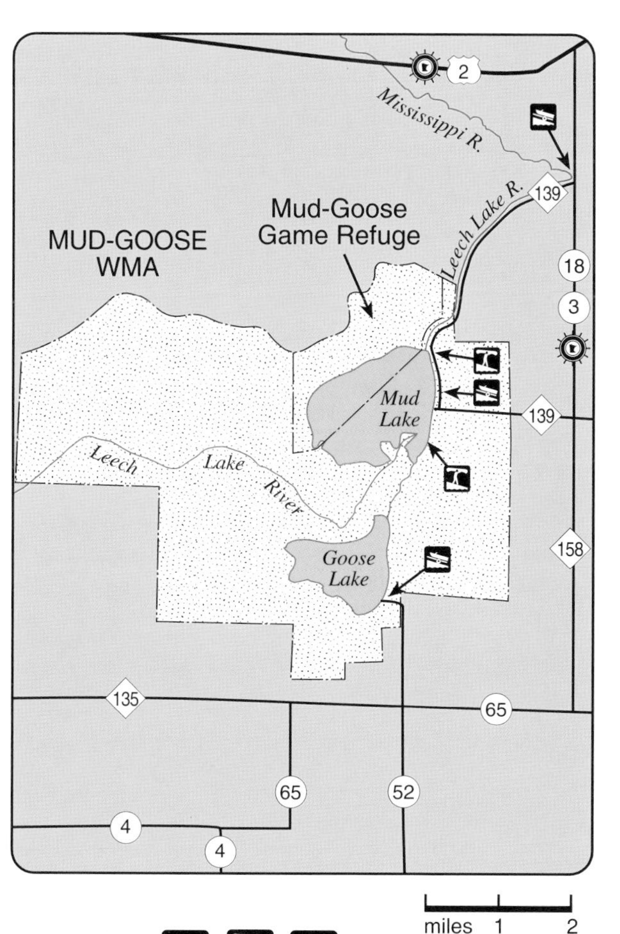

Facilities: 

Recreational Opportunities:

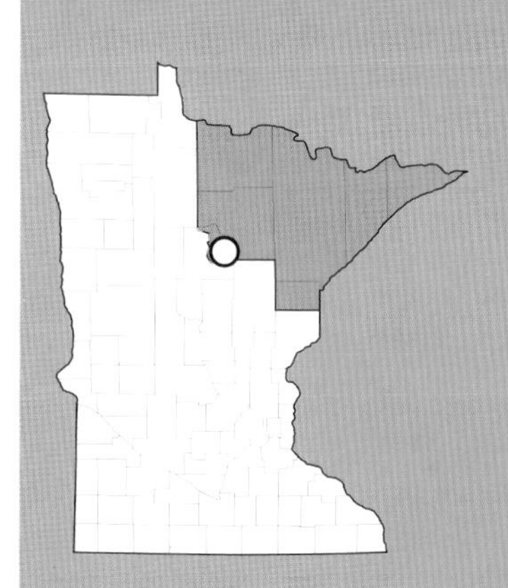

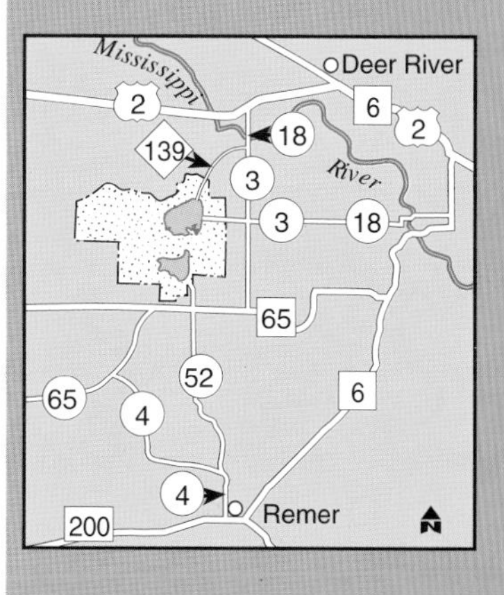

Contact:

DNR Area Wildlife Office
1201 East Highway 2
Grand Rapids MN 55744
(218) 327-4428

31–Suomi Hills Recreation Area

Lynn and Donna Rogers

White-tailed deer

Why is this area special?

Suomi Hills in Itasca County offers the solitude of a nonmotorized forest in a world that is increasingly dominated by the sound of motorized equipment and vehicles. Experience the "teacher-teacher-teacher" call of ovenbirds, the drumming of ruffed grouse, the peenting of woodcocks and the distinctive cackling of pileated woodpeckers in one of this region's few remaining high-quality stands of northern hardwood forest.

Unlike northern coniferous forest dominated by red and white pine, spruce, fir and tamarack, this forest is characterized by maple, basswood and oak in a beautiful setting of lakes and rolling hills. Acorns and hazelnuts provide important fall and winter food for deer, black bears, gray and flying squirrels and many birds.

This hardwood forest provides excellent opportunities for wildflower photography in May and great fall colors in late September through early October. While looking for spring ephemeral wildflowers you may encounter or hear wood frogs and gray tree frogs.

Other wildlife includes spring migrant warblers such as American redstarts, black-and-white, chestnut-sided and bay-breasted warblers. This is an excellent place to look and listen for scarlet tanagers and local raptors including broad-winged hawks and barred owls.

Adele, Spruce Island, Big Horn, Hill, Lucky and Kremer Lakes offer canoeing and fishing opportunities, as well as the chance to see bald eagles, ospreys, common loons, common goldeneyes, beavers and river otters.

There are 21 miles of forest trails, so watch for the tracks and scats of timber wolves. While camping, try some nocturnal howling to elicit a response from nearby pack members.

Note:

This area is open to hunting from September through November. There are some pack-in primitive campsites available at a few of the lakes. Highway 38 is a narrow, curving road with small to nonexistent shoulders, so drive with care. No motorized vehicles are allowed in Suomi Hills.

Best viewing time:

Hunting allowed. Call ahead for hunting season dates.

How do I get there?

Maps: MN Highway Coordinate: I-7
PRIM Area: Grand Rapids
DeLorme MN Atlas Grid #: 73 D-9

Additional directions:

From Grand Rapids, take Highway 38 north for 13 miles. From this point, Highway 38 forms the eastern boundary of Soumi Hills for 6 miles. Look for the designated parking areas on the west side of Highway 38.

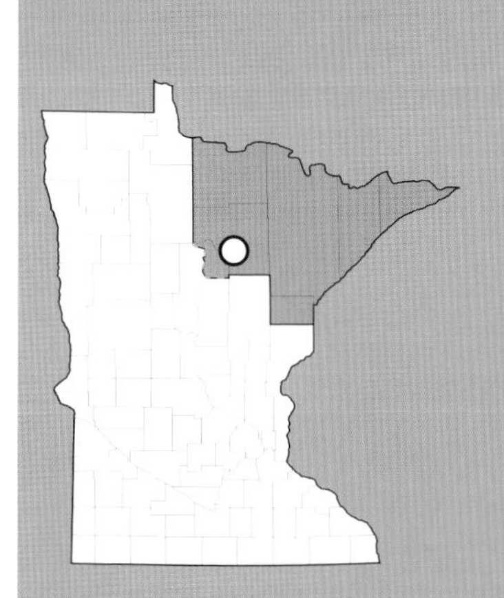

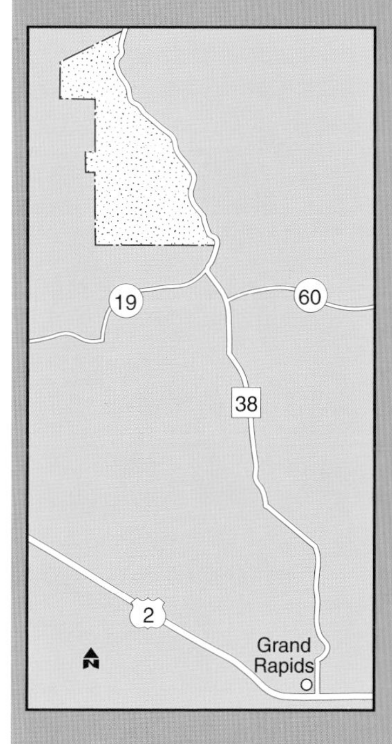

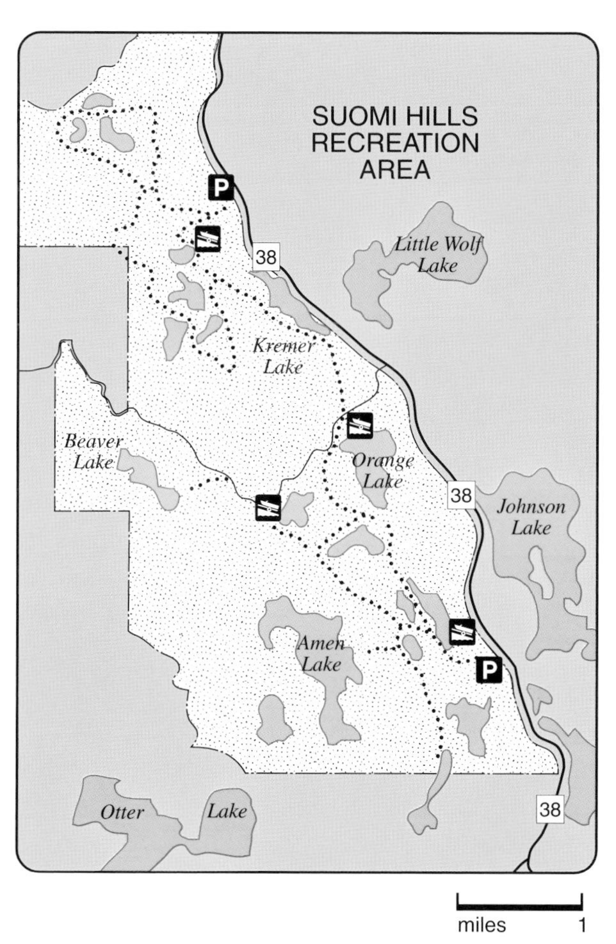

Contact:

Marcell District
Chippewa National Forest
HC 1 Box 600
Marcell MN 56657
(218) 832-3161

Facilities: 

Recreational Opportunities:     

32–Bass Brook WMA

C. Henderson
Yellow-bellied sapsucker

Why is this area special?

This 300-acre wildlife management area along the south shore of the Mississippi River is only minutes from Grand Rapids and Cohasset, an ideal day trip. Bass Brook Wildlife Management Area was purchased by the Nongame Wildlife Program to preserve habitat for forest songbirds along the Mississippi River. This is a forest of aspens, birch and firs with some stands of jack pine, scattered red and white pine and a spruce-cedar bog.

If you hike along the river, you'll see many forest songbirds, great blue herons and small forest mammals. An outing in May can provide opportunities to see a multitude of warblers: black-throated green, Wilson's, Tennessee, black-and-white, golden-winged, American redstart and bay-breasted. Listen for the flute-like songs of wood thrushes and veeries or the "teacher-teacher-teacher" calls of ovenbirds.

Forest raptors in the area include Cooper's, broad-winged and sharp-shinned hawks and great-horned and barred owls. You can watch waterfowl on the water in the early spring and late fall.

White-tailed deer, river otters, beavers, ruffed grouse, bald eagles, red-winged blackbirds and wood ducks are some of the species you might find here.

Along the hiking trail, you'll find beautiful views of the river and you'll also get a good look at a Pokegama quartzite bedrock outcrop.

Note:

The WMA adjoins private property on the south and west, so respect the boundaries. Off-road motor vehicles are not permitted.

There are camping and picnic areas at the Corps of Engineers facility. The WMA is also adjacent to a city park in Cohasset, which is a good spot for a picnic lunch.

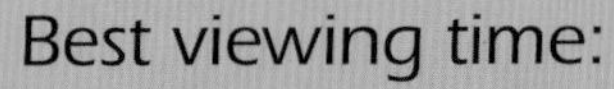
Best viewing time:

Barney Oldfield
Mink frog

How do I get there?

Maps: MN Highway Coordinate: I-8
PRIM Area: Grand Rapids
DeLorme MN Atlas Grid #: 73 E-9

Additional directions:

From Grand Rapids, drive west on Highway 2 to County Road 63. Turn left and continue to Lake Street. Turn right onto Lake Street until you see the Portage Park parking lot. The Bass Brook WMA is east of the park.

You can also access this area from the north off Highway 2 through the U.S. Army Corps of Engineers Pokegama Lake Recreation Area.

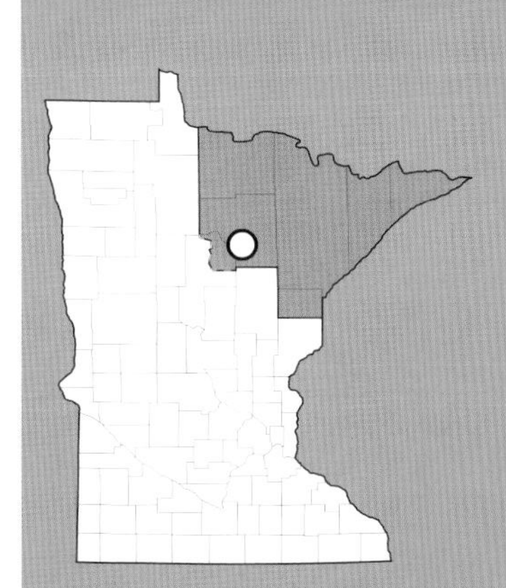

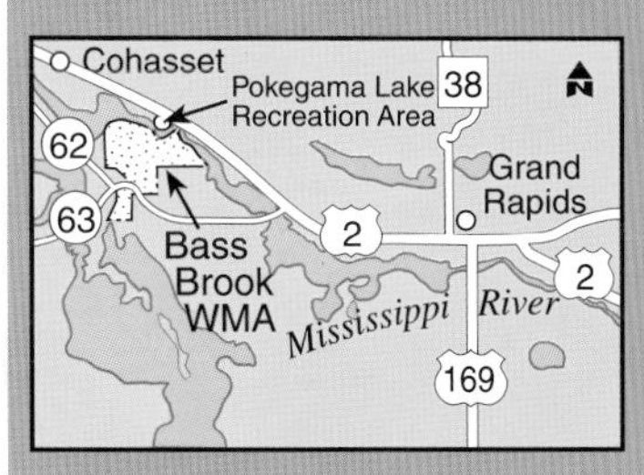

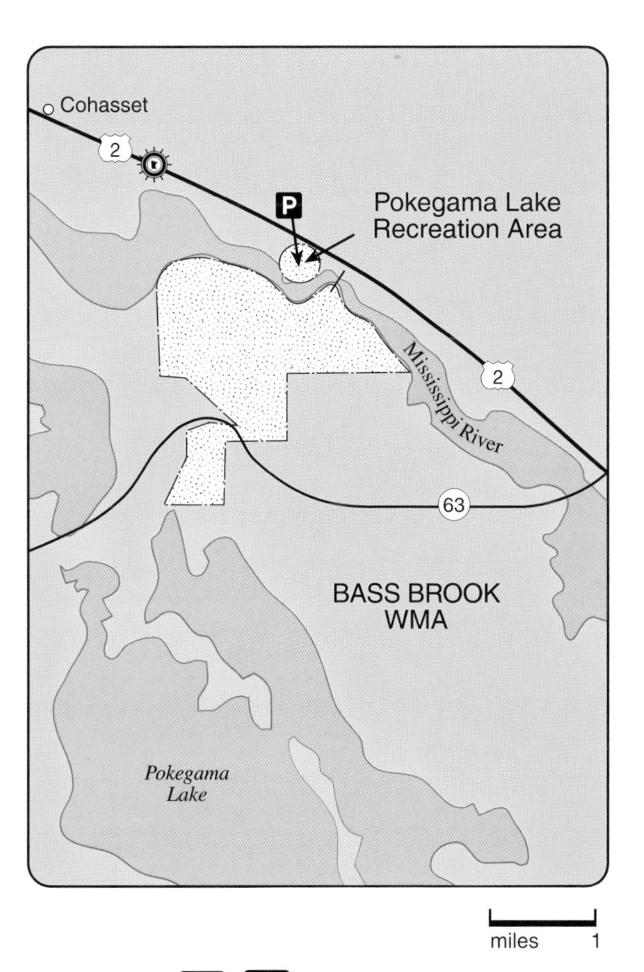

miles 1

Facilities:

Recreational Opportunities:   

Contact:

DNR Area Wildlife Office
1201 East Highway 2
Grand Rapids MN 55744
(218) 327-4428

33–Mississippi River

Why is this area special?

This eight-mile stretch of the Mississippi River is peaceful and flat for easy canoeing and boating. You can also explore vast areas of floodplain forest made up of silver maple, black ash, northern red cedar and bur oak.

C. Henderson
Great blue heron

With these forests come wildlife species such as belted kingfishers, wood ducks, bald eagles, great blue herons, mallards, common mergansers, black bears, soft-shelled turtles and white-tailed deer. Northern and walleye pike are common in this stretch of the river.

Note:

Put your canoe in at the Blackberry public access on the south side of County Road 441. Take out at Herb Beer's public access off Highway 3 (River Road).

Fishing is best during low water conditions, but low water may be a problem for outboard motors in some locations.

There are no developed campsites on this stretch of the river. Campsites are available both above and below this stretch.

County Road 3 is part of the Great River Road that starts at Lake Itasca and ends at New Orleans.

C. Henderson
Western painted turtle

Best viewing time:

How do I get there?

Maps: MN Highway Coordinate: J-9
PRIM Area: Grand Rapids
DeLorme MN Atlas Grid #: 64 B-2

Additional directions:

From Grand Rapids, travel south on the Great River Road (Highway 3) for 5 miles to County Road 441 east. Drive for 1.5 miles across the Mississippi River to the Blackberry public access on the right.

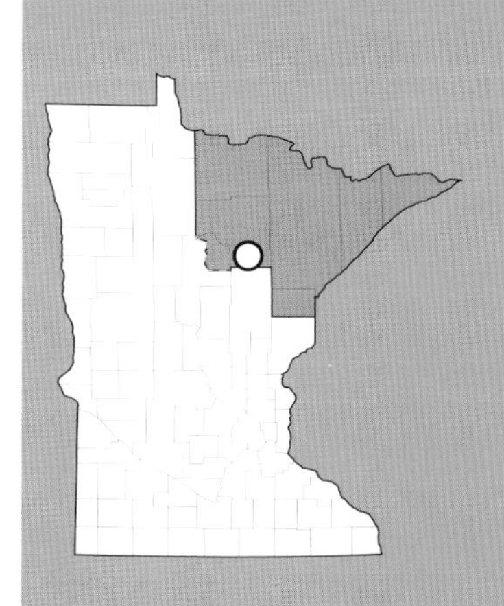

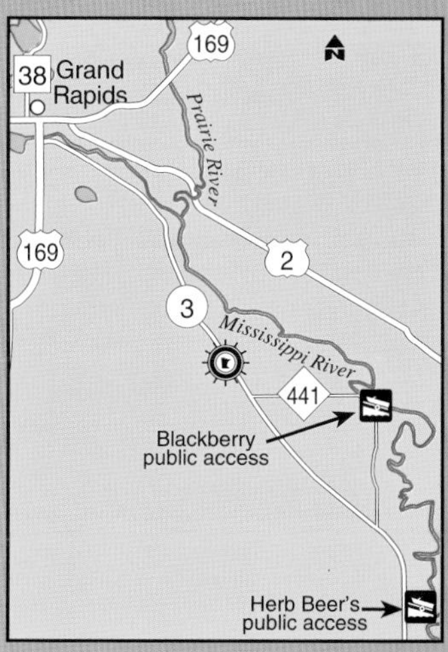

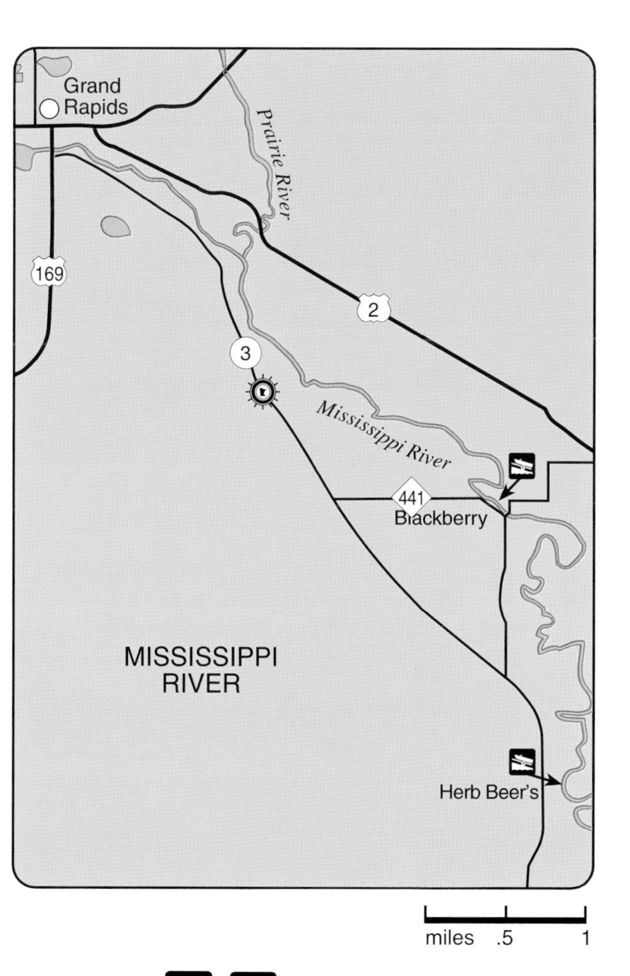

Contact:

Trails and Waterways Unit
DNR
Grand Rapids MN 55744
(218) 327-4408

Nongame Wildlife Program
DNR
1201 East Highway 2
Grand Rapids MN 55744
(218) 327-4267

Facilities: 

Recreational Opportunities:

34–Sax-Zim Bog

Why is this area special?

Accessible yet vast conifer bog areas are not common in Minnesota, but one is located a mere three-hour drive from the Twin Cities. Northwest of Duluth, this area covers approximately 200 square miles, so it can accommodate you if you're just passing through or if you want to stay for a few days.

Northern hawk-owl

Sax-Zim has long been known to birders as an excellent spot to see northern wildlife. The habitat consists of a mix of spruce, tamarack and northern white cedar bogs. There are also lowland hardwood species such as black ash, as well as isolated hayfields and sedge meadows. You can see these from various township and county roads or you can venture out into the bogs themselves. You might find stemless lady's slippers or other species of bog vegetation such as sundew, pitcher plant, leatherleaf and bog birch.

Birds to look for in the winter include northern goshawks, snowy and great gray owls and northern hawk-owls. Summer possibilities include winter wrens, golden-winged warblers, sharp-tailed grouse, white-crowned sparrows, Connecticut and pine warblers, yellow-bellied flycatchers, black-backed woodpeckers and gray jays. Black bear are common and pine martens and timber wolves have been spotted here.

Note:

The name Sax-Zim comes from old "towns" in the vicinity: the hamlet of Sax named after an Eveleth man, and Zim named after a Zimmer man who managed a logging camp. Land in the vicinity is both state and privately owned.

From County Roads 202 and 203 you can see conifer-dependent species such as boreal chickadees. County Road 319, one and a half miles east of County Road 7, is a good place to see yellow rails. Sharp-tailed grouse can sometimes been seen at the junctions of County Roads 208 and 52.

See the Featured Species section on page 22 for more information on Northern Winter Owls.

Best viewing time:

How do I get there?

Maps: MN Highway Coordinate: L 8/9
PRIM Area: Hibbing
DeLorme Mn Atlas Grid #: 65 A-8, 75 E-8

Additional directions:

From Duluth, follow Highway 53 north to St. Louis County Road 133 (the Meadowlands turnoff). You could also use County Roads 319, 232 and 208.

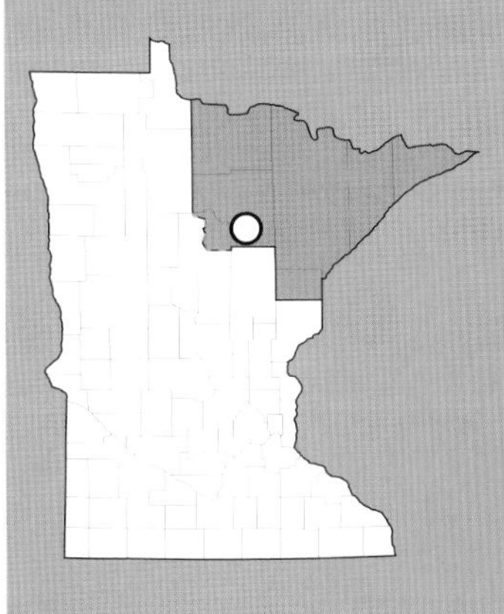

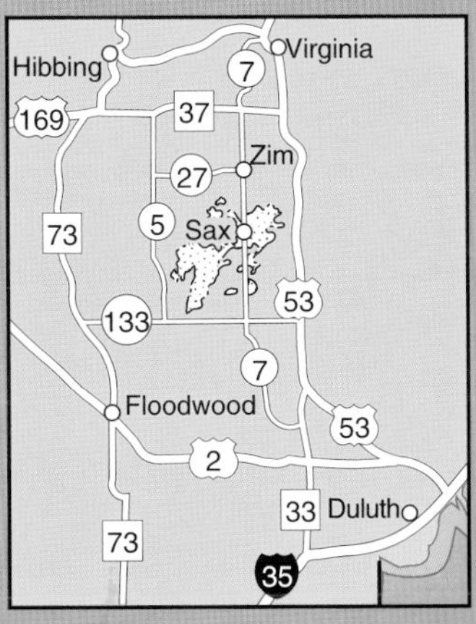

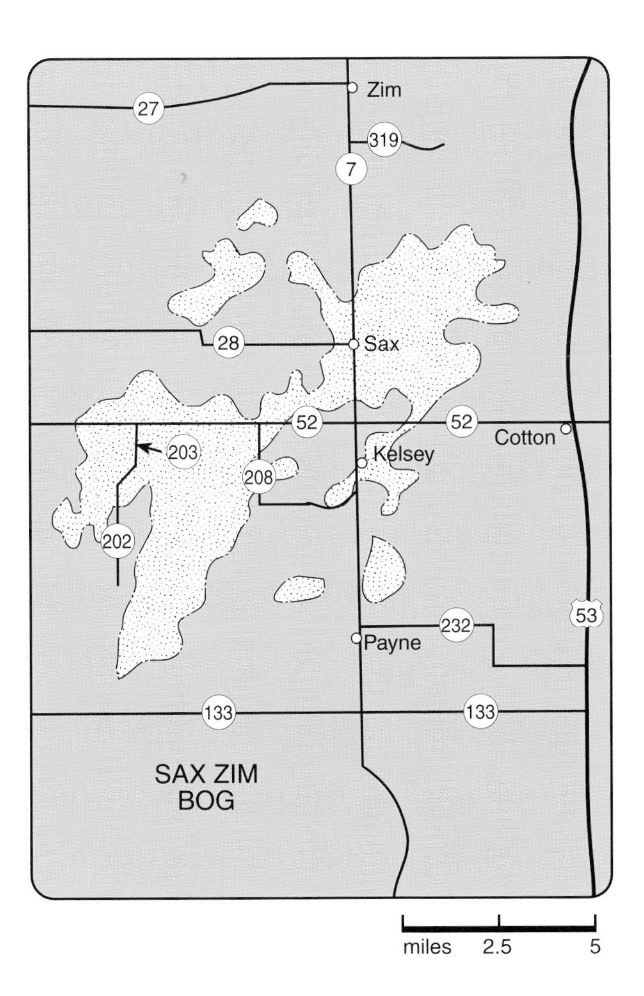

Facilities:

Recreational Opportunities:

Contact:

Forest Ecologist
DNR
2005 Highway 37
Eveleth MN 55734
(218) 744-7447

35–Murphy City/Stoney River Grade

Why is this area special?

One of the most impressive wildlife species in Minnesota is the moose. Large bulls may exceed 1,000 pounds in weight and carry antlers with a spread that exceeds four feet. An excellent place to watch and photograph moose is from a highway in the Murphy City vicinity.

Another good moose-watching spot is at an old railroad bed called the Stoney River Grade Forest Road. From there you might also see rare wildlife species associated with lowland conifer forests, particularly great gray owls and timber wolves. You can also look for other wildlife of the northern boreal forest, such as boreal chickadees, red-breasted nuthatches and gray jays.

Note:

This area is primitive, with no facilities nearby. The nearest minimal services are at Finland or Isabella, and you can camp in Superior National Forest.

The Stoney River Grade is not always open during the winter.

See the Featured Species section on page 34 for more information on moose.

Plan extra time to explore other sites (26–29) along the North Shore for viewing vistas and more wildlife.

C. Henderson

Blackpoll warbler

Best viewing time:

Hunting allowed. Call ahead for hunting season dates.

How do I get there?

Maps: MN Highway Coordinate: 0-7
PRIM Area: Ely & Two Harbors
DeLorme MN Atlas Grid #: 77 C-9

Additional directions:

From Ely take Highway 1 for 45 miles south to Murphy City.

From Duluth and Highway 61 go north to Illgen City. Take Highway 1 for 20 miles to Murphy City.

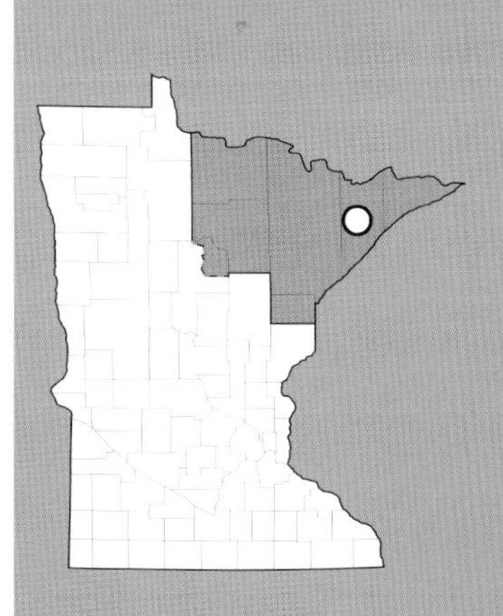

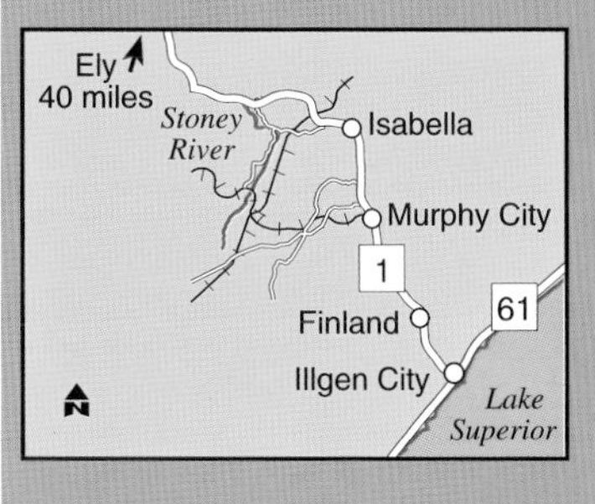

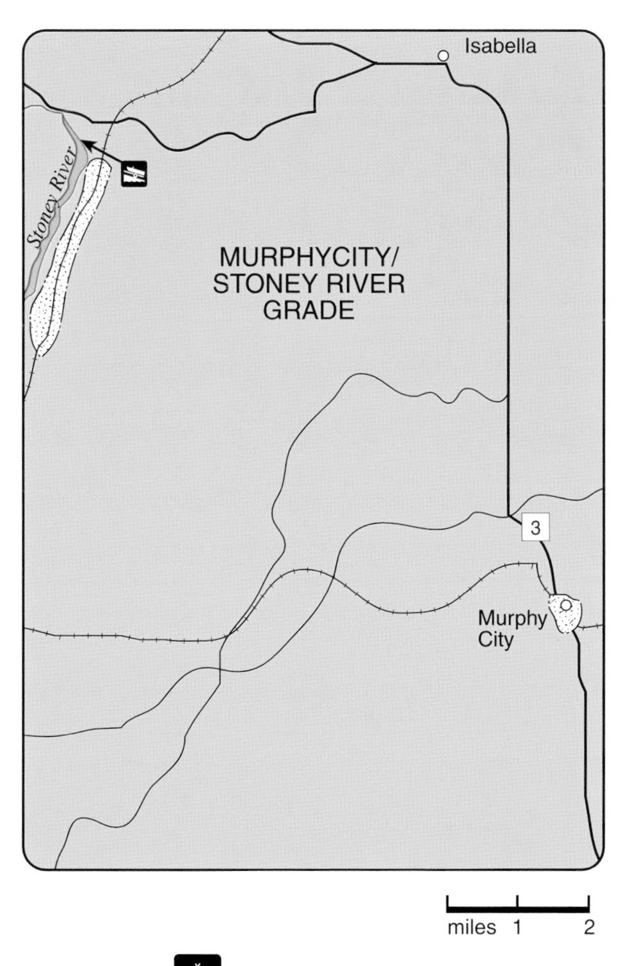

Facilities:
Recreational Opportunities:

Contact:

DNR Area Wildlife Office
1429 Grant McMahon Road
Ely MN 55731
(218) 365-7280

36–Hawk Ridge Nature Reserve

C. Henderson

Why is this area special?

Hawk Ridge is one of the best and most famous raptor migration sites in North America. More than 15 species of migrating birds of prey take advantage of the updrafts along the shore of Lake Superior as they migrate south from mid-August through mid-November. Broad-winged hawks are the most numerous; more than 3,000 can be seen on a good day. Between September 10 and 20, the numbers of broad-wings peak at more than 20,000.

Visit this site to practice raptor identification and to learn about birds from Duluth Audubon members. Watch the release of banded birds on weekends, participate in some of the site's educational programs and enjoy the beautiful view of Duluth and Lake Superior.

Birds are reluctant to fly over Lake Superior, so they tend to follow the shoreline, funneling right through the Hawk Ridge Nature Reserve.

Nineteen different raptor species have been observed at Hawk Ridge over the years, including sharp-shinned, red-tailed, rough-legged and Cooper's hawks, northern harriers, northern goshawks, bald eagles, ospreys, turkey vultures, American kestrels and merlins.

Note:

Binoculars or spotting scopes are essential in this area. Bring a camera with a telephoto lens in order to get good pictures. Bring warm clothing, too, as the wind can get very cold.

See the Featured Species section on page 20 for more information on Fall Hawk migration.

Visit Snively and Magney City Parks (site 37) and Park Point Recreation Area/Minnesota Point Forest (site 38) in Duluth for more wildlife watching.

Best viewing time:

C. Henderson

Peregrine falcon

How do I get there?

Maps: MN Highway Coordinate: M-10
PRIM Area: Duluth
DeLorme MN Atlas Grid #: 66 D-3

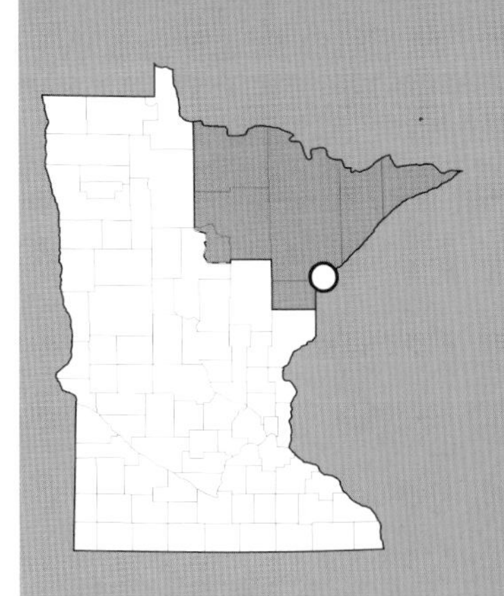

Additional directions:

From State Highway 61, exit at 43rd, 45th, 47th or 60th Avenues East. Follow any of these north to Glenwood Avenue. Turn left, and take Glenwood to Skyline Parkway. Turn right onto Skyline Parkway.

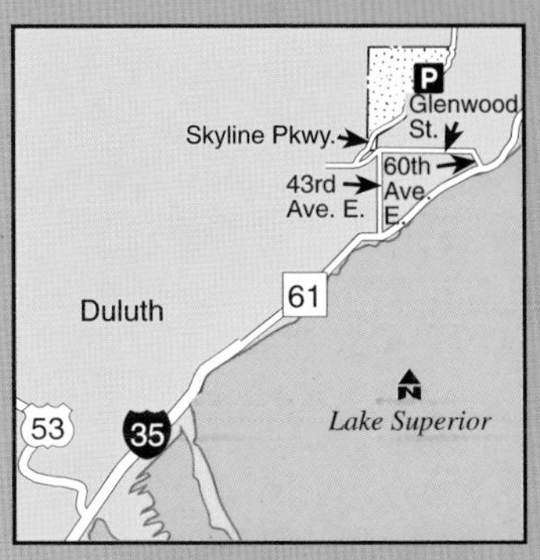

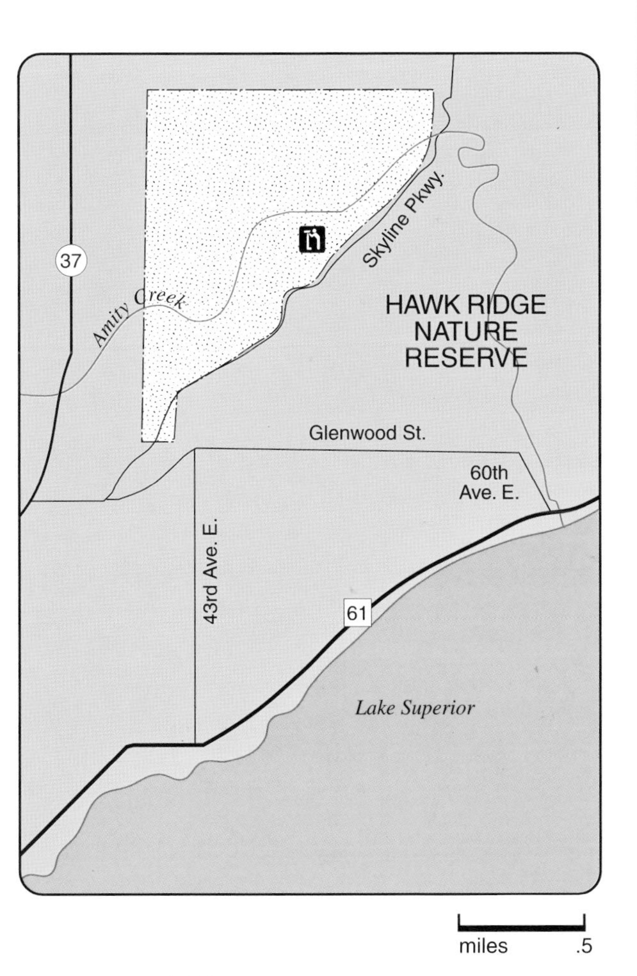

Facilities:

Recreational Opportunities:

Contact:

Hawk Ridge Nature Reserve
Duluth Audubon Society
Biology Department
University of Minnesota
Duluth MN 55812

Duluth Audubon Hotline
(218) 525-5952 (recorded message)

Duluth Parks & Recreation
Central Hillside Community Center
12 E 4th St.
Duluth MN 55802
(218) 723-3337

37–Snively and Magney City Parks

Why is this area special?

Although Hawk Ridge and Park Point get more attention from birders, Snively and Magney City Parks provide an excellent forest habitat for birding in Duluth. Because these parks have been preserved, their understory flora is intact and the conditions are probably very similar to those experienced by early European explorers and settlers.

C. Henderson
Blackburnian warbler

Except for ski trails, there is very little development in these outstanding old northern hardwood forests filled with massive maple, oak and basswood trees. Fall leaf colors are spectacular, and you'll get great views of West Duluth and the St. Louis River from Skyline Parkway. This is a good place to see spring and early summer wild flowers typical of maple-basswood forests. Look especially for trillium, bloodroot, leatherwood and baneberry. Watch for hardwood forest songbirds, wood warblers and woodpeckers from spring through fall. Examples would be the indigo bunting, wood thrush, chestnut-sided warbler and great crested flycatcher.

Note:

Biting insects are abundant in the summer so bring insect repellent. Spring and fall days may be very cool due to winds from Lake Superior.

While in the area, allow time to visit Hawk Ridge (site 36) and Park Point (site 38).

C. Henderson
White-tailed deer

Best viewing time:

How do I get there?

Maps: MN Highway Coordinate: M-10
PRIM Area: Duluth
DeLorme MN Atlas Grid #: 66 D-2

Additional directions:

From State Highway 2, exit at Becks Road. Follow Becks Road south to Skyline Parkway.

From I-35 exit at Proctor at Becks Road (County Road 13). Go south and turn east on Skyline Parkway which passes the Spirit Mountain Recreation Area.

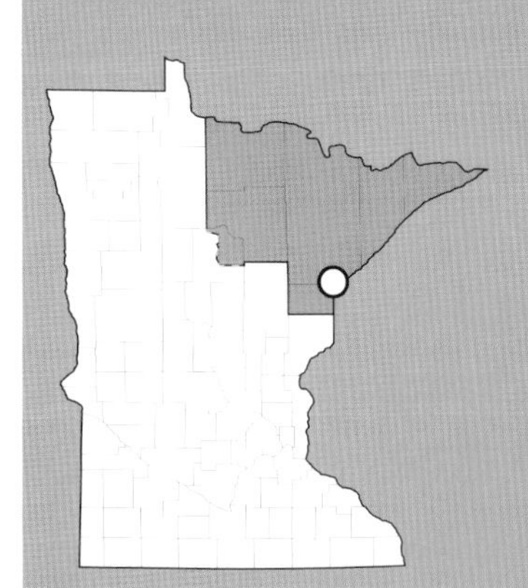

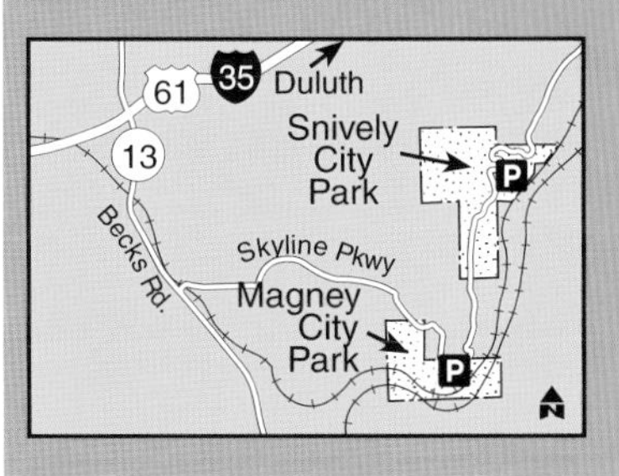

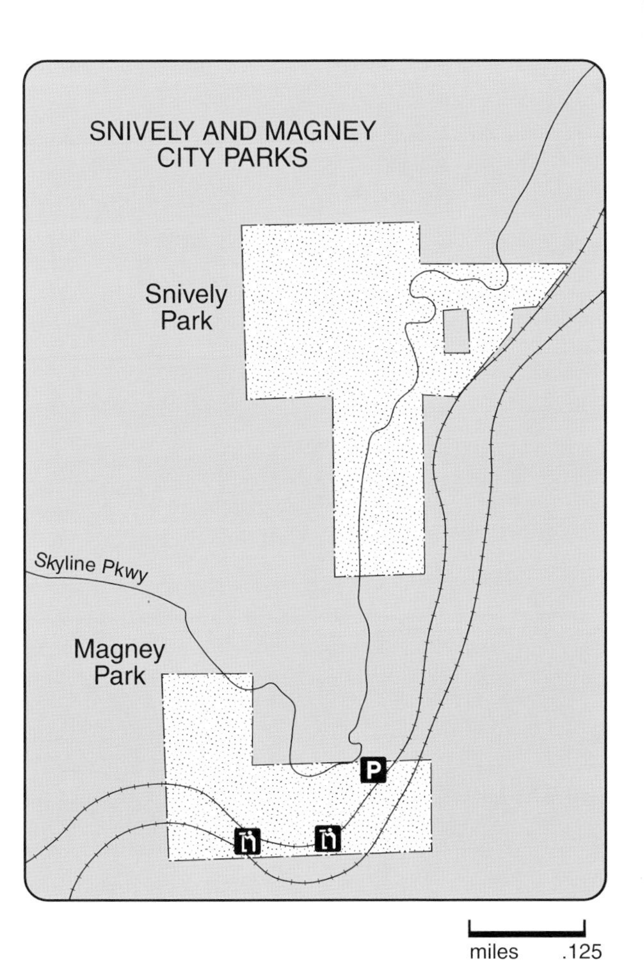

Contact:

Duluth Parks and Recreation
Central Hillside Community Center
12 E 4th St.
Duluth MN 55802
(218) 723-3337-

Facilities:  

Recreational Opportunities: 

38–Park Point Recreation Area/ Minnesota Point Forest

Why is this area special?

This long sand dune sandwiched between Duluth and Lake Superior separates the lake from Duluth Harbor. The area has been protected, so it retains some interesting old great lakes pine forests. Explore the open parkland, dense hardwood-pine forests, red and white pine forests and sand dune beach habitats.

Spring and fall offers excellent birding as large numbers of migrating birds move around Lake Superior. Many shorebirds and other migrants stop to rest on Park Point during their yearly travels. In addition to songbirds, look for common terns, and an occasional peregrine falcon. Some of the best birding will be on days with fog, rain or wind, because the birds are forced to stop there until the weather improves.

Note:

You can gain access to the area beyond Sky Harbor Airport by entering through a gate on the northeast side of the buildings and runway. Make sure to have a jacket—Lake Superior is known for its cool weather conditions.

See the Featured Species section on pages 18–21 for more information on peregrine falcons and fall hawk migration.

Stephen Maxson

Common tern

Best viewing time:

How do I get there?

Maps: MN Highway Coordinate: M-10
PRIM Area: Duluth
DeLorme MN Atlas Grid #: 66 E-3

Additional directions:

From I-35, take the Lake Avenue/Canal Park exit. On Lake Avenue, drive to the first traffic light and turn right. Then take the first left onto Minnesota Avenue. Take Minnesota Avenue across Aerial Lift Bridge to the Park Point Recreation Area.

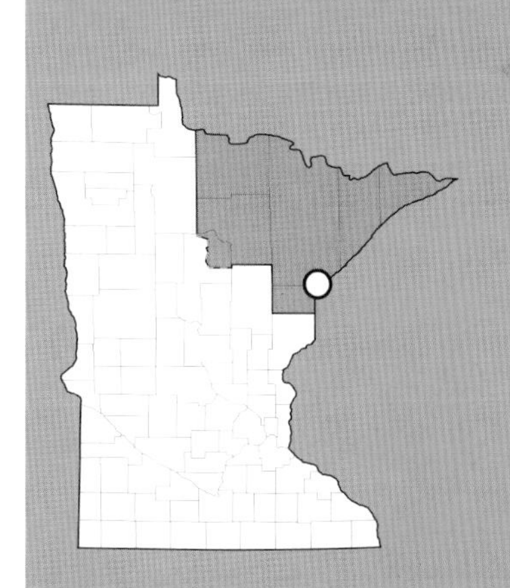

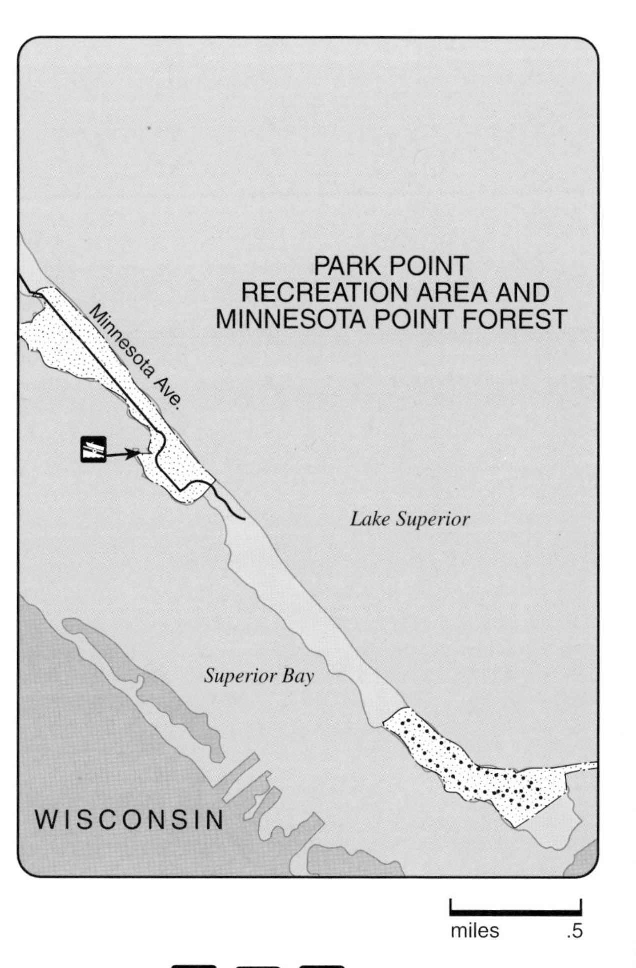

Contact:

Duluth Parks and Recreation
Central Hillside Community Center
12 E 4th St.
Duluth MN 55802
(218) 723-3337

Facilities: 

Recreational Opportunities:

39–Sharp-tailed Grouse Dancing Grounds

Why is this area special?

This dancing ground or "lek," as it is referred to by biologists, is a displaying area where male sharp-tailed grouse gather at sunrise to compete for the attention of local sharp-tailed hens. The pattering of the birds' feet as they lower their heads, spread their wings, raise their tails and rotate their bodies back and forth have given them the nickname "typewriter bird."

Like the better-known greater prairie chickens, sharp-tailed grouse are a native grouse species in Minnesota. Their preferred habitat is brushland–grasslands interspersed with thickets of aspen. Because there has been inadequate attention to the loss of brushland habitats in the past, sharp-tailed grouse have become increasingly uncommon.

The DNR Section of Wildlife maintains an observation blind for viewing the sharptails in April. They begin their display between 4:15 to 4:30 a.m. You will need to be in the blind before 4 a.m. to avoid flushing the birds off the site. That may seem early, but the experience is one that you will value for a lifetime!

A. B. Sheldon

Sharp-tailed grouse

Note:

This site is on private land and the observation blind is maintained by the DNR with the permission of the landowner. You need reservations; contact the DNR Area Wildlife Manager in Cloquet at (218) 879-0883. The manager will provide you with details about reaching the site.

See the Featured Species section on page 24 for more information on sharp-tailed grouse.

See site 25 for another opportunity to reserve a blind.

Best viewing time:

How do I get there?

Maps: MN Highway Coordinate: K-11
PRIM Area: Sandstone
DeLorme MN Atlas Grid #: 57

Additional directions:

The Carlton County site is near Kettle River.

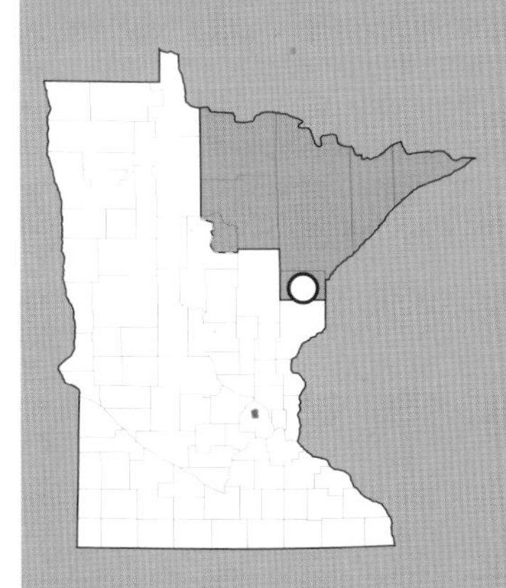

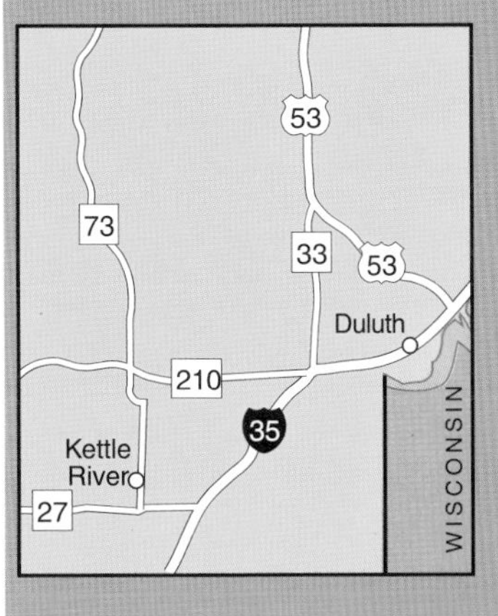

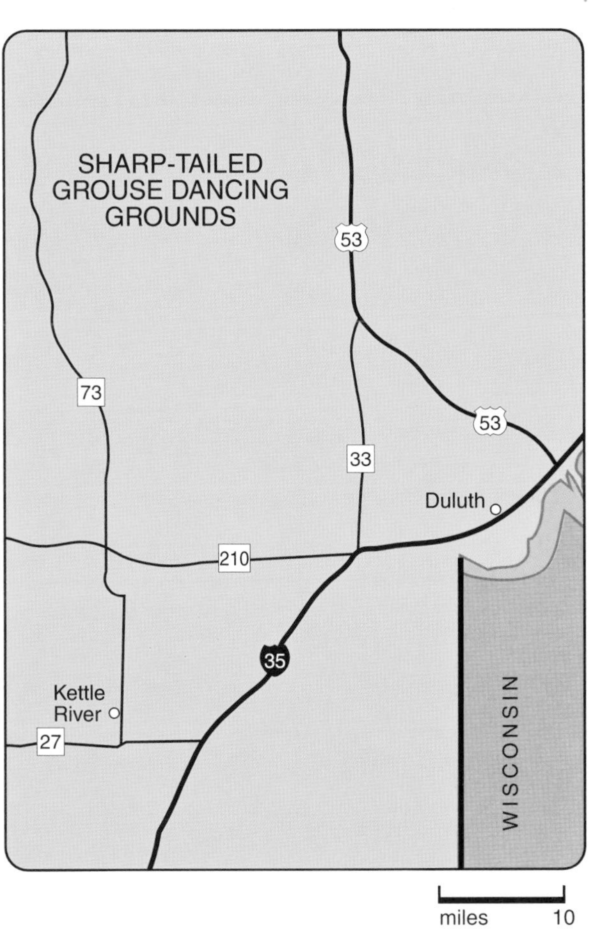

Facilities:

Recreational Opportunities:

Contact:

DNR Area Wildlife Office
1604 South Highway 33
Cloquet MN 55720
(218) 879-0883

40–Moose Lake State Park

Why is this area special?

Moose Lake State Park offers the unique setting of meadows and wetlands in a region otherwise dominated by northern forests. The park was originally a farm used to raise food for patients at the nearby Moose Lake State Hospital. Management by the state park system has allowed old fields to revert to grassland. Forests of pine and spruce are being restored. Natural succession processes are featuring the regrowth of aspen, birch, basswood and maple.

A. B. Sheldon

Smooth green snake

In May, the meadows adjacent to the woodlands are a good place to watch and listen at dusk for woodcocks doing their spring courtship flights. Spring woodlands are characterized by the drumming of ruffed grouse and the songs of migrant warblers. Watch for common loons, bald eagles and ospreys at Moose and Echo Lakes. Restored wetlands are used by migrating waterfowl, as well as resident Canada geese, wood ducks, beavers, mink and muskrats.

Note:

A daily or annual vehicle permit is needed to enter the state parks.

C. Henderson

American woodcock

Best viewing time:

How do I get there?

Maps: MN Highway Coordinate: L-11
PRIM Area: Sandstone
DeLorme MN Atlas Grid #: 57 B-7

Additional directions:

Take Interstate 35 to the Moose Lake exit (Hwy 73). The park headquarters is located on the east side of the highway. Follow the signs.

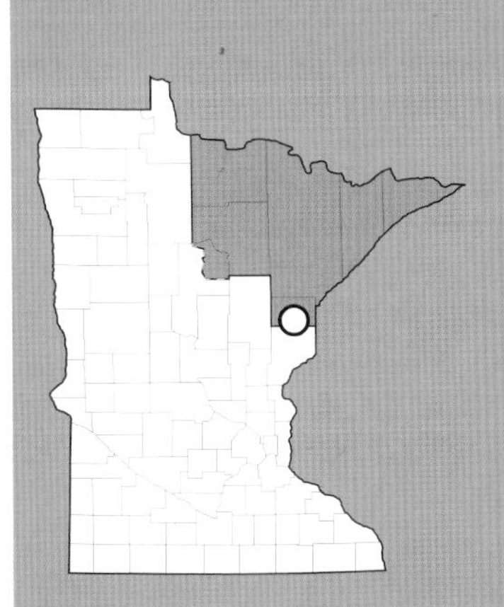

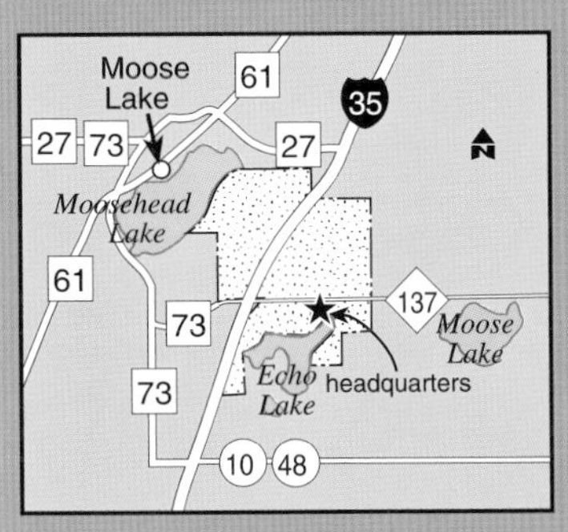

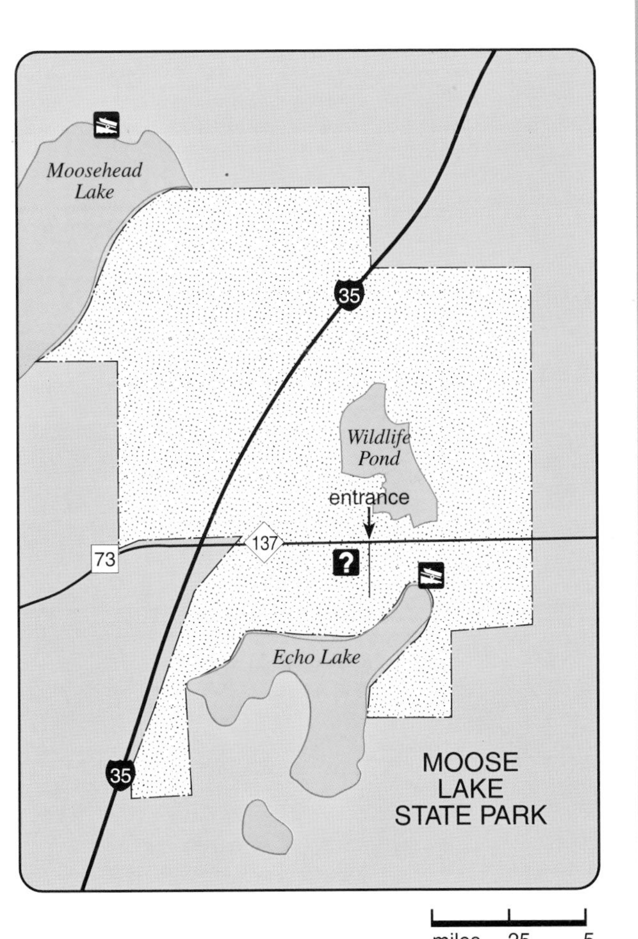

miles .25 .5

Facilities:

Recreational Opportunities:   

Contact:

Moose Lake State Park
4252 Co. Rd. 137
Moose Lake MN 55767
(218) 485-5420

Division of Parks & Recreation
DNR
500 Lafayette Rd
St. Paul MN 55155
(612) 296-9223 or
888-MINNDNR

Central-Heartland Lakes Country

The central Minnesota region boasts a wide variety of wildlife species, numerous outdoor recreational opportunities and exceptional tourism facilities. The great variety of habitats found in this region is due to central Minnesota's position at the junction of three major biomes: the northern coniferous forest, the eastern deciduous forest, and the tallgrass prairie.

In the northern part of the region, Aitkin County is famous for its lakes, bogs and wetlands, and is considered one of the premier birdwatching areas in the state. Northern species such as great gray owls, loons, eagles and bears are often seen here. Wild rice paddies attract large flocks of waterfowl in April and hardwood forests provide excellent habitat for numerous species of warblers.

The Mississippi River runs through the heart of central Minnesota and provides a major travel corridor and migration route for many species, especially waterfowl. Some areas along the river are part of the Anoka Sand Plain. Exceedingly well-drained sandy soils can be found that produce rolling sand hill conditions (see Sand Dunes State Forest /Uncas Dunes Scientific and Natural Area, site 59). Before European settlement, much of this area was oak and jack pine savanna. Prairie grasses and wild flowers are often found along the highways and the railroad grades. Savannas are sparse woodlands with prairie plants for a ground cover. To see a jack pine savanna, visit The Nature Conservancy property within the Northland Arboretum (site 44).

C. Henderson

Common loon

In the western part of the region, you will find small towns and farmland. Lake Osakis in Todd County has the largest nesting colony of western grebes in the state. During spring and summer, many other water birds might be observed. To experience what the original tallgrass prairie was like, visit the Roscoe Prairie SNA (site 54) in Stearns County.

Some of the largest and best known resorts in Minnesota (Madden's, Cragun's, Ruttger's Bay Lake Lodge and Grand View Lodge) are located in the lakes region north and east of Brainerd. There are also numerous small resorts, motels and bed & breakfasts for the traveler. The many lakes in this area provide a popular summer home locale. Wildlife watching is considered a part of the tourism industry with loons, deer and ducks portrayed as symbols of the area.

The Mille Lacs Lake area is also a prime destination for many visitors whether they fish (one of the best walleye lakes in the state), birdwatch or visit state parks. The Mille Lacs Band of Ojibwe operates one casino on the west side of the lake, and another near Hinckley. Excellent restaurants and lodging are nearby.

For summer visits, don't forget to bring some insect repellant. From late May through July, expect mosquitos near wetlands and in forested areas. In wet years, mosquitos will be more abundant. In July and August deer flies are common, especially in dry open areas.

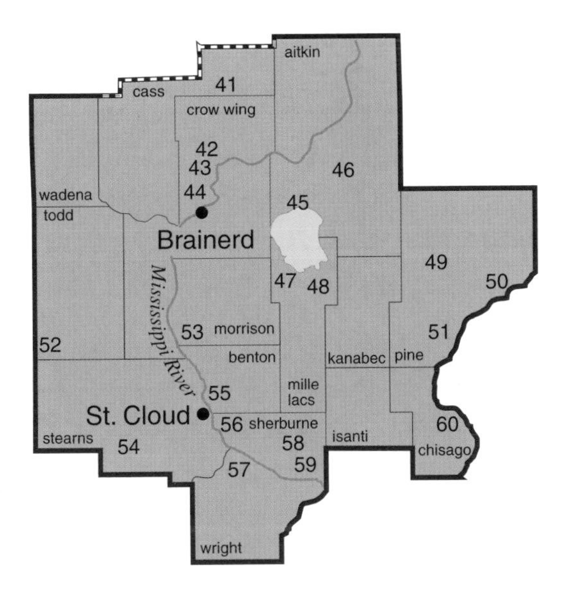

Sites

41. Washburn Lake Solitude Area
42. Big Island Natural & Recreation Area
43. Uppgaard WMA
44. Northland Arboretum/ Paul Bunyan Jack Pine Savanna
45. Mille Lacs Lake-North Shore (Highway 18)
46. Rice Lake NWR/ Kimberly WMA/ McGregor Marsh SNA
47. Mille Lacs Lake Area & Kathio State Park
48. Mille Lacs WMA
49. Banning State Park
50. St. Croix State Park
51. Chengwatana State Forest
52. Lake Osakis
53. Crane Meadows NWR/ Rice-Skunk & Crane Meadows WMAs
54. Roscoe Prairie SNA
55. Graham's Island in the Mississippi River
56. Sand Prairie WMA
57. Lake Maria State Park
58. Sherburne NWR
59. Sand Dunes State Forest/ Uncas Dunes SNA
60. Wild River State Park

41–Washburn Lake Solitude Area

Why is this area special?

Open only to hikers, mountain bikers, horseback riders and cross-country skiers, the 2500-acre Washburn Lake Solitude Area was set aside for people who seek the quietude of the forest. Twenty-six miles of trails wind through lake and lowland habitat, providing ideal wildlife watching.

In the 1880s this area was logged by the Pine Tree Lumber Company. Logs were driven into Washburn Lake and eventually into the Mississippi until the company completed their cutting around 1907. Fires followed the early loggers, and parts of the region burned over yearly, causing the forest cover to grow back slowly. However, no serious fires have occurred since the 1930s. Today the greater Land O'Lakes Forest totals nearly 50,000 acres of lush wildlife habitat.

C. Henderson

Scarlet tanager

White-tailed deer, red fox, raccoon, black bear and beaver reside in the tranquil setting—and keep an eye out for signs of moose and the shy, elusive timber wolf, both of which are occasionally sighted. You might spot scarlet tanagers, Baltimore orioles, ruby-throated hummingbirds, wood thrushes, evening and rose-breasted grosbeaks and a variety of warblers, as well as ruffed grouse, broad-winged hawks and bald eagles.

The forest is comprised mostly of aspen and birch, but you'll also see pine, spruce, oak, maple, balsam fir, basswood, tamarack, willow, white cedar and ash. Visit in autumn when the mixture of leaves forms a spectacular kaleidoscope of rich, royal colors.

Note:

The Area's Clinton Converse Campground, used as a depression-era Civilian Conservation Corps camp, has 33 well-kept, handicapped-accessible campsites nestled among the trees. A nominal camping fee is charged. The groomed Washburn Lake Ski Trail has off-road parking, a posted map and an outhouse. A cross-country ski pass is required.

Be sure to check out the Land O'Lakes Forest lookout tower and the 24-mile Ben Draper Recreational Trail for additional wildlife viewing.

Best viewing time:

Hunting allowed. Call ahead for hunting season dates.

How do I get there?

Maps: MN Highway Coordinate: H-10
PRIM Area: Aitkin
DeLorme MN Atlas Grid #: 63 D-7

Additional directions:

The Washburn Lake Solitude Area is a small tract separate from the main Land O'Lakes State Forest. From Outing take Highway 6 north two miles, turn west on Cass County Road 48. The headquarters is just south of that junction.

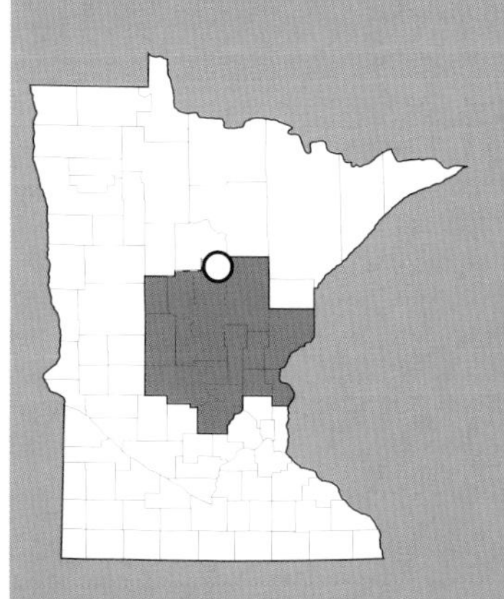

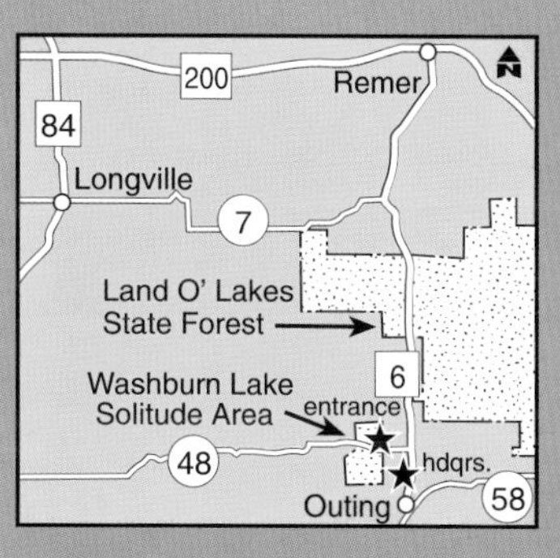

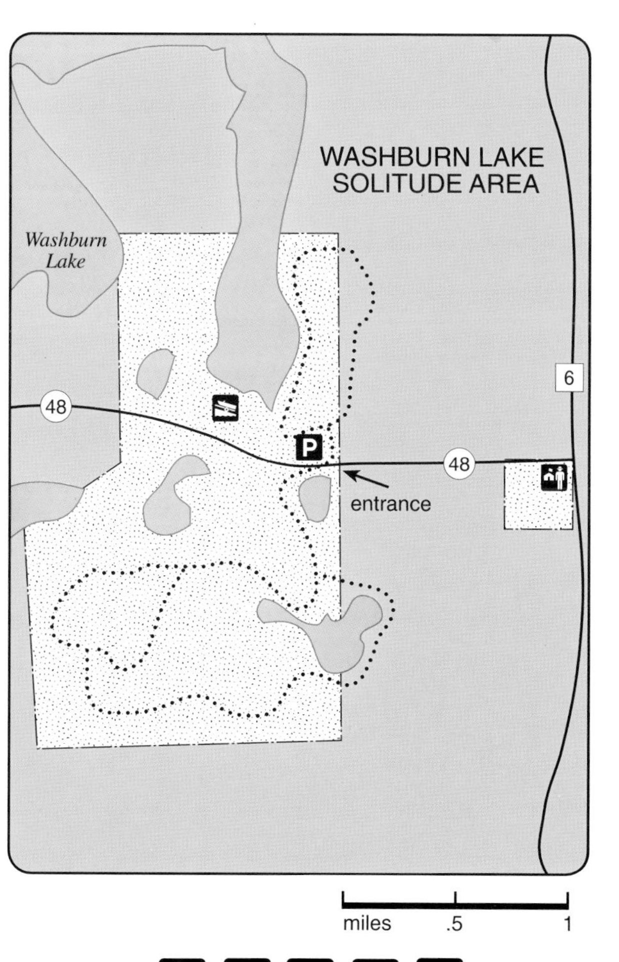

Facilities:    

Recreational Opportunities:

Contact:

Washburn Lake
DNR District Forestry Office
HCR-Box 370
Outing MN 56662
(218) 792-5383 or the

DNR Area Forestry Office
Pequot Lakes MN 56472
(218) 568-4566

42–Big Island Natural & Recreation Area

Why is this area special?

Big Island in Whitefish Lake is a rare example of an undisturbed old-growth maple-basswood forest, which is unique in this area of pine, aspen, birch and oak. Look up to see 150-year-old trees forming a dense canopy 100 feet above the forest floor and sheltering a rich assortment of flowering plants unusual this far north in Minnesota. For the butternut, this island is the northwestern-most point of its North American range. Other trees include red maple, northern white oak, slippery elm, hackberry and white pine.

In May and early June scan the island for large-flowered and nodding trillium, wild ginger, bloodroot, wild geranium, jack-in-the-pulpit and other spring ephemerals. Once summer arrives, patches of maidenhair fern carpet the woods.

Lynn and Donna Rogers

Listen for chorus frog and spring peeper symphonies in spring and as the season progresses, peruse the forest floor for these small frogs. Red-eyed vireo, ovenbird, chestnut-sided warbler, bald eagle, pileated woodpecker, wood duck, Caspian tern and great blue heron are just a few of the resident birds.

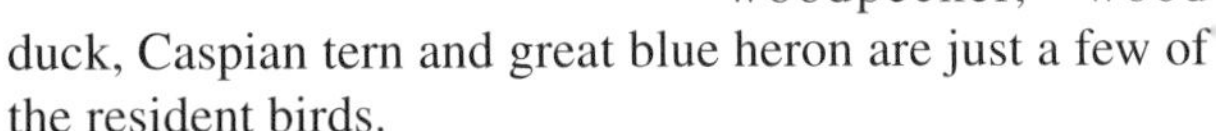

If the island escapes catastrophic disturbance, such as fire, tornado or human impact, this remarkable plant community may prosper for hundreds of years.

Note:

Access to the island is only by boat. Once you're there, a self-guided nature trail will provide you with information about the site.

Please stay on the trails and do not pick wildflowers or harvest firewood. Use the firewood and fire rings provided and douse the embers completely when you're finished.

While in the vicinity, stop at the Uppgaard WMA (site 43) for additional wildlife watching opportunities.

Best viewing time:

How do I get there?

Maps: MN Highway Coordinate: H-10
PRIM Area: Pine River
DeLorme MN Atlas Grid #: 62 E-4

Additional directions:

You can get to the island through the Whitefish chain of lakes, located about 30 miles north of Brainerd. Contact the Chambers of Commerce in Pequot Lakes, Pine River or Crosslake for information on accesses, lodging, boat rental and maps.

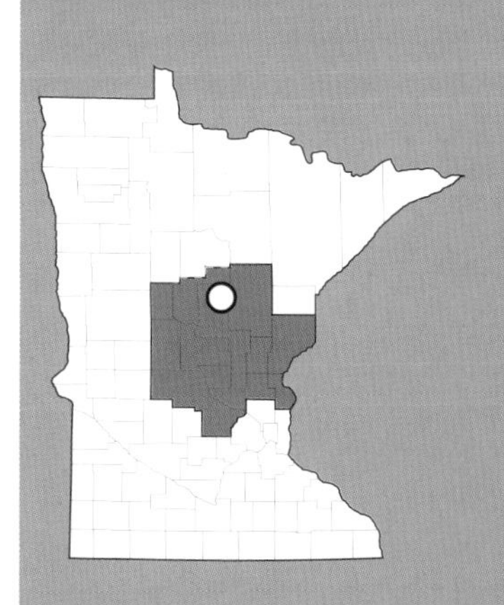

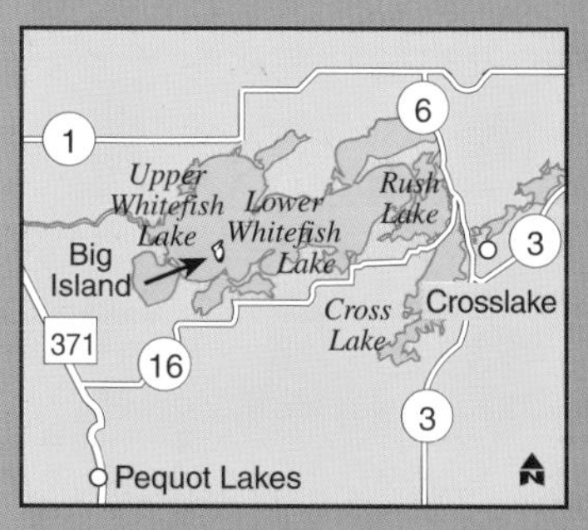

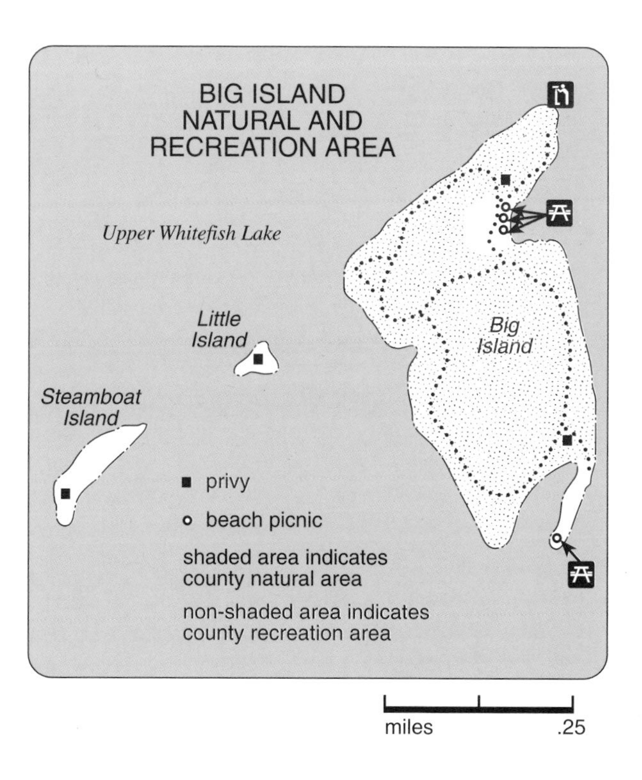

Contact:

Nongame Wildlife Program
DNR
1601 Minnesota Drive
Brainerd MN 56401
(218) 828-2228

Facilities: 

Recreational Opportunities:  

43–Uppgaard WMA

Why is this area special?

Wildlife observation blinds, well-maintained trails and scenic overlooks with benches make this site delightful for easy wildlife watching. A restored prairie and wildflower garden enhance the area, which is named after land donors Bob and Barbara Uppgaard.

In the heart of the lakes country, this 110-acre tract of gently rolling woods and wetlands offers not only the opportunity to view wildlife, but shows how you can attract wildlife to your property. As Minnesota's first "Landscaping for Wildlife" Demonstration Area, this newer approach of habitat management consists of adding plants valuable for wildlife, feeders, nest boxes, dust beds, brush and rock piles and snags to attract animals.

C. Henderson

Silvery checkerspot butterfly

Look for white-tailed deer, western painted turtle, ruffed grouse, beaver, porcupine, great blue heron, broad-winged hawk, American redstart, ovenbird, great crested flycatcher and summer butterflies who call this acreage home. Watch for eastern bluebirds and tree swallows around the nest boxes in the parking area and upper meadow. Listen for the common yellowthroat by the observation blind at the end of Hidden Blind Trail and look for beaver near their lodge.

A blend of mixed coniferous and deciduous forest, two small lakes, meadow and marshland offers a potpourri of plant life. Aspen, birch, oak and Minnesota's three species of pine—jack, red and white—can be seen here. Check out the sunny wildflower garden, which features a seasonal parade of pasque flower, black-eyed Susan, purple coneflower, blazing star, pearly everlasting, American columbine, wild phlox and butterflyweed.

A great place to enjoy a leisurely walk, watch wildlife and learn!

Note:

Information map and bird checklist are available at the entrance. Although not groomed, you may use the trails for cross-country skiing in winter. Ski passes are not required.

While in the vicinity, check out Big Island Natural and Recreation Area (site 42) for additional wildlife watching opportunities.

Best viewing time:

Hunting allowed. Call ahead for hunting season dates.

How do I get there?

Maps: MN Highway Coordinate: H-11
PRIM Area: Pine River
DeLorme MN Atlas Grid #: 62 E-5

Additional directions:

Located about 30 miles north of Brainerd, this area is just off County Road 16 between Pequot Lakes and Crosslake.

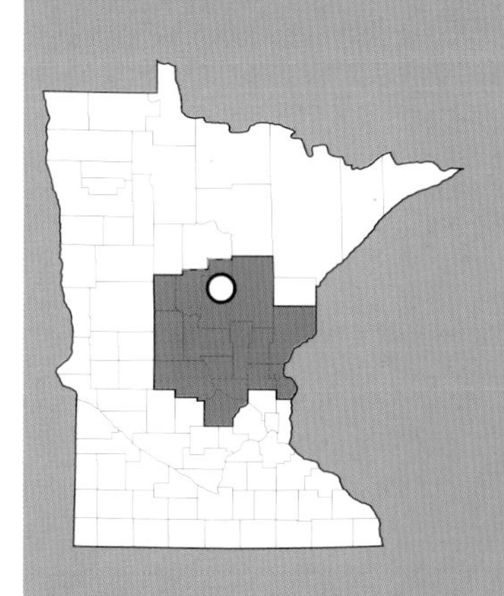

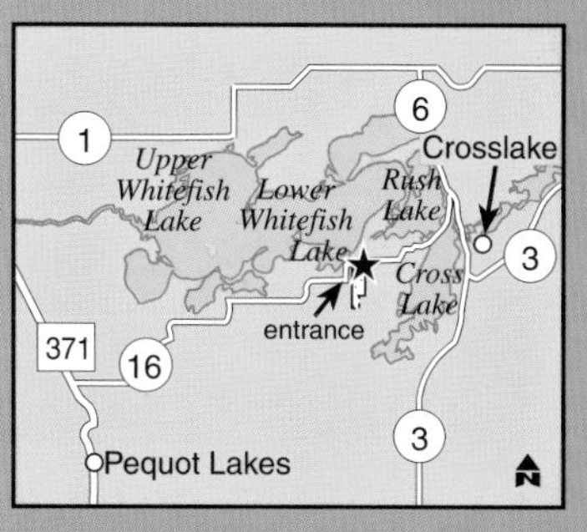

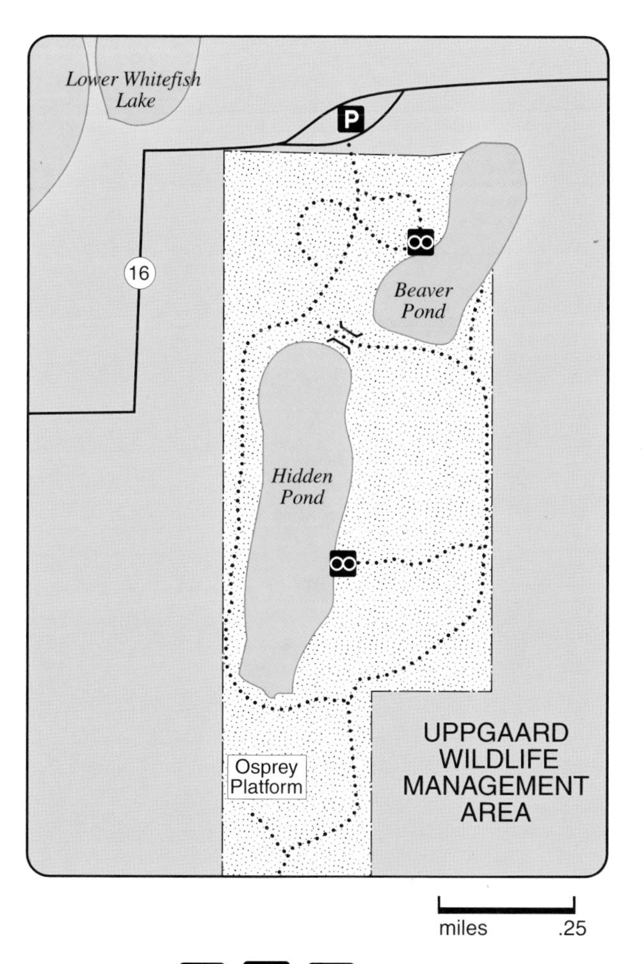

miles .25

Facilities:

Recreational Opportunities:

Contact:

Nongame Wildlife Program
DNR
1601 Minnesota Drive
Brainerd MN 56401
(218) 828-2228

44–Northland Arboretum/Paul Bunyan Jack Pine Savanna

Why is this area special?

Bluebirds and butterflies flitting about, a replica of Monet's garden pond and backyard wildlife landscaping sites make this songbird sanctuary special. Sit in the gazebo, linger on the bridge, stroll along a path or wind through the winter woods on skis—whether you have an hour or a day, tranquillity will surely envelop your visit.

Look and listen for eastern bluebird, downy woodpecker, black-capped chickadee, white-breasted nuthatch, blue jay, ovenbird, American goldfinch and ruffed grouse. Watch for beaver, mink, white-tailed deer and other small mammals who call the Arboretum home in the heart of the city. If luck has it, it's possible you may spot a beaver, river otter or even a bear! Be sure to scan for signs of wildlife too—holes excavated in trees, tracks in the mud or snow, chiseled tree stumps, scat on the trails and freshly dug dirt indicate animals are in the vicinity.

C. Henderson

Native jack pine and bur oak dominate the sand plain, and beautiful gardens of wild and cultivated flowers have been carved into the setting. Depending on the season, enjoy marsh marigold, blue flag, hoary puccoon, birds-foot violet, prairie phlox, pipsissewa, black-eyed Susan, blazing star, harebell, aster, swamp milkweed, lupine, cardinal flower, cosmos, coneflower and a host of other cheery comrades, along with water lilies, native orchids and ferns dotting the landscape.

Note:

Fifteen miles of summer trails and walkable roads are groomed in winter for cross-country skiing. There's even a lighted ski trail. A nominal entrance fee is charged. Ski passes are required. Mountain bikes are permitted only on marked trails and on the bordering Paul Bunyan Trail.

The 600+ acre site, collectively now referred to as the Paul Bunyan Conservation Area, is comprised of the Northland Arboretum, the Paul Bunyan Jack Pine Savanna (owned by The Nature Conservancy) and the Fremling Tree Farm.

Best viewing time:

How do I get there?

Maps: MN Highway Coordinate: H-12
PRIM Area: Brainerd
DeLorme MN Atlas Grid #: 54 C-5

Additional directions:

The Arboretum is on the north side of Brainerd behind the Westgate Mall. From Highway 210 look for the brown signs and turn north onto 7th Street NW, proceed a half-mile to the entrance.

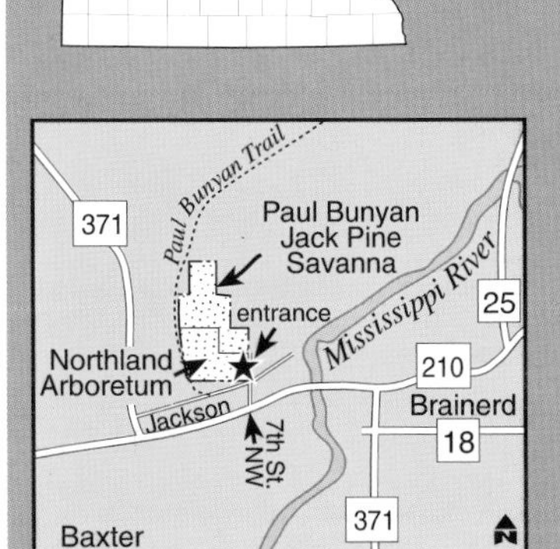

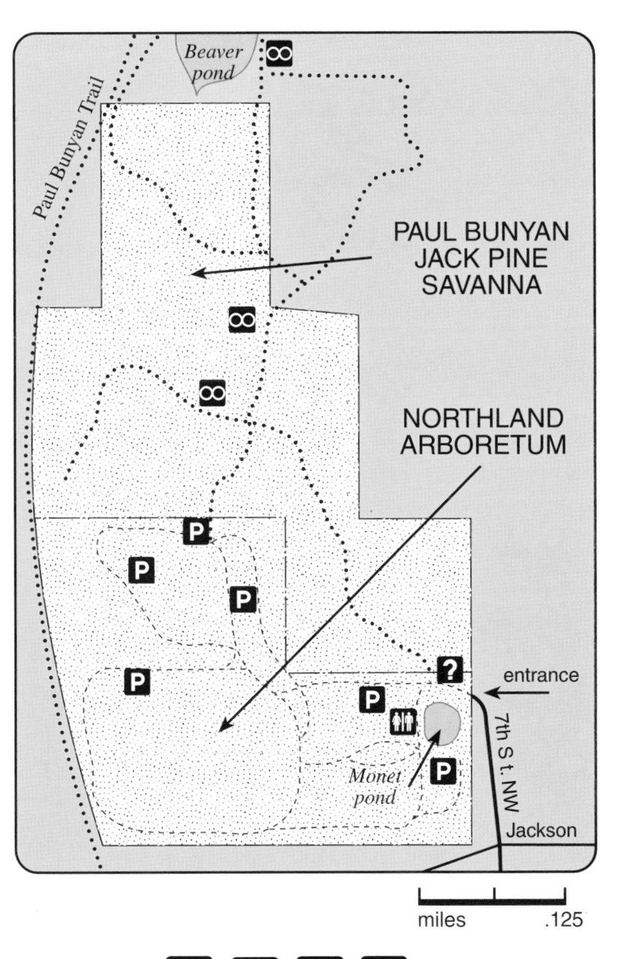

miles .125

Facilities:

Recreational Opportunities:   

Contact:

Northland Arboretum
P.O. Box 375
Brainerd MN 56401
(218) 829-8770

45–Mille Lacs Lake-North Shore (Highway 18)

Why is this area special?

If you're looking for easy birdwatching, then this drive along the north shore of Mille Lacs Lake is perfect. Terns and gulls drift above the big lake and shorebirds scurry along the rocky shore. Look for eagles sitting in trees bordering the highway—at peak times there may be one every 100 yards.

You could spot ospreys, double-crested cormorants, common and Caspian terns and ring-billed and herring gulls near the shore of this 132,000-acre lake. During migration, watch for American white pelicans, tundra and trumpeter swans, as well as concentrations of common loons and Bonaparte's gulls–particularly in the fall. Bring along a pair of binoculars and a bird book to identify a few of the many birds you'll be seeing.

C. Henderson
Bald eagle

The adjacent Wealthwood State Forest provides habitat for white-tailed deer, black bears, gray squirrels and other small mammals, ruffed grouse and many songbirds. You might even see a sharp-tailed grouse, sandhill crane or short-eared owl.

Maple, basswood and oak dominate the forested shoreline and tamarack, black spruce, aspen and black ash prevail in the lowlands. Highway 18, along with the entire 76-mile shoreline, is a spectacular drive in autumn when the forest is painted in shades of rust, scarlet, pumpkin and gold.

Note:

While the north shore is residential and has extremely narrow shoulders in some places, there are some areas where you can pull over. There is also a swimming beach and a municipal park near Malmo. Parking areas and rustic roads into the interior of the Wealthwood State Forest are used by birders, hikers, loggers and hunters.

See the Mille Lacs Lake Area-Kathio State Park (site 47) and the Mille Lacs WMA (site 48) for other wildlife watching opportunities. Garrison, Malmo, Isle and many businesses around the lake offer lodging, food, boat rental and gas.

Best viewing time:

How do I get there?

Maps: MN Highway Coordinate: I-12
PRIM Area: Mille Lacs Lake
DeLorme MN Atlas Grid #: 55 C-8/9

Additional directions:

Follow Highway 18 northeast from Garrison along the north shore of Mille Lacs Lake.

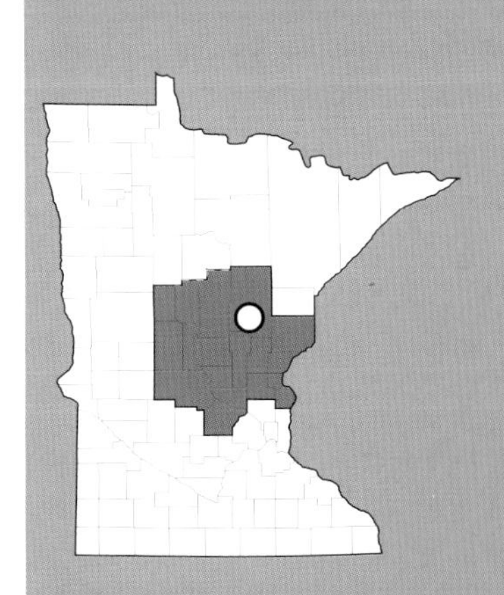

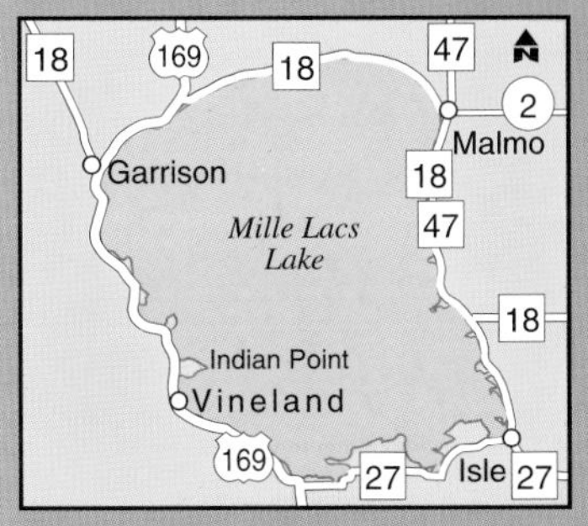

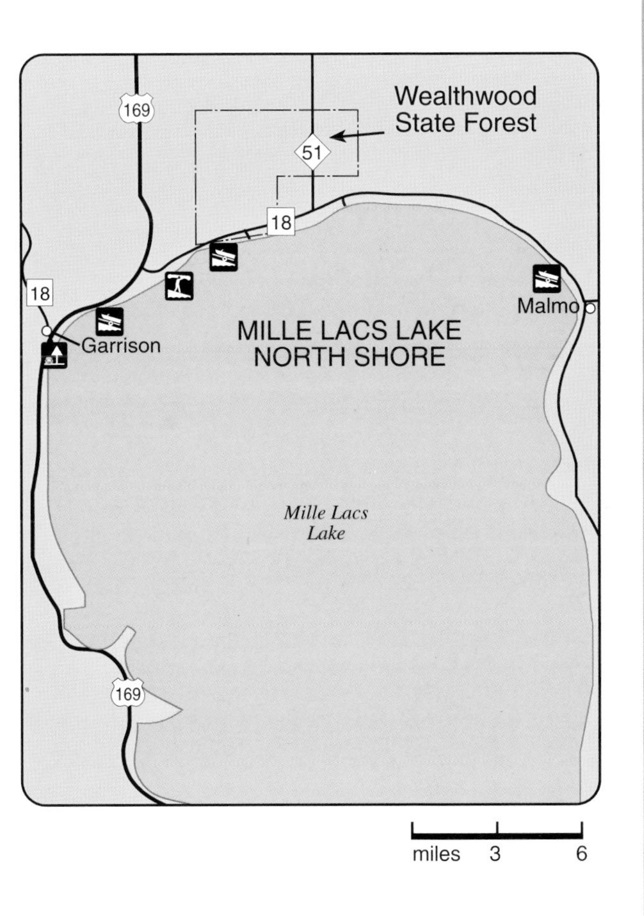

Facilities:

Recreational Opportunities:   

Contact:

Nongame Wildlife Program
DNR
1601 Minnesota Drive
Brainerd MN 56401
(218) 828-2228

46–Rice Lake NWR/Kimberly WMA/McGregor Marsh SNA

Best viewing time:

Why is this area special?

If you're interested in waterfowl, then this 18,000-acre refuge, located in the bog country of north central Minnesota, is the place for you. Not only do numerous species nest at the site, but it's estimated more than 100,000 birds migrate through the area in October, including up to 75,000 ring-necked ducks.

During spring migration, warblers and other songbirds are abundant along edges and in forested areas. Look and listen for palm, yellow-rumped, chestnut-sided, black-throated green, Nashville, black-and-white, blackburnian and Cape May warblers. You might spot savannah sparrows and bobolinks in the open fields, eastern bluebirds near fringes of fields and forests, northern flickers in the woods and sharp-tailed grouse near the cropped farm fields. Black terns, common loons, bald eagles, ruffed grouse and northern harriers also frequent the area. Mallards, ring-necked ducks, blue-winged teal, wood ducks, hooded mergansers and Canada geese are among the common waterfowl. More than 235 species are on the refuge bird list, which you may pick up at the office.

The refuge is located in the transition zone between the coniferous forests of northern Minnesota and the hardwood forests of the southern part of the state. A mixture of cedar swamps, tamarack bogs, forested uplands, scattered grasslands and small lakes harbor countless plants. As the name implies, Rice Lake produces large quantities of wild rice, which is utilized by waterfowl.

The Rice Lake vicinity is rich in history. Ancient people, thought to have inhabited the area 1300 years ago, lived and buried their dead in mounds within the present-day refuge. Please remember the remains are fragile, irreplaceable and strictly protected by law.

Attracted by wild rice, sugar maple trees, berries and plentiful game, Eastern Dakota Native Americans occupied the region more than 300 years ago. Ojibwe, pushed out of the East by European settlement, drove out the Dakota. As time went on, Europeans continued to press westward bringing with them axes, plows, cattle and the railroad. Life was never the same for the native people or the wildlife that resided near Rice Lake. However, the tide turned, at least for the latter, when the refuge came into being.

A branch of the Soo Line Railroad, known as the Cuyuna and Iron Range, was constructed in 1910. This line carried ore from the iron mines of the nearby Cuyuna Range and timber from the surrounding area to Lake Superior ports until it was abandoned in the 1920s. A portion of the rail bed later became part of the main Rice Lake Refuge road.

Established in 1935 by President Franklin Roosevelt to provide habitat for migratory waterfowl, the refuge provides habitat for all wildlife. Watch for white-tailed deer, black bear, raccoons, mink and striped skunks. If you're very lucky you may even spot a badger or bobcat. Near the pools and potholes, look and listen for muskrat, beaver, frolicking river otters, basking turtles and the serenades of western chorus frogs and spring peepers. In winter, scan the trees for "porkies" (porcupine), snowshoe hares in the brush and deer in the fields. A mammal checklist is also available at the office.

Maintained and unimproved trails plus logging roads cross nearly every habitat type found on the refuge. Hike

John and Karen Hollingsworth

Yellow rail

the two-mile Mandy Lake loop, the three-quarter-mile Twin Lakes loop or the nearly three-mile Rice Lake Pool Trail to get a good layout of the land and its inhabitants. Roll slowly along the splendid 9-1/2 mile Wildlife Drive and stop at the observation deck overlooking Rice Lake to greatly increase your chances of spotting wildlife.

Adjacent to the Refuge on the north is the 8500-acre **Kimberly WMA,** which is managed for sharp-tailed grouse, white-tailed deer and waterfowl. Dikes and unmarked, minimally-maintained trails run through the unit. Pay attention to avoid getting lost. There are two entrance points: the north access off Highway 210 and the impoundment access south of Highway 210 on County Road 245 (Portage Lake Road).

The 400-acre **McGregor Marsh SNA,** an extensive marsh land in the former bed of Glacial Lake Aitkin, is

continued...

nearby. A well-known birding spot, it contains the very specific habitat requirements of the sedge wren, Nelson's sharp-tailed sparrow and the rare and reclusive yellow rail. Look and listen for these species as well as American bitterns and red-winged blackbirds. During the winter, look for northern hawk-owls and the signs and sounds of other winter visitors. To hike across the area, park just off the highway and walk along the old rail-road grade, which is now the recreational Soo Line Trail.

D.E. Heffernan, U.S. Fish and Wildlife Service

Note:

You can use the Rice Lake refuge road and other public facilities only during daylight hours and the inside phone during office hours. The Wildlife Drive beyond the cross-country ski trailhead is closed from December to mid-April. Biting insects are abundant from June to September. There is an accessible fishing area along the Rice River. Hunting is permitted during season.

Kimberly WMA and McGregor Marsh SNA offer no facilities other than a place to park. Hunting and trapping are allowed in the Kimberly unit. Strict rules protect McGregor Marsh.

 Hunting allowed. Call ahead for hunting season dates.

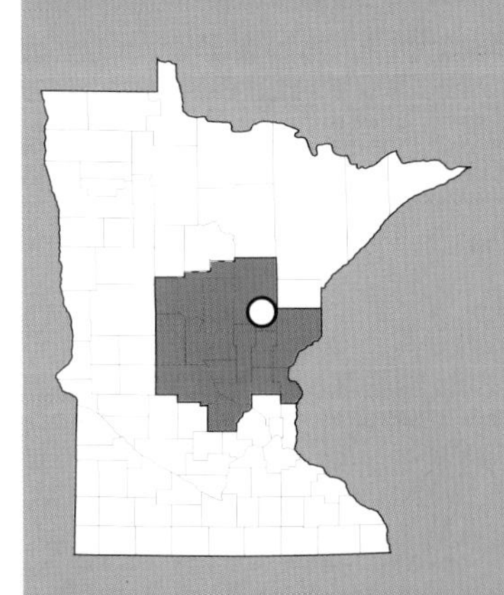

How do I get there?

Maps: MN Highway Coordinate: J-11
PRIM Area: Aitkin
DeLorme MN Atlas Grid #: 56 A-2

Additional directions:

The Rice Lake Refuge headquarters and entrance road are located five miles south of McGregor on the west side of Highway 65.

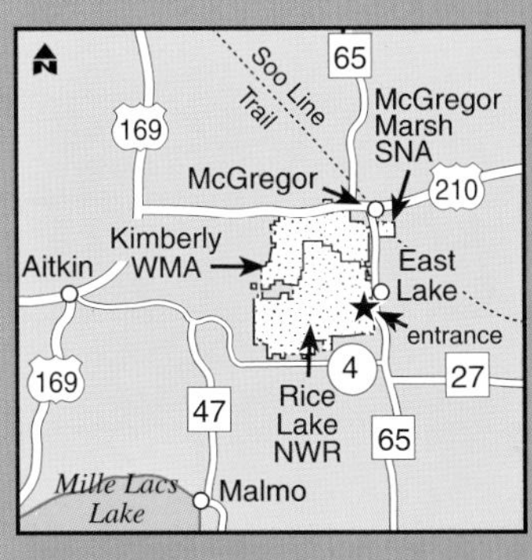

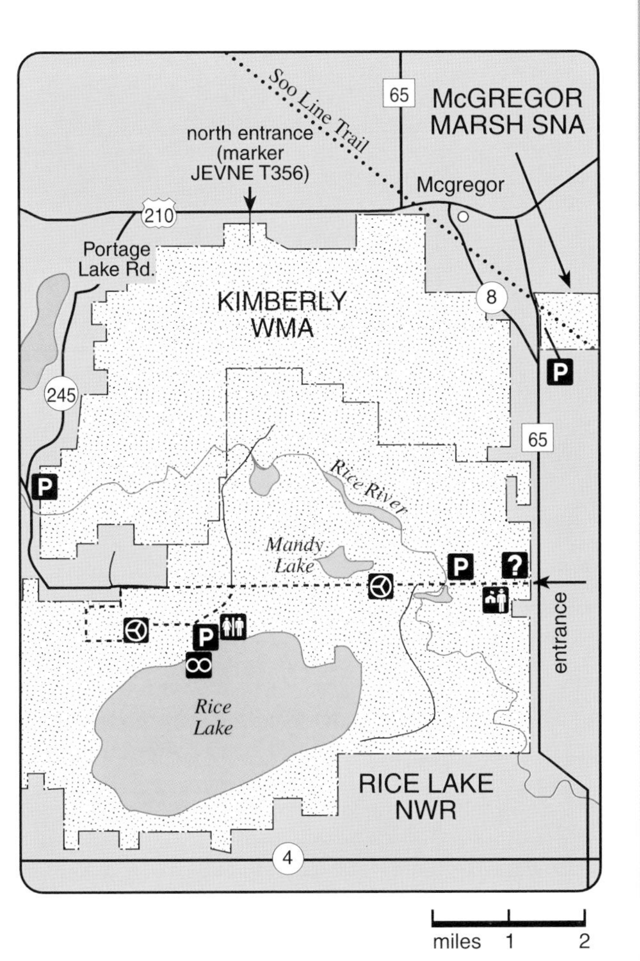

Facilities:

Recreational Opportunities:    

Contact:

Rice Lake NWR
RR 2 Box 67
McGregor MN 55760
(218) 768-2402

Kimberly WMA
DNR Area Wildlife Office
P.O. Box 138
Aitkin MN 56431
(218) 927-6915

Scientific and Natural Areas Program
DNR
Box 25
500 Lafayette Road
St. Paul MN 55155
(612) 297-2357

47–Mille Lacs Lake Area & Kathio State Park

Why is this area special?

Soaring eagles and osprey, staging loons, gliding gulls and migrating waterfowl and warblers are just a few of the highlights of Mille Lacs Lake. This is one of the largest lakes in Minnesota, encompassing 132,510 acres and 76 miles of shoreline. In conjunction with the thousands of acres of undeveloped woods and wetlands surrounding it, the area provides choice wildlife watching.

In early spring before the ice breaks up on the "big lake", the inlet creeks teem with thousands of northern pike, muskie and carp. Look for opportunistic eagles that perch in nearby trees to take advantage of easy hunting.

C. Henderson

White-tailed deer

In May, forest floors carpeted with ephemeral wildflowers in dappled light, are home to spotted fawns and warblers are on the wing. Spring and summer wildflowers, from spectacular waves of large-flowered trilliums to showy lady's slippers to black-eyed Susan's, abound. Other wildflowers, such as bloodroot, hepatica, nodding trillium, trout lily, blue flag iris, wild calla, Indian paintbrush, small purple-fringed orchis and yellow and pink lady slippers reward the eye.

Scan the large flocks of birds on the water during the summer. Ring-billed gulls are common—but see if you can spot some herring gulls in the group. Both common and Caspian terns are present, so be on the look out for those too. Don't forget to watch the roadsides for white-tailed deer, black bears, raccoons, porcupines and gray squirrels.

Shorter day length and cooler weather bring not only changing leaf color, but rafts of migrating loons, congregating Bonaparte's gulls and waterfowl, especially common goldeneyes, to Mille Lacs Lake. Several species of birds not normally found in Minnesota, such as red-throated and Pacific loons, have been seen here during fall migration. Wild rice is ubiquitous, so wherever you see rice beds, look for ducks feeding and seeking shelter from cold whipping winds that are common for the season.

At **Mille Lacs Kathio State Park,** scout for black terns on Ogechie Lake and red-winged blackbirds in the vast cattail marsh that lies between Shakopee and Onamia Lakes. Rent a canoe and spend an entire day on the lakes and Rum River.

Forest songbirds are abundant—watch for indigo buntings, Baltimore orioles, American redstarts, black-capped chickadees, red-breasted and white-breasted nuthatches,

Best viewing time:

cedar waxwings, fox and white-throated sparrows, dark-eyed juncos, pine and evening grosbeaks, common redpolls, pine siskins, American goldfinches, purple finches and red-headed, red-bellied, downy, hairy and pileated woodpeckers. Don't be surprised if you scare up a ruffed grouse while walking in the woods. Pick up a bird checklist at the visitor center and read bulletin boards for naturalist activities, films and programs.

During most of the year the best way to see animals is to drive slowly through the park at dawn or dusk. Look for deer along meadow edges and porcupines lumbering across the road. Black bears are common, but tend to be reclusive during the park's busy times. Although beavers are not often seen, you might notice their lodges and chiselings. In addition, explore miles of hiking and horseback riding trails that roam through the park.

In autumn scan the skies for winged migrants, the forest floor for tracks, tree bark for deer rubs and sheltered spots for critters basking in the waning heat of the season. Climb the observation tower for a panoramic view of the spectacular, color-splashed foliage. The forests are primarily northern red oak, aspen, birch and maple, although a few isolated remnant conifer stands give a hint of what the forest looked like a century ago. Bog forests with slender spruce and tamarack, which turn to muted gold in autumn, provide habitat for wildlife and a home for unique plant species.

Snowflakes signal the commencement of the cold quietude of winter. It means hibernation for some species, but other hardy residents remain active. Look for footprints, scat, wing marks and bedding sites in the snow. Stop by the park's visitor center where wildlife is drawn to stocked feeders. If you're able, you may get in closer proximity to wildlife by gliding along groomed cross-country ski trails.

Jane Norris

Trillium

By 1920, Spirit and Hennepin Islands, near the south end of Mille Lacs Lake, were designated as the Mille Lacs NWR as a haven for colony-nesting birds. Early recognition of the importance of protecting this fragile boulder environment for the not-so-common, common tern was critical.

The common tern population dropped dramatically through the years, from more than 2600 nesting pairs in Minnesota to fewer than 400 pairs in 1992. Efforts to monitor and manage the population and habitat have brought some success. There are now about 800 nesting

continued...

pairs and of these, a dozen or so use Spirit Island and about a hundred pairs occupy Hennepin Island.

Early in this century, the islands had a natural colony of purple martins nesting among the rocks. In recent years it has been one of the only places where Caspian terns nest in Minnesota.

To continue to protect the sensitive sanctuaries, marker buoys instruct people to stay 100 feet from the shoreline. But, that need not discourage you from experiencing these special assets—use binoculars or telescopes to see from a boat or the main lake shore.

Snuggled on the southeastern shoreline, the 316-acre Father Hennepin State Park is another treasure. Exquisite ferns under a canopy of maples, remnant scattering of pines, aspen stands, small clearings and wetlands provide diverse wildlife habitat. Watch for tracks of beaver, raccoon, mink and deer in the snow or soft earth, listen to squirrels and chipmunks scurry in the leaves and anticipate ruffed grouse to explode into the air as you walk the trails. There's a sandy beach for swimming, strolling and searching the sky and waterfront for shorebirds, gulls, terns, ospreys and eagles.

Note:

Daily or annual vehicle permits are required to enter state parks. Be respectful of Indian Tribal lands within the Kathio Park boundaries. Whenever possible along Highway 169, take the frontage roads since they run closer to the water's edge and give a better view of bays and inlets. You'll be able to go slower than on the main highway and it'll be easier to spot and enjoy birds and wildlife. These roads provide great birding in September and October. Check sites 45 and 48 for additional wildlife watching opportunities.

This area is a rich tapestry woven with threads of geology, biology and history of ancient inhabitants, American Indians, European explorers, fur trappers, traders, loggers, missionaries and settlers.

No commentary about Mille Lacs would be complete without mention of the people who have lived in this area for more than 4000 years. American Indians and their ancestors recognized the wealth of the woods, wetlands, waters and wild rice and made it one of their important settlements. Today, the Ojibwe live, work and maintain an active cultural community. The new Mille Lacs Indian Museum (320/532-3632) showcases their history. Restored to its 1930s vintage, the Trading Post (320/532-3694) captures the essence of that era. Open daily May–October, and Thursdays–Sundays in the off season.

How do I get there?

Maps: MN Highway Coordinate: I-11
PRIM Area: Mille Lacs Lake
DeLorme MN Atlas Grid #: 55 C/D-8, 9
56 C/D-1

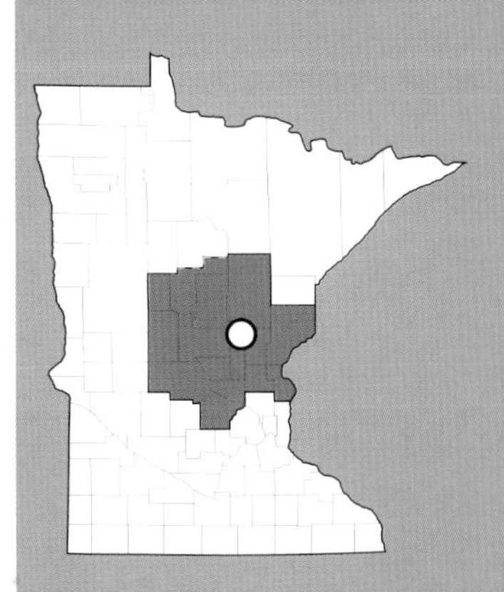

Additional directions:

Mille Lacs Lake is about 95 miles north of Minneapolis-St. Paul, bordered on the west by MN Highway 169, on the south and east by Highway 47 and 18, on the north by Highway 18. The Park is near the southwest corner of the Lake off 169; take County Road 26 one mile to reach the entrance.

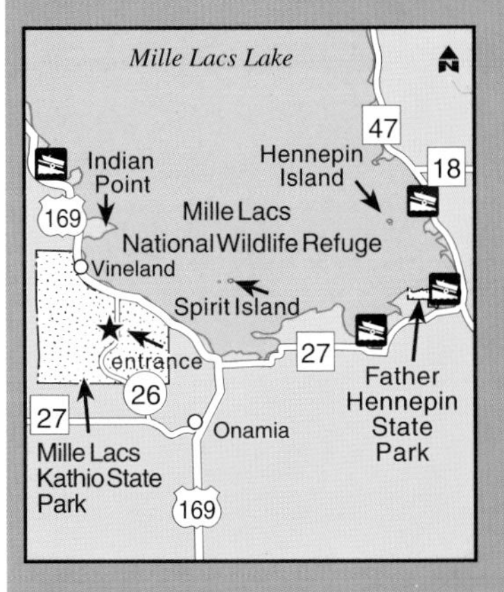

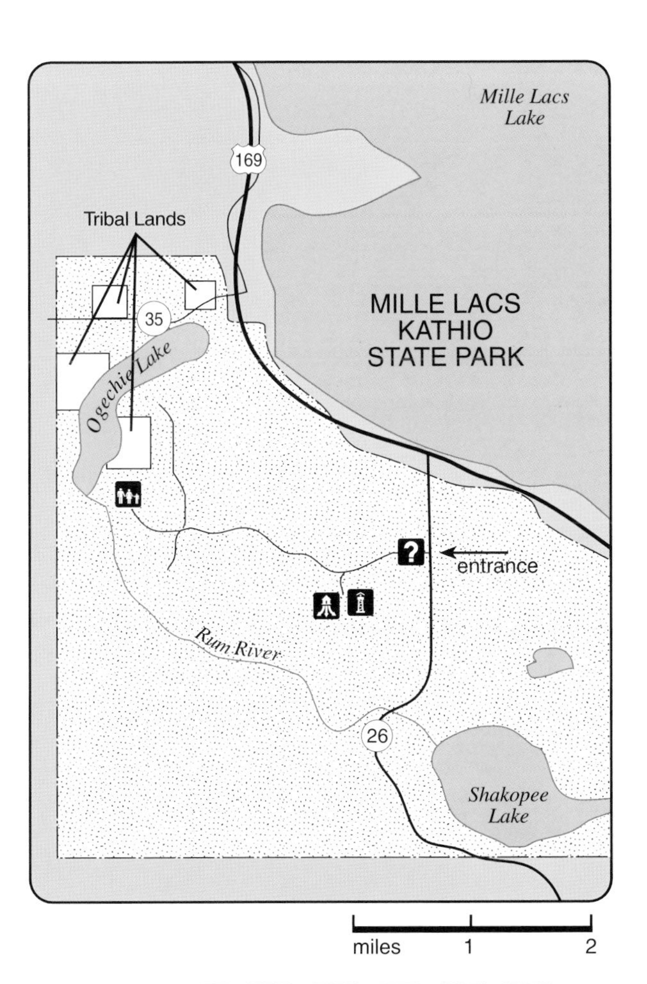

Contact:

Mille Lacs Kathio St. Park
15066 Kathio St. Park Road
Onamia MN 56359
(320) 532-3523
Visitor's Center 532-3269

Facilities:

Recreational Opportunities:     

48–Mille Lacs WMA

Why is this area special?

Much of the area's attraction is due to the variety of wildlife found here, including ruffed grouse, red-tailed and rough-legged hawks, waterfowl, owls, song and marsh birds, white-tailed deer, raccoon, beaver, mink and muskrat. Check out Dewitt or Ernst Pools to see a bald eagle, osprey or possibly even a trumpeter swan or frolicking otter. Listen for the low, loud musical rattle of the sandhill cranes, which nest on the unit, and look for signs of the black bear as you hike or bike the trails. Everything from woodcock to warblers to woodpeckers frequent the woods and wetlands. Be sure to ask for the bird checklist at the headquarters.

D.E. Heffernan, U.S. Fish and Wildlife Service

Ruffed grouse

One hundred and fifty miles of trails, firebreaks and roads criss-cross the site. Spring (before leaf out), early summer (before biting bugs invade) and autumn (before hunting begins) are the best times to visit. Whether you're hiking, mountain biking or cross-country skiing, a good starting point is the loop trail that begins near the headquarters. Although this trail is not groomed, winter skiing offers solitude, as well as wildlife sightings and signs.

The 39,000-acre area supports biodiversity because of its "patchwork distribution" of marshes, bogs, streams, forests and fields. It's about 60 percent forested with aspen, oak, maple, basswood and ash. Food plots for wildlife are planted through agreements with local farmers.

The WMA was established in 1949 largely from tax-forfeited lands. For nearly 25 years the University of Minnesota studied the responses of grouse to various forest clear-cutting patterns.

Note:

Bugs are bad during the summer and deer ticks are plentiful, so be prepared. Bring both mosquito and tick repellent. Primitive camping is an option from September through February.

Additional wildlife watching may be found at the Rum River State Forest, Mille Lacs Lake-North Shore (site 45) and Mille Lacs Lake Area-Mille Lacs Kathio State Park (site 47).

 Hunting allowed. Call ahead for hunting season dates.

Best viewing time:

How do I get there?

Maps: MN Highway Coordinate: I-12/13
PRIM Area: Mille Lacs & Mora
DeLorme MN Atlas Grid #: 47 A-9

Additional directions:

Located 11 miles south of Isle the area may be reached by taking Mille Lacs County Road 20 east off Highway 169 or Kanabec County Road 26 west off Highway 47. The headquarters is one mile north of the intersection of County Roads 19 and 20.

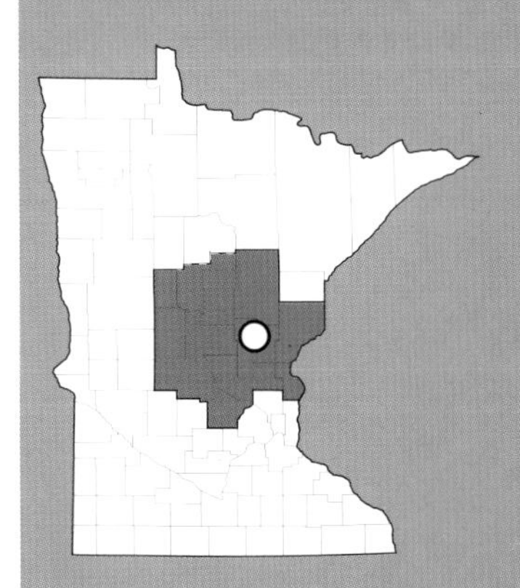

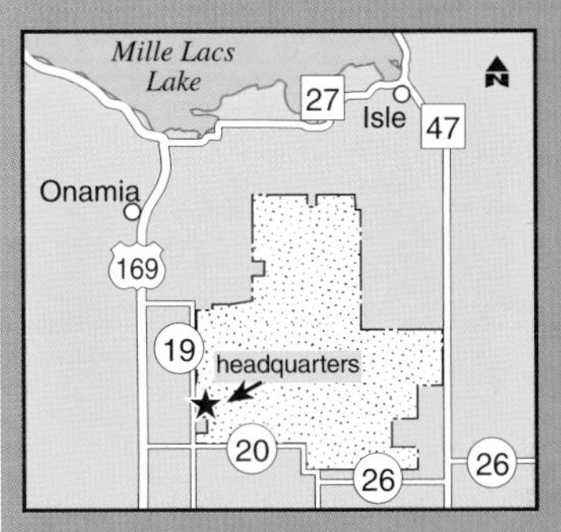

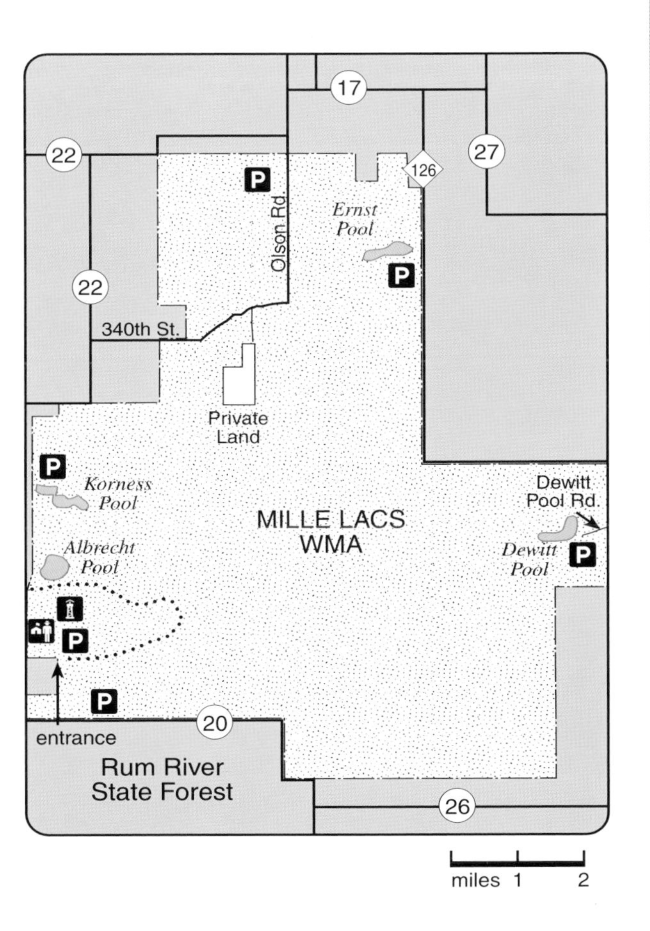

Contact:

DNR Wildlife Area Office
Mille Lacs WMA
29172 100th Avenue
Onamia MN 56359
(320) 532-3537

Facilities:  

Recreational Opportunities:   

49–Banning State Park

Why is this area special?

Breathtaking vistas abound at this 6,237-acre park, which hugs a ten-mile stretch of the wild and scenic Kettle River. In the northern section of the rugged Banning Rapids the river flows through a shallow, slender valley. Within a few miles, the valley narrows to a river-worn gorge of sandstone to a depth of 100 feet. At the end is "Hell's Gate", where the water flows through sheer 40-foot cliffs.

C. Henderson

Rose-breasted grosbeak

When you explore the 17 miles of hiking and 11 miles of ski trails that wind through the picturesque park, you may get a glimpse of a white-tailed deer, black bear or beaver. Towards evening, look for beneficial bats that venture forth from cracks, crevices and caves in pursuit of a meal of moths and mosquitoes. Skim the sky for a soaring bald eagle, turkey vulture or a variety of hawks. Ruffed grouse and forest songbirds, such as the beautiful rose-breasted grosbeak, are plentiful. Throughout the year, you can see more than 180 species of birds from warblers to waterfowl in this area.

Originally the landscape was primarily composed of red and white pine interspersed with aspen and birch. Today it's dominated by aspen and birch, although stands of pine remain along the river corridor. Aquatic and cliff plant and animal communities are found along the river and adjacent tributaries.

Note:

Look for the park's historic sites: ruins of the former Banning townsite and sandstone quarries, which employed 500 stonecutters in the 1880s. In 1894 the great Hinckley forest fire swept through the area, inflicting heavy financial losses on the company and the railroad line serving it. By 1905 steel replaced sandstone and all quarry work ceased. The town declined, fires continued to plague the village and by 1912 Banning was deserted.

Daily or annual permits are required for vehicles entering a state park.

Best viewing time:

How do I get there?

Maps: MN Highway Coordinate: K-12
PRIM Area: Sandstone
DeLorme MN Atlas Grid #: 57 D-6

Additional directions:

Located four miles north of Sandstone, the park entrance is off Interstate 35 and Highway 23.

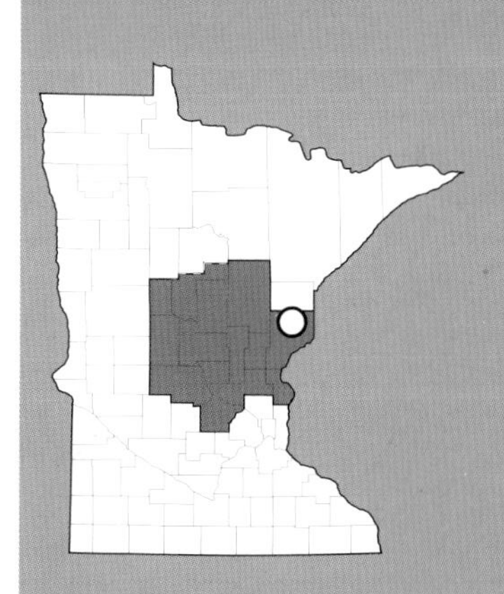

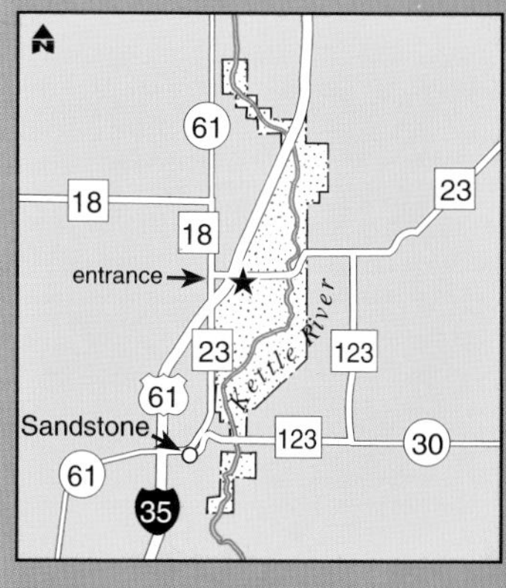

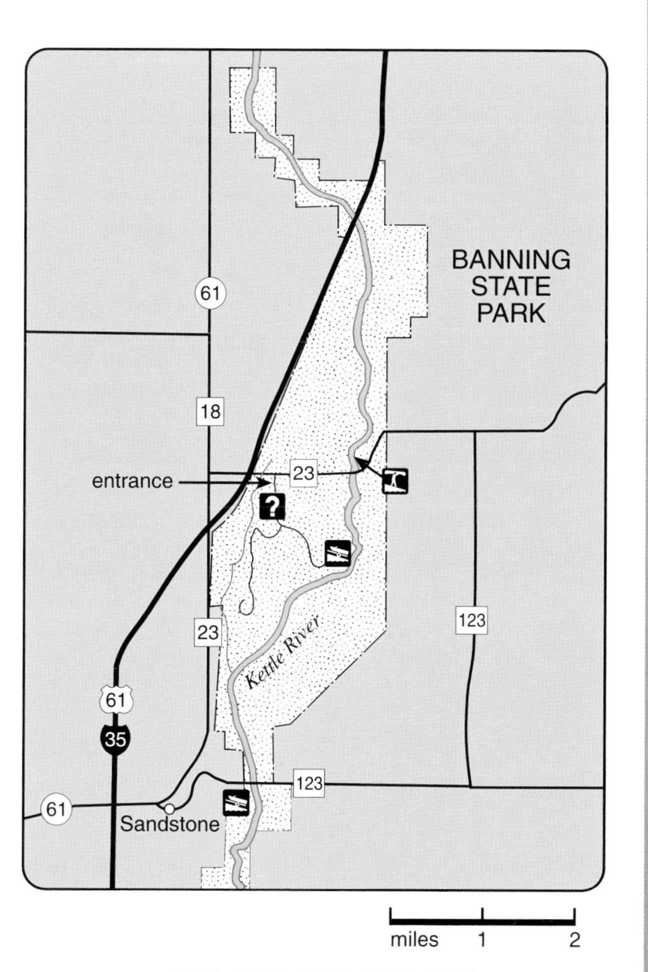

Facilities:

Recreational Opportunities:

Contact:

Banning State Park
P.O. Box 643
Sandstone MN 55072
(320) 245-2668

50–St. Croix State Park

Why is this area special?

Noted for its wealth of wildlife, St. Croix State Park is a hideaway for many species. More than 34,000 acres of meadows, marshes, streams and forests provide habitat for deer, black bears, coyotes, gray and red foxes, squirrels and a variety of songbirds including warblers and flycatchers.

White-tailed deer sightings are quite possible and black bear are commonly spotted during the spring and summer. A great diversity in habitats provides homes for a variety of wildlife from aquatic animals such as Blanding's turtle, beaver and river otter to land dwellers like porcupine, bobcat and timber wolf. Birds, such as the bald eagle, barred owl, eastern bluebird and red-eyed vireo are often seen throughout the park.

Lynn and Donna Rogers

Black bear

Twenty-one miles of the St. Croix River, a national wild and scenic riverway, form the eastern boundary of the park, while Minnesota's first wild and scenic river, the Kettle River, joins the St. Croix to form the western boundary. At least ten other streams flow through the park, creating a watershed of hundreds of square miles.

The landscape is dominated by communities of jack pine, aspen, birch, black spruce swamp, tamarack, northern and lowland hardwoods, white and red pine and some cedar. St. Croix is home to 5,000 acres of a unique jack pine plant community that includes the rare jack pine barrens, with its jack pine canopy and prairie plant understory. Look for big bluestem and blazing star here, as well as the stemless orchid, blueberry and blackberry.

No matter what your means of transportation, miles of trails and waterways wind through the park for those on foot, horse, bicycle, skis, snowmobile, kayak, canoe or car. There are 127 miles of foot, 75 miles of horseback, six miles of paved bicycle and two self-guided interpretive trails, so you'll have plenty of opportunity to spot wildlife. The multiple-use Willard Munger State Trail, consisting of a complex system of interconnecting trails, winds through the park. In addition, an observation tower and three scenic overlooks will give you memorable views of the vicinity.

Best viewing time:

To spot wildlife on and around the waterways and springs, bring your own canoe or rent one at the park. Enjoy the flat water and easy rapids of the St. Croix or the more challenging Kettle River, but do check with park officials to get updated reports on current river conditions.

You can learn more about park history, both natural and cultural, with the help of a park naturalist. Stop by the interpretive center and check program schedules posted throughout the park for hikes, talks, demonstrations, canoe and bike caravans and special events. It's a family-friendly place.

Note:

The geological history of the Valley, like most of Minnesota, is among the most complex in the world. During the last glacial period, about 10,000 years ago, the St. Croix River Valley served as a major drainage channel for glacial meltwater. As these waters carved the way for the river seen today, the waters left behind a variety of

C. Henderson

Tennessee warbler

soils and sediment that cover the ancient lava bedrock far below. One of the most common types being red and yellow clay, and sand. These soils may be seen along the River Bluff Trail, where the St. Croix has cut away the riverbank. In fact, one area along the river has such a large deposit of yellow clay, it is commonly called Yellow Banks.

Long before railroads, the St. Croix served as a major highway—for ancient people, the Dakota, Objibwe and Fox, and later French fur trappers, traders, loggers and settlers. Around 1800, a French fur post was established in the vicinity of the park.

continued...

50-continued

In the late 19th century, the demand for timber virtually eliminated the giant red and white pine. St. John, a colorful logging camp operator, had his base camp near the present site of the Group Camp. By 1915 when logging ended, settlers moved into the newly cleared land. Although they struggled to make a living from the poor soil, many left in deep despair during the 1930s.

Fortunately, one of the many government relief programs included purchasing poor farmland and converting it to recreational use. In 1934, 18,000 acres of land was purchased by the National Park Service and a year later it became the St. Croix Recreational Development Area. The Civilian Conservation Corps (CCC) and Works Progress Administration (WPA) transformed the land into group camps, roads and campgrounds with all the necessary buildings and structures.

Much of their work remains today and many of the buildings and structures have been added to the National Register of Historic Sites. Interpretive signs at a restored CCC campsite near the Yellow Banks area describe the lives of the workers. In time, St. Croix became the largest state park in Minnesota.

The Chengwatana State Forest (site 51), adjacent to the park on the south, offers additional wildlife watching opportunities.

Daily or annual permits are required for vehicles entering a state park.

C. Henderson

How do I get there?

Maps: MN Highway Coordinate: L-13
PRIM Area: Mora
DeLorme MN Atlas Grid #: 57 E-9

Additional directions:

St. Croix State Park is 16 miles east of Hinckley on Highway 48. Park headquarters are on Pine County Road 22, five miles south of the park entrance.

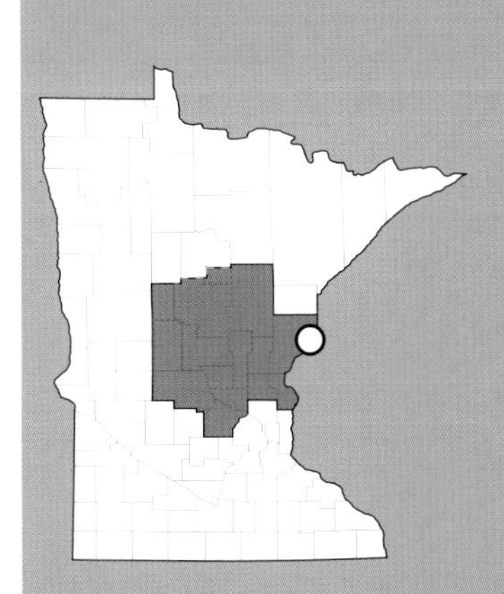

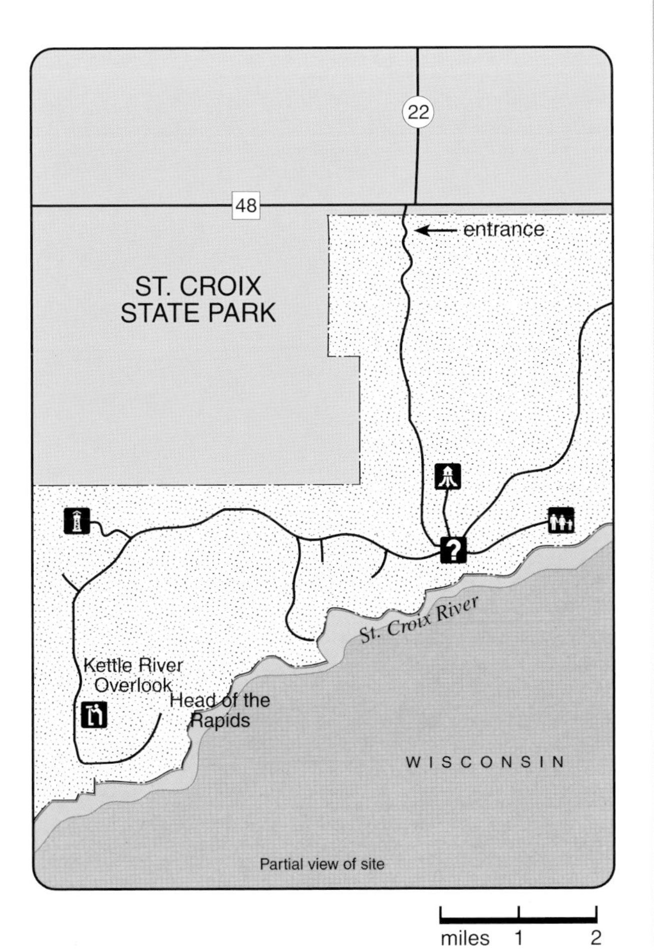

Facilities:    

Recreational Opportunities:

Contact:

St. Croix State Park
RR 3 Box 450
Hinckley MN 55037
(320) 384-6591

51– Chengwatana State Forest

Why is this area special?

Uniquely situated, the Chengwatana has three bordering rivers—the rough and untamed Kettle River on the north, the meandering Snake River on the south and the St. Croix National Scenic Riverway on the east.

Magnificent white and red pines covered this area when European immigrants first arrived. In the late 1800's, the quietude of the forest gave way to the noise of the saw as millions of logs were cut and floated down these rivers to sawmills at Stillwater. Today, the Chengwatana is managed for timber production, wildlife management, recreation and environmental protection.

C. Henderson

Mocassin flower

Drive down into the valley on the south end for picnicking and hiking along the river's edge or camp in the pines just steps away from the rock-strewn rapids of the Snake River. Look for blue jays, scarlet tanagers and squirrels among the oaks, raccoons by the shoreline and ruffed grouse, fox and white-tailed deer along the trails.

In spring this site is a virtual paradise for lovers of migrating warblers and ephemeral wildflowers.

The majority of the 29,000-acre forest is made up of aspen and birch, with smaller areas of pine, spruce, balsam fir, tamarack and oak. In the middle of the Chengwatana is a mosaic of forested upland "islands" surrounded by marsh and brush. Check out this area for northern harriers flying low over the marshland, beaver, mink, muskrat and especially in the spring and fall, migrating waterfowl. To increase your chances of spotting wildlife, trek the Willard Munger State Trail, which runs the length of the forest, or the eight-mile hiking and cross-county ski trail winding alongside Redhorse Creek.

Note:

Eventually the Willard Munger Trail will connect the Twin Cities to Duluth. A nominal camping fee is charged. Private canoe and kayak rental and shuttle services are available and there is a primitive boat access. See St. Croix State Park (site 50) for more wildlife watching possibilities.

Hunting allowed. Call ahead for hunting season dates. Target practice is allowed in designated areas.

Best viewing time:

How do I get there?

Maps: MN Highway Coordinate: K-13
PRIM Area: Mora
DeLorme MN Atlas Grid #: 49 A-6

Additional directions:

From Interstate 35, take the 324/County 7 exit, go east on 324 into Pine City. At the stop light, turn north on County 61, go one block to the stop sign (8th Ave. E./Co. 65), turn east to get on County Road 8. This road becomes Township Rd. 118 and gravel before entering south end.

To enter in the middle of the Forest, take County Road 9 (off County 8) to the north and turn east onto County 10. When County 10 turns north, turn south for about a quarter block, look for a brown DNR sign and turn east.

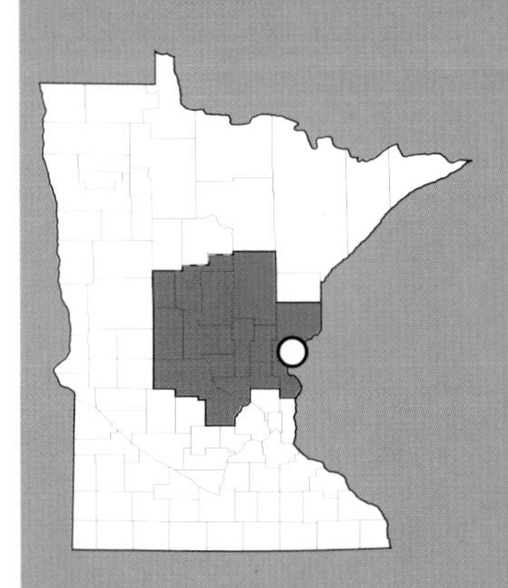

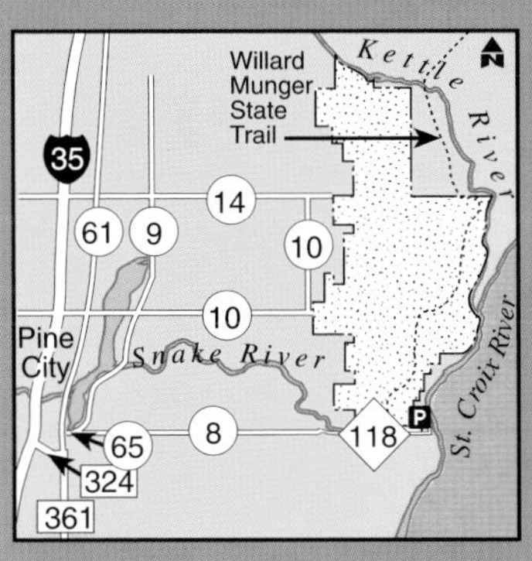

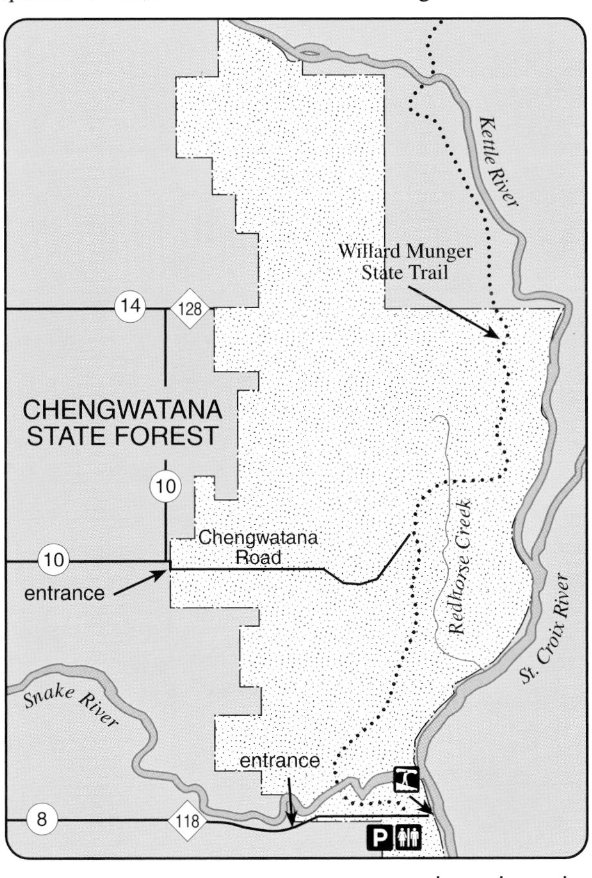

Facilities:  

Recreational Opportunities:   

Contact:

DNR Area Forestry Office
RR 2
701 Kenwood S.
Moose Lake MN 55767
(218) 485-5400

52–Lake Osakis

Why is this area special?

"A great day!" would sum up a visit to Lake Osakis to witness western grebes perform their spectacular courtship dance on the water. Clearly, there are few birding experiences that would surpass such sight and sound. Occurring on the eastern edge of their range, this is the largest nesting population of western grebes in Minnesota.

Gary Nuechterlein

Western grebe

And as if that weren't enough, another species of grebe, the red-necked, bob, dip and dive along the shoreline. Look for Forster's terns as they hover, skim and swoop through the air near their reedy nests, as well as American white pelicans, double-crested cormorants, ring-billed gulls, Caspian terns and great blue herons.

Check out the protected bay on the southwest end of the lake for grebes and waterfowl, such as wood and ruddy ducks and American coots. On the lake margin—watch for purple martins, tree swallows, warbling vireos, killdeer and red-winged and yellow-headed blackbirds. With fields and farmlands nearby, it's not unusual to spot red-tailed hawks or other birds of prey searching for a meal of mice.

This 6,000-acre lake is 11 miles long, so the best way to see birds is to rent a pontoon or boat. Rental rates are reasonable, making viewing easy, especially where dense emergent vegetation makes it hard to spot birds from shore. Bring binoculars, bird book and a box lunch. Don't forget sun screen and a cap. Lake maps are helpful and available at the visitor center, resorts and retailers.

If time doesn't allow for a water outing, highways circle the lake. There's a park and swimming beach on the south end and four public accesses, where you may walk to the water's edge to look for birds. The Battle Point access also has a short trail on a spit of land that juts out into the water.

Best viewing time:

Note:

For information stop at the Visitor and Heritage Center, located off Highway 27.

How do I get there?

Maps: MN Highway Coordinate: F-13
PRIM Area: Alexandria
DeLorme MN Atlas Grid #: 45 A-6/7

Additional directions:

Lake Osakis is about twelve miles east of Alexandria.

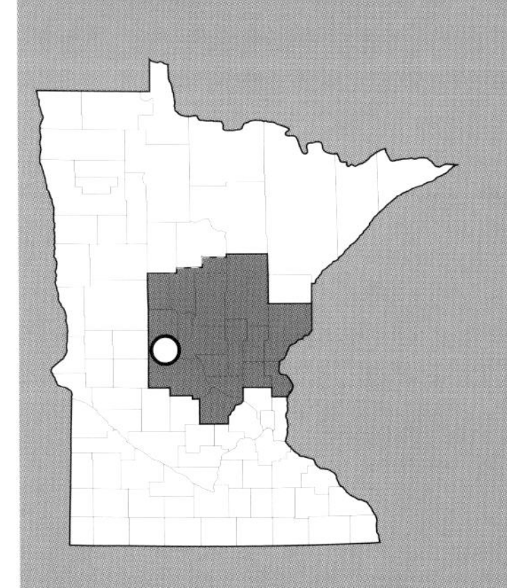

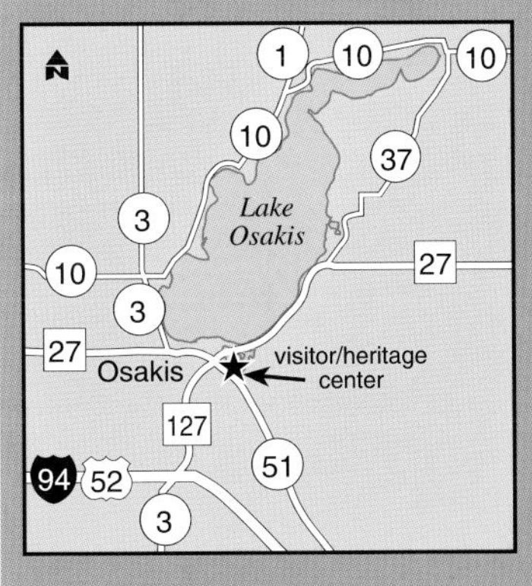

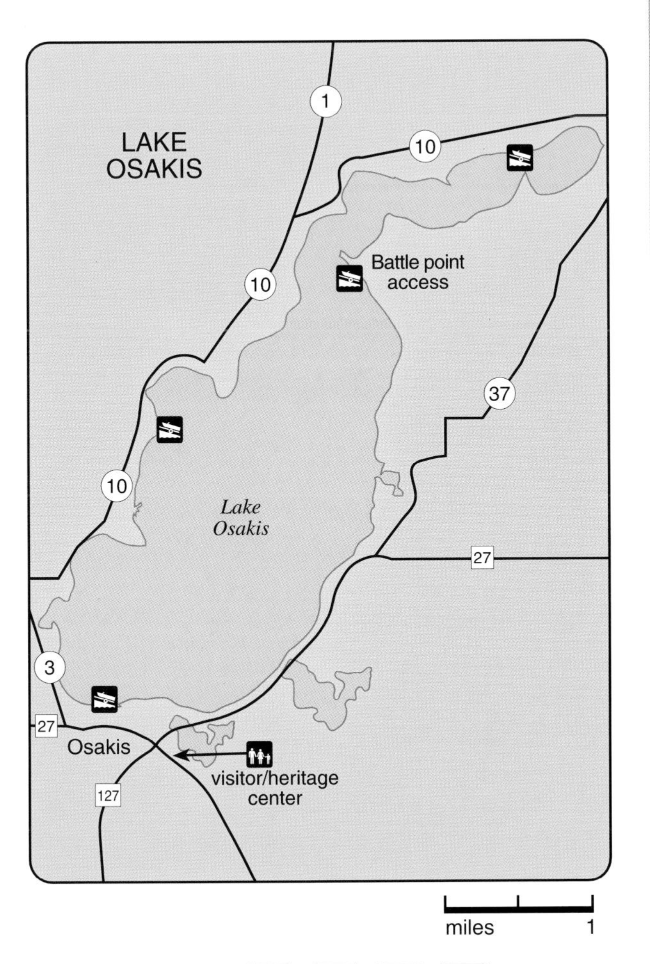

Facilities:

Recreational Opportunities:

Contact:

Nongame Wildlife Program
DNR
1601 Minnesota Drive
Brainerd MN 56401
(218) 828-2228

Lake Osakis Resort Association
Dept. DD6
P.O. Box 327
Osakis MN 56360
(800) 422-0785

53–Crane Meadows NWR/ Rice-Skunk & Crane Meadows WMAs

Sandhill crane

Best viewing time:

Why is this area special?

Visit this site in April, May and early June and again in September and October to see and hear sandhill cranes. More than 30 pairs nest in the vicinity and groups, ranging from a few to more than 400, congregate in autumn prior to migration. Look for these graceful birds in the meadows near the headquarters and along the township roads.

In addition, hosts of other birds and rafts of waterfowl reside in the Crane Meadows NWR and Rice-Skunk and Crane Meadows WMAs. Bald eagle, northern harrier, short-eared owl, American bittern, great blue heron, mallard, blue-winged teal and canvasback are among the species you might see. Watch for resident and migrating warblers such as the yellow-rumped, common yellowthroat, American redstart, yellow and black-throated green. House wrens, least flycatchers, great crested flycatchers, tree and chipping sparrows and red-eyed vireos may also be spotted. Look near nesting boxes for eastern bluebirds, American kestrels and wood ducks. Watch for ring-necked pheasants along the roadsides and tree and barn swallows, as well as eastern bluebirds near the headquarters.

Intersected by the Platte River and Skunk, Rice and Buckman Creeks, these acres of marsh, meadow and open water provide ideal wildlife habitat. There are low-land sedge meadows with willow clumps and red and bur oak that share the savanna with prairie grasses and purple prairie clover. Both Rice and Skunk Lakes have an abundant supply of wild rice that supply a staple food for waterfowl.

Birds are not the only residents. Look for beavers, minks, muskrats, raccoons, river otters and snapping and Blanding's turtles near the water. Scan the open fields for white-tailed deer, fox, coyotes and badgers. Don't forget to search for their tracks, scat and burrows too.

Note:

Three miles of groomed cross-country ski trails on the Refuge serve hikers during the other seasons. You'll want to check out the WMAs from spring through fall because winter access is extremely limited. Roads entering Rice-Skunk from the east are minimum maintenance and after rains may be impassable by car.

The WMAs are within the proposed boundaries of the enlarging Crane Meadows National Wildlife Refuge, which will eventually add thousands of acres and consequently, offer additional viewing opportunities.

 Hunting and trapping are allowed only in the WMAs.

How do I get there?

Maps: MN Highway Coordinate: H-13
PRIM Area: St. Cloud
DeLorme MN Atlas Grid #: 46 A-5

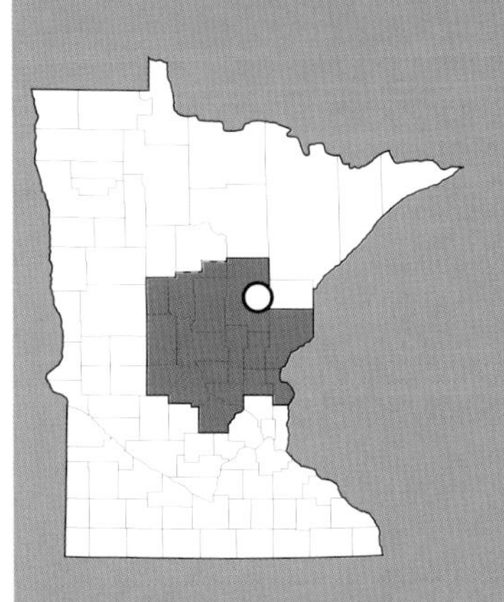

Additional directions:

This site is southeast of Little Falls. From Highway 10, go four miles east on County Road 35, turn north on Morrison 256 (Inca Road/190th Avenue) to get to the river access (Marker 12246) or continue on County 35, cross the Platte River bridge, take the second road (Marker 19502) north to the NWR Headquarters.

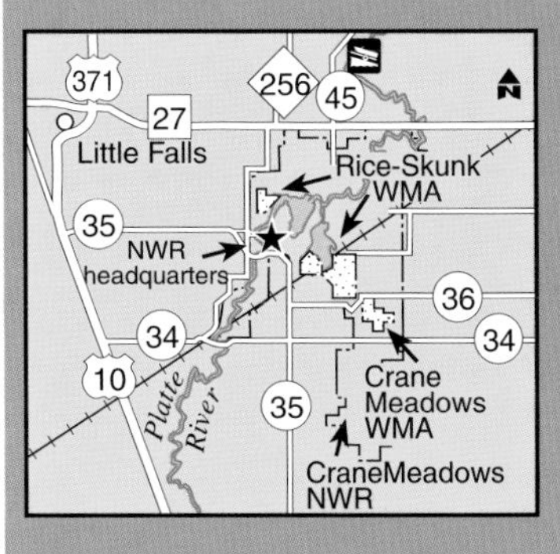

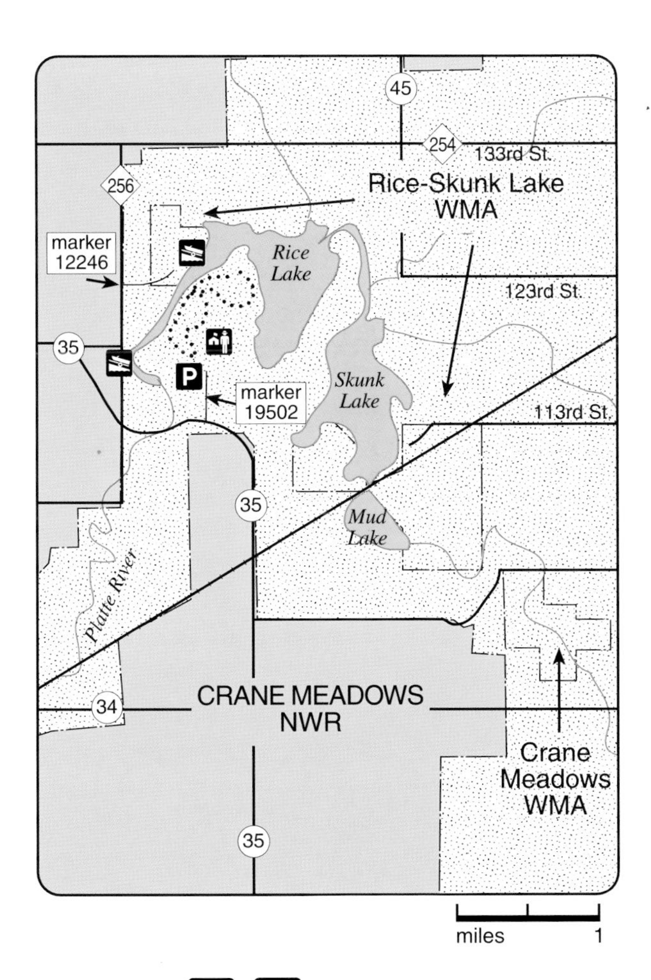

Facilities:  

Recreational Opportunities: 

Contact:

Crane Meadows NWR
RR 6 Box 171A
Little Falls MN 56345
(320) 632-1575

DNR Area Wildlife Office
RR 4 Box 19A
Little Falls MN 56345
(320) 616-2450

54–Roscoe Prairie SNA

Why is this area special?

The sighting of Dakota skipper butterflies on this prairie patch led to the designation of the 57-acre Roscoe Prairie Scientific and Natural Area in 1966. Living only in remnant tallgrass prairies, this insect is very rare in North America. Purple coneflowers supply nectar for adult skippers, while prairie dropseed, Indian grass and big bluestem provide prime breeding habitat.

Although native prairie once covered fully a third of Minnesota, undisturbed prairie is now uncommon. Roscoe sits on the eastern edge of what was an unbroken expanse of prairie. Evidence of past agricultural activity is disappearing and prescribed burns are taking the place of wild fires that once scorched the land.

C. Henderson

Sedge wren

In spring you may see the pale blue petals and wispy seeds of pasqueflowers. As the weeks progress, look for puccoon, spiderwort, prairie smoke, purple prairie clover, spiked lobelia, three gentian species and two rare plants, the small white lady's slipper and Hill's thistle.

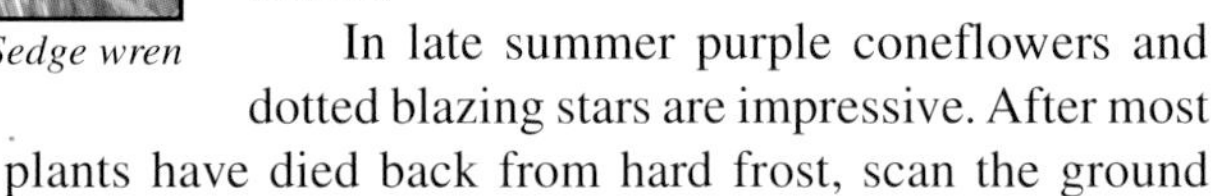

In late summer purple coneflowers and dotted blazing stars are impressive. After most plants have died back from hard frost, scan the ground carefully for purple downy gentians.

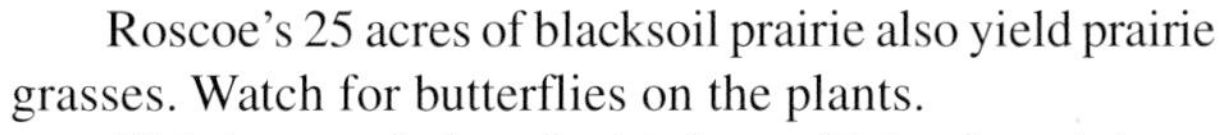

Roscoe's 25 acres of blacksoil prairie also yield prairie grasses. Watch for butterflies on the plants.

This is a good place for birds too. Upland sandpipers nest in the grass, red-tailed hawks soar overhead and ring-necked pheasants strut across the fields. Also look for American goldfinches, gray catbirds, marbled godwits, American woodcocks, eastern kingbirds, horned larks, short-billed marsh wrens, bobolinks, western meadowlarks, and savanna, grasshopper, clay-colored, swamp and song sparrows.

As you walk, you can't miss the piles of black dirt called mima mounds—apparently created by the burrowing activities of pocket gophers. Other residents include thirteen-lined ground squirrels, short-tailed weasels, white-tailed jackrabbits, leopard frogs and grasshoppers native to the prairie.

Best viewing time:

Note:

There are no trails except the abandoned railroad grade. This land is owned by The Nature Conservancy.

How do I get there?

Maps: MN Highway Coordinate: G-15
PRIM Area: Litchfield
DeLorme MN Atlas Grid #: 46 E-2

Additional directions:

From Highway 23, turn onto County Road 10, go through the tiny town of Roscoe and turn west on County Road 16. Travel a short distance, passing 263rd Avenue to the south and 265th Avenue to the north before reaching 273rd Avenue, a gravel cross road. Turn south onto this minimum maintenance road for about a half mile, park near the wooden Nature Conservancy sign near the south end of the preserve.

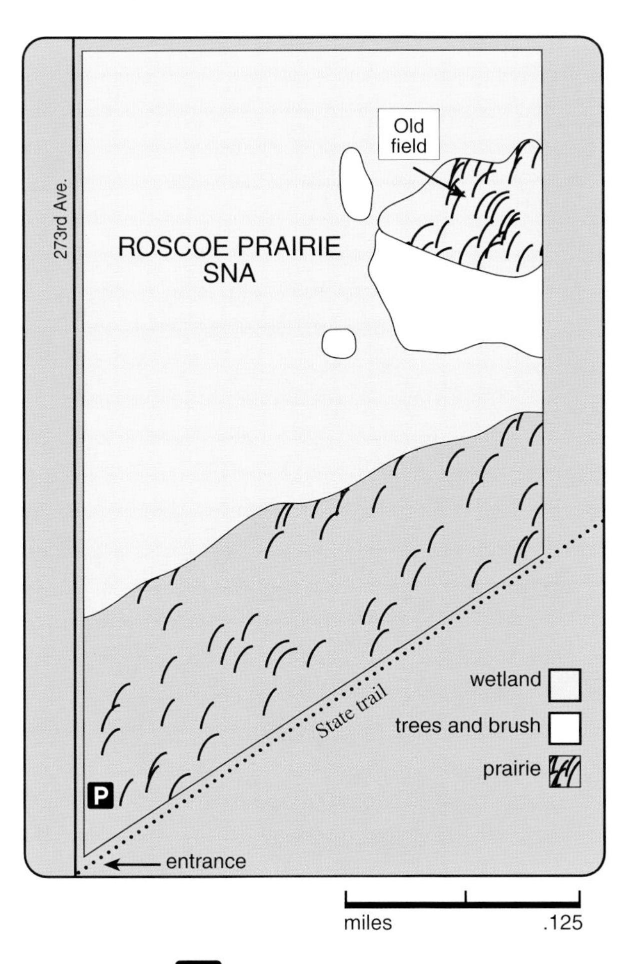

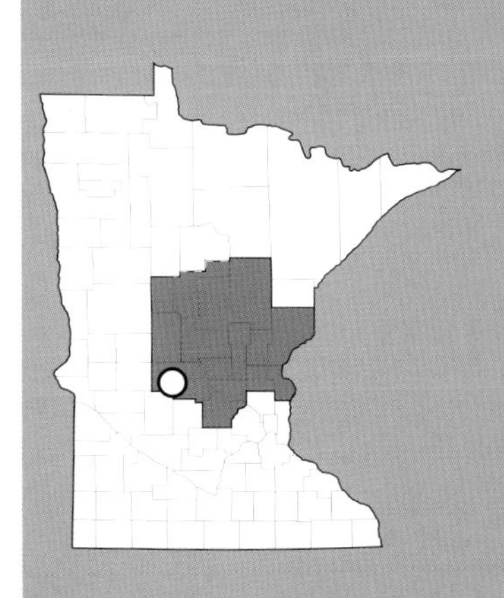

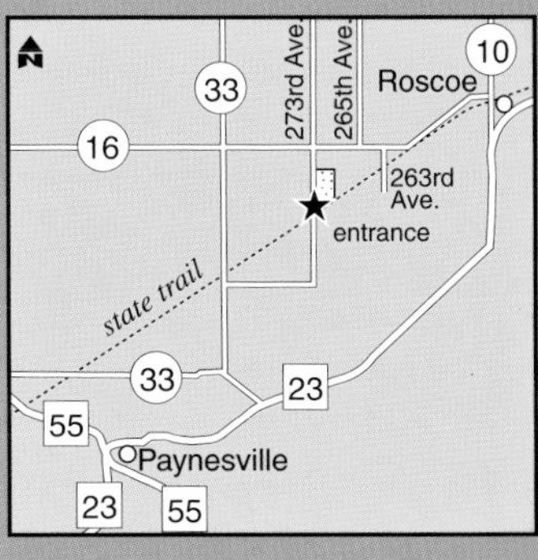

Facilities: P
Recreational Opportunities:

Contact:

Scientific and Natural Areas Program
DNR
Box 25
500 Lafayette Road
St. Paul MN 55155
(612) 297-2357

55–Graham's Island in the Mississippi River

Why is this area special?

Spring bustles when great blue herons, great egrets, Canada geese and songbirds, such as the Baltimore orioles and brown thrashers, arrive on this Mississippi River island sanctuary. As soon as the ice breaks up, look for common loons, common golden-eyes and common, red-breasted and hooded mergansers.

A heron colony housing about 200 birds is located on the north end of the island and great egrets have been seen in the vicinity. Watch for bald eagles soaring along the river corridor. At this point the riverbed is boulder-strewn and the current is swift, making it prime habitat for small-mouth bass and walleye.

Note:

Because of the Island's fragile nature, it's best to watch from the Sauk Rapids side of the river, including under the massive stately arches of the new bridge. River Avenue runs along the bank and ends just north of the bridge. The new bridge, which crosses the south end of the island, spans a 1,710-foot section of the Mississippi. It was built according to guidelines that protect herons, bald eagles and fish habitat. Bridge construction also preserved an area where archaeologists have found evidence of living sites dating back 8,000 years.

C. Henderson

Great blue heron

Follow the road south to a riverside municipal park offering restrooms, picnic and play areas, as well as places to sit and contemplate this mighty river and its inhabitants.

Sauk Rapids is planning to construct a bike and pedestrian trail along the water's edge, which also follows a portion of the Mississippi's Great River Road. Interpretive signs and a viewing platform will be included as part of that project.

Best viewing time:

How do I get there?

Maps: MN Highway Coordinate: H-14
PRIM Area: St. Cloud
DeLorme MN Atlas Grid #: 46 D-5

Additional directions:

The island is near Sauk Rapids, on the east bank of the Mississippi River where Highway 15 meets County Road 33 (Benton Drive). From Benton Drive, turn on 10th Street North. Drive toward the river, cross the railroad tracks, turn onto River Avenue. Turn right to go under the bridge or left to get to the park.

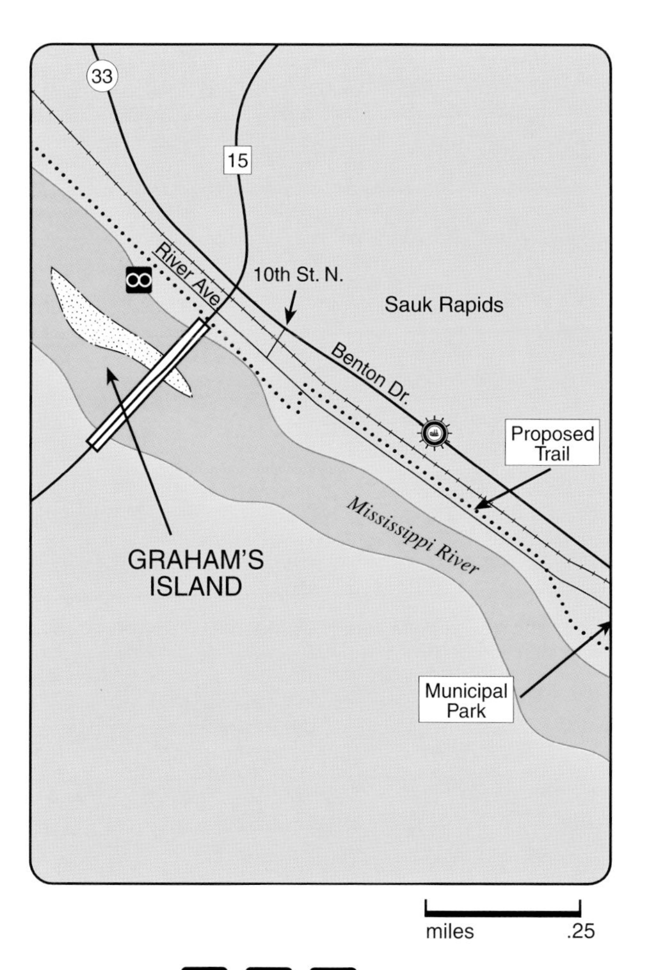

miles .25

Facilities:

Recreational Opportunities:  

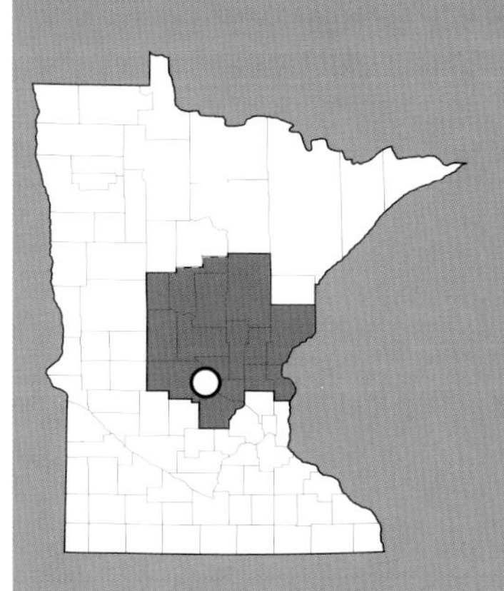

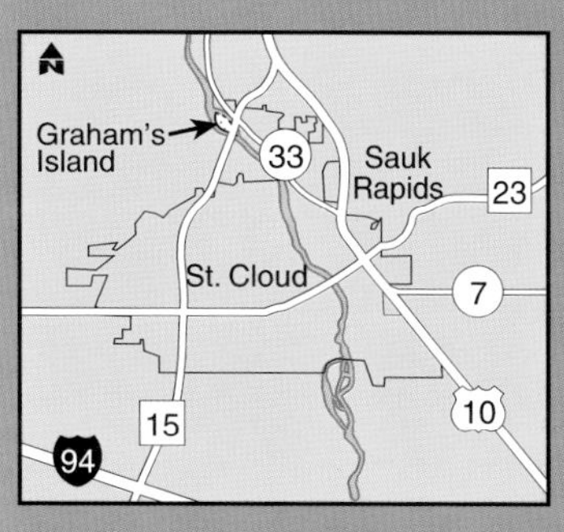

Contact:

Nongame Wildlife Program
DNR
1601 Minnesota Drive
Brainerd MN 56401
(218) 828-2228

56–Sand Prairie WMA and Environmental Education Area

Why is this area special?

Almost 70 years ago this extensive prairie-wetland complex—once a channel of the Mississippi River—was drained for cropland. Now its abandoned fields are being recolonized by native prairie plants. The 700-acre site encompasses two major wetland restorations and a tract of restored prairie, plus native prairie brushlands and woods.

The flat terrain makes it an easy three-quarter mile walk to the observation deck. Bring binoculars to spot belted kingfishers, great egrets, green herons, black terns, soras, marsh wrens, lesser yellow-legs, American woodcock, common snipes, pied-billed grebes, mallards, wood ducks, blue-winged teal, lesser scaup, American wigeons, northern shovelers and Canada geese.

C. Henderson

In May watch for warblers, such as the yellow, black-and-white, palm, yellow-rumped, and common yellow-throat, flitting about in the willows. Ruffed grouse, red-tailed hawks, Cooper's hawks, pileated woodpeckers, northern flickers, brown thrashers, eastern kingbirds, mourning doves, bobolink and ruby-throated hummingbirds may also be seen. Listen for the loud musical trill of the sandhill cranes.

Keep an eye out for chorus frogs, beavers, muskrats, white-tailed deer and foxes, as well as less common prairie skinks, western hognose snakes and Blanding's turtles.

Look for birds, butterflies and frogs too, as you stroll the prairie trail. Enjoy the sights and scents of blazing star, prairie clover, prairie smoke, lead plant, wild bergamot, harebell, goldenrod, golden alexander, downy phlox, mountain mint, wood lily, big bluestem and Indian grass.

Note:

The DNR manages this area for wildlife, environmental education and field research. Unlike most WMAs, hunting and trapping are not permitted.

Best viewing time:

How do I get there?

Maps: MN Highway Coordinate: H-14
PRIM Area: St. Cloud
DeLorme MN Atlas Grid #: 46 D-5

Additional directions:

Sand Prairie is near the southeastern edge of St. Cloud, south of County Road 7. Signs mark the entrance on the east side of Highway 10.

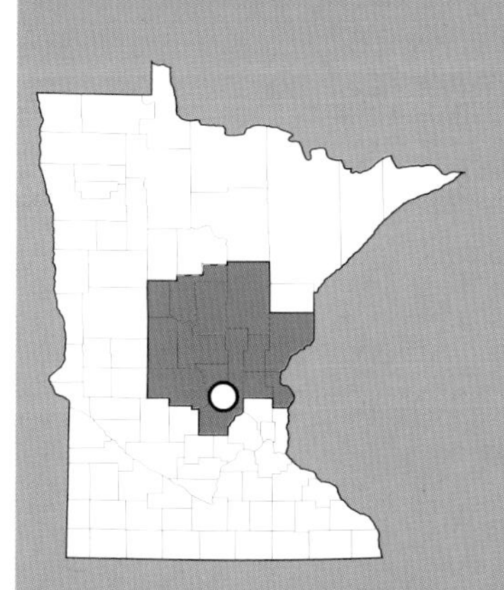

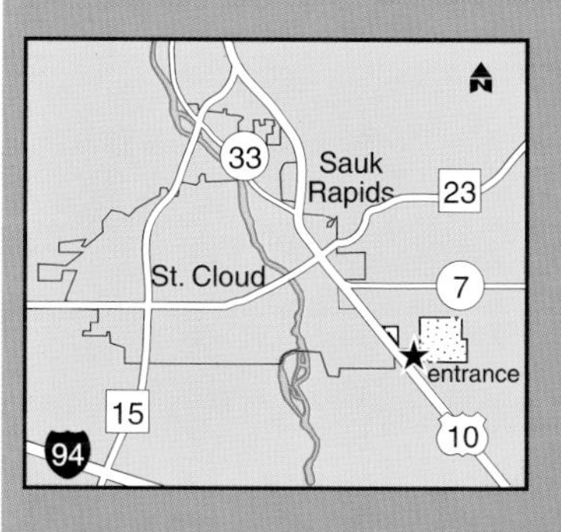

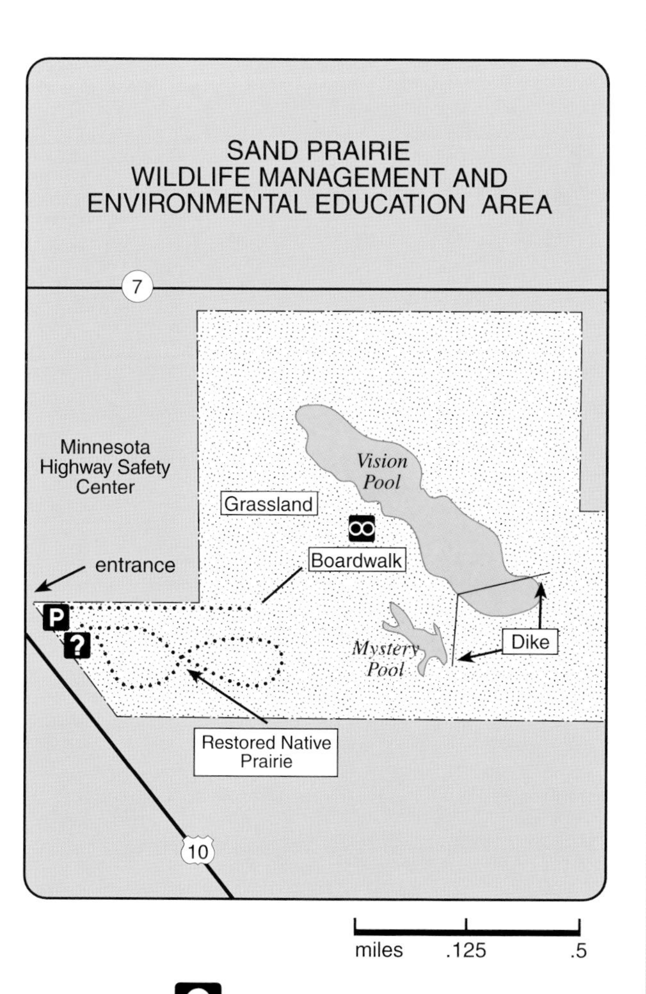

Facilities: 

Recreational Opportunities: 

Contact:

DNR Area Wildlife Office
4140 Thielman Lane
St. Cloud MN 56301
(320) 255-4279

57–Lake Maria State Park

Why is this area special?

Lake Maria State Park was designed for hikers, backpackers and horseback riders looking for a wilderness experience. Three major landscapes are found within the park: wetland, remnant prairie and the oak-maple forest known as the "Big Woods". Here the northern hardwood forest meets the southern prairie. This mixed habitat of rolling woods, cattail marsh, sedge meadow, small lakes and tallgrass prairie attracts a variety of wildlife.

You may spot white-tailed deer, beaver and fox, as well as eastern hognose, bull and garter snakes. The park is known for Blanding's turtles, a state threatened species. Your chance of spotting one of these unique yellow-throated individuals is increased if you look around the ponds where turtle-crossing signs are posted. Check out the turtle display near Lake Maria to speed your search for Blanding's, painted, snapping and spiny softshell turtles.

C. Henderson

Blanding's turtle

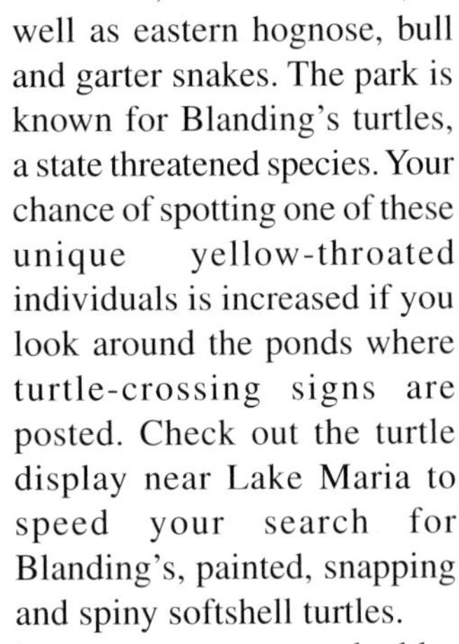

Watch for great blue herons, great egrets, double-crested cormorants, common loons, green herons, pied-billed grebes, American bitterns, soras, barred owls, ospreys and broad-winged and red-shouldered hawks. Look for forest songbirds, such as wood thrushes, scarlet tanagers, Baltimore orioles, ovenbirds, veeries, hermit thrushes and migrant warblers. A bird list is available.

There's lots to do here—take the self-guided trail featuring a 300-foot wetland boardwalk and observation deck or hike up Anderson Hill for a panoramic view of the area or rent a canoe for an excursion on Maria Lake. Explore the 14 miles of hiking, 27 miles of cross-country ski trails and six miles of horseback trails to encounter more reclusive wildlife.

Be sure to stop at the nature center for seasonal programs such as maple syruping, bird hikes, workshops and candlelight skiing.

Best viewing time:

Note:

Insects may be ferocious in July and August, so repellent and protective clothing are recommended. A vehicle permit is required and if skiing, you'll need a ski pass. Backpack and group camping sites and a few log cabins are available. Boat/canoe rental runs May–October.

How do I get there?

Maps: MN Highway Coordinate: L-15
PRIM Area: North Metro
DeLorme MN Atlas Grid #: 40 A-2

Additional directions:

Lake Maria State Park is about 35 miles northwest of the Twin Cities, just south of Interstate 94. The park may be reached from the north via Wright County Road 111 or from the east from County Road 39.

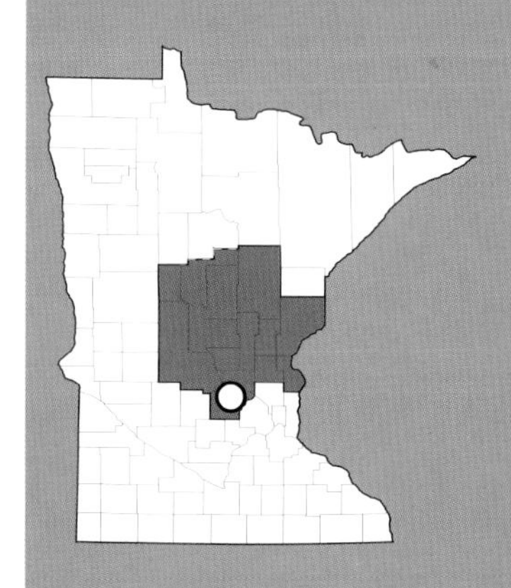

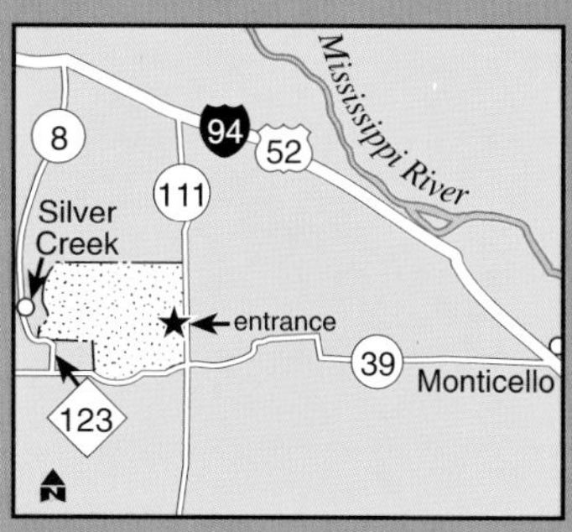

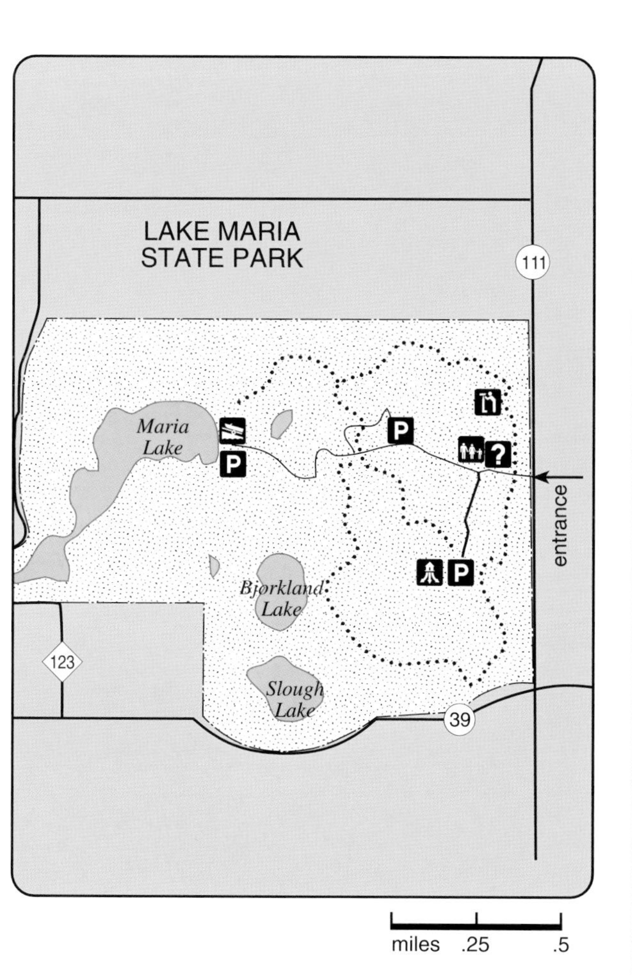

Facilities:

Recreational Opportunities:     

Contact:

Lake Maria State Park
11411 Clementa Avenue NW
Monticello MN 55362
(612) 878-2325

58–Sherburne NWR

Why is this area special?

At Sherburne discover the excitement that might have been felt nearly 150 years ago, as early pioneers stepped out of the "Big Woods" and onto the edge of Minnesota's magnificent tallgrass prairie. The refuge is a mosaic of prairie, wetlands, oak savanna and woodlands set in this transition zone between forest and prairie. Set aside in 1965 to preserve this vanishing heritage and restore the St. Francis River Valley, the refuge encompasses nearly 31,000 gently rolling acres.

C. Henderson

Trumpeter swan

To start, take at a snail's pace the superb Prairie's Edge Wildlife Drive. It's an eight-mile auto tour featuring interpretive displays, a couple of short trails and two observation decks, where you're guaranteed to spot wildlife.

Search the lakes and impoundments for basking painted and Blanding's turtles, tiger and blue-spotted salamanders, beaver, muskrat, great egrets, great blue herons and shorebirds, including 11 species of sandpiper. Waterfowl abounds—look for ring-necked ducks, hooded mergansers, mallards, wood ducks, blue-winged teal, northern shovelers, ruddy ducks, greater and lesser scaup, ring-necked ducks and buffleheads, as well as pied-billed and eared grebes. Keep an eye out for common loons, bald eagles and trumpeter swans that also frequent the refuge.

On a late spring evening discover the enchanting symphony created by chorus frogs and spring peepers, listen to the trill of red-winged blackbirds, the low pitched "karoo" of the sandhill cranes, the honk of Canada geese or the cry of a red-tailed hawk high overhead.

Two scenic hiking trails, Blue Hill and Mahnomen, will take you through fields, forests and along a lake, so watch for signs of pocket gophers, bull and garter snakes, prairie skinks, white-tailed deer, coyotes, foxes and occasionally bears. A multitude of birds including woodcock, field and song sparrows, eastern bluebirds, scarlet tanagers, Baltimore orioles, indigo buntings, as well as

Best viewing time:

red-headed and red-bellied woodpeckers may readily be seen. These trails are open in the winter for cross-country skiing and snowshoeing—a wonderful time to appreciate the unique beauty and quietude of the area. Look for tracks and signs of hardy winter residents, such as deer, and visitors like the northern shrike.

Surrounding Sherburne's wetlands are scattered woods, prairie grasses and wildflowers that once dominated the oak savannas found by pioneers. Oak savannas and grasslands are maintained by prescribed burns, which encourage the growth of native flowers and warm-season grasses. These fires also reduce competition from non-native, cool-season grasses and encroaching trees and shrubs.

Enjoy the sway of big and little bluestem, switch, Indian, cord and porcupine grasses in summer breezes. Look for wildflowers, such as pasque flower, hoary puccoon, penstemon, blazing star, butterfly weed, Indian paintbrush, blue lupine, gentian, lead plant and prairie smoke that add seasonal dabs of color.

Humans have lived in this area for more than 10,000 years, with Indian village sites on the refuge dating back to 1300 A.D. When European settlers arrived in the 1870s,

C. Henderson

Indigo bunting

continued...

the St. Francis River watershed, with its interspersion of habitats, was considered one of the finest wildlife areas in the state. But much of this valuable habitat was lost as settlers concentrated on their own survival. Oak forests were logged, wetlands drained and oak savannas were invaded by woody vegetation. These activities greatly reduced the wildlife value of the basin. In the early 1940s, with the creation of the refuge, efforts commenced to restore the area for wildlife.

C. Henderson

Sandhill cranes

Note:

The refuge is open only during daylight hours and the headquarters is staffed Monday-Friday, 8 a.m. to 4:30 p.m. all year. The Wildlife Drive is open from mid-April through late October. Maps and leaflets are available at information kiosks located at the main entrance points.

Bicycling is permitted only on the refuge roads and bicyclists are advised no fresh drinking water is available on the route. Canoeing, fishing and berry and mushroom picking are permitted, but check with the office first for details.

Hunting allowed. Call ahead for hunting season dates.

How do I get there?

Maps: MN Highway Coordinate: I-15
PRIM Area: North Metro
DeLorme MN Atlas Grid #: 47 D-9

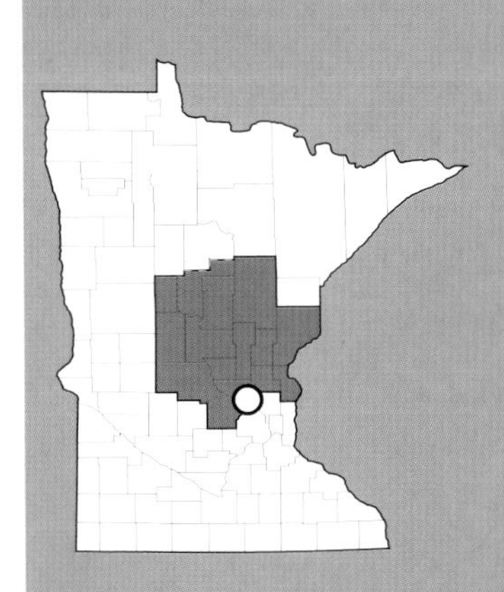

Additional directions:

From the Twin Cities: Take Highway 169 north to four miles north of Zimmerman. Turn west on Sherburne County Road 9, which will turn into gravel as you enter the Refuge.

From St. Cloud: Take MN Highway 23 east, turn south onto Highway 95 east, turn south onto Mille Lacs Co. Rd. 7, which becomes Sherburne Co. Rd. 5. Turn east onto Sherburne County Rd. 9 into the Refuge.

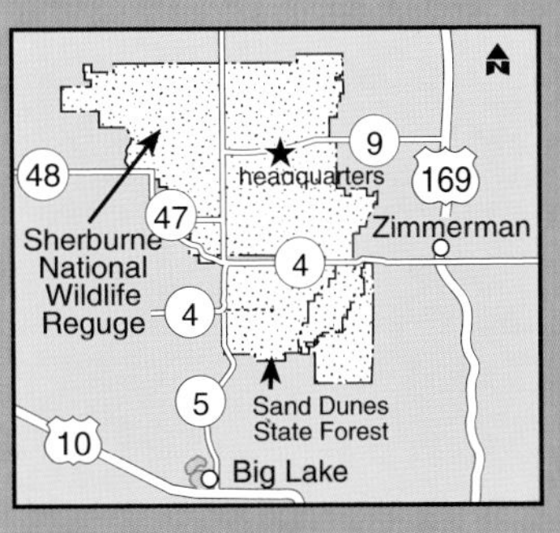

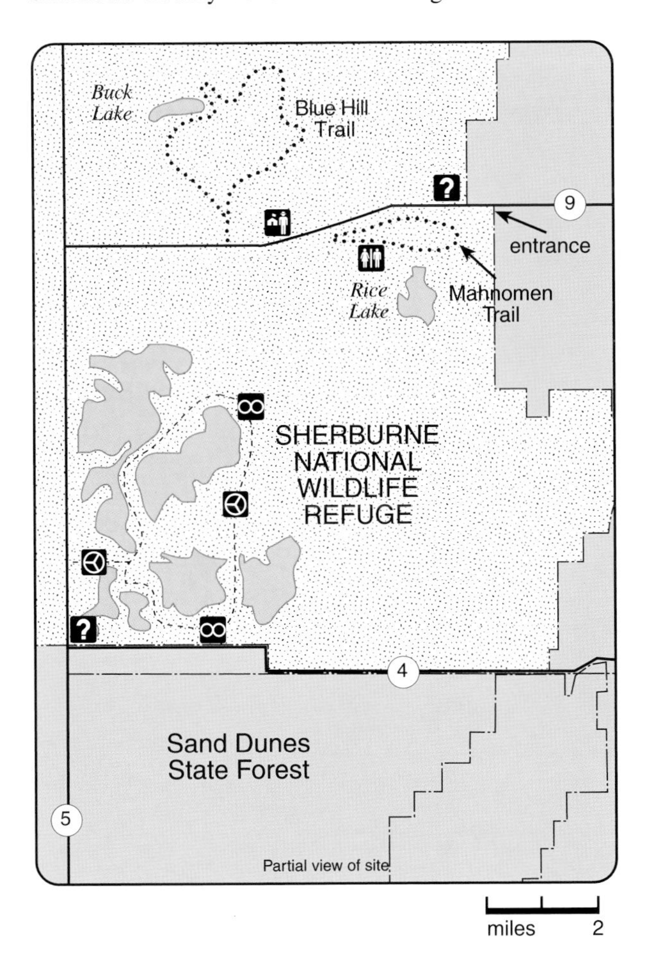

Facilities:

Recreational Opportunities:     

Contact:

Sherburne NWR
17076 293rd Avenue
Zimmerman MN 55398
(612) 389-3323

59–Sand Dunes State Forest/ Uncas Dunes SNA

Why is this area special?

In this quiet setting, you may spot a seldom seen skipper butterfly, a Blanding's turtle or a strutting wild turkey. Listen for blue jays and chipping sparrows in the woodlands and ring-billed gulls and ospreys calling over Ann Lake. Watch for red fox, coyotes and white-tailed deer roaming through the forest and keep your eyes open for signs of beaver.

This area was once open prairie and oak savanna, but since the days of settlement the oaks have closed in to create extensive woods.

When European settlers arrived in 1857, plows broke the prairie, but the sandy soil was never conducive to high yields. Economic depression in the 1930s and drought brought an end to most farming. The light, worn-out soils took to the air and drifted like snow over roads and onto front porches. In the '40s, concerned citizens started planting trees to stabilize the shifting sand. Today the area is thick with those pine plantations.

C. Henderson

White-tailed deer

There are two segments to the state forest, separated by the St. Francis River, a leg of the Sherburne NWR and private acreage. Explore one of the forest trails, including the three-mile interpretive trail, to improve your chances of seeing wildlife.

Take the trail that begins at the interpretive sign near camp site 28, go through the woods and up over a small hill before the path disappears into the dunes. From there on, tread lightly in this fragile environment. You can also admire the goldenrod, aster, puccoon, butterfly weed, lead plant, little bluestem and other grasses dotting the dunes.

The 600-acre **Uncas Dunes Scientific and Natural Area** adjacent to Ann Lake features relic sand dunes and oak savannas.

Note:

Watch out for patches of plentiful three-leafed poison ivy. And don't be fooled by its pale green berries that cluster on woody stems in fall and spring—the oil can still irritate those susceptible.

The state forest offers trails for hikers, skiers, horseback riders and snowmobilers. Ann Lake campground has spacious sites spread out among the oaks and pines. To protect the delicate Uncas Dunes landscape, use is restricted. See Sherburne NWR (site 58) for nearby wildlife watching opportunities. Strict rules apply to the SNA. No collecting of butterflies, plants, or other wildlife is allowed. Check signs there for details.

Best viewing time:

How do I get there?

Maps: MN Highway Coordinate: I-15
PRIM Area: North Metro
DeLorme MN Atlas Grid #: 47 E-9

Additional directions:

Located west of Zimmerman and north of Big Lake, Sand Dunes State Forest and Uncas Dunes SNA may be reached by taking County Road 5 north from Big Lake, off of Highway 10 OR by following County Road 4 west from Zimmerman off of Highway 169.

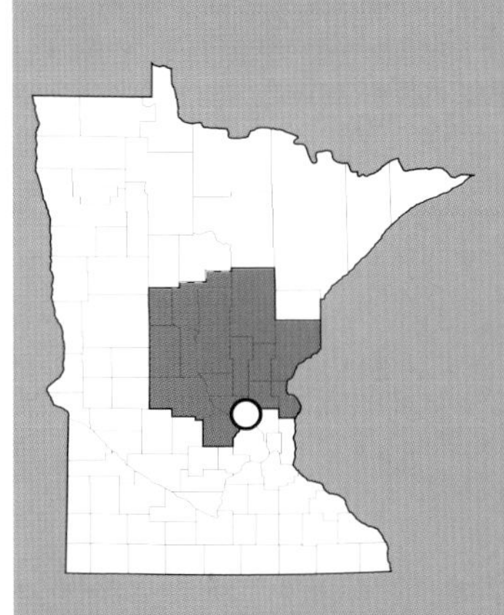

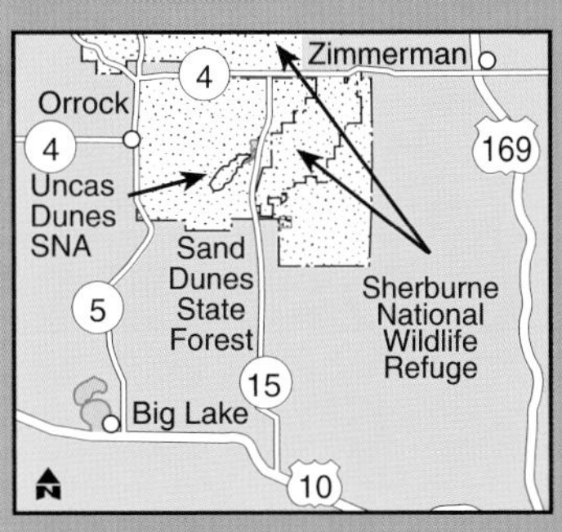

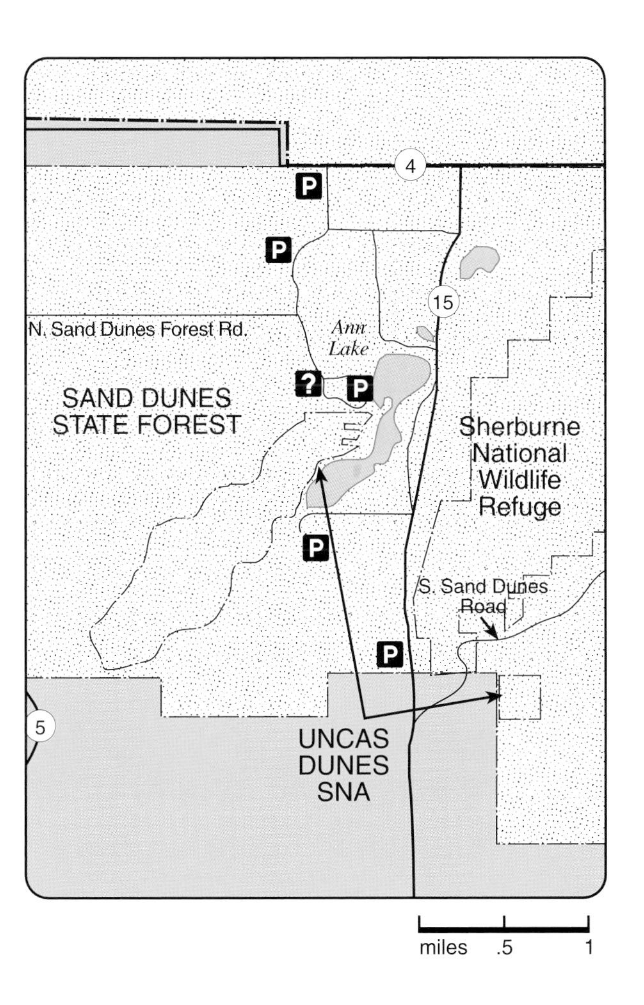

Facilities:

Recreational Opportunities:

Contact:

DNR Forestry
12969 Fremont Avenue
Zimmerman MN 55398
(612) 856-4826

Scientific and Natural Areas Program
DNR
Box 25
500 Lafayette Road
St. Paul MN 55155
(612) 297-2357

60–Wild River State Park

Why is this area special?

Turn the clock back a few hundred years and imagine yourself standing in the St. Croix River Valley amid a stretch of 100-foot white pine trees. If you're successful, you'll have a mental picture of what the riverway looked like then. If you are having a little trouble coming up with a clear picture, a unique outdoor exhibit set in a 20-acre pine plantation will give you a feel for the immensity of the vanished pines.

C. Henderson

Wild River State Park also preserves a long cultural heritage. The St. Croix Valley was first occupied by nomadic people 6000 years ago and in relatively more recent times, Dakota, Ojibwe, Sauk and Fox Indians all lived in the area. As time passed, two trading posts, built within present-day park boundaries, flourished. Traces of the Hastings to Superior Military Road, constructed in the 1850s, are still visible in the park.

Lumberjacks and settlers from Sweden and New England came in the mid 1800s to log, farm and plat two town sites that never developed. Nevers Dam, said by some to have been the largest timber-crib dam ever built, was constructed in 1890 to regulate the flow of huge white pine logs en route to Stillwater sawmills. The dam was demolished in 1955, but the old Nevers Dam site is still an attraction.

Today, this narrow, diverse sanctuary hugging the wild and scenic St. Croix remains a wonderful place for wildlife watching. Wetlands and the river offer both food and protection for marsh birds and waterfowl, as well as a haven for muskrats, beavers and river otters. Look closely to discover signs or tracks in the snow or soft earth left by these animals, plus those of the raccoons, badgers, coyotes, black bears or white-tailed deer. Watch for deer in open prairie or meadow settings during early morning and evening hours.

Best viewing time:

Scout for bald eagles and turkey vultures riding the thermals and red-shouldered and broad-winged hawks and northern harriers winging over forests and fields. Zoom in on barred owls, great blue herons and songbirds such as the scarlet tanagers, eastern bluebirds, golden-winged warblers, Louisiana waterthrushes, ovenbirds and common yellowthroats. In spring and autumn count on seeing migratory birds in large numbers. Just for fun, pick up a bird checklist at the visitor center and see how many species you can spot.

In winter watch for trumpeter swans that frequent the open water near the Deer Creek outlet and south of the Nevers Dam site. Cross-country ski trails run close to these spots and a packed walking trail leads from the picnic area to the dam site. Use binoculars to get a glimpse of these graceful white birds.

The park terrain varies from level sand plains to steep river bluffs and lowland floodplains. Forests are mostly pin oak, but also include red, bur and white oak, aspen, sugar and silver maple, basswood, paper birch, tamarack and white pine. Hazelnut, dogwood, raspberry and blackberry are common and provide food for many birds and animals.

Search out the exquisite spring ephemerals such as trillium, bloodroot, hepatica and blue phlox on the forest floor and the summer prairie flowers, including wild lupine, Carolina and hoary puccoon, spiderwort, oxeye daisy, aster and blazing star in the meadows.

C. Henderson

Golden-winged warbler

continued...

Note:

Inquire about the year-round naturalist programs and seasonal events such as maple syrup demonstrations, birding walks, prairie tours, hikes, campfires, fall color programs, snowshoeing, animal tracking and moonlight skiing. The visitor center overlooks the valley and features a weather station, bird feeding area, biodiversity display and a landscaping for wildlife demonstration garden. There are also historical and cultural exhibits and slide presentations.

Hikers and cross-country skiers will find 35 miles of fairly level trails. The Amiks Pond self-guided trail is one of the more popular hikes. Cross-country ski rental is an option for those who want to do more winter wildlife exploring. Twenty miles of horseback trails make this one of the premier places to ride. Several of the loops give views of the river, including one that is part of the old military road.

Daily or annual permits are required for vehicles entering a state park.

CAUTION: High water levels and swift river currents may develop overnight. Be extremely careful when in and around the water and mindful of slippery rocks and soil.

C. Henderson

Black phase-tiger swallowtail

How do I get there?

Maps: MN Highway Coordinate: K-14
PRIM Area: Mora
DeLorme MN Atlas Grid #: 49 D-7

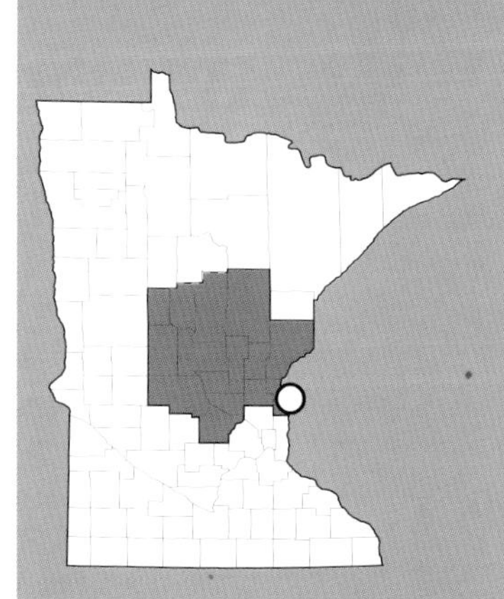

Additional directions:

The main entrance to the Park is located 13 miles east of Interstate 35, north of Highway 95, at the north end of Chisago County Road 12.

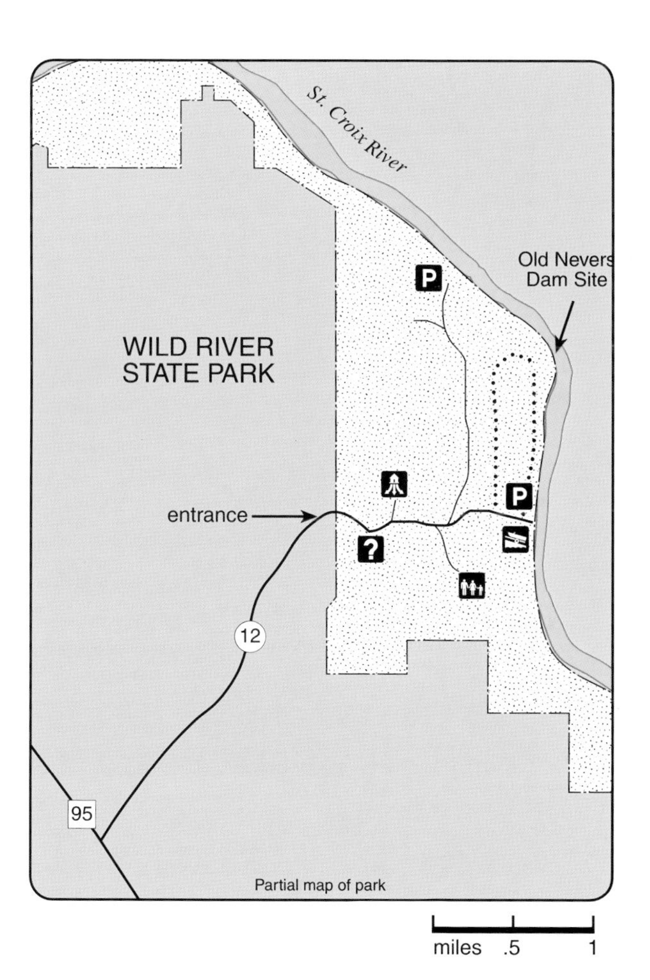

Facilities:

Recreational Opportunities:

Contact:

Wild River State Park
39755 Park Trail
Center City MN 55012
(612) 583-2125

Southwest-Prairie and Wetland Country

Minnesota's remaining prairies and wetlands make up some of the best wildlife habitats in southwest Minnesota. Although the area is dominated by row-crop agriculture, it is dotted with islands of natural grasslands, wetlands and woodlands. Explore this region for broad vistas of prairie and stunning spectacles of waterfowl migration.

C. Henderson

American white pelicans

This region is a transition zone between western grasslands, eastern deciduous forests and northern lake country. It has habitats and wildlife characteristic of all three areas.

Topography and soil varies from the southwest to northeast. The soil of the southwest can be light and rocky and the topography is well-sloped. In the southwest corner of the state, the Coteau des Prairie, or highland of the prairie, forms a dividing line between the Missouri and Minnesota River systems.

To the northeast of the coteau lies some of the richest farmland in the state. The gently rolling to flat landscape was once covered by a vast sea of prairie grasses. The prairie land is characterized by rich soil. Topography in the northern part of the region is not as level as that in the south and the soil is not as rich. The hilly, glaciated landscape of this area is dotted with lakes typical of central Minnesota.

Although the landscape, plant and animal communities in the southwest have been heavily altered by people, wildlife still abounds and many viewing opportunities exist for the wildlife enthusiast.

White-tailed deer, red foxes, red-tailed hawks, pheasants, wild turkeys, herons, ducks, geese, grebes, terns, gulls and many waterbirds make the wetlands of southwest Minnesota their home. Occasionally there are visitors from the west: pronghorns, mule deer and burrowing owls.

Prairie grasslands provide nesting habitat for marbled godwits and upland sandpipers. Restoration projects for trumpeter swans and river otters have brought these species back to southwest Minnesota in recent years. Some areas provide the opportunity to see blue grosbeaks, sandhill cranes and ospreys.

Each spring and fall, hundreds of thousands of waterfowl pass through southwest Minnesota to and from their breeding and wintering grounds. Several areas, such as Lac Qui Parle, Talcot Lake and North Heron Lake, are resting sites for thousands of waterfowl during their southbound fall migration. If you explore the Minnesota River at Lac Qui Parle in early May, you might see flocks of golden plovers streaming northward above the prairie, as they have done for thousands of years.

Forests along the Minnesota River valley are a migratory corridor for songbirds not normally associated with prairie. Even bald eagles now nest there and can be seen flying along the river valley as they migrate or winter near open water.

Roads throughout the entire area are good and in many areas are located on section lines that are one mile apart. Gravel roads are well-maintained and usually passable. However, blowing snow and prairie winds can cause blizzard conditions during inclement winter weather.

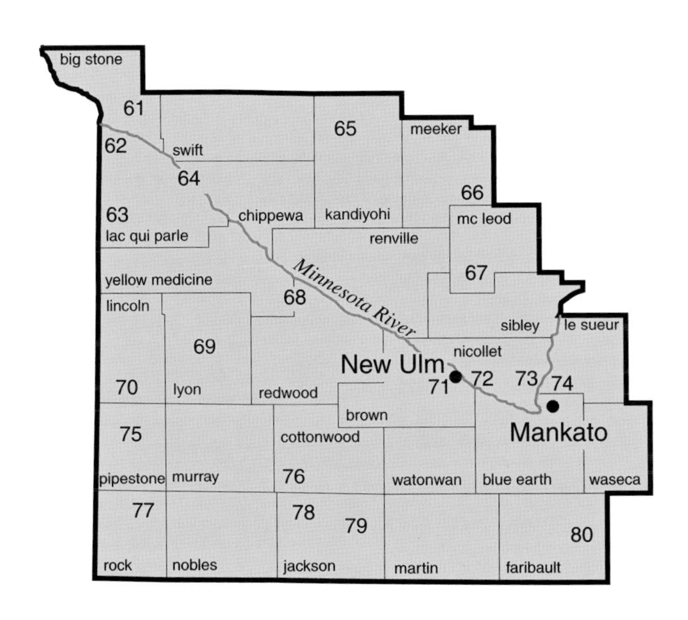

Sites

61. Thielke Lake WMA
62. Big Stone NWR
63. Salt Lake WMA
64. Lac Qui Parle WMA/ State Park
65. Sibley State Park
66. Pigeon Lake Rookery
67. Schaefer Prairie
68. Swede's Forest SNA
69. Camden State Park/ Prairie Marshes WMA
70. Hole-in-the-Mountain WMA/ TNC/Co. Park
71. Flandrau State Park
72. Swan Lake
73. Seven Mile Creek County Park
74. Kasota Prairie SNA
75. Pipestone National Monument/ WMA
76. Talcot Lake WMA
77. Blue Mounds State Park
78. Heron Lake
79. Kilen Woods State Park/ Prairie Bush Clover SNA
80. Walnut Lake WMA

61–Thielke Lake WMA

Why is this area special?

Thielke Lake is well known as home to a nesting colony of western grebes. Minnesota marks the eastern edge of the western grebe's range in the United States.

Each spring, western grebes perform a mating display in which pairs rise up and run across the water. With neck curved and wings partially flared, the pair, in almost perfect unison, runs across the surface of the water for 100 yards or more.

After hatching, chicks can be observed riding on the back of their parents in order to rest, stay warm and be protected from predatory fish. You can hear grebes' sharp, screechy whistle as they announce to begging chicks that they have just captured a meal of fish.

Gary Nuechterlein

Western grebe

Spring is one of the best times to visit Thielke Lake and the surrounding wetland areas of Big Stone County, where you may also observe a variety of other birds, including waterfowl, great blue herons, great egrets, American white pelicans, black terns, Forster's terns and ring-billed gulls.

Note:

Due to the many lakes and diverse topography in this area, it has not been as severely ditched, tiled and drained as other areas in southwest Minnesota. When visiting Thielke Lake, be sure to seek out nearby WMAs and federal Waterfowl Production Areas (WPAs) to see additional wetland and grassland birds.

Best viewing time:

How do I get there?

Maps: MN Highway Coordinate: B-15
PRIM Area: Big Stone Lake
DeLorme MN Atlas Grid #: 43 E-6

Additional directions:

Located six miles north of Ortonville, Thielke Lake can be observed from a gravel road bordering the lake's south shore. From Ortonville, take Highway 75 north for six miles. Turn east on gravel road 62 for one and a quarter miles. The gravel curves around the south shore of the lake.

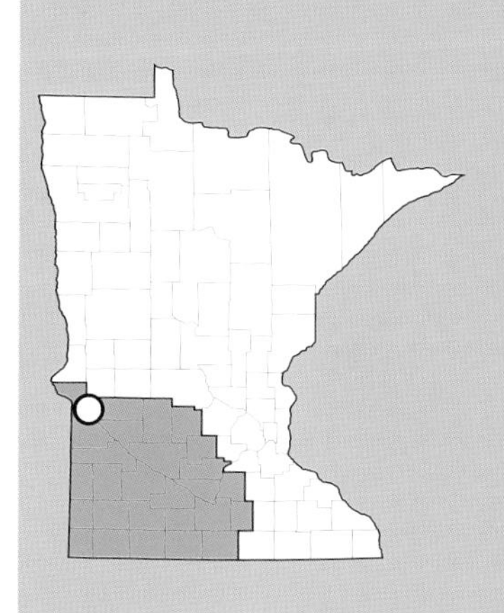

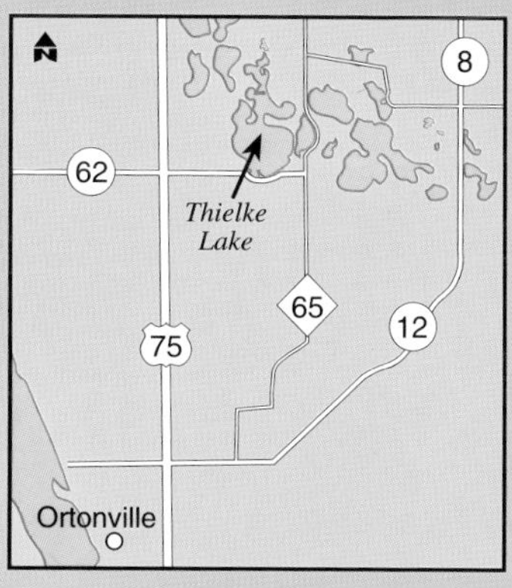

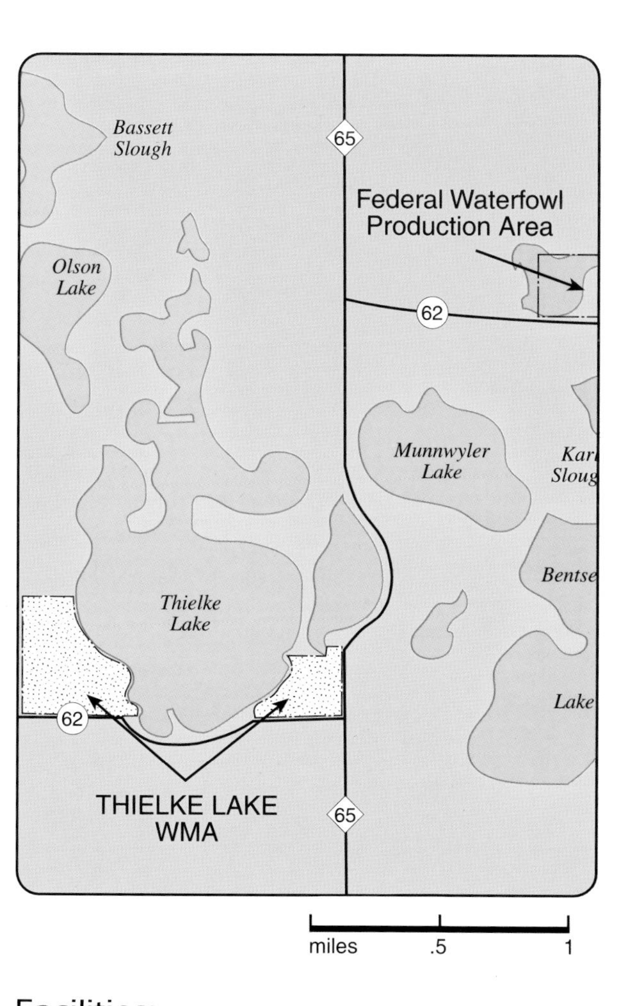

Facilities:

Recreational Opportunities:

Contact:

DNR Area Wildlife Office
Appleton Civic Center
323 W. Schlieman Ave.
Appleton MN 56208
(320) 289-2493

62–Big Stone NWR

Why is this area special?

This 10,000-acre NWR is located along the Minnesota River near the South Dakota border. The reservoir and surrounding land offer a variety of habitats, including native prairie, floodplain forest, wetlands and granite rock outcrops. Plant communities in this area include elm, ash, maple, bur oak, big bluestem, prickly pear and mamillaria cactus.

This is one of the only breeding grounds for snowy egrets in Minnesota. Smaller size and black legs with yellow feet are keys to identify this egret from its larger relative, the great egret.

You might also see western grebes, great blue herons, American white pelicans, wood ducks, hooded mergansers, many kinds of prairie ducks, Swainson's hawks, bald eagles, short-eared owls, loggerhead shrikes, bobolinks, common nighthawks, American woodcocks, white-tailed deer, red fox, river otters and muskrats.

Four miles of refuge roads have been opened to create an auto route with a good view of the reservoir and its pelicans, herons, egrets, grebes and waterfowl. A brochure describes special features along the route.

The rock outcrop hiking trail provides a look at different habitat types and historical features plus several species of songbirds, small mammals, cactus, prairie plants and skinks.

C. Henderson

Coyote

Note:

Walking conditions can be difficult and rocky areas may be slippery in the early morning or after a shower. Stay on established trails.

Hunting allowed. Call ahead for hunting season dates.

Best viewing time:

How do I get there?

Maps: MN Highway Coordinate: B-15, C-15
PRIM Area: Big Stone Lake
DeLorme MN Atlas Grid #: 36 A/B-1, 2

Additional directions:

To use the auto tour trail, take Highway 75 for one mile south of Ortonville, and then take County Road 17 that cuts back to the southwest into the refuge. There are several places to park on the east side of the refuge along Highway 75.

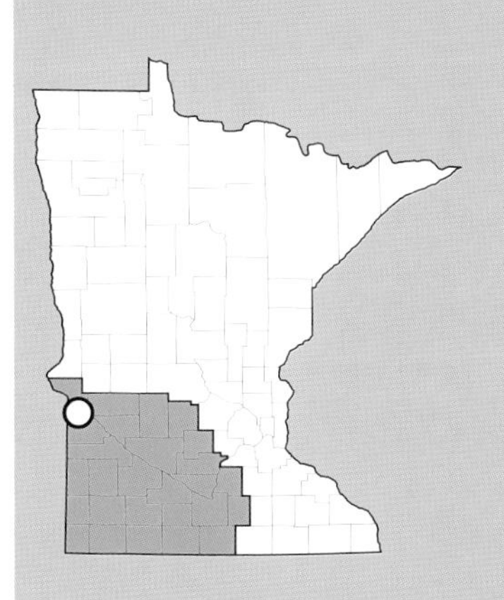

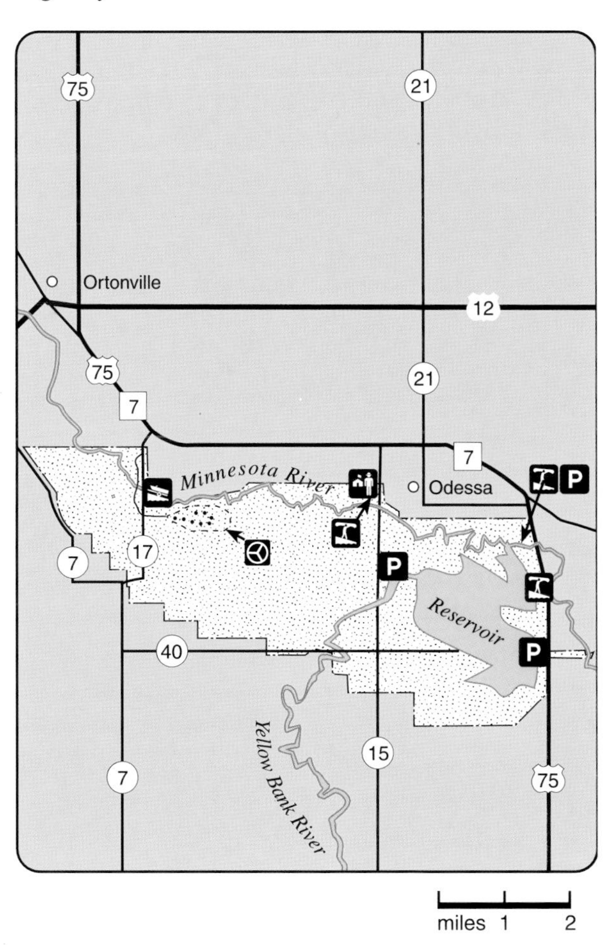

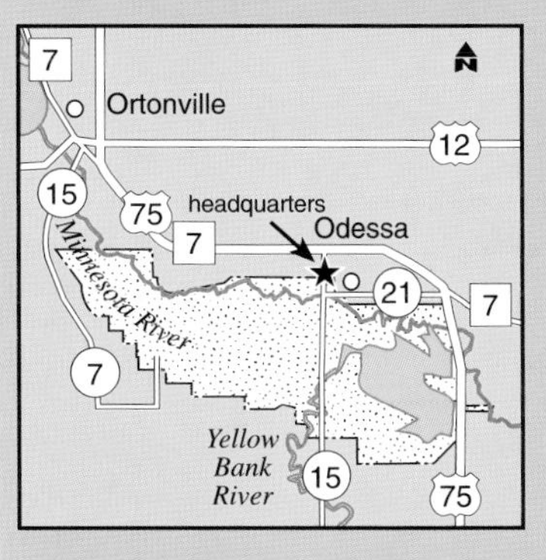

Facilities:

Recreational Opportunities:    

Contact:

Big Stone NWR Headquarters
25 NW 2nd Street
Ortonville MN 56278
(320) 273-2191

63–Salt Lake WMA

Why is this area special?

Salt Lake, on the border of Minnesota and South Dakota in Lac Qui Parle County, is Minnesota's only alkaline wetland. The water in Salt Lake is one-third as salty as sea water. Although it's not one of the largest lakes in the region, Salt Lake is an oasis for waterbirds in western Minnesota. From a birder's perspective, it may be one of the most impressive lakes in the state.

Each spring, many species stop at Salt Lake to feed and rest while they make their way to northern breeding grounds. The lake is particularly attractive to shorebirds such as willets, piping plovers and sandpipers. More than 140 species of birds have been identified on Salt Lake. It also has one of the few Minnesota breeding records for the American avocet. These birds normally nest in the saline prairie wetlands of the Dakotas and Canada, and Salt Lake is one of the few places in Minnesota where a suitable habitat exists for them.

W. L. Penning

Avocet

While the migration of shorebirds in April may be the highlight at the Salt Lake WMA, other species offer wildlife viewing from late spring through fall. You might find western grebes, American white pelicans, tundra swans, Hudsonian godwits and marbled godwits near the lake. Eared grebes are common summer residents. You can see these small grebes constructing nests on vegetative mats in the lake.

Public upland areas within the WMA area provide a potential habitat for loggerhead shrikes. Open grassy areas with scattered trees in Lac Qui Parle County offer opportunities to observe these uncommon birds.

Note:

The Minnesota Ornithologists' Union annually sponsors Salt Lake Weekend on the third or fourth weekend of April. Contact the MOU for details on upcoming events at Salt Lake.

Best viewing time:

 Hunting allowed. Call ahead for hunting season dates.

How do I get there?

Maps: MN Highway Coordinate: B-16
PRIM Area: Montevideo
DeLorme MN Atlas Grid #: 36 D-1

Additional directions:

Drive west of Dawson on Highway 212 for 17 miles. Turn north on County Road 7, which takes you to the community of Mehurin. Drive two miles north of Mehurin, and then turn west on a gravel township road. Drive one mile to a T' intersection that overlooks Salt Lake.

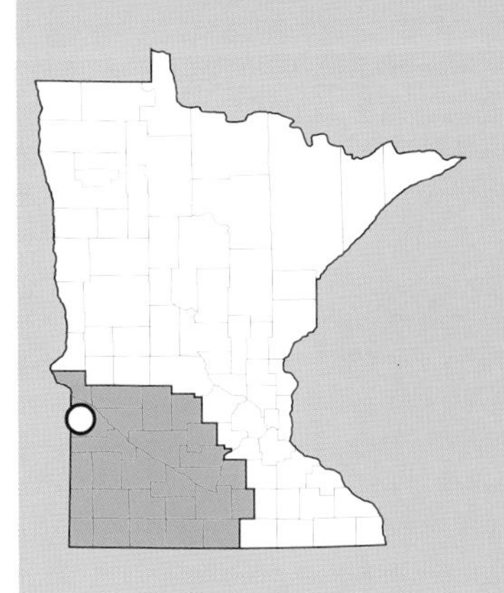

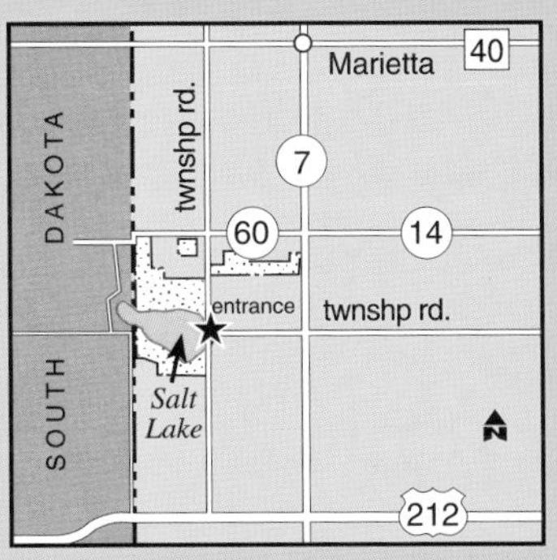

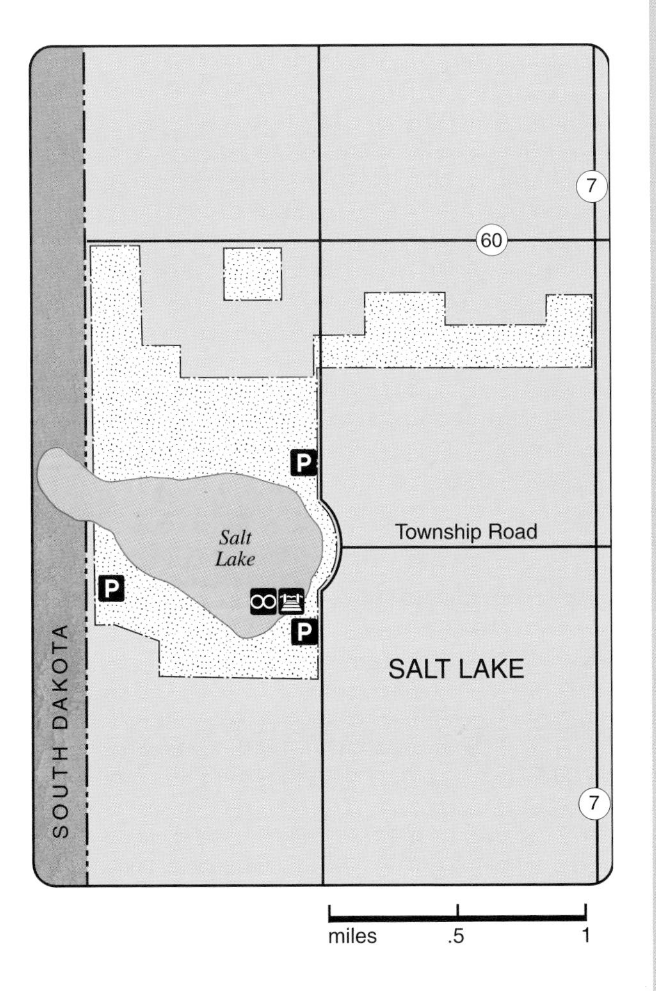

Facilities: 
Recreational Opportunities:

Contact:

DNR Area Wildlife Office
504 3rd St.
Madison MN 56256
(320) 598-7641

64–Lac Qui Parle WMA/ State Park

Why is this area special?

The Lac Qui Parle Wildlife Management Area is one of the most diverse in the state. It contains 31,238 acres of wildlife habitats and exceptional wildlife viewing opportunities.

This area is located in one of the major waterfowl flyways in North America. Waterfowl and other migratory birds from Alberta, Manitoba, North Dakota and Minnesota travel through the area. The floodplain forests of the state park and WMA are used by migrating neotropical songbirds such as warblers and vireos. As many as 50 bald eagles use the area during the spring and fall and a few pairs nest there. Prairie parcels south of Appleton are great in early May for watching golden plovers migrating north to Arctic nesting grounds.

C. Henderson

Canada goose

Lac Qui Parle is home to the largest American white pelican nesting colony in Minnesota. It's easy to spot pelicans below the dams at Marsh Lake, near Appleton, and Lac Qui Parle Lake, near Watson. As many as 10,000 pelicans, as well as double-crested cormorants and ring-billed gulls, nest here. Up to 150,000 Canada geese have stopped at the WMA during fall migration. Tundra swans, snow geese, wood ducks and sandhill cranes can also be seen in migration here. Look too for western grebes, Forster's terns, cattle egrets, loggerhead shrikes, upland sandpipers and marbled godwits. River otters have been reintroduced on the WMA, and white-tailed deer are common here.

Plant communities at this site include big bluestem, Indian grass, switch grass, prairie coneflower, stiff goldenrod, white and purple prairie clover, sunflowers, lead plant, bur oak, willows, elm and green ash.

Note:

The Nature Conservancy owns the Chippewa Prairie south of Appleton. Its prairie holdings total more than 1,600 acres adjacent to the Lac Qui Parle WMA. These areas are also open to the public for wildlife viewing and photography. You can go hunting, fishing, birding, boating and camping on the WMA, but hunting is not allowed on the Chippewa Prairie.

Best viewing time:

 Hunting allowed. Call ahead for hunting season dates.

How do I get there?

Maps: MN Highway Coordinate: C-16, D-16
PRIM Area: Willmar
DeLorme MN Atlas Grid #: 36/37 C-5

Additional directions:

Situated near the South Dakota border, Lac Qui Parle is between Appleton and Montevideo. It can be reached by taking Highway 59 north of Montevideo for seven miles. Turn west on County Road 13 for two miles. Go north on Township Road 32 for two and a quarter miles, then west on Township Rd. 33 to reach the WMA headquarters. The State Park is located along County Road 33 on the south end of Lac Qui Parle Lake.

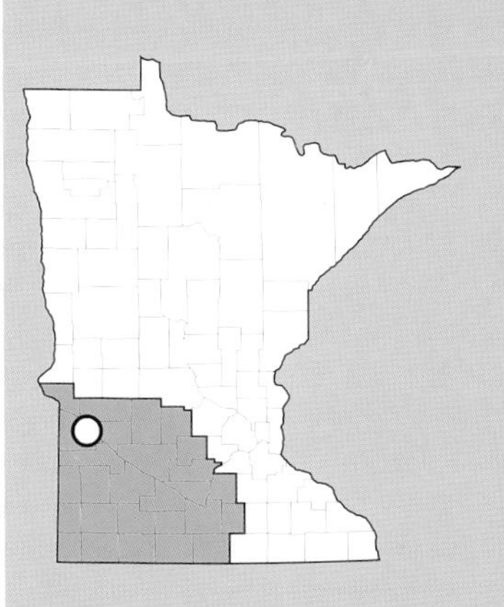

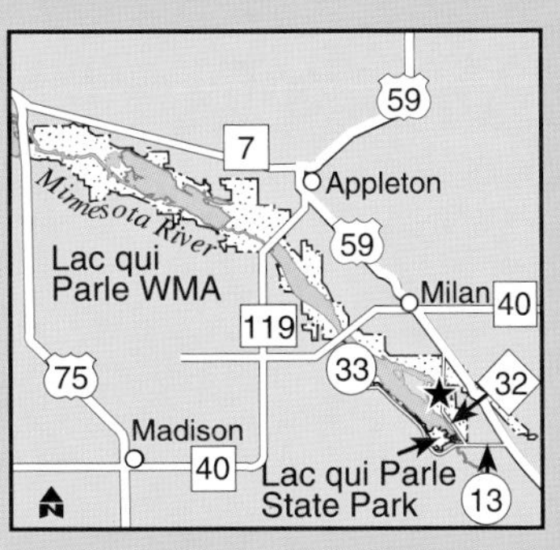

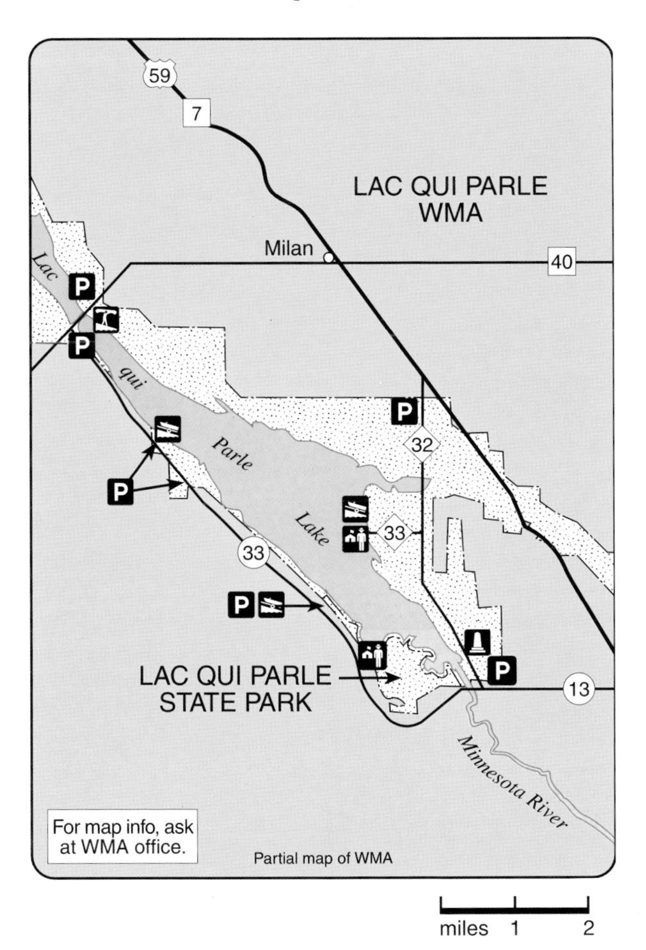

Facilities: 

Recreational Opportunities:   

Contact:

Lac Qui Parle State Park
RR 5 Box 74-A
Montevideo MN 56265
(320) 752-4736

DNR Wildlife Area Office
Lac Qui Parle WMA
RR 1 Box 23
Watson MN 56295
(320) 734-4451

65–Sibley State Park

Why is this area special?

Sibley State Park lies in a transition zone between two ecosystems; it's where the Big Woods of the east meet the grasslands of the west. Plants and animals found here are representative of both areas. The area's lakes were formed about 10,000 years ago as glaciers passed through the state and deposited rock, gravel and sand .

Large tracts of prairie developed where the land was unprotected from fire or too dry for forests to grow. Most of these areas were subsequently grazed or converted to agricultural land, but attempts are being made to restore prairie areas in the park.

C. Henderson

White admiral butterfly

The park's Lake Andrew is one of the few places in the region where you can regularly hear the call of the common loon. Sibley's woodlands are home to ruffed grouse and wild turkeys, while its grassland areas offer habitat to bobolinks, grassland sparrows and other prairie birds. The lakes and marshes are home to great blue herons, great egrets, mink, beavers and waterfowl.

Look for broad-winged, Cooper's and sharp-shinned hawks, great horned, barred and eastern screech-owls, great blue herons, great egrets, American white pelicans, American redstarts, red-eyed vireos, gray foxes, red foxes and white-tailed deer. Plant life includes bur oak, ironwood, basswood, hackberries, green ash, aspens, grassland plants and wetland communities.

Note:

Mt. Tom, a large hill, rises 1,375 feet above sea level inside the park. It is the highest point for 50 miles around and offers an exceptional view of the surrounding forest, prairie, lakes and farmland. At nearby Monson Lake State Park you might see red-necked grebes.

Best viewing time:

How do I get there?

Maps: MN Highway Coordinate: F-15
PRIM Area: Willmar
DeLorme MN Atlas Grid #: 38 A-3

Additional directions:

Located north of Willmar, Sibley State Park can be reached by taking Highway 71 eleven miles north of Willmar. Turn west on County Road 48. Drive for one mile to the park headquarters.

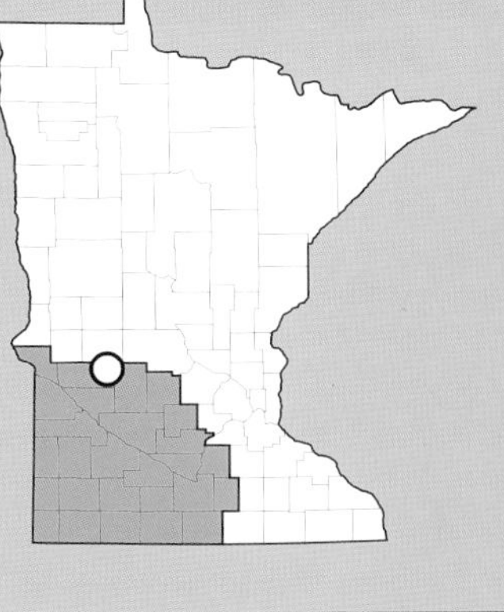

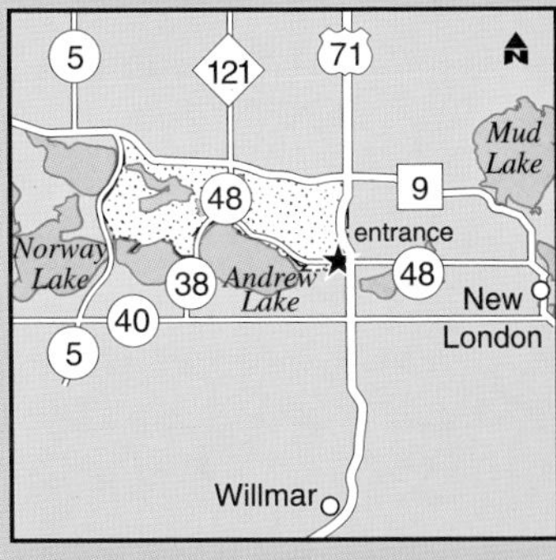

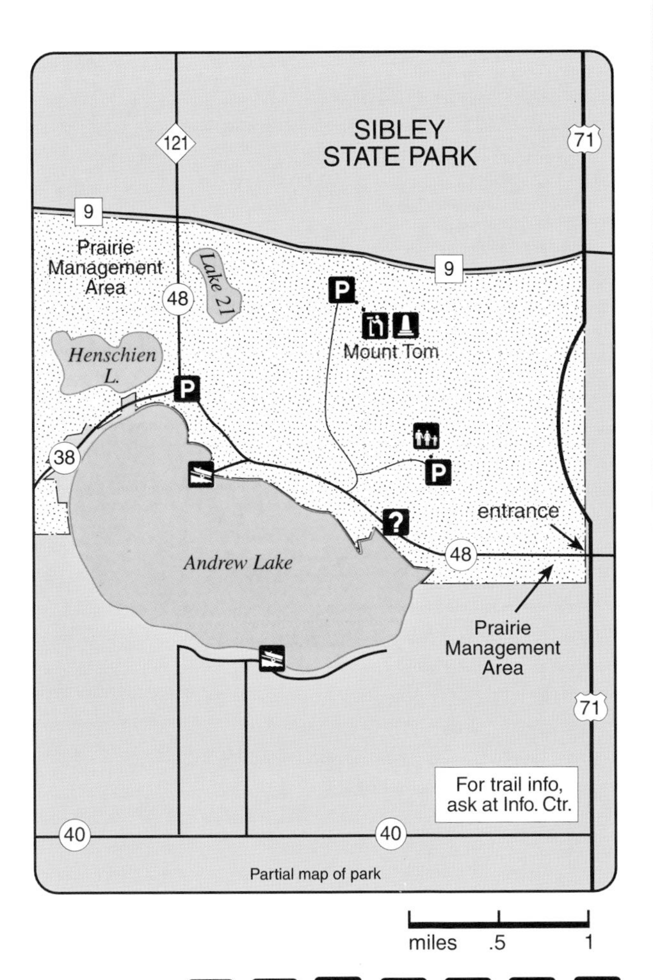

Facilities:

Recreational Opportunities:

Contact:

Sibley State Park
800 Sibley Park Rd. NE
New London MN 56273
(320) 354-2055

66–Pigeon Lake Rookery

Why is this area special?

The abundant lakes, marshes and small streams of the northeastern part of this region provide an excellent habitat and nesting ground for herons, egrets and cormorants. You can often see them feeding on area lakes and marshes, but it's difficult to spot their treetop nests. Great blue herons tend to occupy the highest tree branches while black-crowned night-herons build nests nearer to the ground. You can observe the young birds throughout the early summer months.

Great blue heron

Heavy use of the northern island by nesting birds has killed much of the original vegetation, which now includes mostly green ash and boxelder. The open areas of the island are commonly used by American white pelicans for loafing sites. Through continued use of the island by nesting birds, vegetation may be further altered, creating an environment which will perhaps one day be suitable for nesting pelicans.

Note:

The island colony is best viewed from a scenic lookout off Highway 15 on the northwest side of the lake. Use binoculars or a spotting scope to get a good look at the island. The young waterbirds do not tolerant disturbance, so do not take a boat out to see them. Frightened herons and egret chicks may fall out of the trees and be deserted by their parents if people enter the colonies.

Great egret

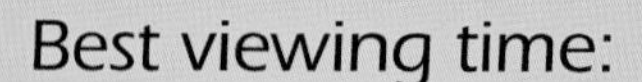

How do I get there?

Maps: MN Highway Coordinate: G-16
PRIM Area: Litchfield
DeLorme MN Atlas Grid #: 39 C-9

Additional directions:

Drive 10 miles north of Hutchinson until you see the island on the east side of Highway 15. This spot overlooks the northwest corner of the lake and one of the island rookeries.

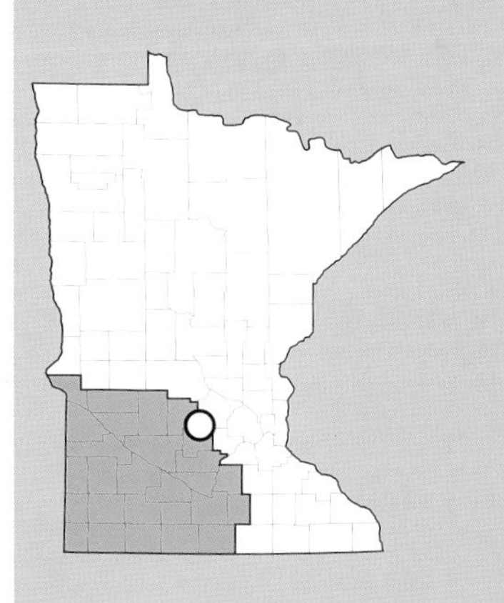

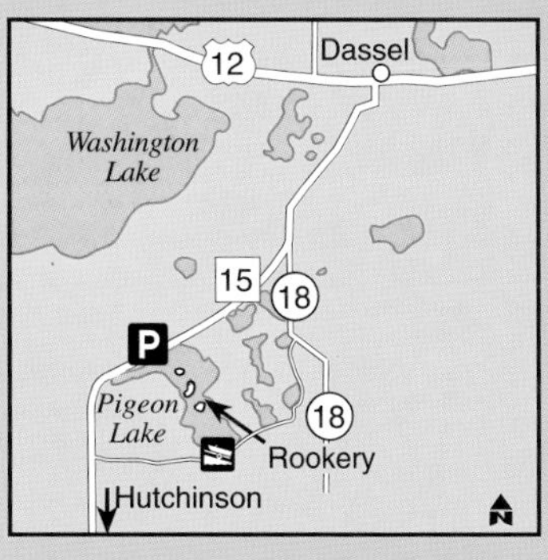

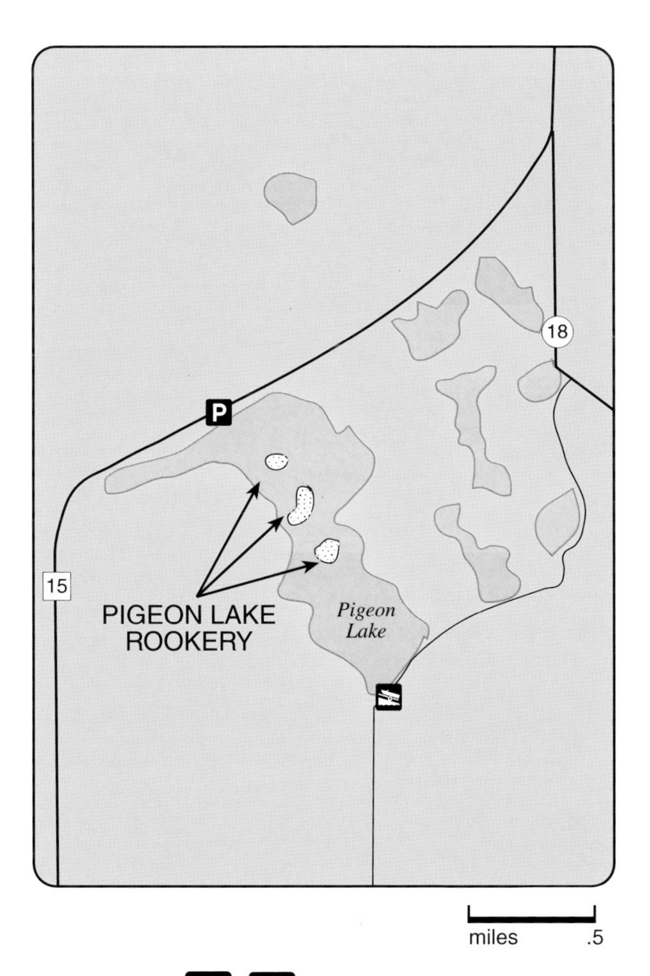

miles .5

Facilities:

Recreational Opportunities:

Contact:

Nongame Wildlife Program
DNR
261 Highway 15 S.
New Ulm MN 56073-8915
(507) 359-6033

67–Schaefer Prairie

Why is this area special?

One third of Minnesota was once covered by grasslands. Now less than one tenth of one percent of the original prairie remains. Schaefer Prairie is one of the only tallgrass prairie areas left in south central Minnesota.

C. Henderson

Bobolink

This 160-acre site contains marshes, several ponds, a creek and its floodplain. While the prairie is not large enough to support the complete prairie ecosystem that once defined the area, blooming prairie wildflowers such as milkweed still attract monarch butterflies. Monarch caterpillars depend largely on milkweed as a major food source even though it's toxic to many other creatures. Bad-tasting chemicals from the milkweed help protect monarchs from the birds.

Other wildlife you might see at this site include savanna and vesper sparrows, ring-necked pheasants, bobolinks and western meadowlarks. Look for plant communities that contain big bluestem, purple prairie clover and sunflowers. Visit this area every few weeks throughout the spring and summer because the colorful wildflowers are constantly changing.

Note:

Though the prairie was mowed annually from 1910–1941, you can still find more than 245 native plants on this Nature Conservancy preserve. Schaefer Prairie's size makes it vulnerable to encroachment by trees but, through proper fire management, the cottonwoods and other undesirable species are controlled.

When you visit this area, disturb it as little as possible and remember that you're not allowed to collect plants, seeds or butterflies. There are no trails or facilities.

C. Henderson

Monarch butterfly

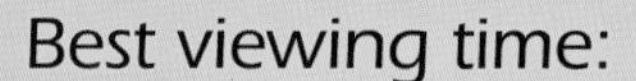

Best viewing time:

How do I get there?

Maps: MN Highway Coordinate: H-17
PRIM Area: Glencoe
DeLorme MN Atlas Grid #: 31 A-9

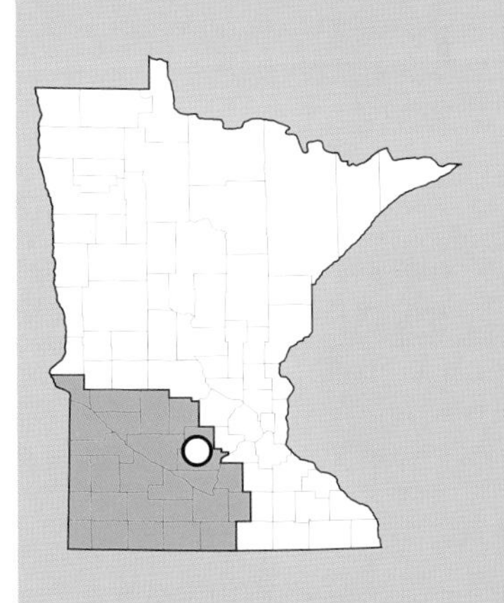

Additional directions:

From Glencoe, drive seven miles west on Highway 212 and turn south on a gravel road (Nature Avenue) opposite County Road 4. Drive for half a mile to the first intersection. The prairie is at the southwest corner of that intersection. Proceed on the gravel road and park on the SE corner field road. Do not park across from the residences on the north and east sides.

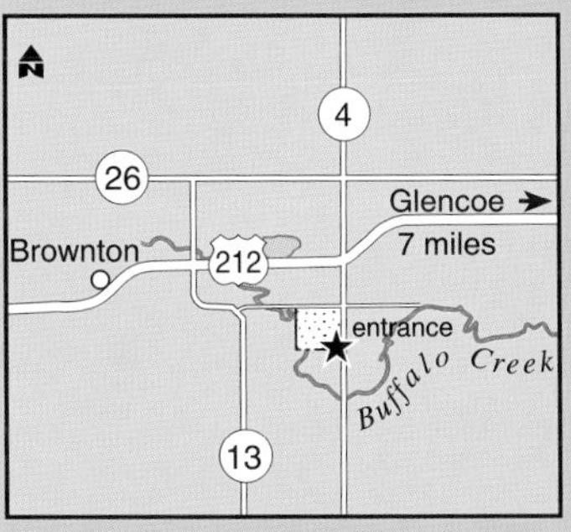

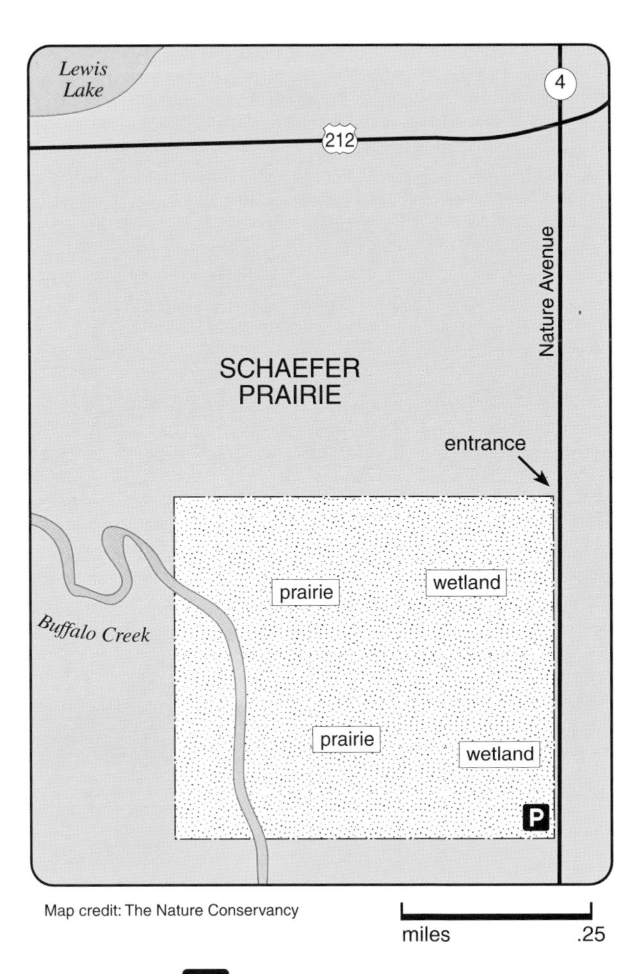

Map credit: The Nature Conservancy

Facilities: P

Recreational Opportunities:

Contact:

The Nature Conservancy
Mn. Chapter
1313 5th St. SE
Minneapolis MN 55414-1588
(612) 331-0750

68–Swede's Forest SNA

Why is this area special?

Within the Minnesota River Valley, the rugged landscape of Swede's Forest Scientific and Natural Area provides habitat for the rare five-lined skink. These small blue-tailed lizards are sometimes called "blue devils".

In our state, this skink is confined to rock outcrops within deciduous woodlands such as those found in the upper parts of the Minnesota River Valley, and in the southeastern part of the state. One of only two lizards to call this area home, these skinks are isolated from the main range of the species in the eastern United States.

C. Henderson

Gray fox

Fire suppression in the River Valley has allowed red cedar to encroach on the open grasslands and reduce skink habitat by covering the open, sunny spots they need. Dense stands of eastern red cedar are being removed by controlled burning and cutting to improve skink habitat and restore a more natural prairie setting.

Small wetlands in the SNA also make the area suitable for painted turtles, waterfowl, great blue herons and red-winged blackbirds. Look also for white-tailed deer, downy woodpeckers, loggerhead shrikes and eastern bluebirds.

Note:

The rock comprising the outcrops in Swede's Forest and the Granite Falls area is known as gneiss (pronounced "nice"). It is believed to be some of the oldest rock in the world, formed nearly 3.5 billion years ago.

A. B. Sheldon

Five-lined skink

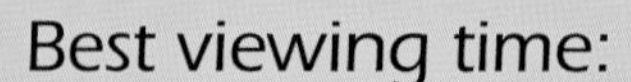

Best viewing time:

How do I get there?

Maps: MN Highway Coordinate: E-17
PRIM Area: Montevideo
DeLorme MN Atlas Grid #: 29 A-9

Additional directions:

Take County Road 7 north of Belview for five miles and turn west on an unmarked gravel road. A parking area is on the south side of the road after about 2 miles.

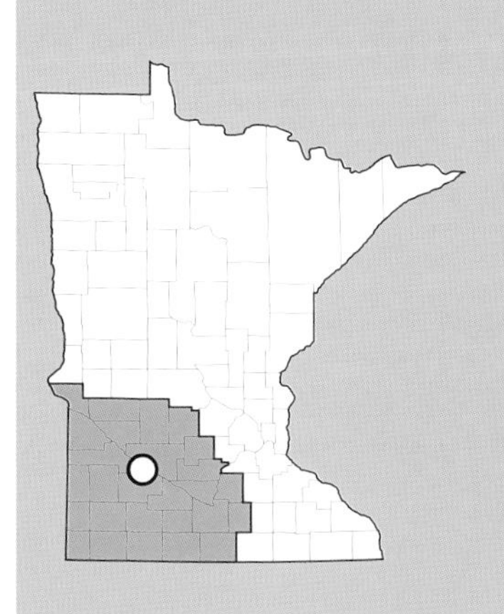

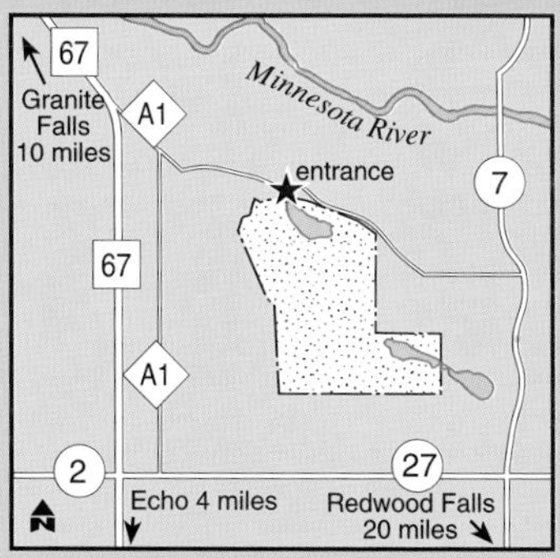

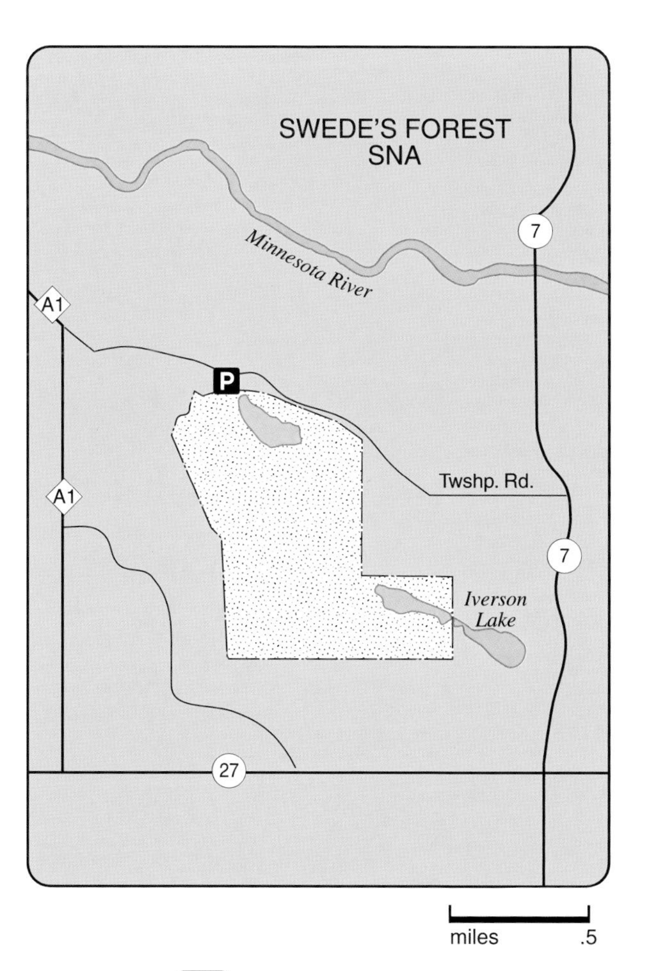

Facilities:

Recreational Opportunities:

Contact:

Scientific and Natural Areas Program
DNR
Box 25
500 Lafayette Rd.
St. Paul MN 55155
(612) 297-2357

69–Camden State Park/ Prairie Marshes WMA

Why is this area special?

Camden State Park is rich in resources and has been used by people for 8,000 years. Bison, elk, wolves and sharp-tailed grouse were all once a part of the ecosystem. Springs entering the Redwood River create a cold water environment. That in turn allows brown trout to be stocked in the Redwood River and provides visitors with a chance to fish. The blooming wildflowers in spring, abundant wildlife in summer, colorful woodlands in the fall and the scenic view of the river valley on a winter day make Camden an enjoyable place to visit any time of year.

R. Dana

Regal fritillary

The park lies on the second highest and easternmost moraine in the Coteau des Prairie. Woodlands, which lie in the 150-foot deep river valley, are relatively rare in southwestern Minnesota and provide an oasis for woodland birds not typically found in the prairie landscape.

Red-bellied woodpeckers, rose-breasted grosbeaks, indigo buntings and pileated woodpeckers are all common here. As a direct result of nest boxes, eastern bluebirds are also breeding in the area. Wild turkeys have been introduced to the park vicinity and are becoming more abundant with each passing season. Look too for vesper sparrows, red-tailed hawks and regal fritillary butterflies. You might also find mammals like mink, raccoons and coyotes. In winter, white-tailed deer congregate in the park.

Wetlands and prairie on the **Prairie Marshes Wildlife Management Area** provide habitat for waterfowl and several other species of grassland wildlife like dickcissels and bobolinks. Look for plants such as pasqueflower, prairie smoke, purple coneflower and blazing star.

Note:

Park trails make viewing wildlife more enjoyable. To protect the park, stay on the trails and obey all signs. There are no major prairie habitats in the state park, but if you want to experience the beauty of a native prairie and wetland complex, visit the nearby 277-acre Prairie Marshes WMA northwest of Camden State Park. There is an excellent variety of prairie wildflowers and butterflies in the spring and summer, and a good variety of prairie waterfowl during the spring, summer and fall on the large marsh.

Best viewing time:

 Hunting allowed on the WMA. Call ahead for hunting season dates.

How do I get there?

Maps: MN Highway Coordinate: D-19
PRIM Area: Marshall
DeLorme MN Atlas Grid #: 29 D-5

Additional directions:

Take Highway 23 for ten miles southwest from Marshall. The park entrance is on the west side of Highway 23 about 2 miles southwest of Lynd. **The Prairie Marshes WMA** is 3 miles north of Russell on Highway 15 and half a mile west on an unimproved field driveway. The field driveway that goes into the Prairie Marshes WMA can be very muddy and impassable after rains. If you have a car with two-wheel drive and low clearance or if it has rained recently, walk in from County Road 15.

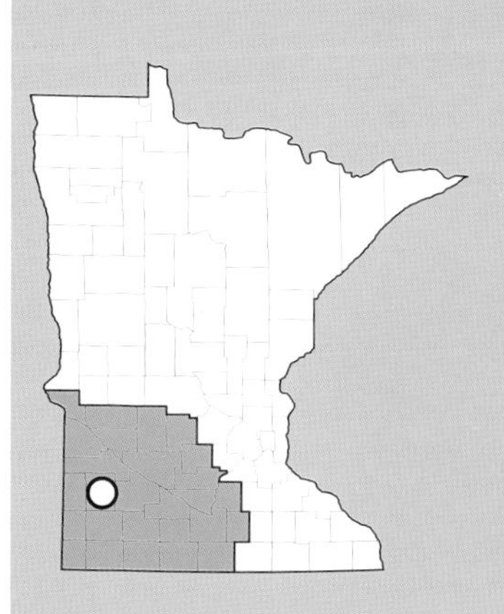

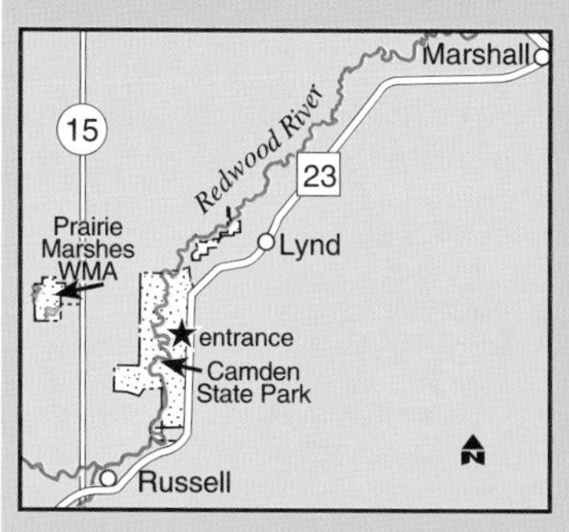

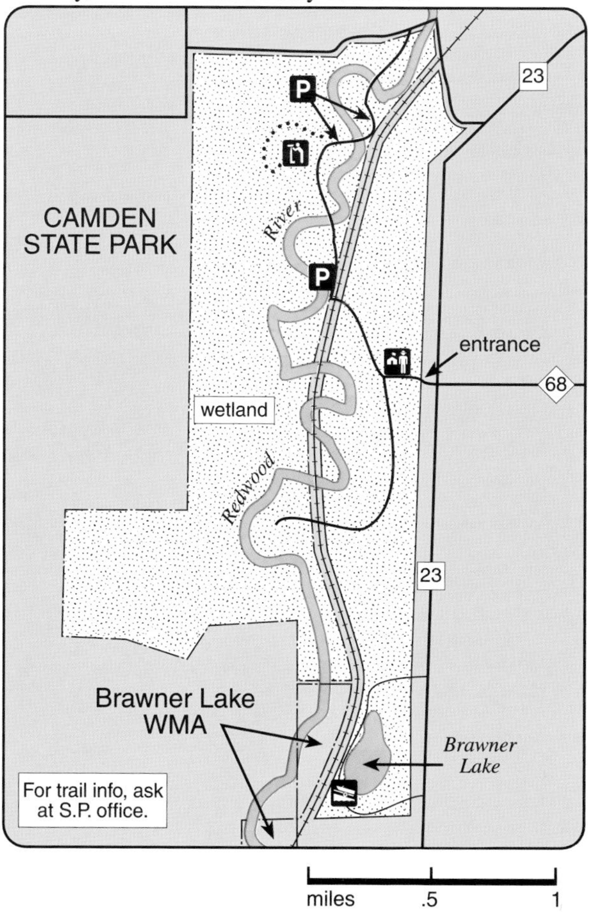

Facilities:

Recreational Opportunities:

Contact:

DNR Area Wildlife Office
1400 E. Lyon St.
Box 111
Marshall MN 56258
(507) 537-6250

Camden State Park
RR 1 Box 49
Lynd MN 56157
(507) 865-4530

70–Hole-in-the-Mountain WMA/TNC/ County Park

Why is this area special?

You could spend a whole day watching the many common and rare butterflies fluttering among the wildflowers of Hole-in-the-Mountain prairie. This prairie provides habitat to more than 25 butterfly species. The Dakota skipper, a Minnesota threatened species, makes its home on this 300-acre site. This spot is one of the state's few remaining areas suitable for the Dakota skipper, dependent on undisturbed, mid-grass prairies with purple coneflower. You may also find Richardson's ground squirrel.

The TNC land, WMA and county park lie within the Coteau des Prairie, a flat highland that formed between the James and Des Moines river basins before glacial times. Its plant communities include 200 species of wild flowers, such as the small white lady's slipper, goldenrod, purple prairie clover, blazing star and purple coneflower. In addition, there are 60 species of native grasses in the area.

C. Henderson

Richardson's ground squirrel

The park's oak woodlands have invaded the prairie and offer habitat for woodland birds. Other species present are Wilson's snipes, savannah, vesper and clay-colored sparrows, bobolinks and dickcissels. You might spot a Blanding's turtle in the wetlands.

Note:

Hole-in-the-Mountain SNA is one of several wildlife areas near Lake Benton. The adjacent WMA and county park also provide habitat for additional wildlife.

Amenities, including camping, are available at the County Park one-half mile west of Lake Benton on the south side of Highway 14.

 Hunting allowed (WMA only). Call ahead for hunting season dates.

Best viewing time:

How do I get there?

Maps: MN Highway Coordinate: B-15
PRIM Area: Marshall
DeLorme MN Atlas Grid #: 28 D/E-2

Additional directions:

From Lake Benton, take Highway 75 south for one and a half miles.

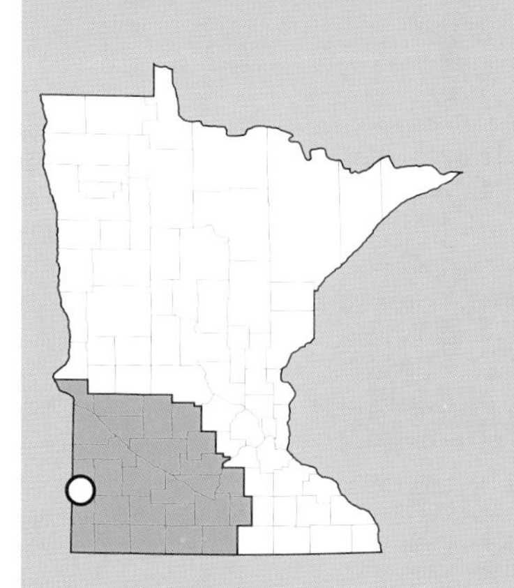

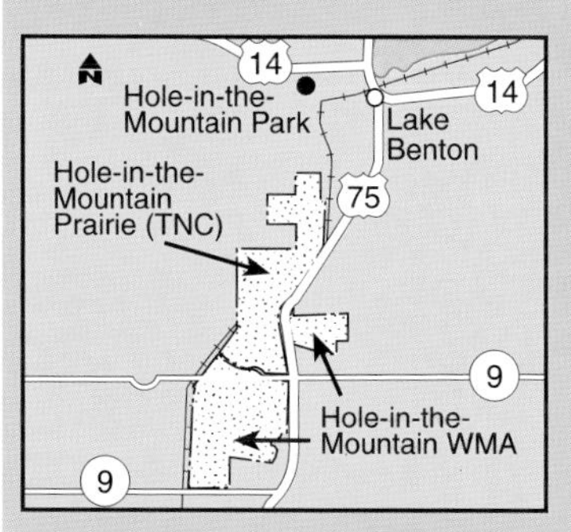

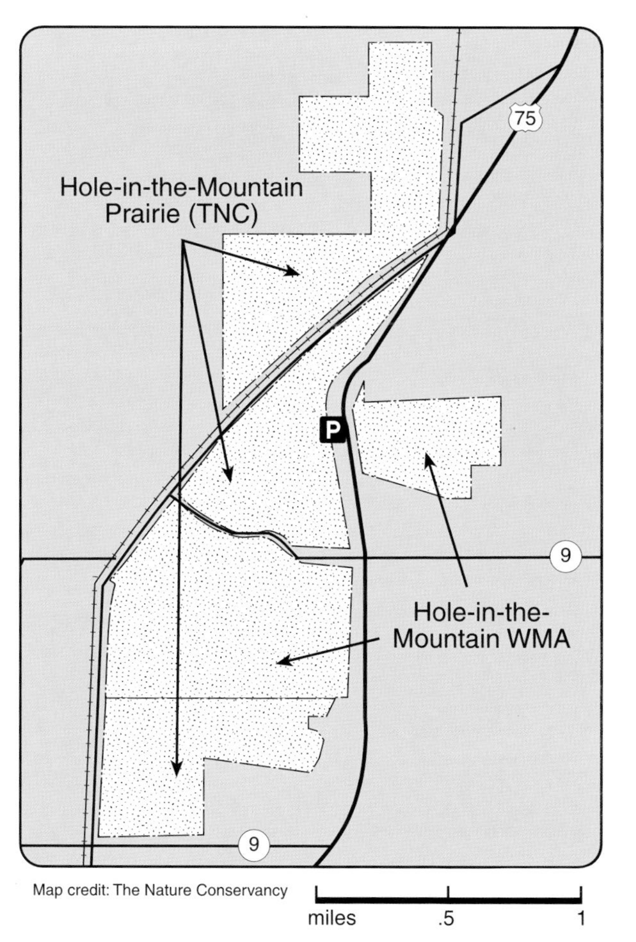

Map credit: The Nature Conservancy

miles .5 1

Facilities:

Recreational Opportunities:

Contact:

DNR Area Wildlife Office
1400 E Lyon St.
Box 111
Marshall MN 56258
(507) 537-6250

The Nature Conservancy
MN Chapter
1313 5th St SE
Minneapolis MN 55414-1588
(612) 331-0750

Hole-in-the-Mountain Park
Lincoln County Parks Dept.
Ivanhoe MN 56142
(507) 368-9350

71–Flandrau State Park

Why is this area special?

Flandrau State Park lies within the Cottonwood River Valley bordering New Ulm. The river flows southeast through the park's 150-foot-deep valley. Several forest communities, prairie knolls and the oxbow marshes, formed by the river's previous path, join together to provide habitat for more than 60 species of birds and 25 mammals.

Minnesota's largest woodpecker, the pileated, can be found in the park. It is a large red-crested, crow-sized woodpecker that feeds on insects in the rotting wood of dead and dying trees. Cavities excavated by pileated woodpeckers provide nesting places for other birds and animals such as wood ducks and fox squirrels.

C. Henderson

Pileated woodpecker

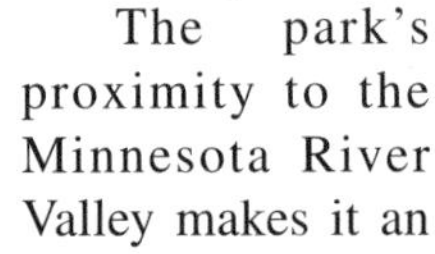

The park's proximity to the Minnesota River Valley makes it an exceptional area to watch woodland wildlife and migrating songbirds. Broad-winged hawks nest in the park and can often be seen circling overhead. Eastern bluebirds inhabit the prairie knolls and large herds of white-tailed deer use the park as a winter refuge.

Other species that make their homes here include indigo buntings, Baltimore orioles, belted kingfishers, ruby-throated hummingbirds, wood thrushes, blue-gray gnatcatchers, beavers, mink and red fox.

The park is home to many species of plant life, too: bur oak, eastern red cedar, aspen, basswood, sugar maple, big bluestem, Indian grass, butterfly milkweed, blazing star and prairie sunflowers are among them.

Note:

Nearby Swan Lake (site72) provides more opportunities for wildlife watching.

Best viewing time:

How do I get there?

Maps: MN Highway Coordinate: G-19
PRIM Area: New Ulm
DeLorme MN Atlas Grid #: 31 D-8

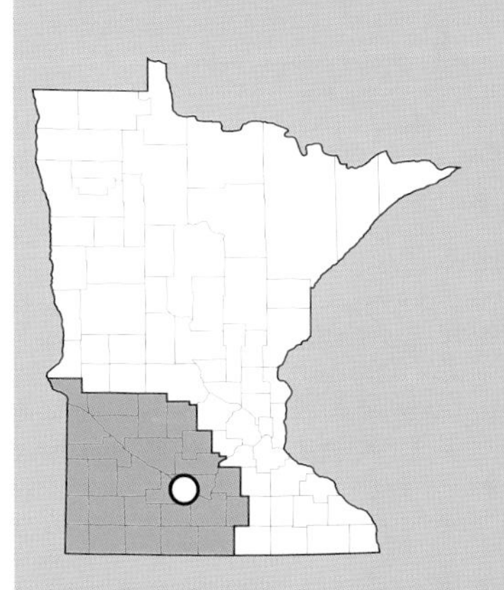

Additional directions:

Located on the southwest edge of New Ulm, Flandrau State Park may be reached by turning southwest on Center Street from Highway 14. Continue on Center Street to Summit Avenue and turn southeast. The entrance to the park is just over one mile from Center Street along Summit Avenue.

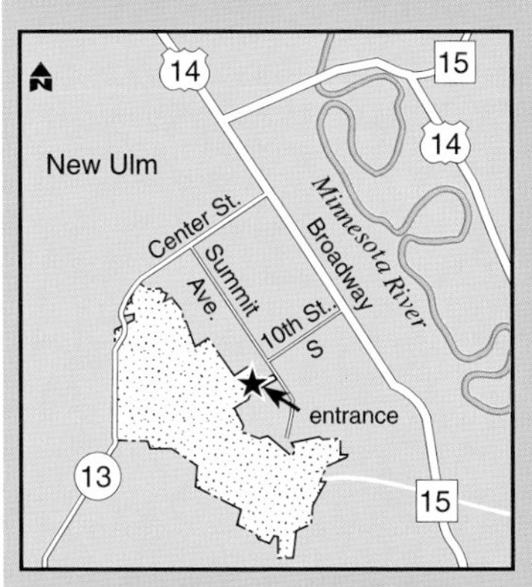

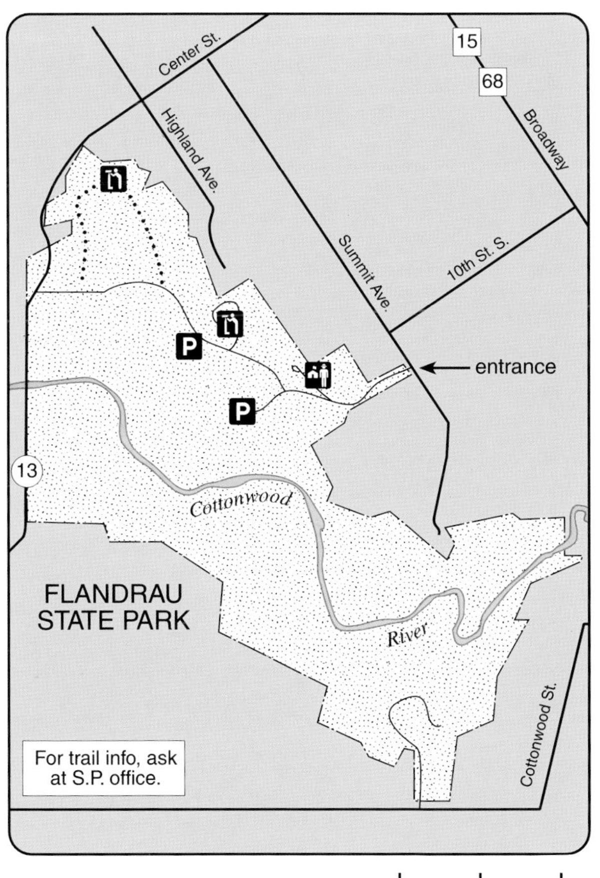

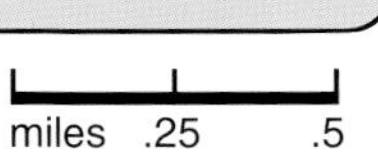

Facilities:

Recreational Opportunities:     

Contact:

Flandrau State Park
1300 Summit Ave.
New Ulm MN 56073
(507) 354-3519

72–Swan Lake

Why is this area special?

In the heart of south central Minnesota is one of the best and largest wetland complexes in North America: Swan Lake. This 10,000-acre, relatively undisturbed marsh wonderland is a place to experience the diversity and beauty of prairie wetlands as they once existed. Serious degradation of natural plant and animal communities has not occurred, and much of the native vegetation is still present. Aquatic plants and shoreline sedges and grasses that are difficult to find in other areas of southwest Minnesota exist here.

C. Henderson

Trumpeter swan

Game refuges and wildlife management areas within the boundaries of the lake provide migrating birds with a safe haven during the fall. The songs and calls of marsh wrens, yellow-headed blackbirds, soras, Virginia rails and American bitterns echo through the spring and summer.

Redheads, mallards, wood ducks, western and eared grebes, black terns and Forster's terns all thrive in this wetland haven. Colonies of more than 100 nesting Forster's terns have been observed here. The open water, land and islands provide nesting habitat for black-crowned night-herons, least bitterns, and yellow-headed blackbirds. Swan Lake has one of the state's largest nesting concentrations of western grebes. Trumpeter swans have been reported in the area, and may once again begin nesting here.

You will find animals such as mink, muskrats and white-tailed deer as well as plants like bulrushes, cattails, phragmites, sedges, willow and water lilies here.

Note:

A canoe trip is the best way to enjoy the lake; however, the vegetation grows quite high and people have become lost in the channels and bays created by cattails and bulrushes. Use landmarks as you travel through the marsh, take a compass or GPS unit, and tell someone where you are going and when you expect to be back.

While in the area, stop by Flandrau State Park (site 71) for additional wildlife watching.

Hunting allowed. Call ahead for hunting season dates.

Best viewing time:

How do I get there?

Maps: MN Highway Coordinate: H-19
PRIM Area: New Ulm
DeLorme MN Atlas Grid #: 31 D-9,10

Additional directions:

Located north of Highway 14 between Nicollet and Courtland, Swan Lake has several public accesses. To access the south side of the lake, take Highway 14 for a quarter of a mile west of Nicollet and turn north at the public water access signs. On the north side of the lake, take Highway 111 north of Nicollet for about four miles. Turn west on County Road 5 for 2.5 miles. Turn south on County Road 64 and continue for a mile. Turn west and follow a gravel road to the public access.

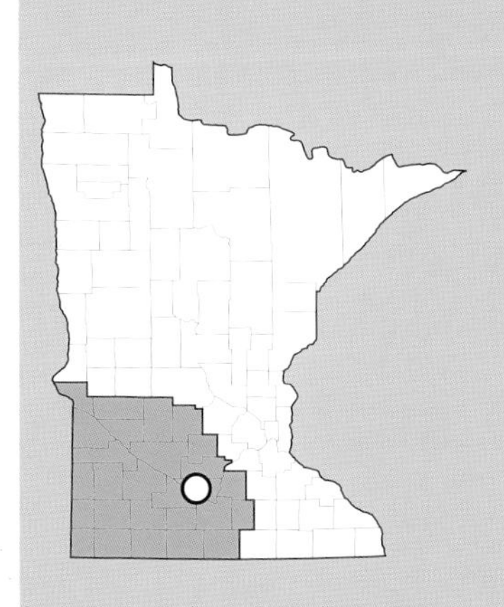

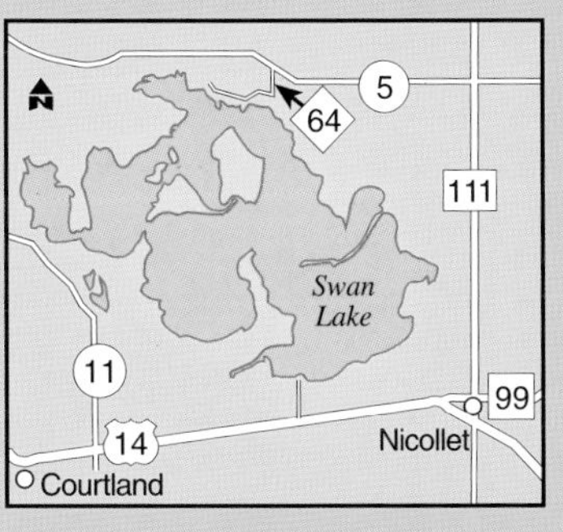

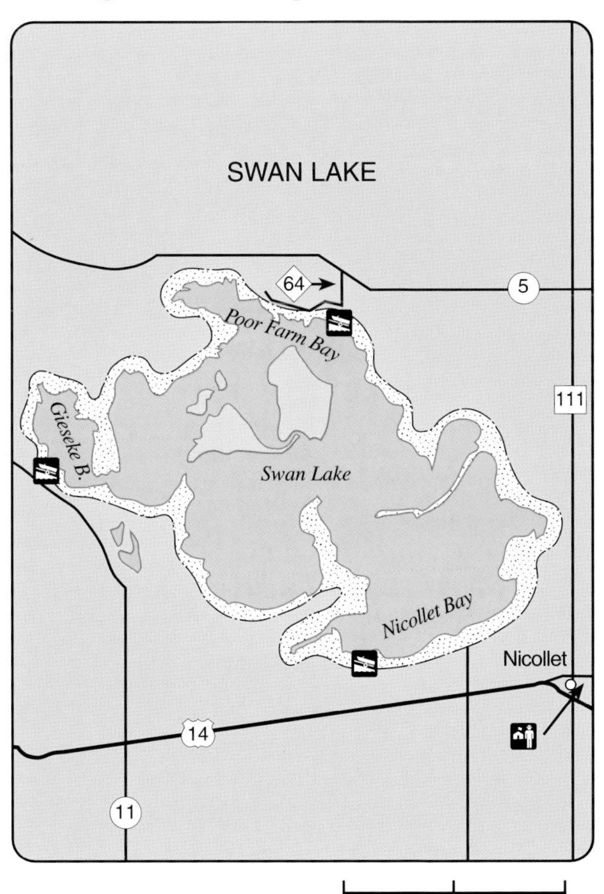

Facilities:

Recreational Opportunities:

Contact:

DNR Area Wildlife Office
501 9th St.
Box 79
Nicollet MN 56074
(507) 225-3572

73–Seven Mile Creek County Park

Why is this area special?

Nestled in the ravines and hills of the Minnesota River Valley, the fast-moving waters of Seven Mile Creek have cut through the land to form a picturesque valley bordering a fast-moving stream.

Lying on the eastern edge of the region, this site is within a transition zone of the grasslands to the west and the deciduous forests to the east. The path cut by Seven Mile Creek offers an excellent place to view wildlife of deciduous woodlands. The forests, home to white-tailed deer and wild turkeys, are also excellent areas to see nesting and migrating bird species.

C. Henderson

Red-headed woodpecker

Of particular interest is the occasional sighting of a cerulean warbler. At the edge of their range, cerulean warblers have nested in the area. These blue-backed and white-breasted warblers prefer deciduous woods near river bottoms or stream sides like those of Seven Mile Creek.

You can see many other woodland songbirds here, like yellow-rumped, chestnut-sided and blackpoll warblers. Keep your eye out for red and gray foxes, cottontail rabbits and pileated woodpeckers. Bur oak, green ash, basswood, sugar maple, hackberries and black cherries are among the tree species found in this region.

Best viewing time:

How do I get there?

Maps: MN Highway Coordinate: H-19
PRIM Area: New Ulm
DeLorme MN Atlas Grid #: 32 D-1

Additional directions:

From Mankato take Highway 169 north for five miles. The county park is located on the west side of Highway 169.

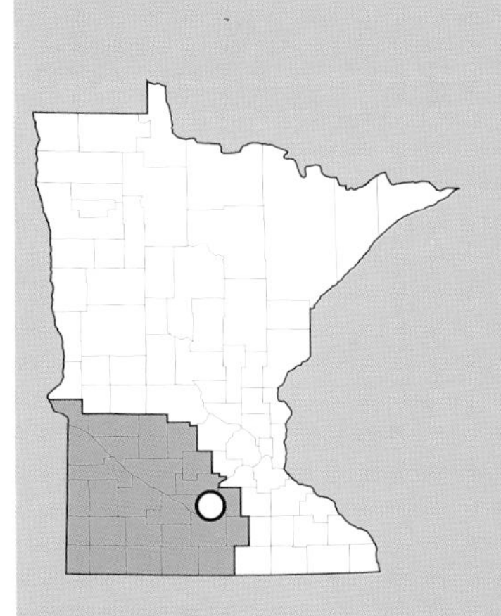

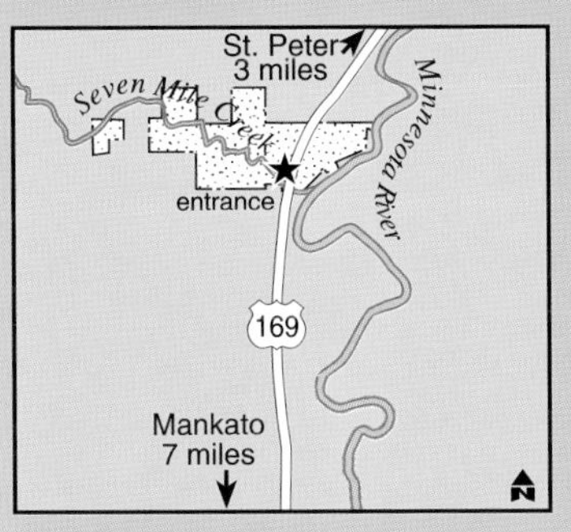

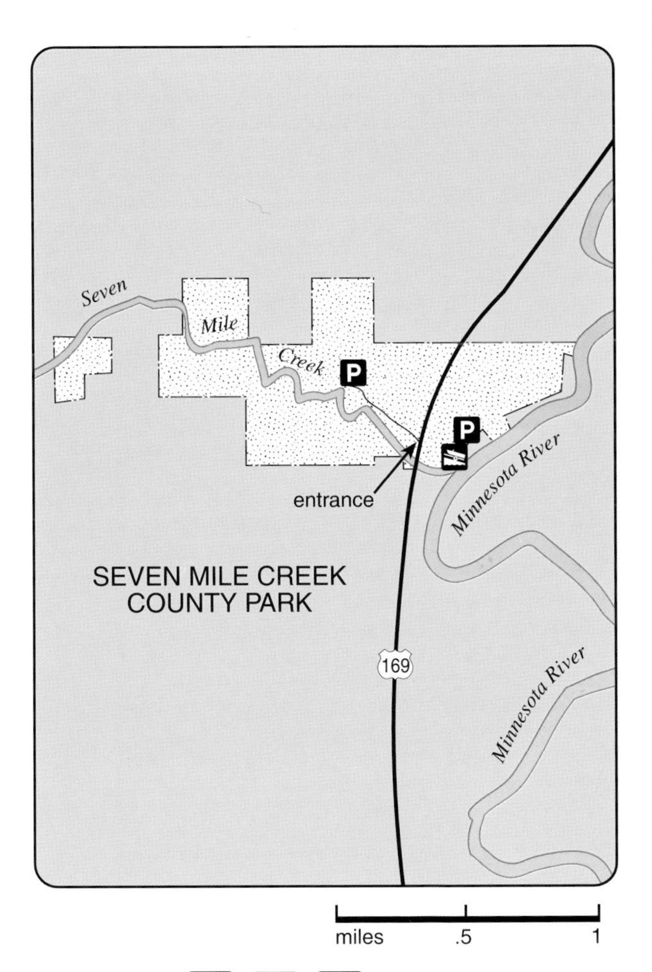

Facilities:

Recreational Opportunities:

Contact:

Nicollet County Public Works
1700 Sunrise Drive
Box 518
St. Peter MN 56082
(800) 247-5044

74–Kasota Prairie SNA

Why is this area special?

Kasota Prairie Scientific and Natural Area and the surrounding prairie are some of the largest remaining shortgrass prairielands in this region. The prairie lies on a rock terrace above the Minnesota River Valley, which in the past was flooded by the Glacial River Warren.

Due to thin soils this prairie was never plowed, but it was mowed for hay.

The soils of the terrace are only about 12 inches deep yet still support wet meadow, oak woodland and hardwood communities. The communities are managed by periodic burning. Other plants in the vicinity include wild plum and wolfberry.

A. B. Sheldon

Eastern milk snake

This site is in almost continuous bloom from the first pasqueflowers in April to the last gentians in October. Visit several times to see other species such as yellow prairie violet, palespike lobelia, sunflowers and yellow nutsedge.

The scattered trees and shrubs of the 38-acre Kasota Prairie SNA and the surrounding Eastern Minnesota Game Refuge provide habitat for the threatened loggerhead shrike. These shrikes have become less common due to the destruction of the open prairie habitat they prefer. Shrikes use the scattered trees and brushy areas for nesting and as perches while hunting for grassland insects, small birds and mammals. They have a peculiar practice of impaling their prey on the branches of trees or on barbed wire fences. They do this so they can tear it apart or store it for later consumption.

White-tailed deer, ring-necked pheasants, blue racers, horned larks, upland sandpipers and butterflies are all common here.

Note:

The surrounding East Minnesota River Wildlife Refuge is a statutory refuge and is all private land.

No trails are marked so tread carefully on this fragile protected environment.

Best viewing time:

How do I get there?

Maps: MN Highway Coordinate: H-19
PRIM Area: New Ulm
DeLorme MN Atlas Grid #: 32 D-2

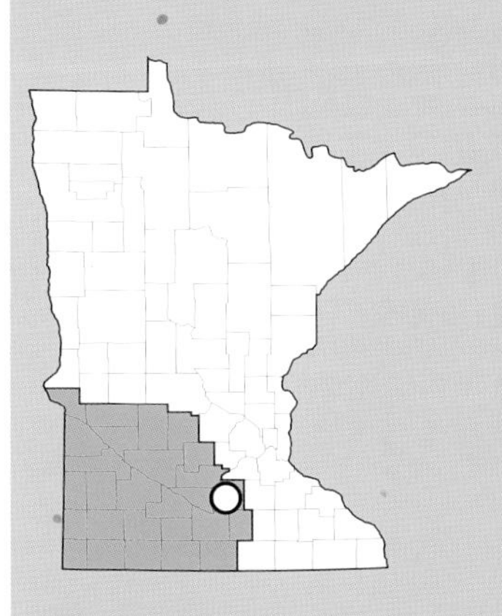

Additional directions:

This site is located on the east side of the Minnesota River. From St. Peter cross the Highway 22 bridge, turn south onto County Road 21 to the small town of Kasota. Take Highway 21 south of Kasota for two miles to County Road 101. Turn west on County Road 101 and drive for one and a half miles. Park on the east side of road.

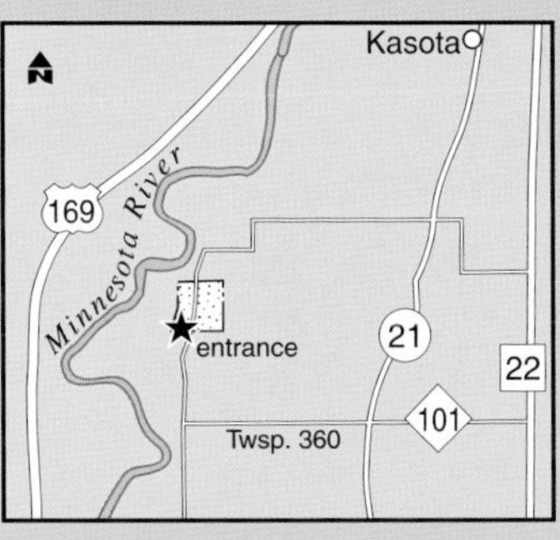

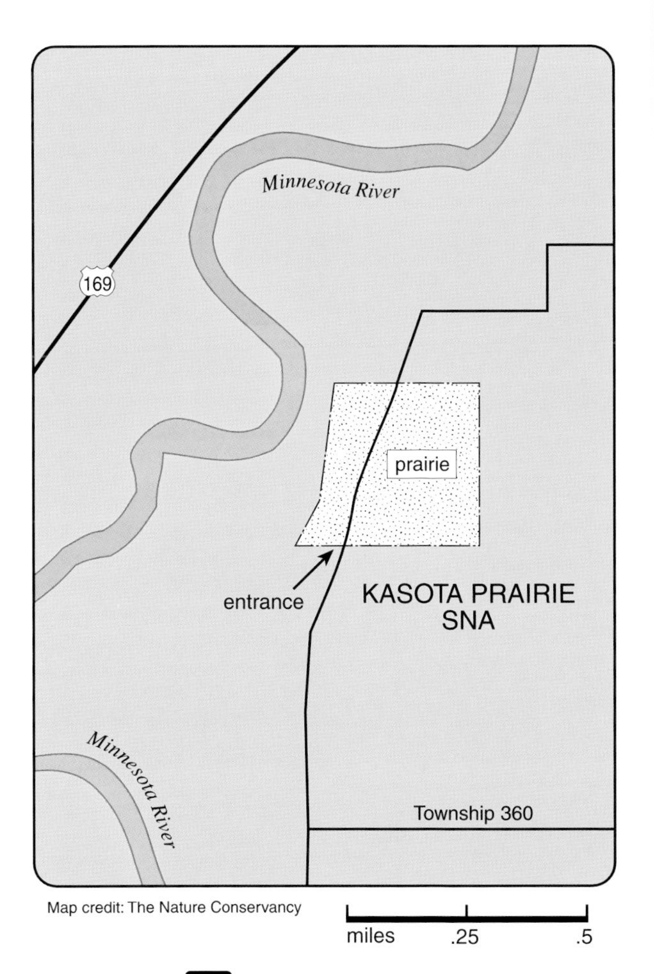

Map credit: The Nature Conservancy

miles .25 .5

Facilities: P

Recreational Opportunities:

Contact:

Scientific and Natural Areas Program
DNR
Box 25
500 Lafayette Rd.
St. Paul MN 55155
(612) 297-2357

75–Pipestone National Monument

Why is this area special?

Pipestone (catlinite) quarries, quartzite bluffs and native tallgrass prairie make Pipestone National Monument a great place to watch wildlife in a historic setting. Listen to the calls and songs of savannah, grasshopper, vesper, and clay-colored sparrows. Bobolinks, horned larks, dickcissels and western meadowlarks also inhabit the area and watch too for field sparrows, downy woodpeckers, eastern goldfinches, Baltimore orioles, orchard orioles and American woodcocks.

C. Henderson

Purple coneflower

Upland sandpipers, related to shorebirds but adapted for life in upland areas, may also be found in the grasslands. Their bubbling calls and wolf-whistles are special sounds in Minnesota's western prairies.

Other animals to look for at this site include white-tailed deer, beavers, muskrats, and painted turtles. Check this area for prairie falcons in winter.

Plant communities include big bluestem, purple prairie clover, yellow lady's slipper, blazing star, purple coneflower, yellow coneflower, Indian grass and prairie cordgrass.

Note:

At one time, American Indians mined the pipestone and used it to make ceremonial pipes and other objects. Due to its cultural significance to American Indians, this area is protected by the federal government. This protection helped preserve the native tallgrass prairie. This expanse of big bluestem and other prairie grasses and wildflowers offer a historic view of one of the largest remaining prairie areas in Minnesota.

Best viewing time:

How do I get there?

Maps: MN Highway Coordinate: B-20
PRIM Area: Marshall
DeLorme MN Atlas Grid #: 19 A/B-2

Additional directions:

From the junction of Highway 30 and Highway 75 in Pipestone, take Highway 75 one mile north. Turn west on 9th Street for a half mile.

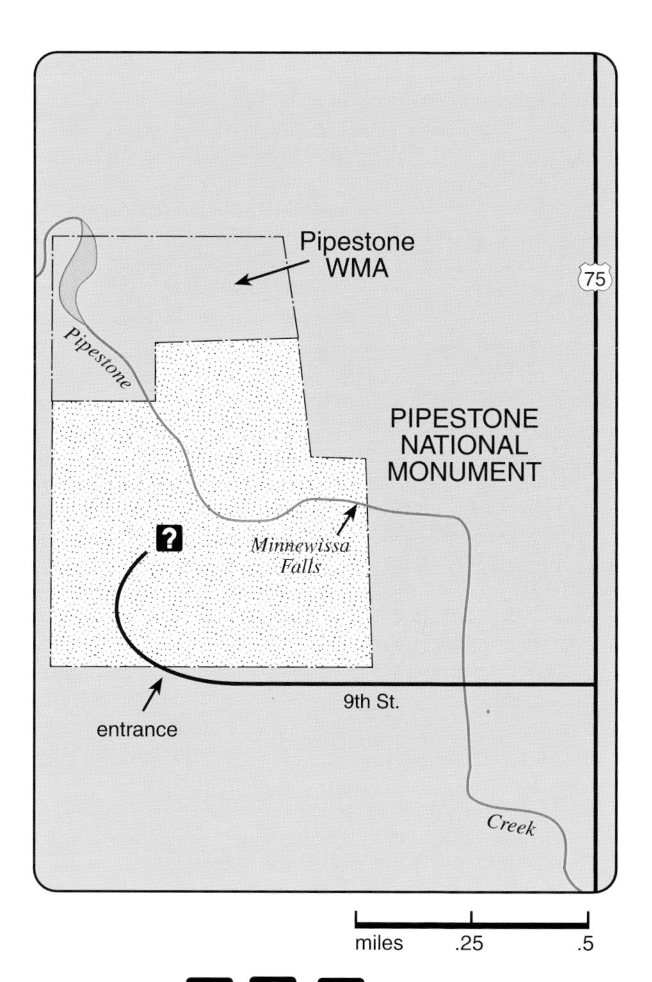

Facilities:

Recreational Opportunities:

Contact:

Pipestone National Monument
P.O. Box 127
Pipestone MN 56164
(507) 825-5464

76–Talcot Lake WMA

Why is this area special?

This 4,000-acre WMA and game refuge found along the West Branch of the Des Moines River consists of marshes, bottomlands, uplands and agricultural areas. Large flocks of migratory waterfowl, particularly Canada geese, use the lake during the fall migration. The eastern prairie population of Canada geese, which nests on the west shore of Hudson Bay, stop to feed and rest at Talcot Lake during migration to wintering grounds in Missouri. You might also see giant Canada geese nesting here in the summer.

C. Henderson

Yellow-headed blackbird

Talcot Lake WMA is one of the largest areas set aside for wildlife in southwest Minnesota. The lake and many marsh areas in the WMA are formed by a dam on the site's east side and by 2,000 feet of dikes within the WMA. Marshes and upland areas are managed to provide nesting habitat for many wildlife species, including American bitterns, sora and Virginia rails, common yellowthroats, northern cardinals, indigo buntings, bobolinks, ring-necked pheasants, gray partridges, northern harriers and several species of sparrows.

Mammals such as beavers, muskrats, white-tailed deer, red foxes and mink make this site their home.

Note:

Parking areas in the WMA allow wildlife to be conveniently viewed from several spots. Use primitive trails to get closer to wildlife. Motorboats are not allowed on the lake when migratory birds are present. Public use of the WMA is encouraged, but sanctuary areas are designated where trespassing is not permitted. A headquarters staffed by a resident wildlife manager is located on the premises.

A county park on the south side of the lake offers recreational opportunities.

Visit nearby Heron Lake (site 78) while you're in the area to see more wildlife.

Best viewing time:

 Hunting allowed. Call ahead for hunting season dates.

How do I get there?

Maps: MN Highway Coordinate: E-20
PRIM Area: Worthington
DeLorme MN Atlas Grid #: 20 B-4

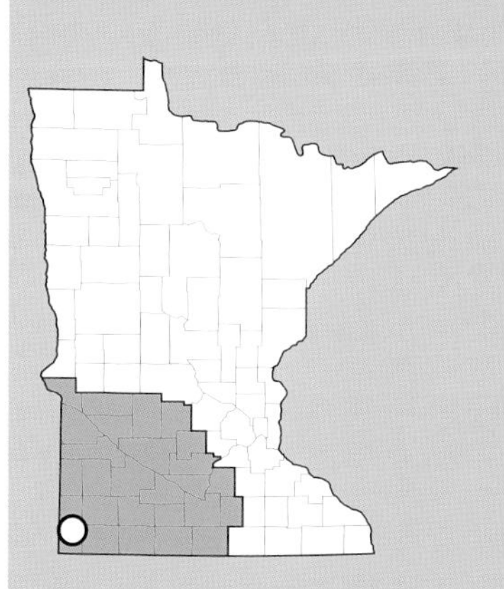

Additional directions:

This WMA is between the towns of Westbrook and Dundee. From Westbrook, take Highway 7 south for nine miles. The management area and headquarters is to the west of County Road 7.

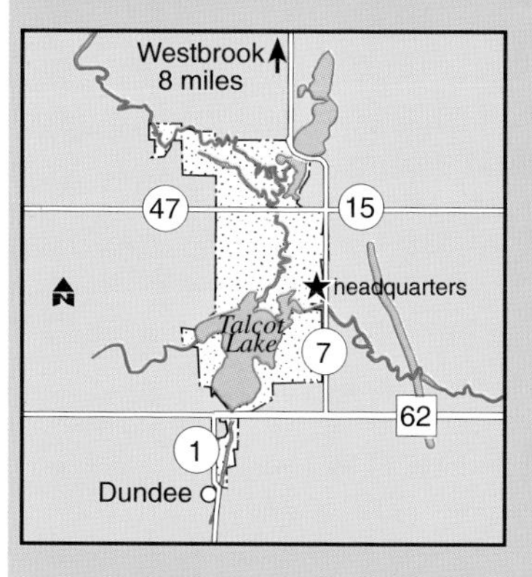

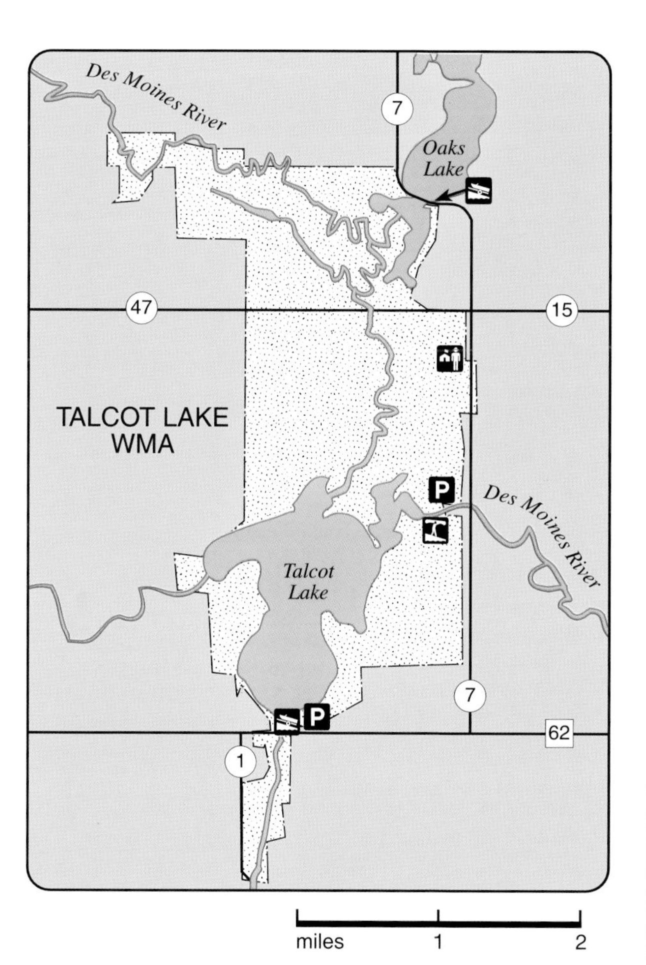

Facilities:

Recreational Opportunities:   

Contact:

DNR Wildlife Area Office
Talcot Lake WMA
RR 3 Box 534
Dundee MN 56131
(507) 468-2248

77–Blue Mounds State Park

Why is this area special?

Approximately 1,500 acres of prairie and grasslands make Blue Mounds one of the largest prairie parks in the state. The park lies on top of a large outcrop of Sioux quartzite that forms a mound almost two miles long and 100 feet above the surrounding land. Lichen, which grows on the exposed rock, is blue and gives the area its name.

A small herd of bison roams the park, giving visitors a glimpse of the area's past prairie heritage. At one time, huge herds of bison naturally managed prairie grasses through grazing.

This site is on the uplands of the Coteau des Prairie which separates the Missouri and Minnesota River drainages. While native prairie is present, it has been altered by heavy grazing and lack of natural prairie fires. Current management will restore the prairie through controlled burns, rotational grazing and noxious weed control.

C. Henderson

Bison

Plants growing here include needlegrass, big and little bluestem, prickly pear cactus and buffalo grass. Look for coyotes, red fox, white-tailed jackrabbits, bull and fox snakes, bobolinks, and savannah, swamp and clay-colored sparrows. Rare species such as blue grosbeaks and lined snakes have been reported, and vagrant species from the west, such as Say's phoebe and burrowing owl, are occasionally spotted in the vicinity. A large herd of deer winters in the park.

Note:

Hiking and skiing trails can be used to view wildlife throughout the park.

Best viewing time:

How do I get there?

Maps: MN Highway Coordinate: C-21
PRIM Area: Worthington
DeLorme MN Atlas Grid #: 19 D-3

Additional directions:

The park can be reached by taking Highway 75 for just over three miles north of Luverne. Turn east on County Road 20 for one mile to the park entrance and headquarters. The visitor center is located on the south end of the park.

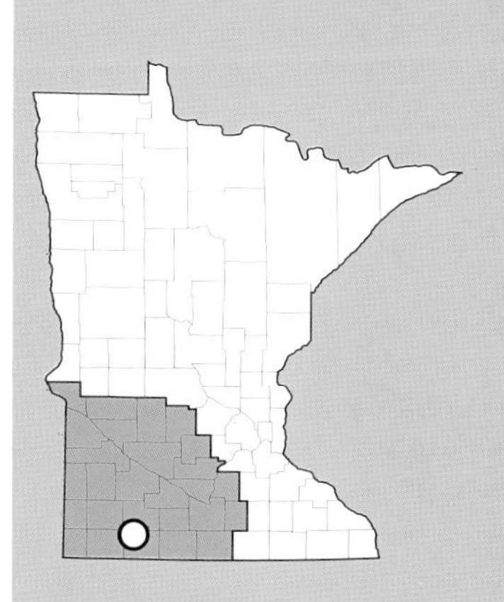

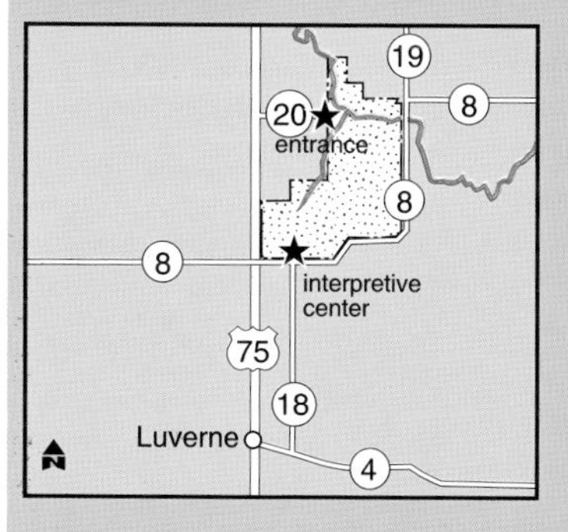

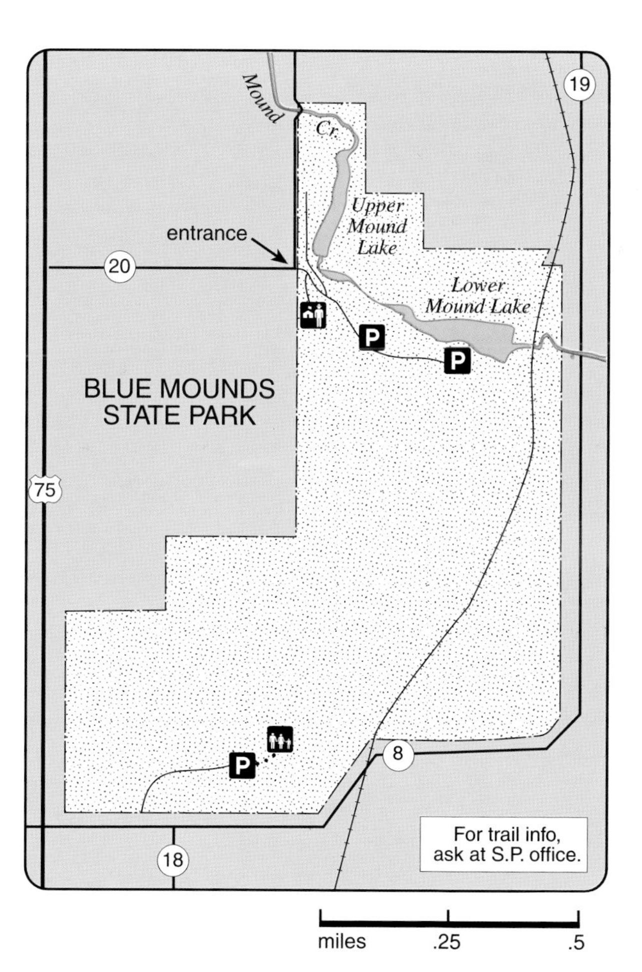

Facilities: 

Recreational Opportunities:   

Contact:

Blue Mounds State Park
RR 1
Luverne MN 56156
(507) 283-4548

78–Heron Lake System

Why is this area special?

Heron Lake is one of the largest prairie marsh systems in North America. This famous chain of wetlands lies in the heart of the prairie pothole region. Though the area has changed greatly, it is still an important migratory path and nesting area for birds. Thousands of waterfowl use the lake each spring and fall. Every spring a spectacular variety of migratory shorebirds rest and feed on the shoreline and mud flats.

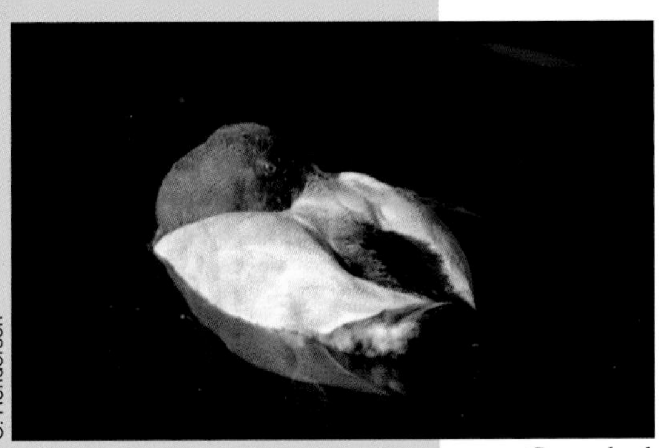

C. Henderson

Canvasback

The Heron Lake chain was once a famous canvasback haven but, due to the loss of wild celery beds, few canvasbacks now use the lake. As recently as the late 1980s, a large colony of Franklin's gulls nested on North Heron Lake. With 10,000 gulls in the area, it had one of the largest concentrations in the world. Fluctuating water levels due to tiling and drainage of adjacent lands destroyed the vegetation that the gulls needed for nesting.

Fortunately, new efforts are being made by the Heron Lake Game Producers Association, The Nature Conservancy and the DNR to improve the water level management of Heron Lake so it is a better habitat for wildlife.

Current summer residents are western grebes, Forster's and black terns, giant Canada geese and many American white pelicans and double-crested cormorants. Look for spotted sandpipers, trumpeter swans, ospreys and yellow-headed blackbirds. You might also see white-tailed deer.

Phragmites, cattails, bulrushes, spikerushes, arrowhead and duckweed make up much of the plant communities.

Best viewing time:

Note:

Both public and private groups have undertaken several projects to enhance the lake and restore native wildlife. In 1995, trumpeter swan releases began in hopes of restoring the swan. Osprey chicks from northern Minnesota have also been released to reestablish the osprey.

County parks on South Heron Lake provide shore viewing and a place to put a canoe in the lake. You can also watch wildlife on two areas owned by The Nature Conservancy on South Heron Lake.

 Hunting allowed. Call ahead for hunting season dates.

How do I get there?

Maps: MN Highway Coordinate: E-15
PRIM Area: Worthington
DeLorme MN Atlas Grid #: 21 C/D-5,6

Additional directions:

To reach the public access and Nature Conservancy land from Lakefield, take Highway 20 for about six miles northwest. Turn north on an unmarked gravel road for one mile, and turn east for another half mile.

To reach Community Point County Park, take Highway 86 north of Lakefield for one mile. Turn west on County Road 71 for nearly two miles.

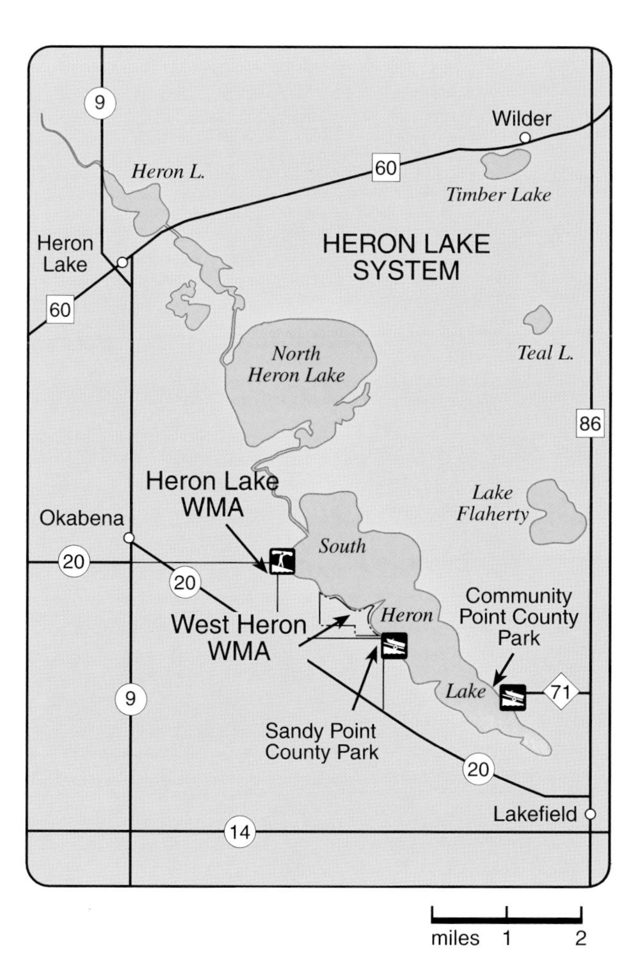

Facilities:   

Recreational Opportunities:  

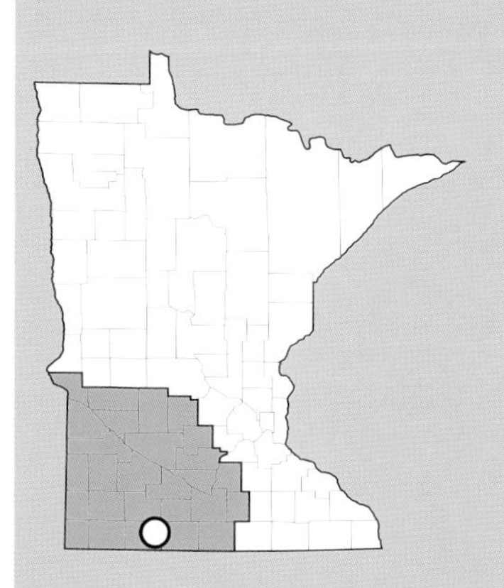

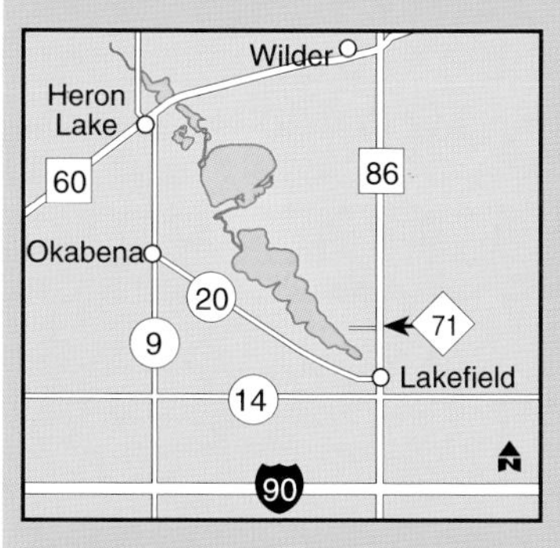

Contact:

DNR Area Wildlife Office
Windom MN 56101
(507) 831-2917

The Nature Conservancy
MN Chapter
313 5th St. SE
Minneapolis MN 55414-1588
(612) 331-0750

79–Kilen Woods State Park/ Prairie Bush Clover SNA

Why is this area special?

Kilen Woods State Park is located where the valley of the Des Moines River changes from a broad, open floodplain into a narrow wooded corridor. The steep hills and thin prairie soil are home to one of the midwest's rarest plants: the prairie bush clover. This is a federally-threatened species that inhabits well-drained and gravelly prairie areas. Evolving in a prairie environment, the prairie bush clover adapted to the frequent fires that were commonplace at one time. The **Prairie Bush Clover SNA** has been established within the state park to protect one of the largest populations of this rare plant.

C. Henderson

Rough blazingstar

The steep bluffs and ravines of the river valley protected the trees of the park from the prairie fires that once roared across the landscape. This topography also prevented cultivation attempts, but provided settlers with fuel, food and shelter in the harsh prairie environment.

The park also contains bottomland meadows and several limestone fens. Plant communities include prairie wildflowers, big bluestem, Indian grass, switch grass, gooseberries, cottonwood, maple, basswood, bur oak, green ash, hackberry, sedges, bulrushes and willows.

The bluffs, ravines and forest floodplain provide habitat for uncommon woodland species such as pileated woodpeckers. You might also see white-tailed deer, beavers, muskrats, weasels, mink, great blue herons, great egrets, wood ducks, belted kingfishers, eastern goldfinches, rose-breasted grosbeaks, field sparrows, brown thrashers, eastern kingbirds, eastern bluebirds and several species of butterflies.

Note:

Trails allow access throughout the park. There is poison ivy along the woodland trails, so wear long pants. Avoid wandering from trails near spongy wetland areas because they are particularly sensitive to disturbance.

Best viewing time:

How do I get there?

Maps: MN Highway Coordinate: F-21
PRIM Area: Worthington
DeLorme MN Atlas Grid #: 21 D-7

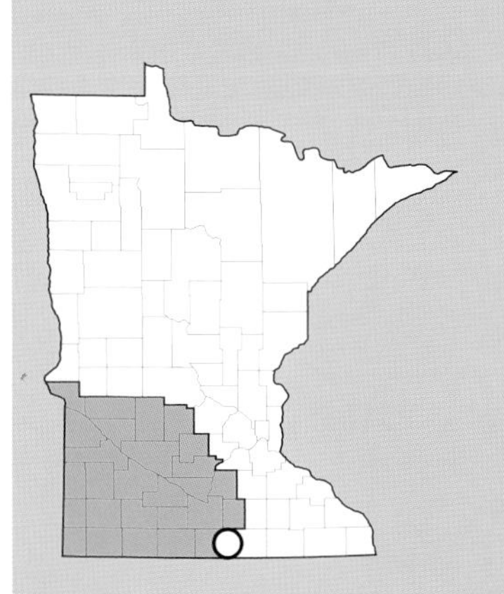

Additional directions:

Situated nine miles northeast of Lakefield, the Kilen Woods State Park entrance can be reached by taking Highway 86 north from Lakefield for three miles and turning east on County Road 24 for 5.25 miles.

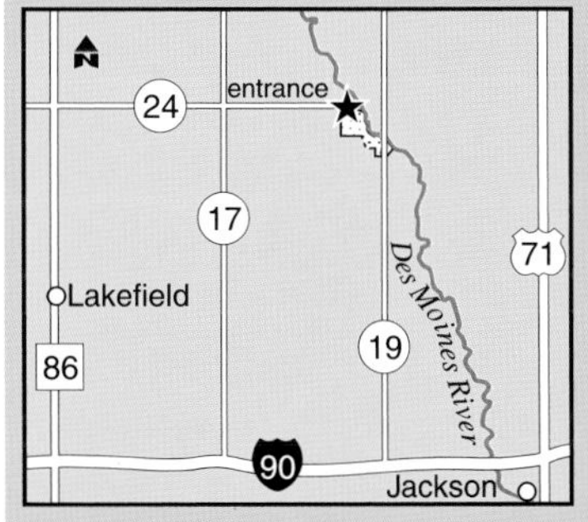

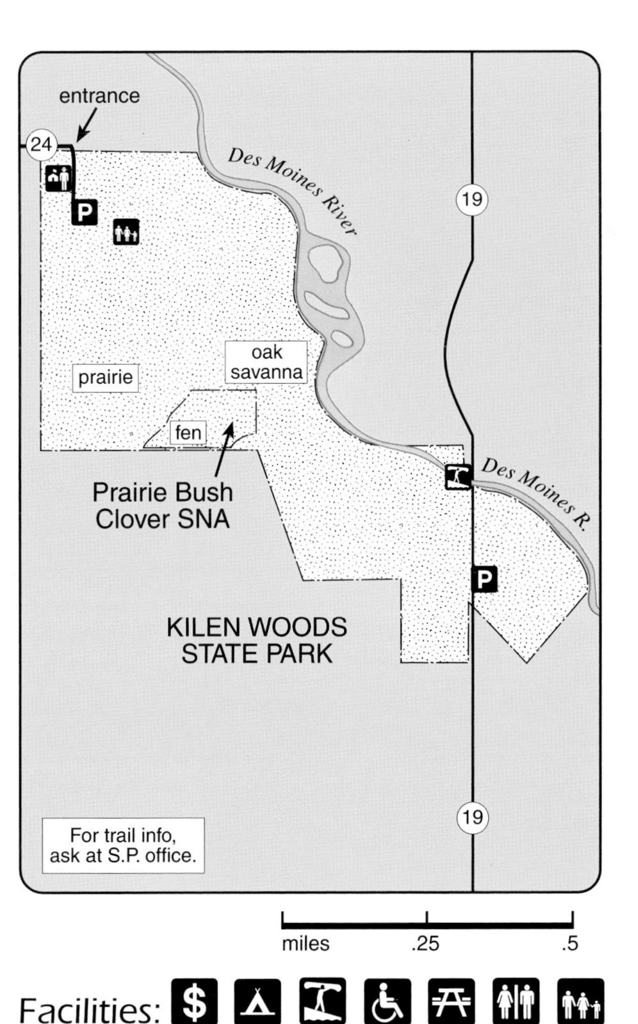

Facilities:    

Recreational Opportunities:

Contact:

Kilen Woods State Park
RR 1 Box 122
Lakefield MN 56150-9566
(507) 662-6258

80–Walnut Lake WMA

Why is this area special?

Just off Interstate 90 in extreme south central Minnesota lies the Walnut Lake Wildlife Management Area. Various habitat types create a scenic area in a highly agricultural environment. Two lakes, grassy upland areas, willow thickets and deciduous woodlands offer habitat for many wildlife species, including muskrats and white-tailed deer.

Walnut Lake and South Walnut Lake, as well as wetland areas of the WMA, provide habitat for wetland birds such as great blue herons, great egrets and spotted sandpipers. Woodland areas offer habitat for songbirds, red-tailed hawks and American kestrels. Shrubby areas provide winter shelter for ring-necked pheasants and American tree sparrows.

C. Henderson

Wood duck family

Each spring a variety of waterfowl stops at lakes and marshes of the WMA during their northward migration. Look for scaup, ringnecks, mergansers, pintail and redheads in early spring. Mallards and blue-winged teal nest in upland areas surrounding the lakes and wetlands. The wood duck, Minnesota's most colorful waterfowl, nests in the tree cavities found in woodlands surrounding the lake. Migrating raptors may also provide good viewing opportunities in September and October.

Note:

When you visit Walnut Lake, remember that parking is not allowed along the Interstate and that you should take care when viewing wildlife from any roadway.

The 2000-acre Walnut Lake WMA also includes a 453 acre refuge to provide wildlife undisturbed sanctuary. This is a no-trespass area and is posted with "Refuge" signs.

Best viewing time:

Hunting allowed. Call ahead for hunting season dates.

How do I get there?

Maps: MN Highway Coordinate: I-21
PRIM Area: Albert Lea
DeLorme MN Atlas Grid #: 23 D-8

Additional directions:

Take I-90 east of Blue Earth for 15 miles. Exit at Highway 21 and drive north for one and a quarter miles. A gravel road to the north bisects Walnut and South Walnut Lake.

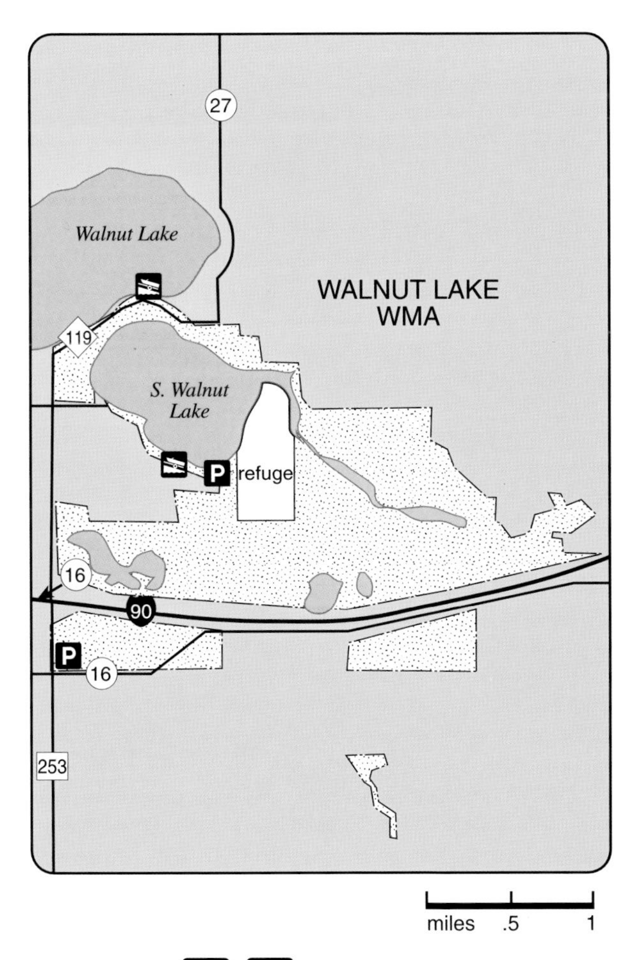

Facilities:

Recreational Opportunities:

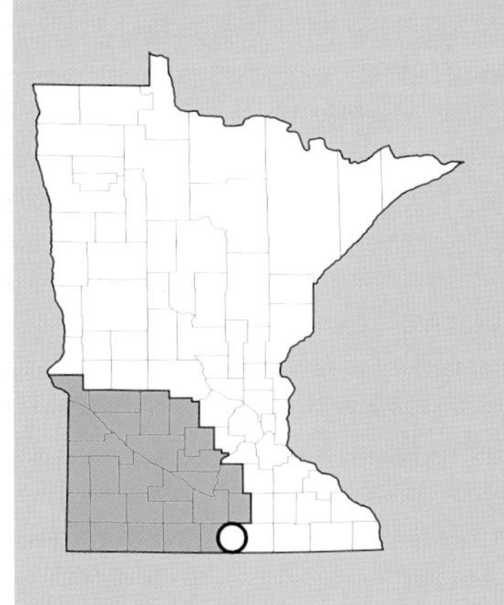

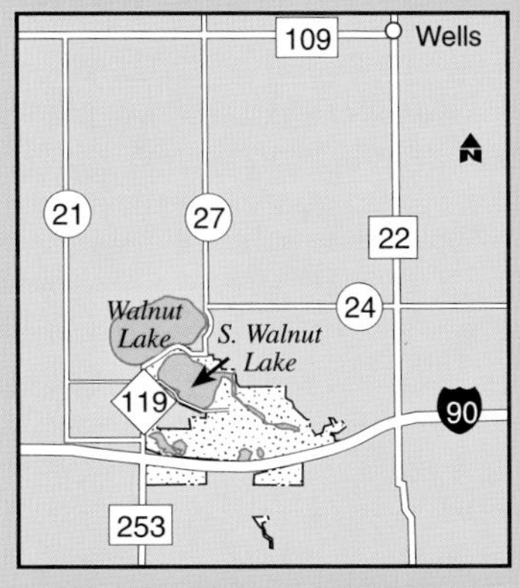

Contact:

DNR Area Wildlife Office
1230 Victory Drive
Mankato MN 56001
(507) 389-5370

Wildlife In and Around the Twin Cities

The native inhabitants and early settlers in this region faced a diverse natural landscape. Extensive floodplain forests were interspersed with lakes, marshes, fens, white pines, sand dunes, prairies and even tamarack swamps. Three major rivers converged in the area's maple, basswood and oak savanna forests, and the variety of wildlife found here was as diverse as the landscape.

Today, the seven counties of the Twin Cities metropolitan area are home to more than half the citizens of the state. Much of the landscape has been pressed into a suburban habitat that can't support some native species such as American bittern, spotted skunk, several turtles, frogs and snakes that once lived here. Many of the more unique wildlife species are now found only in the wilder habitats described in these site accounts.

Fortunately, Twin Cities residents have recognized the importance of natural areas, parks and other open spaces. As a result of progressive open space planning, Minneapolis, St. Paul and the surrounding counties maintain one of the largest urban county and regional park systems in the country. The metro area's estimated 50,000 acres of wildlife habitat include regional parks and park reserves, wildlife management areas, a national wildlife refuge that extends for 34 miles, a national wild and scenic riverway, three state parks and one state-owned wildlife management area covering 23,000 acres.

C. Henderson

Wild turkey

Many public land sites in the metro area are open to the public free of charge, but some require modest user fees. These sites are often associated with rivers, lakes, marshes and other wetlands. Some contain a mix of habitats and ecosystems that have been restored through burning, pollution cleanup, exotic species control and native species restoration projects.

Wildlife remains remarkably diverse. Species once lost from the area, such as peregrine falcons, sandhill cranes, coyotes, bald eagles, river otters and trumpeter swans, now occupy the remaining habitat. Gopher snakes, spring peepers and ospreys have been reintroduced into the park reserves.

There is good fishing in the restored rivers and lakes, enhanced by a network of public fishing piers and water access sites. You can see "wilderness" species such as common loons and bald eagles within a half-hour drive of either downtown.

You will find a warm and informative welcome at any of the nearly 30 nature centers. The Blue Heron Bookstore at the James Ford Bell Museum of Natural History in Minneapolis is among the well-known natural history bookstores in town. The museum's wildlife dioramas offer a great opportunity to practice bird and wildlife identification skills.

Even the Mall of America recognizes our fascination with wildlife; it has recently opened an aquarium featuring both native fish and exotic saltwater species.

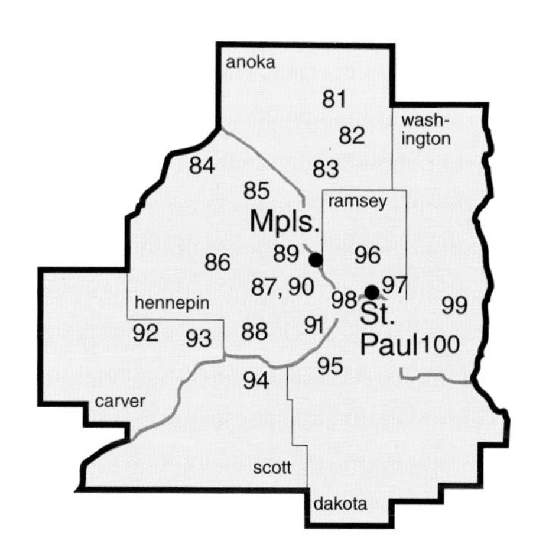

Sites

81. Boot Lake SNA
82. Carlos Avery WMA
83. Springbrook Nature Center
84. Crow-Hassan Park Reserve
85. Elm Creek Park Reserve
86. Wolsfeld Woods SNA
87. T. S. Roberts Bird Sanctuary
88. Wood Lake Nature Center
89. Eloise Butler Wildflower Garden & Bird Sanctuary/ the Quaking Bog
90. Lakes Calhoun & Harriet
91. Minnesota Valley NWR/ Louisville Swamp Black Dog Preserve SNA
92. Carver Park Reserve
93. Minnesota Landscape Arboretum
94. Murphy-Hanrehan Park Reserve
95. Lebanon Hills Regional Park
96. Lake Vadnais/Sucker Lake
97. Battle Creek Regional Park
98. Crosby Farm/Hidden Falls Parks
99. Afton State Park
100. Lost Valley Prairie SNA

81–Boot Lake SNA

Why is this area special?

Boot Lake is an ice-block lake formed by the pressure and erosion of a subglacial river. Extending from the lake are areas of wetland, wooded bog, white pines and oak forest. Several rare plant species including water willow, sea-beach grass and long-bearded hawkweed are found here.

More than 146 bird species have been recorded in this 600-acre site, including nesting alder and least flycatchers, golden-winged, Nashville and pine warblers, northern waterthrushes and sandhill cranes. You might also spot a Blanding's turtle, characterized by a dome-shaped shell and a yellow chin.

Note:

The southwestern part of this area is a posted sanctuary accessible by research permit only. The Carlos Avery WMA (site 82) is adjacent to Boot Lake SNA and also provides numerous opportunities for viewing wildlife.

Hiking trails are not developed; the only trails are those made by deer.

Jane Norris

Best viewing time:

How do I get there?

Maps: MN Highway Coordinate: J-15
PRIM Area: North Metro Area
Delorme MN Atlas Grid #: 41 A-8

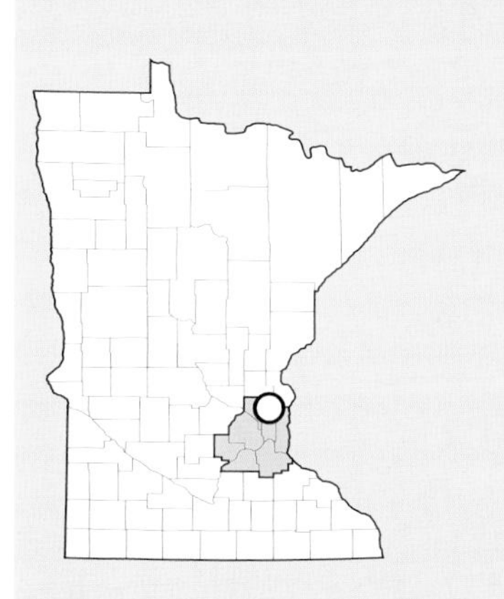

Additional directions:

From the Minneapolis/St. Paul area, head north on either 35W or 35E to the Wyoming exit. Drive west on County Road 22 until you reach County Road 17 and turn left. Continue on County Road 17 until you reach Jordell Road. Turn left and watch for the SNA boundary signs on the left. Use the Wildlife Management Area parking lot on the right.

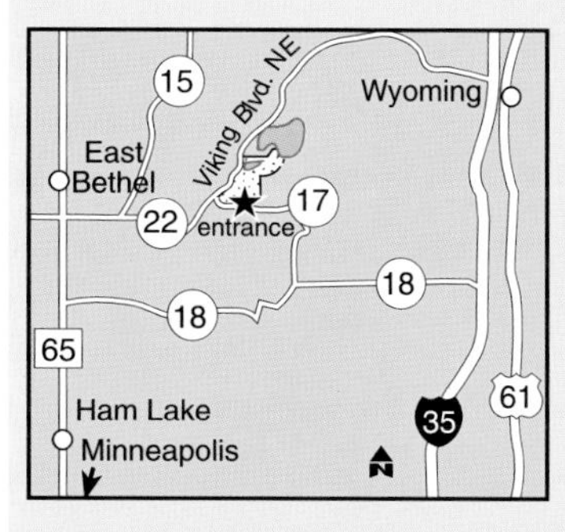

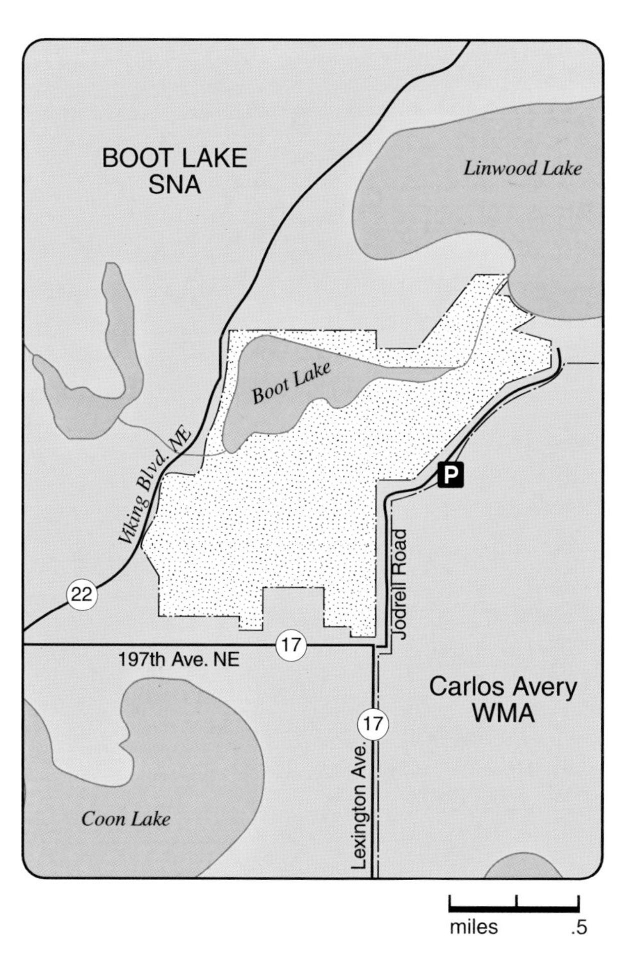

miles .5

Facilities:

Recreational Opportunities:

Contact:

Scientific and Natural Areas Program
DNR
Box 25
500 Lafayette Road
St. Paul MN 55102
(612) 297-2357

82–Carlos Avery WMA

Why is this area special?

The Carlos Avery Wildlife Management Area encompasses more than 23,000 acres, representing the largest public land tract in the seven-county metro area. The land, once owned by the Crex Carpet Company, was managed for the wiregrass used to make rugs. In 1933, the land became tax-forfeited and was purchased by the Minnesota Conservation Commission.

Jane Norris

Carlos Avery WMA lies on the Anoka Sand Plain, a landscape characterized by poorly drained, sandy soils. About two thirds of the management area is wetland, a mixture of emergent marsh and open water.

The Sunrise Unit, east of Stacy, is a vast stretch of tamarack bog that borders the Sunrise River and provides an excellent opportunity to see aquatic birds. The upland areas are primarily old fields, grasslands, oak woodlands and food plots.

A highlight of your visit to Carlos Avery WMA will be the chance to see sandhill cranes, magnificent birds not often spotted in the metro area. This is a great spot to view migrant ducks, geese and warblers in April and May. You might also see American bitterns, green herons, belted kingfishers, bald eagles, wild turkeys, vireos and many species of waterfowl, as well as mammals like deer, coyotes, river otters and an occasional black bear.

Note:

Carlos Avery WMA is managed for wildlife. There is minimal development except for approximately 57 miles of roads, 23 miles of trails and 21 miles of dikes that provide access to this vast area by hiking or by car. A 7-mile self-guided auto tour begins at the WMA headquarters and provides an excellent view of the area. Part of this area near the headquarters is posted as sanctuary—no trespassing. Because of the area's large size, it's a good idea to obtain a WMA map or an auto tour brochure before you explore.

Hunting allowed. Call ahead for hunting season dates.

Best viewing time:

How do I get there?

Maps: MN Highway Coordinate: X-23
PRIM Area: North Metro Area
Delorme MN Atlas Grid #: 41 A-9, 49 E-5

Additional directions:

Carlos Avery is located 30 miles north of the Twin Cities. Take 35E or 35W north to Forest Lake. Go west on County Road 18 for about 8 miles and watch for signs indicating the headquarters.

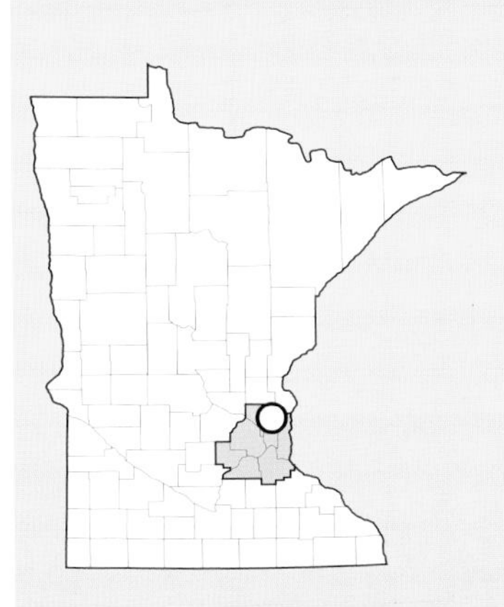

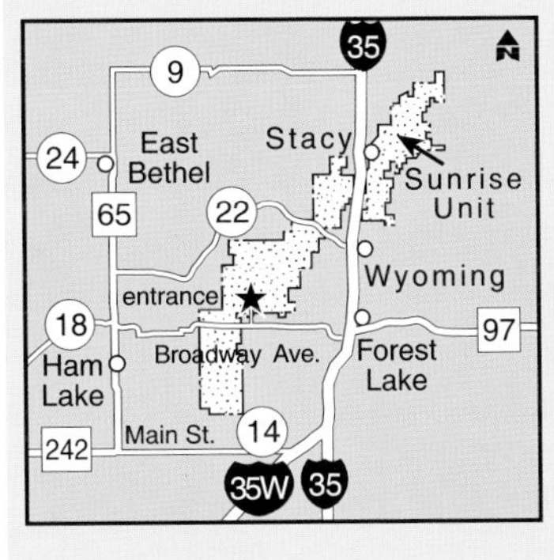

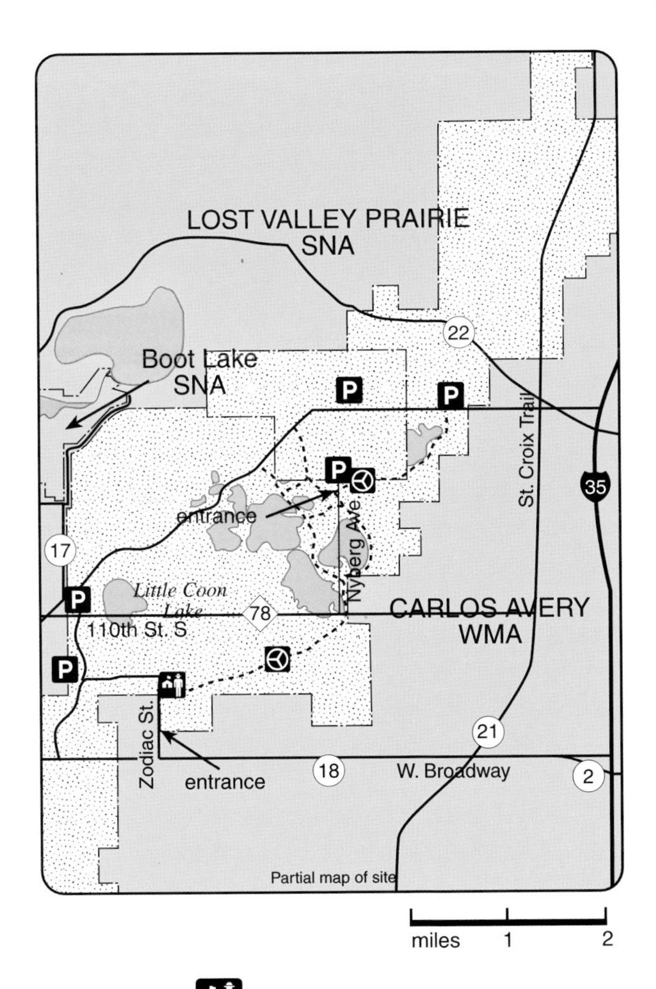

Facilities: 

Recreational Opportunities: 

Contact:

DNR Wildlife Area Office
Carlos Avery WMA
18320 Zodiac Street
Forest Lake MN 55025
(612) 296-5290

83–Springbrook Nature Center

Why is this area special?

If you want to see an American woodcock's courtship display or listen to the call of frogs and toads, Springbrook Nature Center is the place for you. Diverse plant communities, from oak and aspen woodlands to wetlands and native prairie, make the nature center an attractive home for many species of wildlife. You might see American woodcocks, belted kingfishers, green herons, nesting great horned owls, muskrats, raccoons, beavers, gray and red foxes and many species of butterflies.

Jane Norris

Springbrook is a good place to listen for frogs and toads in spring and to scout for northern shrikes and mammal tracks in the winter. Both coyotes and bobcats have been documented here.

A boardwalk over a marsh provides great wildlife watching opportunities during the spring waterfowl migration.

Note:

The nature center has a wonderful display of live reptiles, amphibians and fish. There is also an interesting display and video about the impact a 1986 tornado had on Springbrook.

This nature center was visited by thousands of people from throughout the United States when a rare boreal owl spent the winter there from January through March of 1997.

Jane Norris

Best viewing time:

How do I get there?

Maps: MN Highway Coordinate: Metro Inset W-25
PRIM Area: North Metro Area
Delorme MN Atlas Grid #: 41 C-7

Additional directions:

Take Highway 47 (University Avenue) north of I-694 to 85th Avenue NE. Turn left (west) and watch for the park entrance on the left.

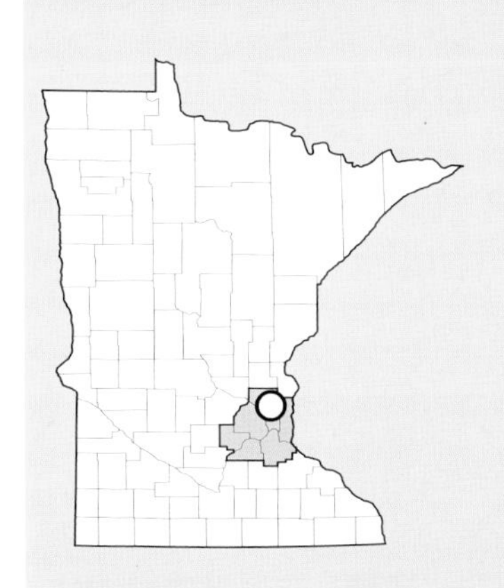

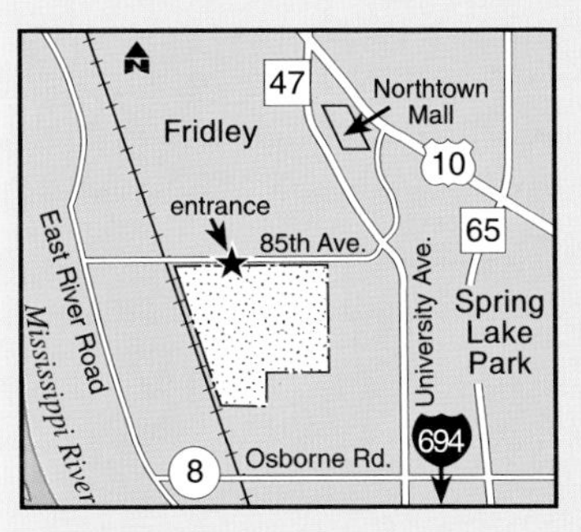

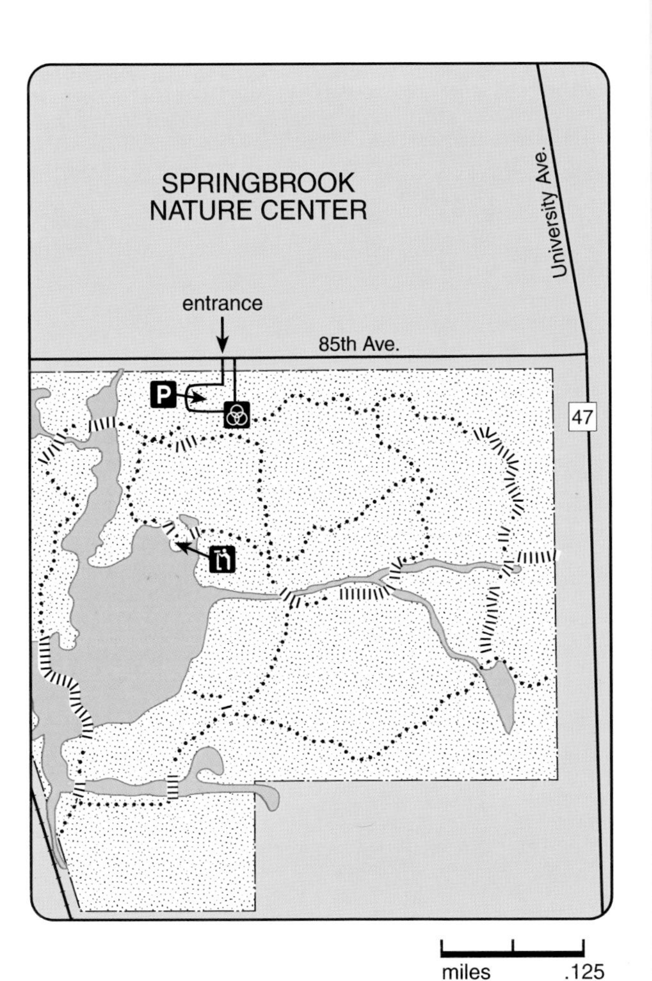

Facilities:

Recreational Opportunities:

Contact:

(mailing address)
Springbrook Nature Center
6431 University Avenue NE
Fridley MN 55432

(location)
Springbrook Nature Center
100 85th Avenue NE
Fridley MN 55432
(612) 572-3588

84–Crow-Hassan Park Reserve

Why is this area special?

Crow-Hassan Park Reserve is one of the prime areas in the metro region for watching grassland birds. Nearly a fourth of the park's 2,600 gently rolling acres are being restored to prairie, and some of the oak woodlands adjacent to the grasslands are burned to create a more natural woodland/prairie edge.

This large tract of restored land will give you a chance to visualize how the area must have appeared to pioneers as they headed out across the prairie. The western edge of the park borders the Crow River, an area noted for an abundance of wildlife including mink, turtles, belted kingfishers, swallows and many other animals.

When you visit the Crow-Hassan Park Reserve you could see grasshopper and vesper sparrows, northern harriers, bobolinks, trumpeter swans, common loons, orchard orioles, coyotes, gopher snakes and Blanding's turtles.

Note:

Daily or annual permits are required for all vehicles entering the park reserve. Canoe access is available at both Crow-Hassan and Lake Rebecca Park Reserve, which is located less than 10 miles upstream on the Crow River.

Jane Norris

Best viewing time:

How do I get there?

Maps: MN Highway Coordinate: U-24
PRIM Area: North Metro Area
Delorme MN Atlas Grid #: 40 B-4

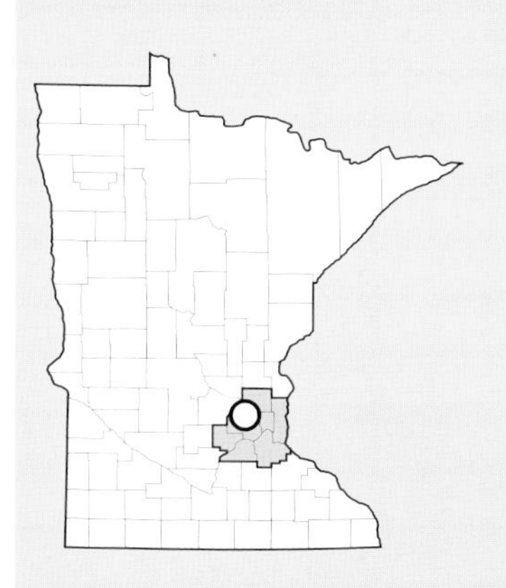

Additional directions:

Crow-Hassan is located northwest of the Twin Cities near Rogers. Take I-94 to the Rogers exit. Drive south on County Road 150 to County Road 116 and turn right. Continue to County Road 203 and turn left. Look for the park entrance on the right.

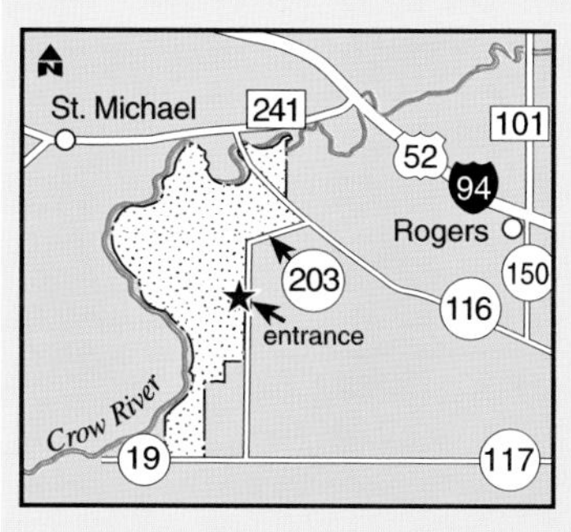

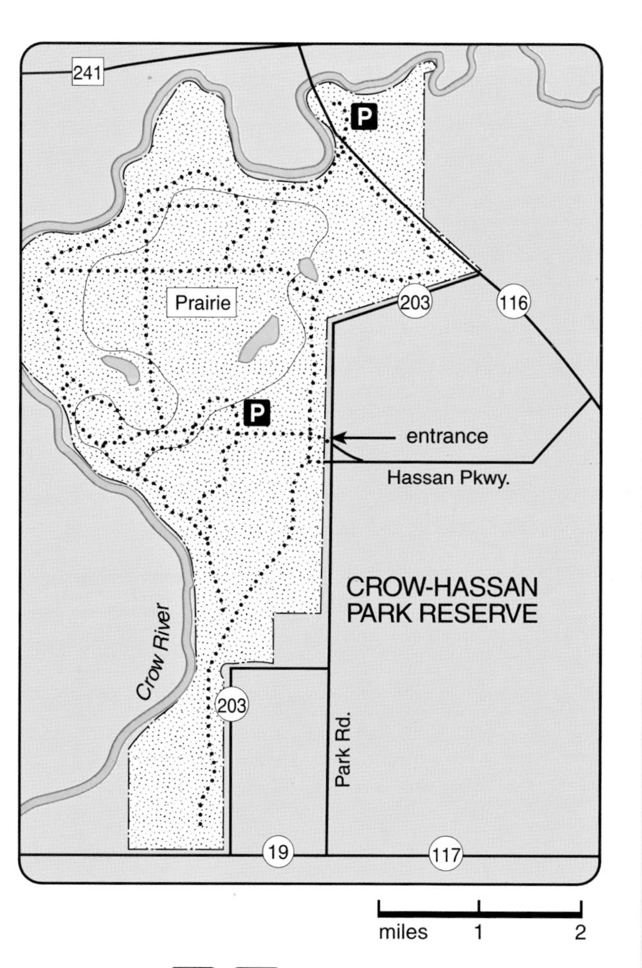

Facilities: 

Recreational Opportunities:    

Contact:

Crow-Hassan Park Reserve
11629 Crow-Hassan Park Rd.
Rogers MN 55374
(612) 428-2765

85–Elm Creek Park Reserve

Why is this area special?

Elm Creek Park Reserve is the largest of the Hennepin Parks. The Hennepin Parks management policy of maintaining 80 percent of each reserve in a natural state ensures that this 5,000-acre preserve will continue to be a haven for wildlife.

Jane Norris

Much of this area was once maple/basswood forest that was converted to farmland. It is now being reverted back to woodland. The park also contains more than 1,500 acres of largely inaccessible wetlands.

Look for wildlife along the streams meandering through the reserve. These streams and the adjacent floodplain forest support wildlife species such as river otters, beavers, mink and coyotes. You might also see bald eagles, sandhill cranes, trumpeter swans, common loons, barred owls, acadian flycatchers, wood thrushes and veeries. The reserve is also home to large populations of wood and green tree frogs.

Note:

Daily or annual permits are required for all vehicles entering the park reserve. Stop first at the Eastman Nature Center, located in Elm Creek Park, for information about the best viewing opportunities.

Watch birds and deer at the feeder stations while you're in the Eastman Nature Center and use the nine miles of paved trails and 4.5 miles unpaved trails for hiking or biking.

C. Henderson

Wood duck

Best viewing time:

How do I get there?

Maps: MN Highway Coordinate: Metro Inset V-24
PRIM Area: North Metro Area
Delorme MN Atlas Grid #: 41 B-6

Additional directions:

Elm Creek Park Reserve is northwest of the Twin Cities near Dayton. Take County Road 81 to County Road 121 and turn right. Drive to Elm Creek Road and turn right. The entrance to nature center is on the right.

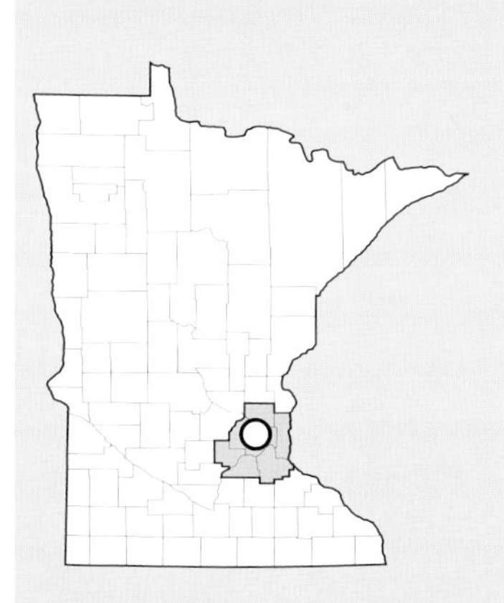

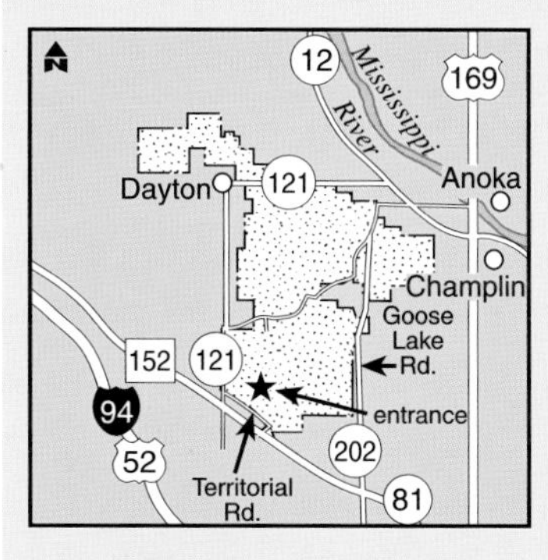

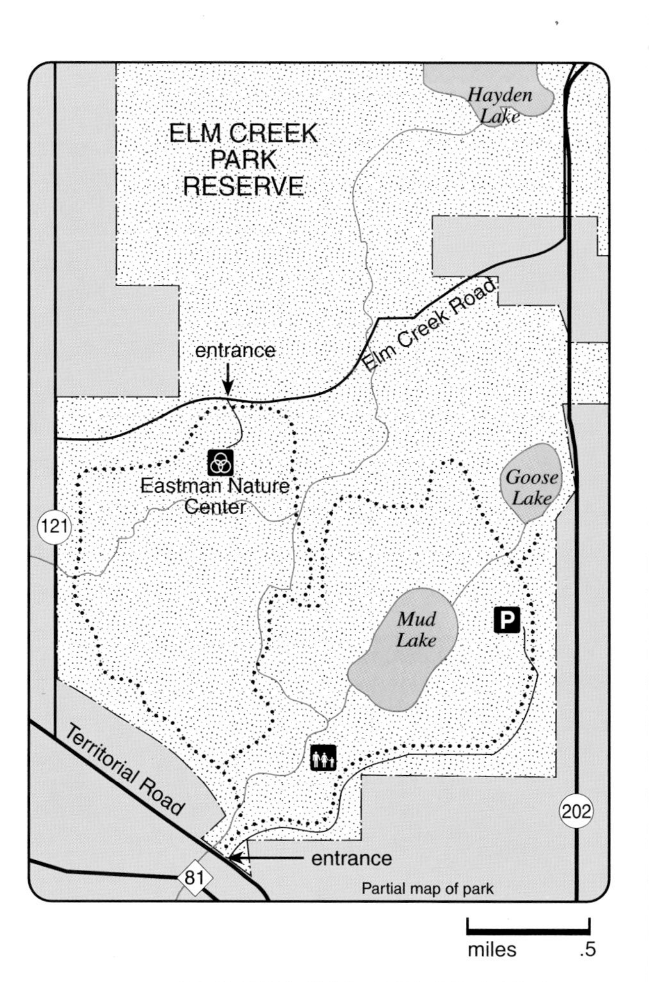

Facilities: 

Recreational Opportunities:    

Contact:

Elm Creek Park Reserve
13351 Elm Creek Park Road
Osseo MN 55369
(612) 424-5511

Eastman Nature Center
(612) 420-4300

86–Wolsfeld Woods SNA

Why is this area special?

Wolsfeld Woods is the best remaining metro-area example of the Big Woods habitat that once covered south-central Minnesota. The large sugar maples—some more than 200 years old—that dominate this 221-acre parcel can give you the feeling of walking through a woodland cathedral. The closed canopy created by these huge trees allows only the most shade-tolerant shrubs and forbs to survive, and wildflowers must bloom in early spring while the sun still reaches the forest floor.

Jane Norris

Wolsfeld Woods was set aside to protect the natural plant and animal community and for scientific and educational purposes. The terrain is fairly steep with many small wetlands occupying the depressions between hills. A large portion of Wolsfeld Lake is surrounded by the preserve.

Animal species at this site include Louisiana waterthrushes, nesting acadian flycatchers, warblers and vireos.

Note:

You are required to stay on the trails when you visit this site, but the trail markers are limited. Request a map and guide for the area from the Scientific and Natural Areas Program before your visit.

DNR File Photo

Best viewing time:

How do I get there?

Maps: MN Highway Coordinate: Metro Inset U-26
PRIM Area: South Metro Area
Delorme MN Atlas Grid #: 40 C-5

Additional directions:

Wolsfeld Woods is west of Minneapolis near the town of Long Lake. From I-494 drive west on Highway 12 to Brown Road in Long Lake. Drive north on Brown Road to County Road 6. Trinity Lutheran Church is located on the north side of this intersection. Park in the northeast corner of the church parking lot, which is where the trail begins.

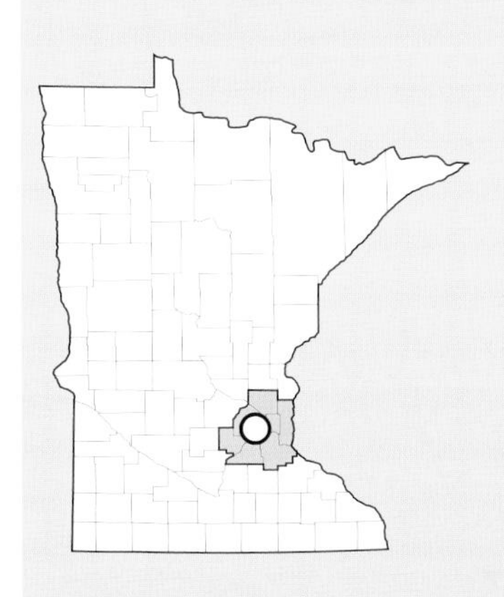

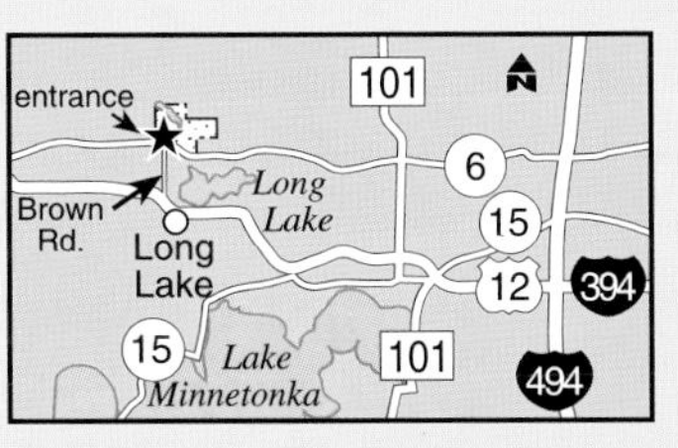

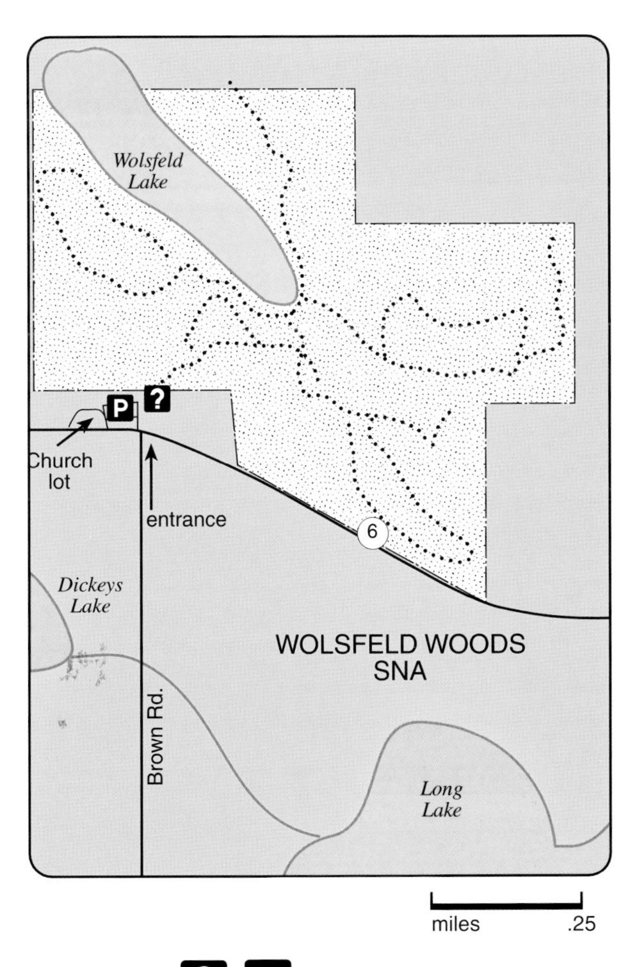

Facilities:

Recreational Opportunities:

Contact:

Scientific and Natural Areas Program
DNR
Box 25
500 Lafayette Rd.
St. Paul MN 55155
(612) 297-2357

87–T.S. Roberts Bird Sanctuary

C. Henderson

Black-capped chickadee

Why is this area special?

Tucked between two of Minneapolis' busiest lakes is a favorite haunt of Twin Cities birders. The sanctuary was named for Thomas Sadler Roberts, the first curator of the University of Minnesota's Museum of Natural History and author of the two-volume 1934 classic *Birds of Minnesota.* This 13-acre sanctuary includes upland woods, dominated by bur oak and sugar maple. The wetland habitat is surrounded by cottonwoods and willows.

Although small in size, this area consistently provides good birding opportunities. You have a good chance of spotting rare birds as well as vireos, pileated and red-bellied woodpeckers, sora, wood ducks, great blue herons and many species of warblers.

Lakewood Cemetery, which borders T. S. Roberts Bird Sanctuary on the north, is also an excellent area for birding, especially for warblers. Townsend's and black-throated gray warblers have been reported here.

Note:

An unpaved trail, including a boardwalk across the marsh, winds through the bird sanctuary and is handicapped accessible. Lakes Calhoun and Harriet (site 90) provides additional wildlife watching opportunities.

Jane Norris

Best viewing time:

How do I get there?

Maps: MN Highway Coordinate: Metro Inset W-27
PRIM Area: South Metro Area
Delorme MN Atlas Grid #: 41 D-7

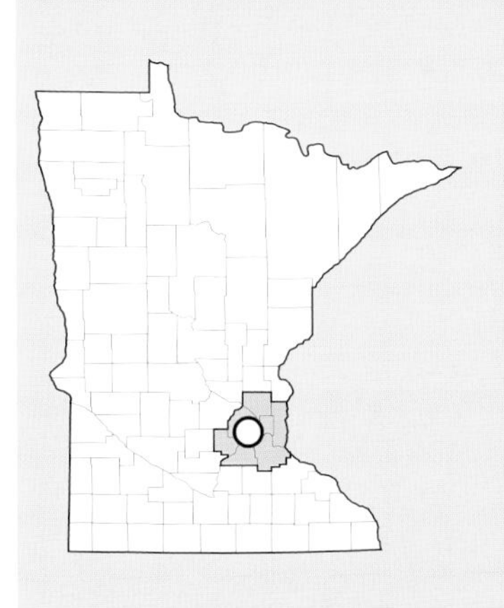

Additional directions:

From Minneapolis, take 35W south and exit west on 46th Street. Continue west on 46th Street to Kings Highway. Turn right and continue to Roseway Road. Turn left. The parking lot is on the right.

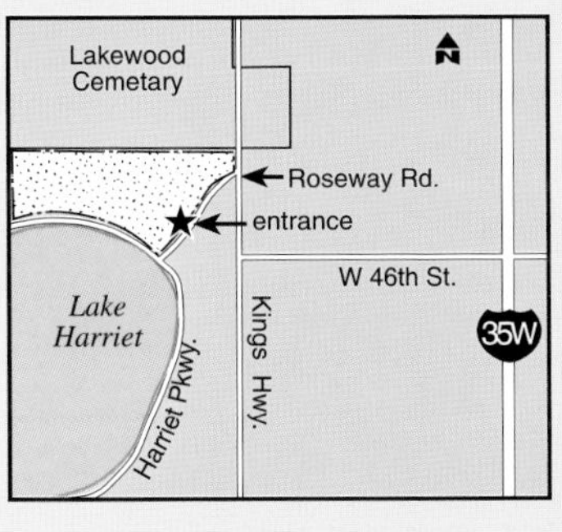

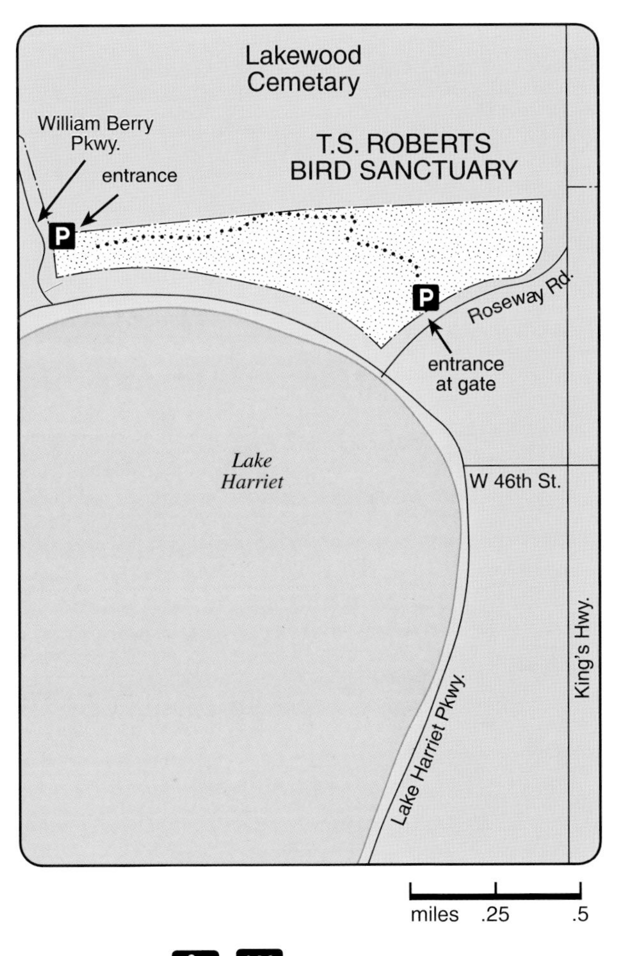

Facilities:

Recreational Opportunities:

Contact:

Minneapolis Park and Recreation Board
3800 Bryant Ave. S
Minneapolis MN 55409-1029
(612) 370-4900

88–Wood Lake Nature Center

Why is this area special?

Adjacent to one of the Twin Cities' most congested freeways is a 160-acre oasis for wildlife. This area attracts more than 200 species of birds, including Virginia rails, soras and American bitterns, and 30 species of mammals. Both black and Forster's terns nest on the Wood Lake marsh. You can frequently spot foxes, white-tailed deer, raccoons, woodchucks, squirrels, skunks and other small mammals from the trails.

This shallow wetland is surrounded by floodplain forest dominated by silver maple, cottonwood and box elder. A floating boardwalk crosses the marsh so you can get an excellent view of the wetland wildlife. Look for wood ducks, blue-winged teal, mallards, ruddy ducks, Canada geese and yellow-headed and red-winged blackbirds.

Note:

The nature center offers many programs about wildlife watching throughout the year. A tally of bird records from Wood Lake Nature Center for the past 20 years is displayed in the visitor center.

C. Henderson

Gray fox

Best viewing time:

How do I get there?

Maps: MN Highway Coordinate: Metro Inset W-27
PRIM Area: South Metro Area
Delorme MN Atlas Grid #: 40 E-7

Additional directions:

Take 35W south from downtown Minneapolis and exit on 66th Street. Turn left, continue to Lake Shore Drive and turn right. The entrance to Wood Lake is on the right.

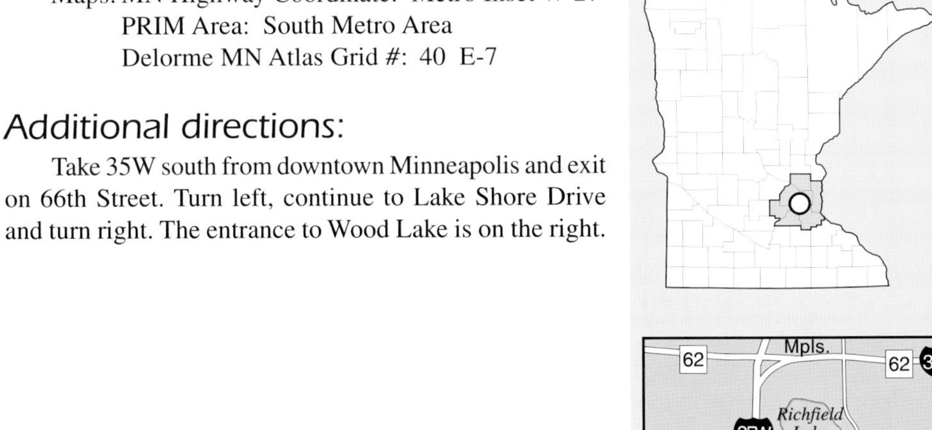

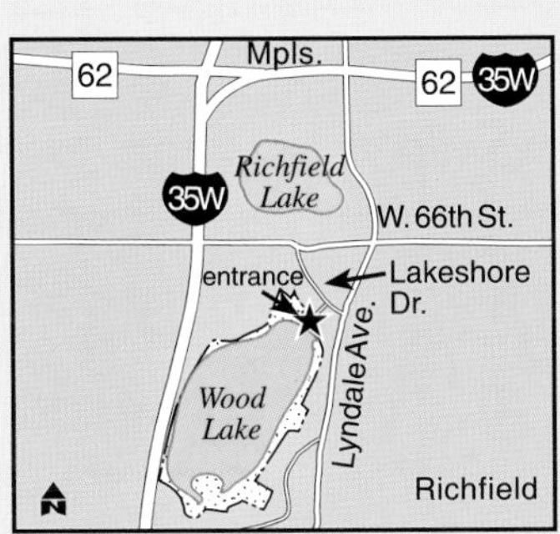

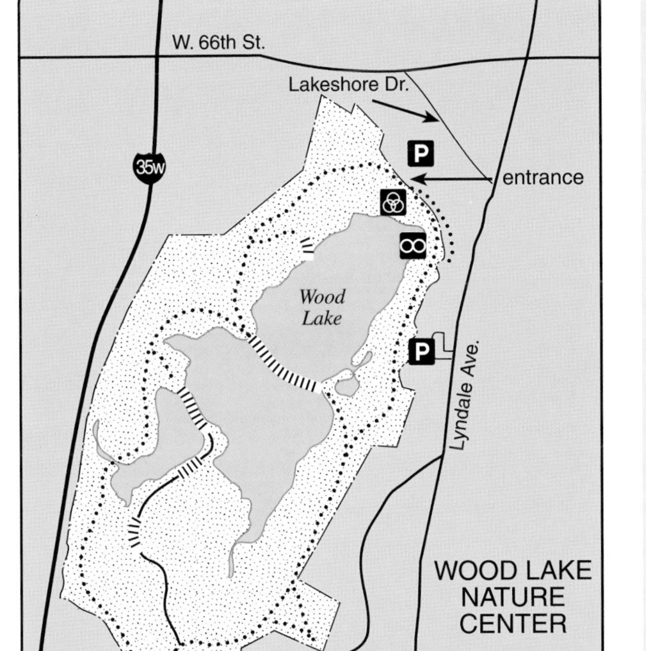

miles .25 .5

Facilities: 

Recreational Opportunities: 

Contact:

Wood Lake Nature Center
735 Lake Shore Drive
Richfield MN 55423
(612) 861-9365

89–Eloise Butler Wildflower Garden and Bird Sanctuary/the Quaking Bog

Why is this area special?

Truly a gem in the Minneapolis Parks system, this 14-acre sanctuary is the oldest public wildflower garden in the United States. The sanctuary includes four habitats: wetland, prairie, mature woodland and open woodland.

Each habitat provides excellent opportunities for birding amid spectacular wildflowers. Look for pileated woodpeckers, great crested flycatchers, indigo buntings, grassland sparrows, barred and great horned owls and many species of migrating warblers.

Theodore Wirth Regional Park, which surrounds the wildflower garden, contains significant additional habitat to explore. Wirth Lake, Bassett Creek and the five-acre tamarack quaking bog are located here.

The **"quaking bog"** is a great place to watch dragonflies in the summer. This is the last of dozens of tamarack bogs that were once found in this part of the city. It is believed to be one of the southernmost bogs in the state.

Feel the ground give underneath your feet as you enter the restored bog and walk on the floating dock. This is a great place to listen to spring peepers and chorus frogs in spring, watch dragonflies in summer, spot migrating songbirds amidst the golden tamaracks in fall and search for the tracks of rabbits, squirrels and voles in winter.

Jane Norris

Note:

Pick up a habitat guide at the start of the one-mile trail winding through the Eloise Butler Sanctuary. Directions to the quaking bog and other areas of interest in Theodore Wirth Regional Park are included in the wildflower garden guide.

Be sure to pay for parking while you visit.

Best viewing time:

How do I get there?

Maps: MN Highway Coordinate: Metro Inset W-26
PRIM Area: North Metro Area
Delorme MN Atlas Grid #: 41 D-7

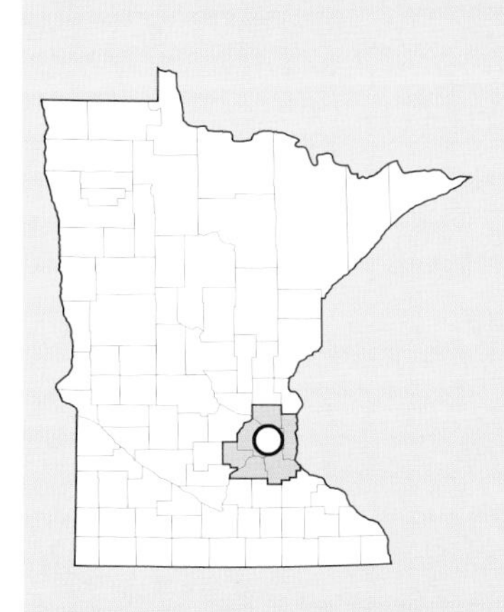

Additional directions:

Eloise Butler Wildflower Garden and Bird Sanctuary is located on the west side of Minneapolis. The entrance is on the east side of Wirth Parkway about 1/2 mile north of I-394. The Quaking Bog is nearby on the west side of the Parkway.

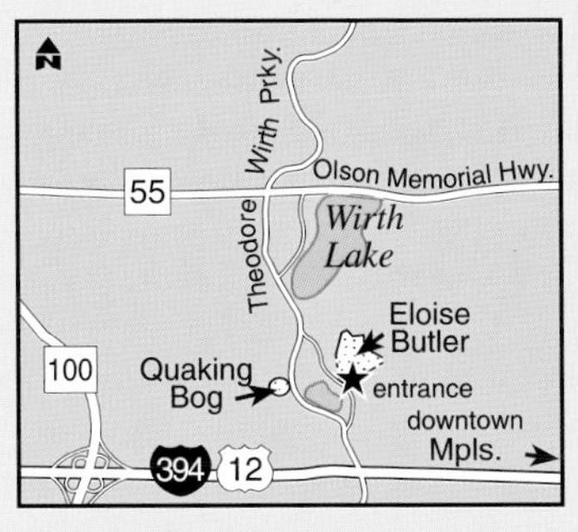

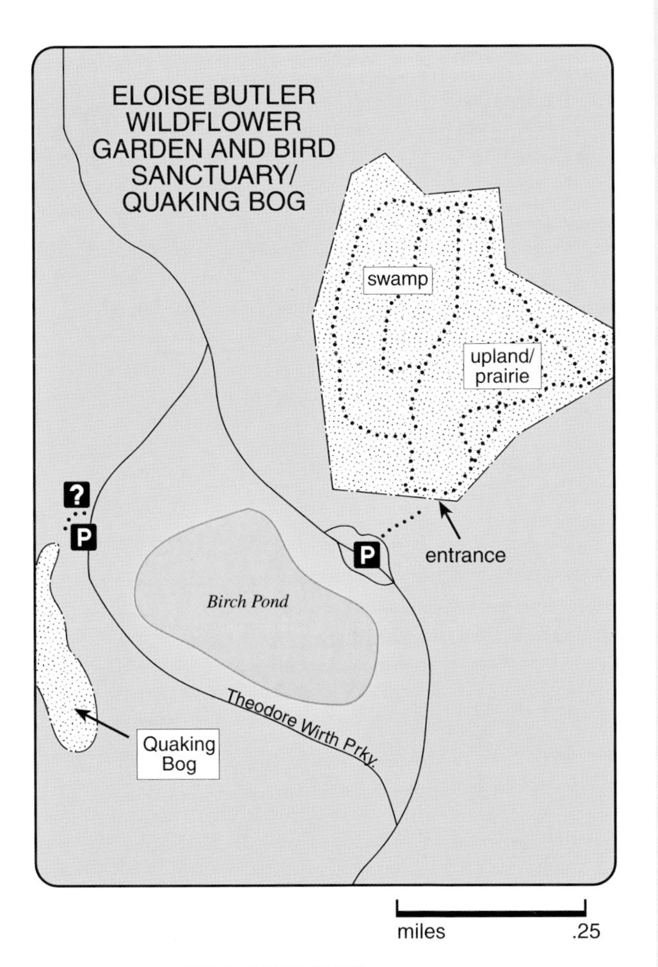

Facilities:

Recreational Opportunities:

Contact:

Minneapolis Park and Recreation Board
3800 Bryant Ave. S
Minneapolis MN 55409-1029
(612) 370-4900

90–Lakes Calhoun & Harriet

Why is this area special?

Minneapolis is renowned for its many lakes, providing abundant recreational opportunities for residents and visitors alike. Two of these lakes, Calhoun and Harriet, host waves of migrating waterfowl and gulls during the spring and fall. You can also see common loons, red-breasted mergansers, hooded mergansers, ruddy ducks, coots, pied-billed grebes, red-necked grebes and northern shovelers. These lakes are used by large numbers of common and rare gulls into late winter. The gulls spend the day at the Black Dog Power Plant and roost here at night. Some visitors have even seen rare red-throated loons, arctic loons and Thayer's gulls.

Note:

Lake Harriet and Lake Calhoun are easily accessible. Biking and hiking paths surround each of the lakes, which are only three blocks from each other.

The T. S. Roberts Bird Sanctuary (site 87) is located just northeast of Lake Harriet and is an excellent spot to watch birds all year long. Parking areas are located along Roseway Road and William Berry Parkway.

C. Henderson

Northern shoveler

Best viewing time:

How do I get there?

Maps: MN Highway Coordinate: Metro Inset W-27
PRIM Area: South Metro Area
Delorme MN Atlas Grid #: 41 D-7

Additional directions:

From downtown Minneapolis, take 35W south. Exit west on 35th Street. Turn left on Lyndale Avenue, drive one block to 36th Street and turn right. Continue along 36th Street, which ends at Lake Calhoun. Park at one of several lots around the lake or along the parkway.

To reach Lake Harriet follow Calhoun Parkway around to the south side of the lake. Drive south on William Berry Parkway and follow this road several blocks to Lake Harriet.

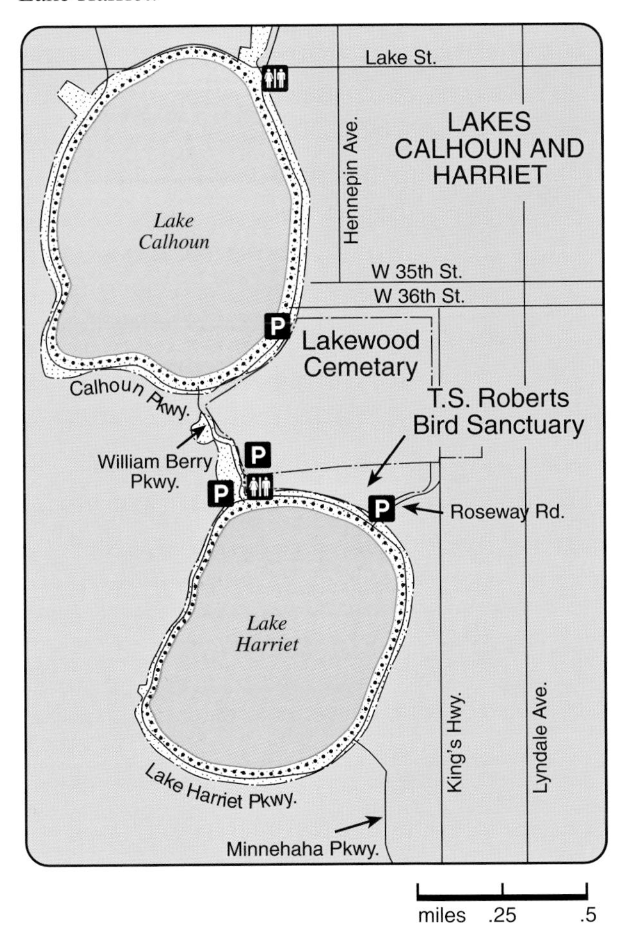

miles .25 .5

Facilities:   

Recreational Opportunities:

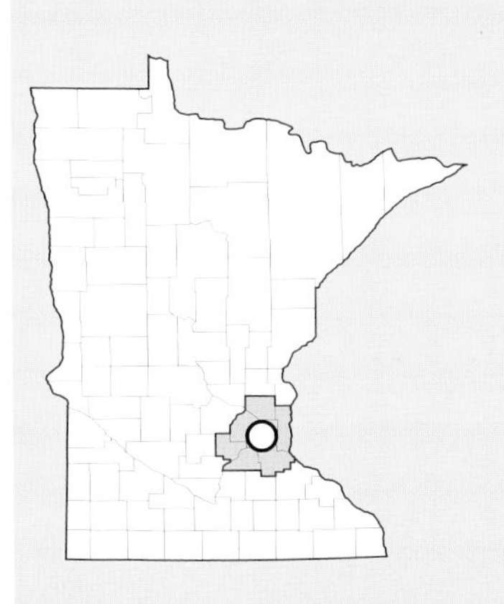

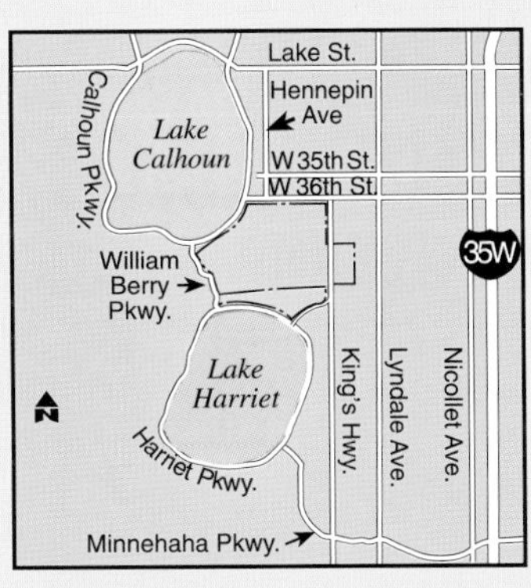

Contact:

Minneapolis Park and Recreation Board
3800 Bryant Ave S
Minneapolis MN 55409-1029
(612) 370-4900

91–Minnesota Valley NWR/ Black Dog Preserve SNA

Why is this area special?

One of the few urban national wildlife refuges in the country is located in the Twin Cities. The Minnesota Valley National Wildlife Refuge stretches 34 miles from Jordan to Bloomington. This vast refuge encompasses 10,500 acres of wildlife habitat ranging from bottomland hardwood forest to a rare calcareous fen community.

The refuge has eight management units. The three most accessible units are described here.

Long Meadow Lake—encompassing 2,200 acres of marshland, floodplain forest and oak savanna—is a great place to watch migrating warblers, waterfowl, bitterns, herons and shorebirds. Two trailheads, at Bass Ponds and Old Cedar Avenue Bridge, provide access to this area, which includes a series of ponds once used for raising fish. Water levels in the ponds are now manipulated to attract waterfowl and shorebirds. People have seen rare birds such as king rail and white-faced ibis in this area.

W. L. Penning

Large flowered bellwort

Black Dog Preserve SNA and Lake derives its name from the Dakota Indian Chief Black Dog. The area includes lake, marsh, prairie, upland and floodplain forest habitats. The prairie here shows no signs of plowing or grazing, and it supports a wonderful assortment of tall grasses and bright flowers.

The calcareous fen, a rare habitat, supports uniquely-adapted plants such as twin-rush and marsh arrow grass. Because of these rare habitats, the area has been designated a Scientific and Natural Area and access is restricted in some places.

A portion of Black Dog Lake remains open all year due to the adjacent power plant, so this area is always worth checking for wildlife. Birds to watch for include Bell's vireos and willow flycatchers. In the winter you can find oldsquaws, Barrow's goldeneyes and Thayer's, glaucous and California gulls in addition to other wintering waterbirds and bald eagles.

Best viewing time:

Louisville Swamp, encompassing 22,000 acres dominated by extensive wetlands, is a good place to find bitterns, herons, egrets, muskrats, beavers, mink and many turtles. On higher ground surrounding the marsh, the prairie, oak savanna, oak woodlands and old fields are home to coyotes, wild turkeys, white-tailed deer and meadowlarks.

Refuge managers are using controlled burning to revitalize the prairie and restore the oak savanna that once covered much of this upland area.

Note:

This refuge is only a ten-minute drive from the Mall of America and the Twin Cities International Airport. It is a delightful destination for Twin Cities visitors before or after a visit to the Mall.

Stop first at the visitor center to pick up maps. The visitor center has displays interpreting the refuge as well as a short slide show, an overlook, a short trail and an excellent bookstore and gift shop. Interpretive programs are regularly scheduled, so ask for a calendar of events.

Jane Norris

continued...

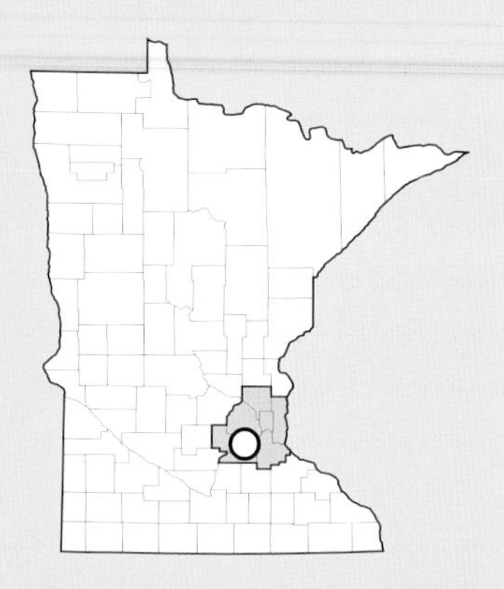

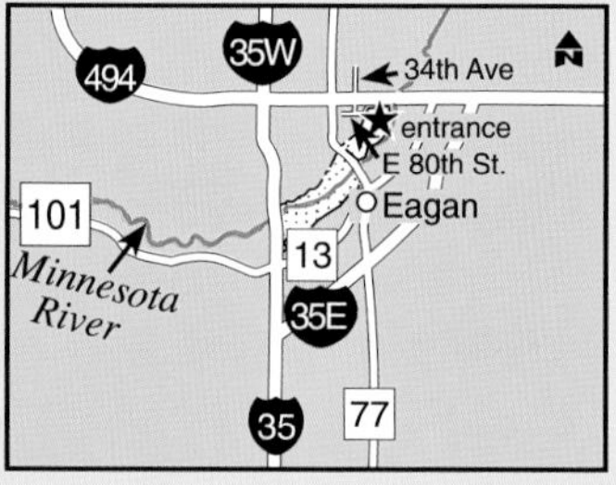

How do I get there?

Maps: MN Highway Coordinate: Metro Inset W-27
PRIM Area: South Metro Area
Delorme MN Atlas Grid #: 40 E-8

Additional directions:

To reach the refuge headquarters and visitor center from I-494 in Bloomington, exit on 34th Avenue. Go south to E. 80th Street. Turn left and follow the road around to the headquarters.

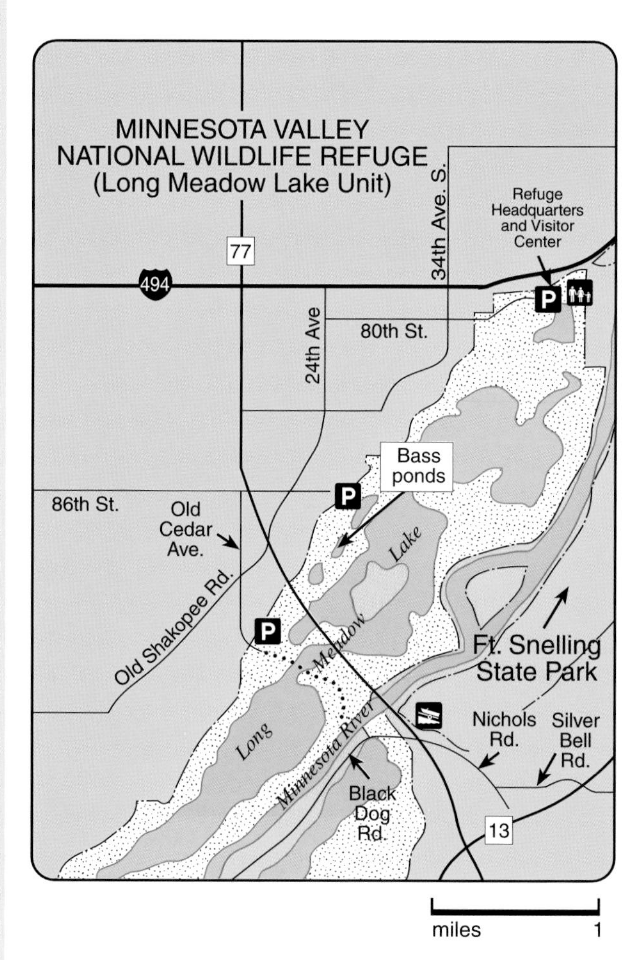

miles 1

Facilities:

Recreational Opportunities:

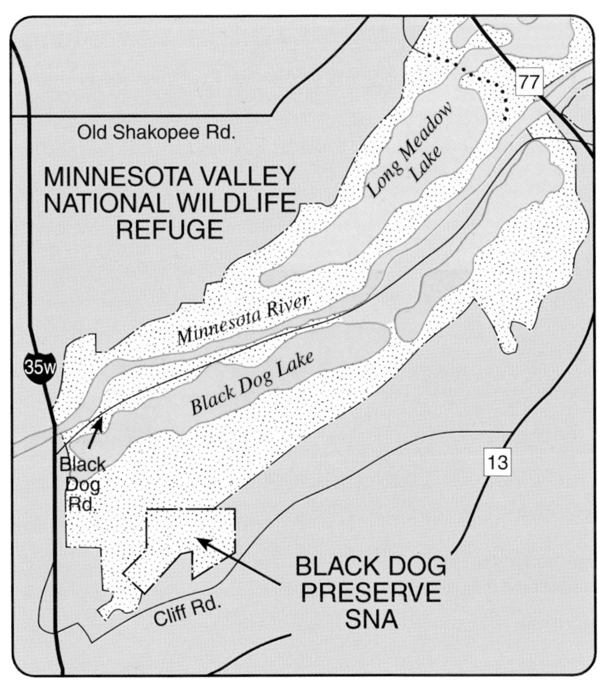

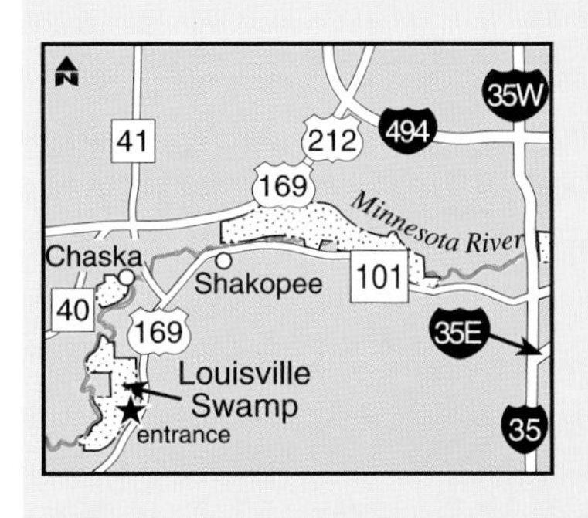

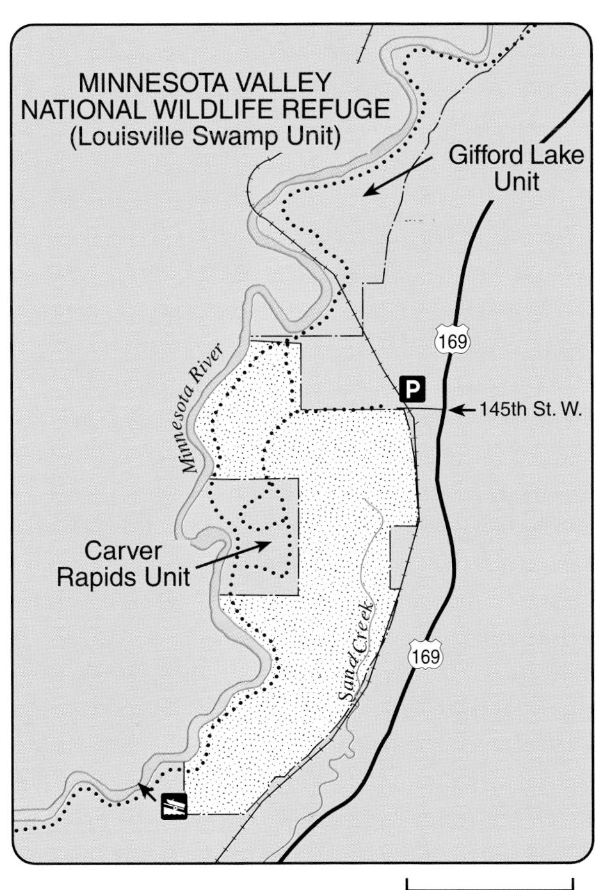

Contact:

Minnesota Valley NWR
3815 E 80th Street
Bloomington MN 55425-1600
General information:
(612) 854-5900

Scientific and Natural Areas Program
DNR
Box 25
500 Lafayette Rd.
St. Paul MN 55155
(612) 297-2357

92–Carver Park Reserve

Why is this area special?

Carver Park Reserve encompasses 3,500 acres of mixed forest, grassland and wetland habitat. It supports a wide variety of wildlife, including osprey, trumpeter swans, common loons, red-tailed hawks, eastern bluebirds, bobolinks and migrating white pelicans. You can find all kinds of habitats here, including lakes and marshes, lowland forest, oak forest, maple-basswood forest and old fields.

Visit the area's three-acre reconstructed prairie with coneflowers, asters, tall grasses and a large butterfly and hummingbird garden. A wildlife watching blind, located at the Fred E. King Waterfowl Sanctuary, overlooks an extensive wetland complex and provides an excellent opportunity to see both migrating and nesting water birds and waterfowl. You can see the successfully-reintroduced trumpeter swans from this spot.

Jane Norris

A feeding station, located at the Lowry Nature Center, attracts many species of birds, as well as deer, raccoons, squirrels, chipmunks, woodchucks and ground squirrels. A shorebird pond, located on the road to the nature center, can have a low enough water level to expose mud flats and attract shorebirds as they migrate in spring and mid-summer.

Note:

You will find easy access to this preserve through the extensive trail system, including paved biking and hiking trails. Daily or annual permits are required for all cars entering the park reserve. Stop at the nature center for information about current sightings and wildlife watching opportunities.

Visit the nearby Minnesota Landscape Arboretum (site 93) to do more wildlife watching.

Best viewing time:

How do I get there?

Maps: MN Highway Coordinate: Metro Inset U-27
PRIM Area: South Metro Area
Delorme MN Atlas Grid #: 40 D-4

Additional directions:

Carver Park Reserve is located southwest of Minneapolis in Victoria. Take Highway 7 west from Minneapolis to Carver County Road 11. Turn left on County Road 11 (also called Victoria Drive) and follow the signs to the nature center.

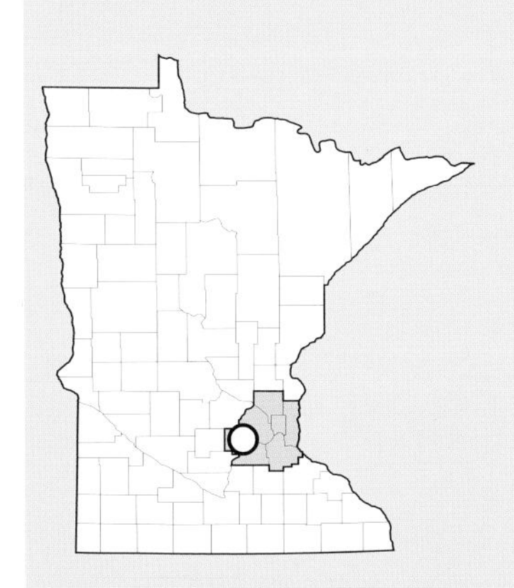

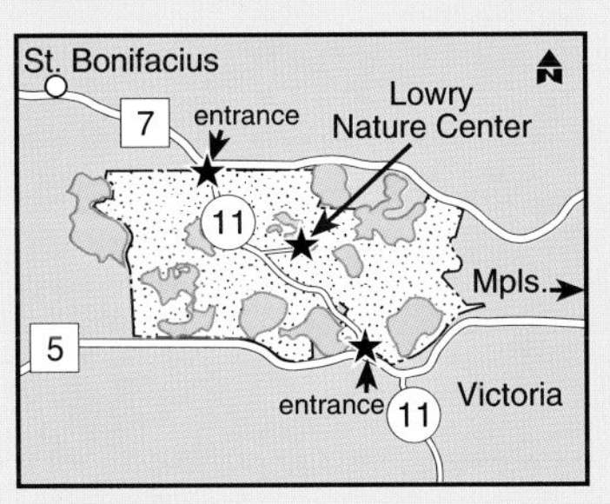

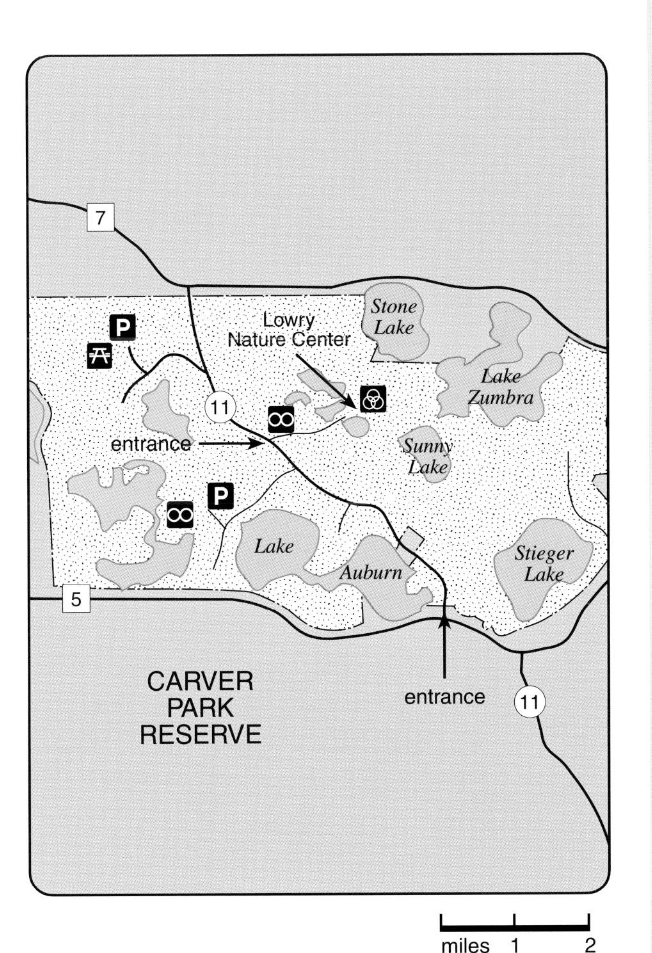

Facilities:

Recreational Opportunities:

Contact:

Carver Park Reserve
Lowry Nature Center
P. O. Box 270
Victoria MN 55386
(612) 472-4911

93–Minnesota Landscape Arboretum

C. Henderson

Tiger swallowtail

Why is this area special?

The Arboretum's 935 acres contain such a variety of plants and plant communities that good wildlife watching is almost always guaranteed. Although most people associate the Arboretum with sculptured formal gardens, a large portion of the site supports natural woodland, marshland and restored prairie areas that are accessible by an extensive trail system.

Animal species you might find here include swallows, vireos, flycatchers, Canada geese, woodpeckers, sora, green heron, Virginia rail, swamp sparrow, butterflies and deer.

In the forested areas, look for eastern wood pewees, blue-gray gnatcatchers, great crested flycatchers and red-eyed vireos. In the prairies, search for sedge wrens and numerous butterflies. The formal gardens also attract many butterflies and hummingbirds. Fireflies, not often seen in the metro area anymore, light up the sky here on summer nights.

Note:

There is an admission fee to enter the arboretum. The Carver Park Reserve (site 93) is close by to do more wildlife watching.

Jane Norris

The Arboretum has miles of hiking trails in summer and cross-country ski trails in winter through northern woodlands, native prairie and natural marshes. Pick up a trail map when you pay your admission fee.\

Best viewing time:

How do I get there?

Maps: MN Highway Coordinate: Metro Inset U-27
PRIM Area: South Metro Area
Delorme MN Atlas Grid #: 40 E-5

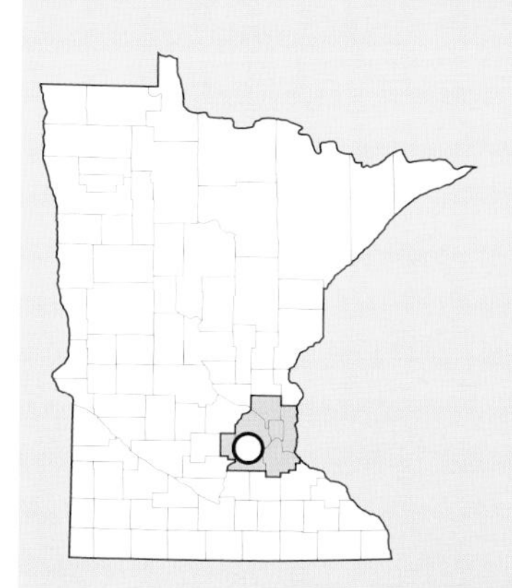

Additional directions:

The Arboretum is located just west of Chanhassen on Highway 5, 9 miles west of I-494.

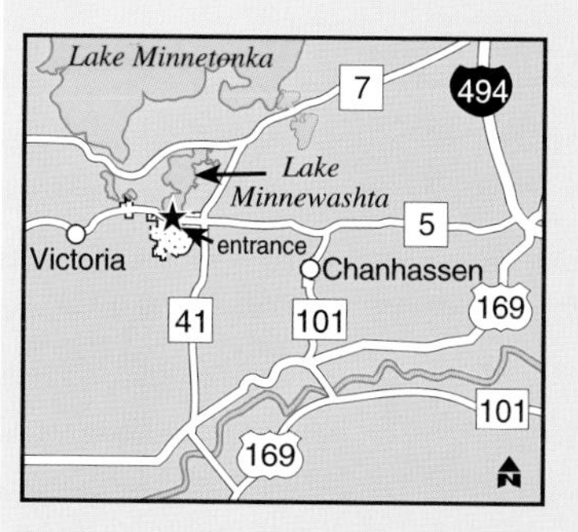

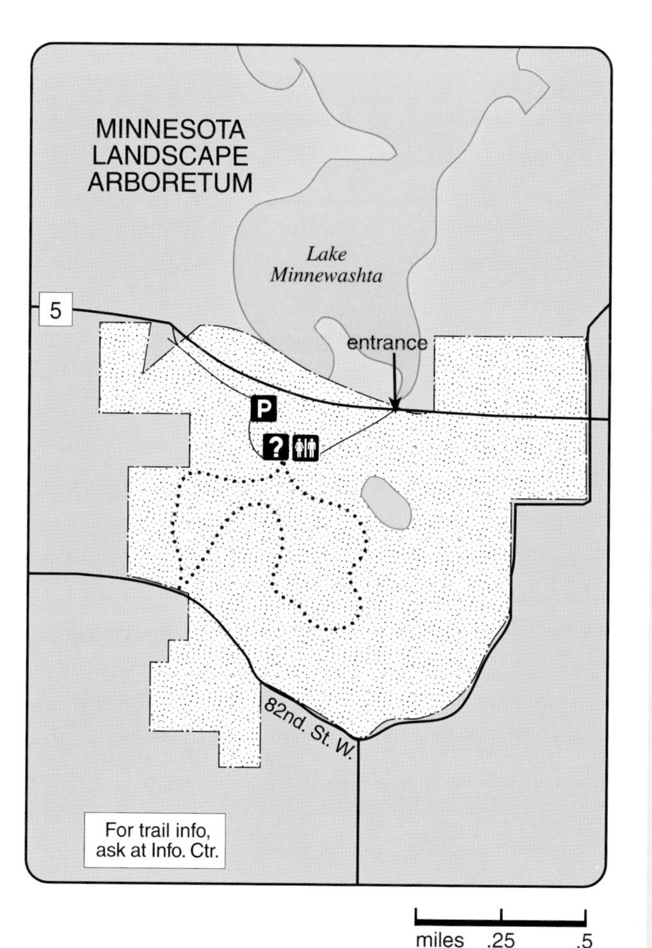

miles .25 .5

Facilities:

Recreational Opportunities:   

Contact:

Minnesota Landscape Arboretum
3675 Arboretum Drive
P. O. Box 39
Chanhassen MN 55317-0039
(612) 443-2460

94–Murphy-Hanrehan Park Reserve

Why is this area special?

Murphy-Hanrehan Park Reserve provides metro wildlife watchers with a prime example of an eastern mixed deciduous forest dominated by oak. Some of the bird species found here are at the northern limit of their range.

This is one of the only known spots in the state for nesting hooded warblers. Also nesting in the area are acadian flycatchers, blue-winged warblers, blue-gray gnatcatchers, American redstarts, ovenbirds, rufous-sided towhees, wood thrushes, scarlet tanagers, red-shouldered, broad-winged and Cooper's hawks. Beavers, rabbits and squirrels are abundant here. Look too for white-tailed deer, coyotes, red and gray foxes, raccoons, striped skunks, woodchucks, long-tailed weasels, mink and muskrats.

W. L. Penning

Red-eyed vireo

The northern part of this 2,800-acre park reserve, which includes Hanrehan Lake, is characterized by steep wooded hillsides interspersed with small, scattered wetlands. In the southern portion, which includes Murphy Lake and a branch of the Credit River, the forests are primarily oak with a much gentler terrain.

The southwest third of the park consists primarily of open fields being restored to prairie. This park is largely undeveloped and has a very remote, wilderness feel.

Note:

You will need a daily or annual permit on your vehicle when you enter the park reserve. The trails in this area are not well marked and pocket maps are not always available at the trailhead. A compass is advisable.

Best viewing time:

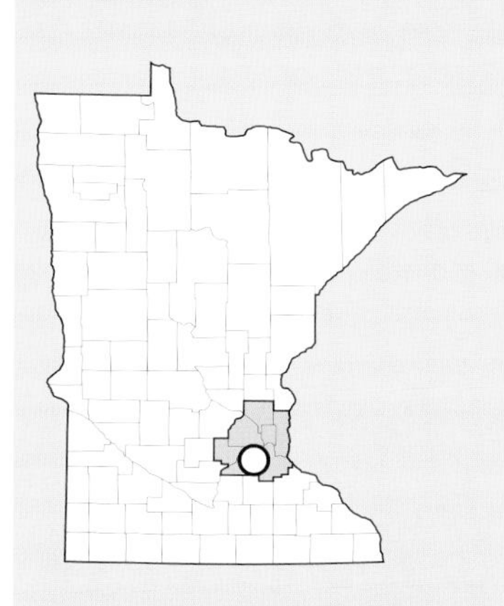

How do I get there?

Maps: MN Highway Coordinate: Metro Inset W-29
PRIM Area: South Metro Area
Delorme MN Atlas Grid #: 33 A-7

Additional directions:

Murphy-Hanrehan is located southwest of Minneapolis in Scott County. Take 35W south to County Road 42. Drive west to County Road 27 and turn left. Follow County Road 27 to County Road 74 and turn left. Turn right on County Road 75. The trailhead is on the left.

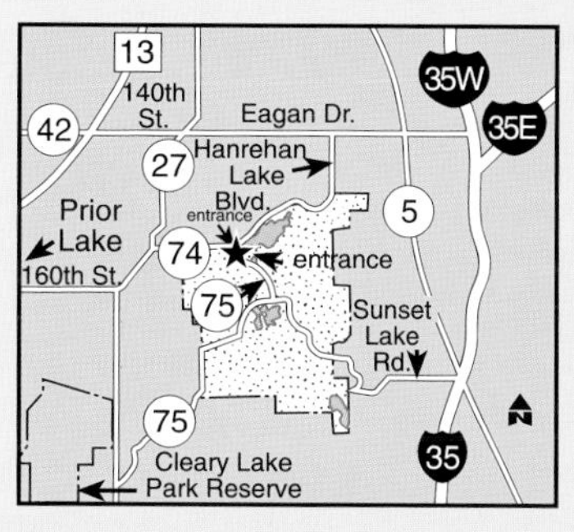

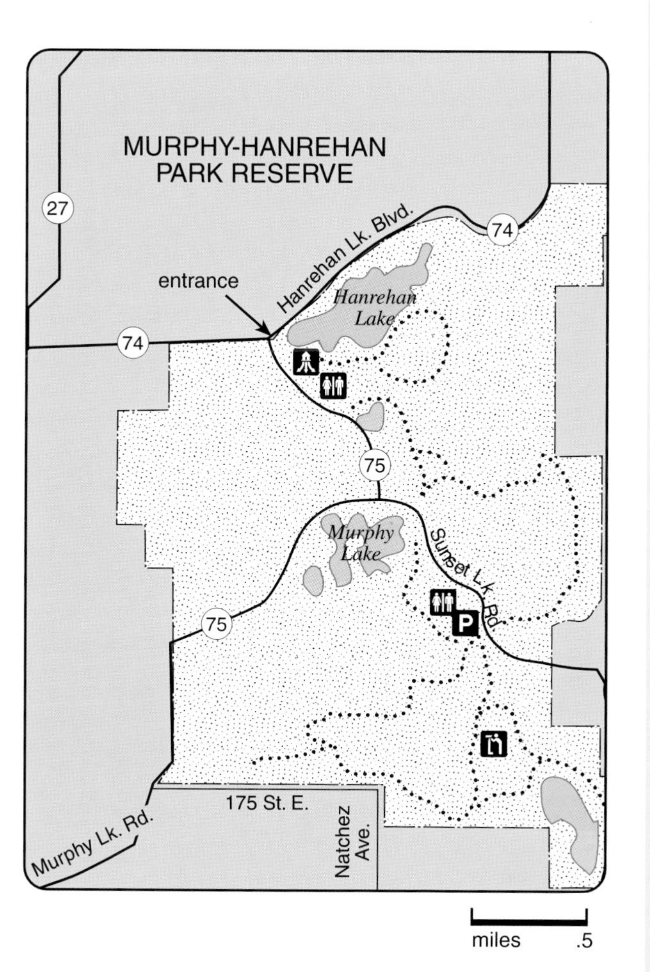

miles .5

Facilities:

Recreational Opportunities:   

Contact:

Murphy-Hanrehan Park Reserve
Hennepin County Parks
12615 County Road 9
Plymouth MN 55441-1248
(612) 447-2171

95–Lebanon Hills Regional Park

Why is this area special?

More than 17 miles of trails meander through the 2,231 acres of woodlands, many lakes, old fields, conifer plantings and marshes that make up Lebanon Hills Regional Park. The enormity of this area makes it a good choice for a day-long or even two-day visit.

The woodlands are primarily red and white oak forests intermingled with red maple, hackberry, elm, aspen, birch and ironwood. Shrubby understory plants like elderberry, chokecherry, raspberry, and dogwood provide fruits for gray catbirds, brown thrashers, American robins, eastern bluebirds and rose-breasted grosbeaks.

Other birds characteristic of eastern hardwood forests are indigo buntings, blue jays, northern cardinals, red-eyed vireos and eastern towhees. Wetland inhabitants include minks, muskrats, raccoons, green herons, western painted turtles, wood ducks and mallards.

Jane Norris

Note:

You can rent horses at a stable in the west section of the park and explore the area by horseback. You can also explore by canoe; a canoe route begins at Jensen Lake and continues east for about 2 miles. Although several small portages are necessary on the route, canoeing allows access to aquatic wildlife not visible from trails.

The Minnesota Zoo is located just west of the park and has many native and exotic animals exhibited in their "natural" habitats.

Best viewing time:

How do I get there?

Maps: MN Highway Coordinate: Metro Inset W-28
PRIM Area: South Metro Area
Delorme MN Atlas Grid #: 41 E-8

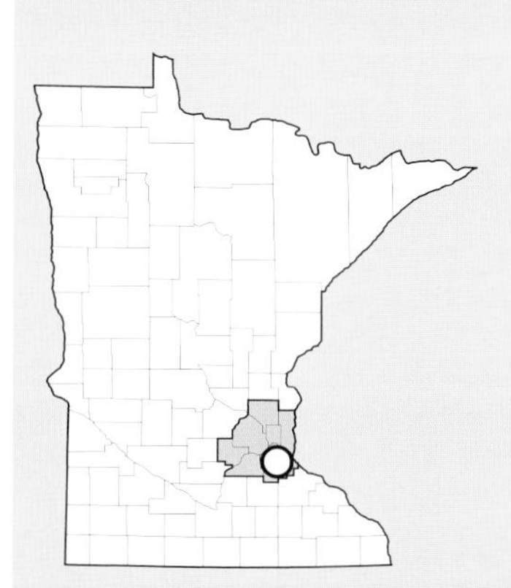

Additional directions:

From the Twin Cities take Highway 77 (Cedar Avenue) south across the Minnesota River. Exit on County Road 32 (Cliff Road) and go east. The Holland Lake entrance is off Cliff Road about 3/4-mile east of Pilot Knob Road.

To reach the Jensen Lake entrance, turn right on Pilot Knob Road and watch for entrance on the left.

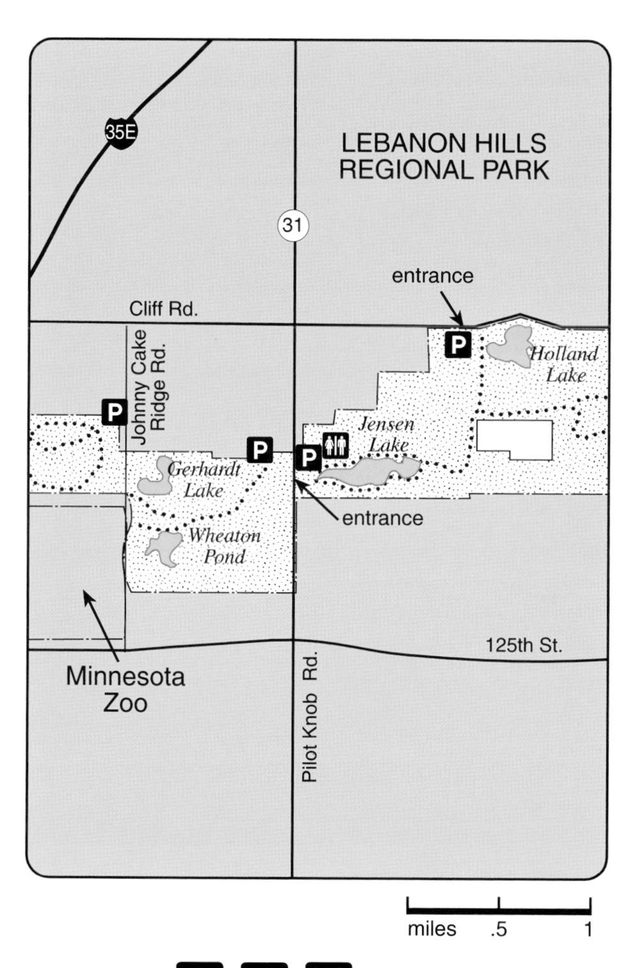

miles .5 1

Facilities:   

Recreational Opportunities:  

Contact:

Dakota County Parks Dept.
8500 127th Street E
Hastings MN 55033
(612) 438-4660

96–Lake Vadnais/Sucker Lake

Why is this area special?

When you visit Lake Vadnais, north of St. Paul, you have an excellent chance of seeing a common loon. This is one of the best places to see loons right in the heart of the Twin Cities. The road that splits the lake provides excellent viewing opportunities. Many other species of waterfowl visit these lakes during migration. You might see double-crested cormorants, hooded mergansers and black-crowned night herons. A rare neotropic cormorant was spotted here in 1992.

Lake and upland forests and conifer plantings on the north and east sides of the lake give this area a northwoods feeling close to the heart of the metropolitan area.

Note:

Facilities are available at Sucker Lake, and you can do shoreline fishing in designated areas. Grass/Snail Lake Regional Park, two miles northwest of Lake Vadnais, offers additional wildlife watching opportunities.

Since this lake provides the water supply for St. Paul, there is no development along the shore and no boat use. The solitude on the lake has contributed to the quality of the wildlife habitat there.

Jane Norris

Best viewing time:

How to I get there:

Maps: MN Highway Coordinate: Metro Inset X-25
PRIM Area: North Metro Area
Delorme MN Atlas Grid #: 41 C-9

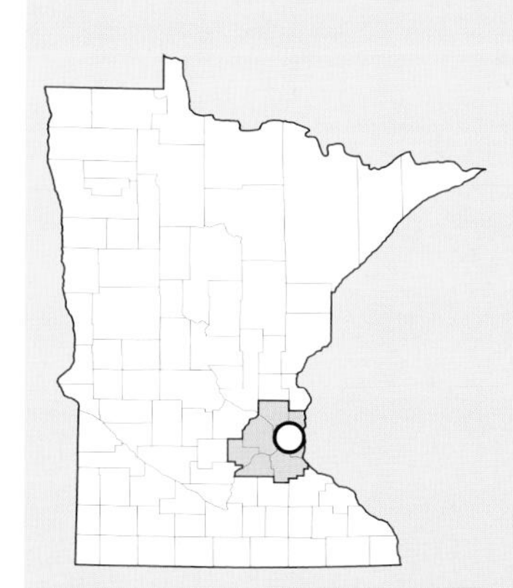

Additional directions:

Lake Vadnais is located in Vadnais Heights north of St. Paul. From I-694, exit north on County Road 49 (Rice Street). Immediately turn right onto the north frontage road (Vadnais Boulevard), follow it to Waterworks Road and turn left. This road cuts across the lake. To get to the west side of the lake, continue north along County Road 49.

To reach Grass/Snail Lake Regional Park from I-694, exit north on Victoria Street and continue to Gramsie Road. Turn right and watch for the parking area on the right.

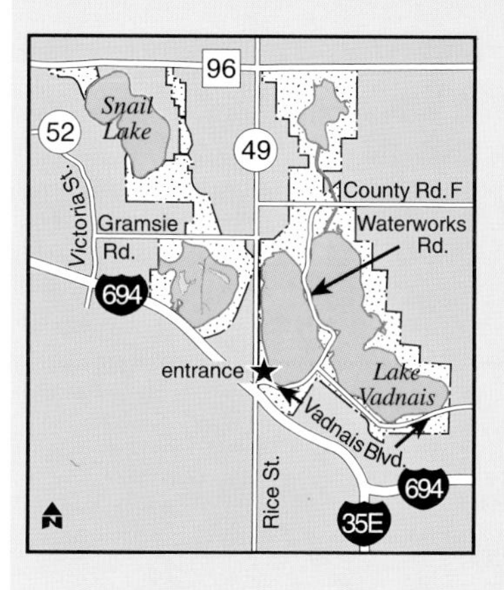

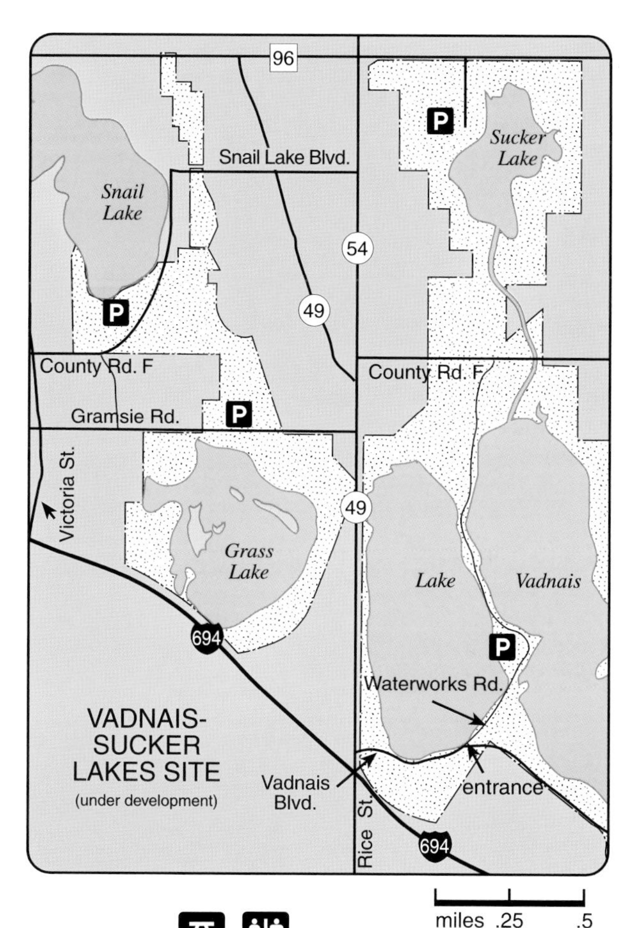

Facilities:  

Recreational Opportunities: 

Contact:

Ramsey County Parks and Recreation Dept.
2015 N Van Dyke Street
Maplewood MN 55109
(612) 748-2500

97–Battle Creek Regional Park

Why is this area special?

Encompassing more than 750 acres of diverse habitats including oak woods, old fields, creek and second-growth woodlands, with some blufftop vistas overlooking the Mississippi River valley, this park is home to a variety of wildlife species.

You can find warblers here during spring and fall migration, as well as great horned owls, pileated woodpeckers and a host of songbirds. Look for white-tailed deer, raccoon, red fox and many small mammals at this site.

Although this site is located less than five miles from downtown St. Paul, it is a year-round destination for local birders and nature enthusiasts.

Note:

The blufftop is accessible off Battle Creek Road, north of Lower Afton Road. The main picnic area is located in the northeast corner of the intersection of Upper Afton and McKnight Road.

C. Henderson

Ovenbird

Best viewing time:

How do I get there?

Maps: MN Highway Coordinate: Metro Inset Y-26
PRIM Area: South Metro Area
Delorme MN Atlas Grid #: 47 D-1

Additional directions:

Exit on McKnight Road off I-94 at the eastern edge of St. Paul. Proceed south to the park. Trailheads are located near the intersections of McKnight and Lower Afton Road, at Winthrop Street just south of Upper Afton Road, and at Point Douglas Road north of Lower Afton Road.

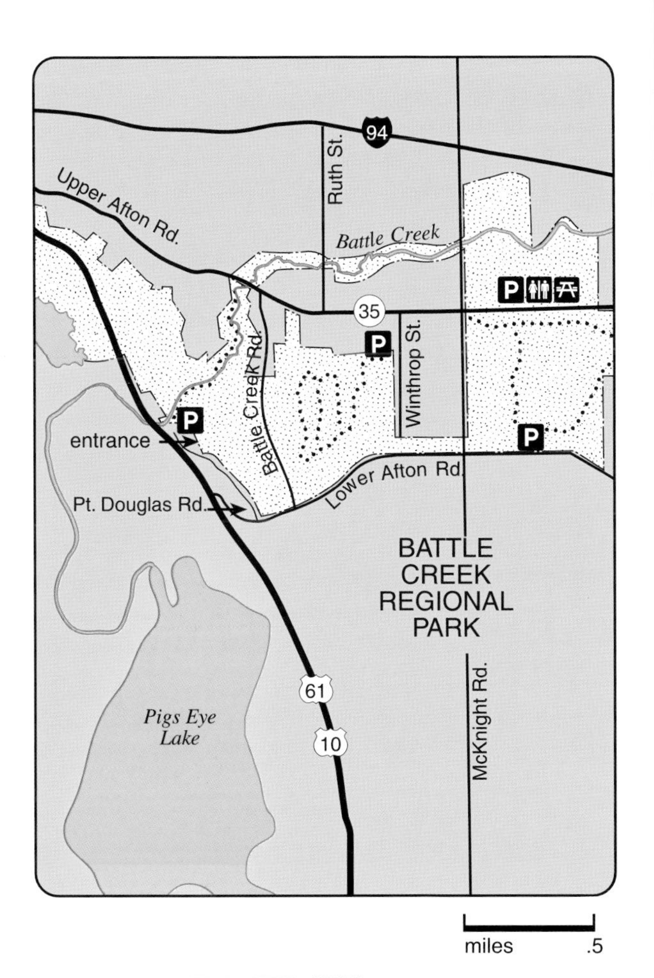

miles .5

Facilities:

Recreational Opportunities:  

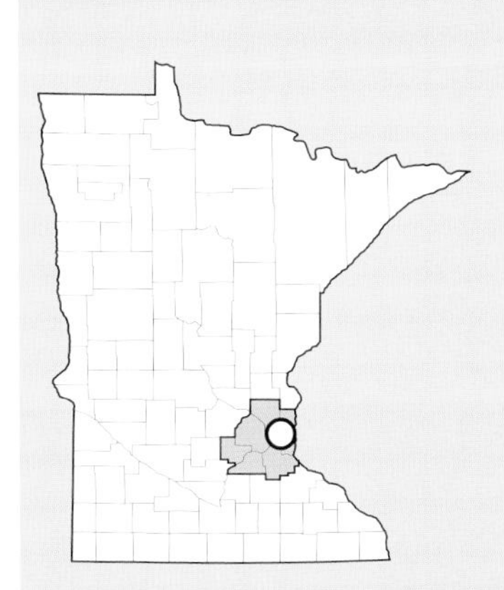

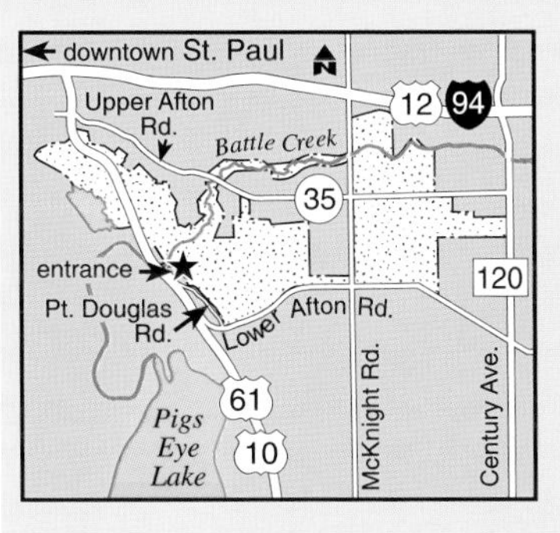

Contact:

Ramsey County Parks and Recreation Dept.
2015 N Van Dyke Street
Maplewood MN 55109
(612) 748-2500

98–Crosby Farm/Hidden Falls Parks

Why is this area special?

Crosby Farm and Hidden Falls Regional Park parallel the east bank of the Mississippi River for five miles in southwest St. Paul. The river here retains much of its natural essence, so as you walk along its banks you might forget that you're in a major metropolitan area.

Hidden Falls Park begins several miles north of the Mississippi's confluence with the Minnesota River and continues south to Crosby Farm Park. The steep, wooded bluffs and rock outcroppings provide a sharp contrast to the floodplain forest along the river.

Animal species to look for include great egrets, belted kingfishers, herons and black-billed cuckoos. There are even records of nesting prothonotary warblers. You could also see bald eagles here during the winter.

Note:

In addition to the trail that follows the east bank of the Mississippi, there is also a paved biking and hiking trail along the bluff, providing good birding opportunities during migration. This is a good spot for wildlife watchers with small children, as most of the trails are stroller accessible.

Crosby Farm Park also offers self-guided nature trails.

Jane Norris

Best viewing time:

How do I get there?

Maps: MN Highway Coordinate: Metro Inset X-27
PRIM Area: South Metro Area
Delorme MN Atlas Grid #: 41 D-8

Additional directions:

To reach Hidden Falls Park from I-94, exit south on County Road 51 (Snelling Avenue). Continue on Snelling to Ford Parkway and turn right. Ford Parkway will end at Mississippi River Boulevard. Turn left. Park entrance is on the right. To reach the Crosby Farm, continue south on Mississippi River Boulevard to the intersection of Gannon and Shepard Road. The entrance is on the right. Continue down the hill past the marina to reach the nature center and additional trails. This road may be closed in winter.

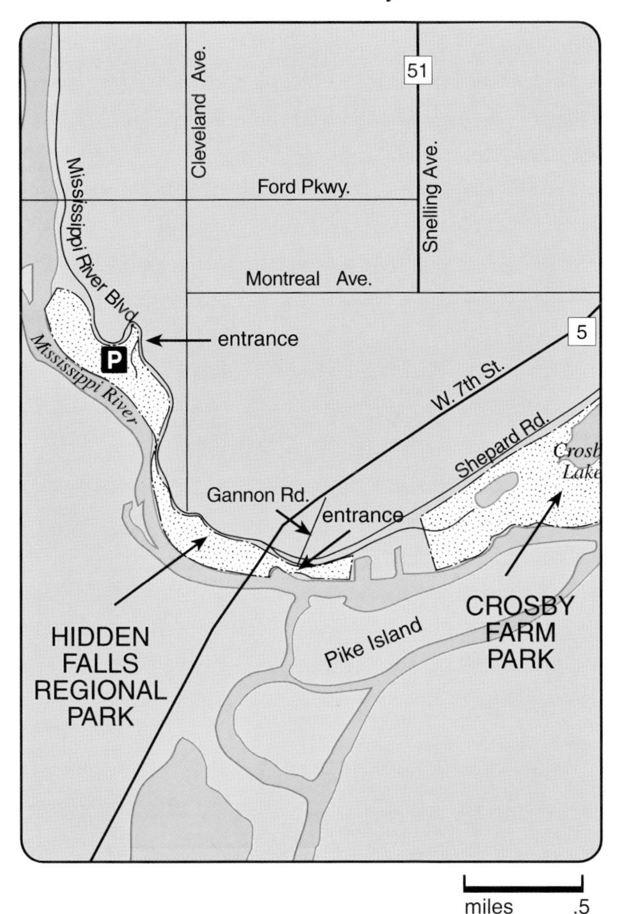

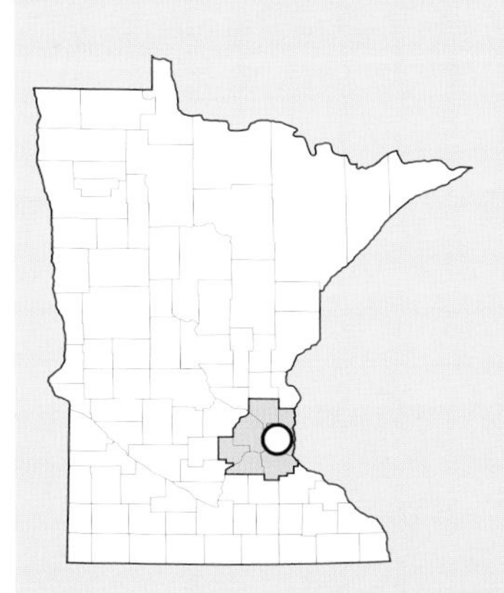

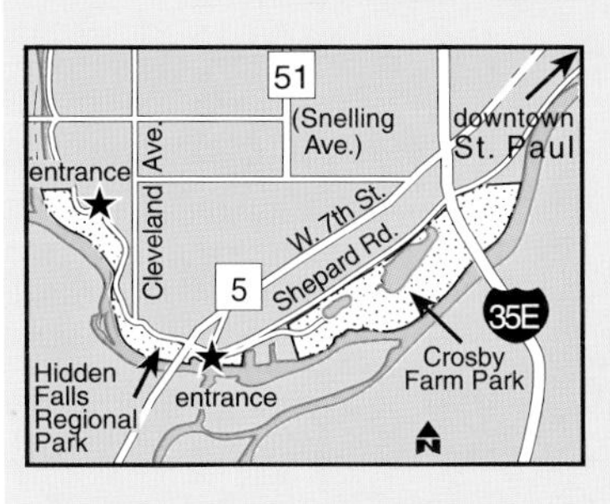

Facilities:

Recreational Opportunities:

Contact:

City of St. Paul
Division of Parks & Recreation
300 City Hall Annex
25 W 4th Street
St. Paul MN 55102
(612) 266-6400

99–Afton State Park

Why is this area special?

Spectacular views, minimal development and rugged terrain are all part of the wildlife watching experience at Afton State Park. Explore the oak savannas, prairies, oak woodlands and floodplain forests. The river overlooks provide excellent vantage points for watching migrating raptors and the Trout Brook Valley area is great for spring warblers and other migrating and nesting songbirds.

You can often see deer along the drive from the gatehouse to the visitor center. Look for field sparrows and savanna sparrows, eastern and western meadowlarks, indigo buntings, blue-gray gnatcatchers, scarlet tanagers, wood thrushes, eastern bluebirds, Baltimore orioles and pileated woodpeckers. Listen as frogs and toads call in the spring.

Note:

Although the terrain here is quite rugged and hiking can be strenuous, you can see many different animal species and great views of the St. Croix River without hiking very far.

A daily or annual permit is needed to enter the state parks.

Jane Norris

Best viewing time:

How do I get there?

Maps: MN Highway Coordinate: Metro Inset Z-27
PRIM area: South Metro Area
DeLorme MN Atlas Grid #: 42 E-2

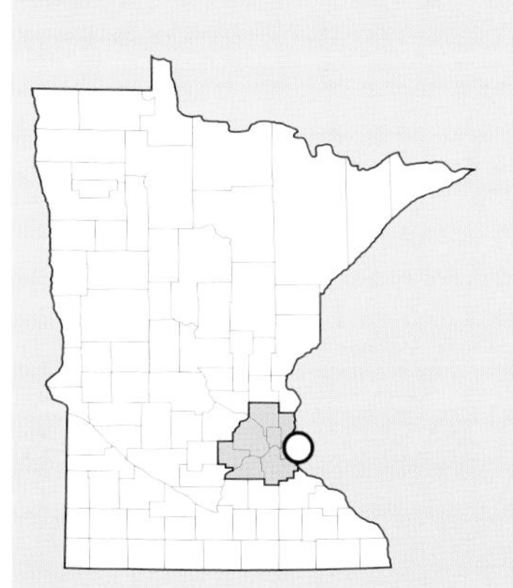

Additional directions:

Afton State Park is located east of St. Paul. Take I-94 east to County Road 15, and then drive 7 miles to County Road 20. Turn left and continue three miles to the park entrance.

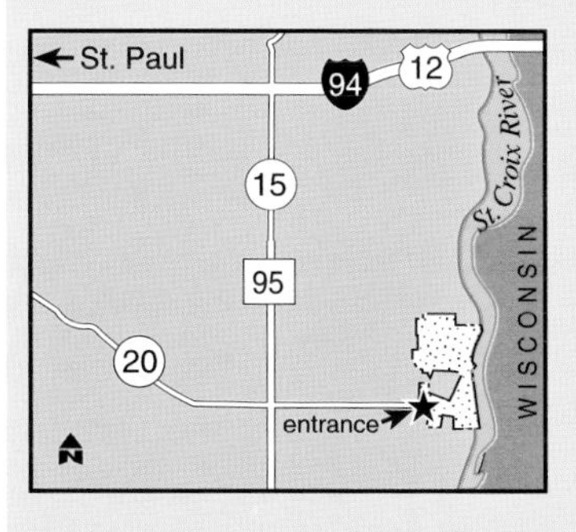

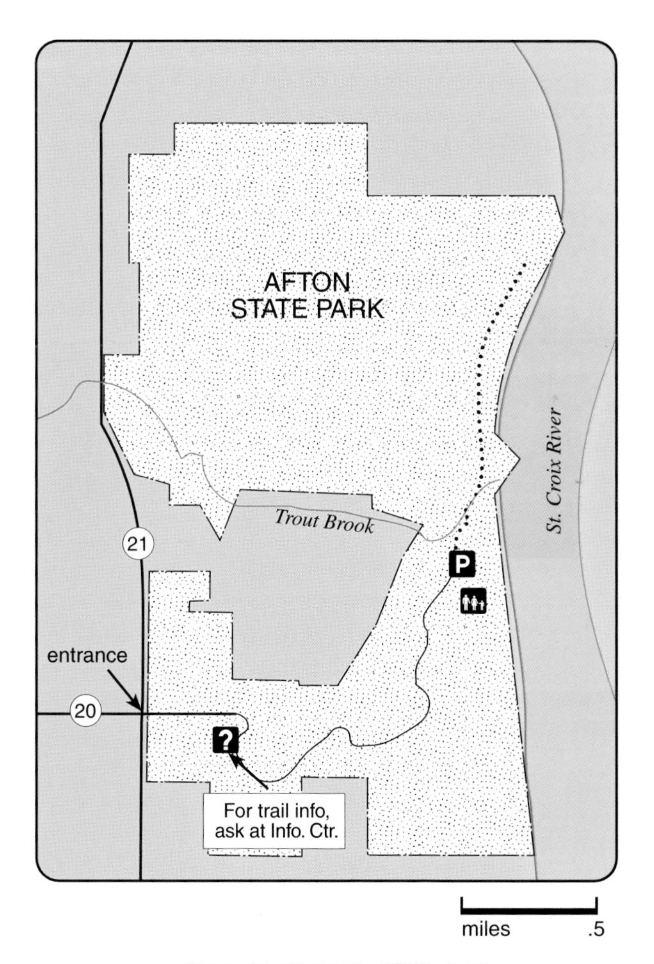

Facilities:    

Recreational Opportunities:

Contact:

Division of Parks and Recreation
DNR
500 Lafayette Road
St. Paul MN 55155-4040
(612) 296-6157
(888) MINNDNR

Afton State Park
6959 Peller Avenue South
Hastings MN 55033
(612) 436-5391

100–Lost Valley Prairie SNA

Why is this area special?

The 200-acre Lost Valley Prairie site contains a series of limestone ridges and dry swales between agricultural fields where a rich collection of native prairie plants thrive. Nearly a hundred species of birds have been recorded in the area, including clay-colored and Vesper sparrows, indigo buntings and raptors. You might find grassland species at this site that have become increasingly rare in the metro area.

Bird surveys on the Lost Valley Prairie SNA in 1990 and 1991 revealed 115 species. About 32 different birds nest here including a pair of red-tailed hawks. There are eastern kingbirds, eastern bluebirds, eastern meadowlarks, gray catbirds, brown thrashers, rose-breasted grosbeaks and indigo buntings. Native sparrows include clay-colored, field, vesper and song sparrows. Turkey vultures and whip-poor-wills also occur in the area.

Shrubby cover comprised of sumac, eastern red cedar, American plum and box elder are being removed from this area as part of a prairie restoration plan. This should cause a shift from shrub-nesting birds to more grassland species in future years.

Jane Norris

Best viewing time:

How do I get there?

Maps: MN Highway Coordinate: Metro Inset Z-28
PRIM Area: South Metro Area
Delorme MN Atlas Grid #: 42 E-1

Additional directions:

From the Twin Cities, drive south on Highway 61 to Highway 95. Drive north on Highway 95, then east on 110th Street (County Road 78) to Nyberg Avenue. The park is at the north end of the road.

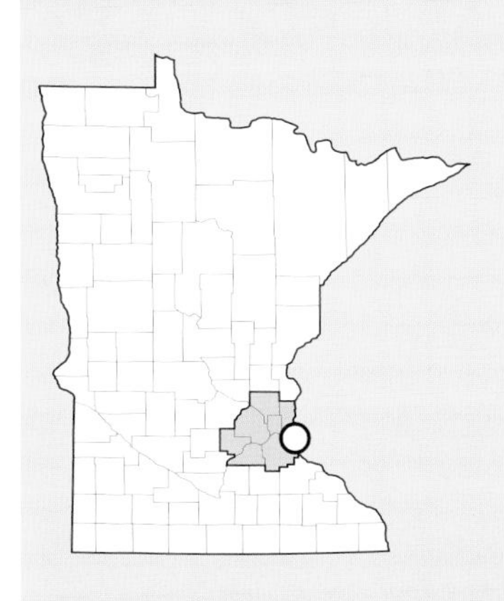

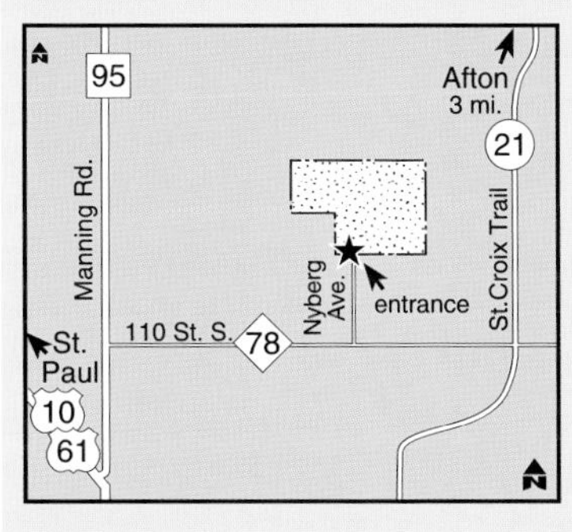

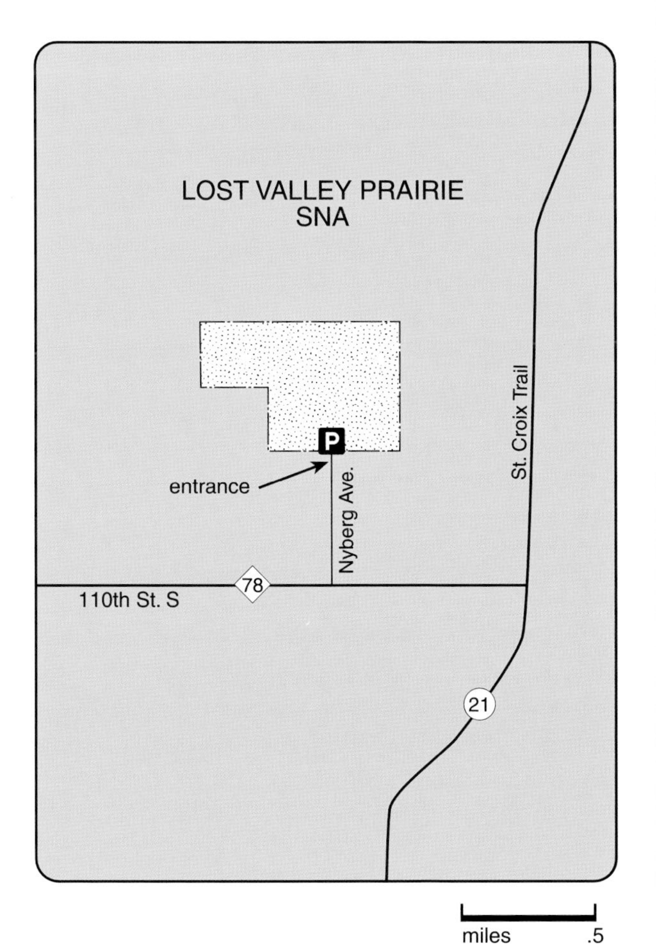

miles .5

Facilities: P

Recreational Opportunities:

Contact:

Scientific and Natural Areas Program
DNR
Box 25
500 Lafayette Road
St. Paul MN 55155-4007
(612) 297-2357

Southeast-Blufflands and Big Woods

From ridges to river bottoms and bluff prairies to Big Woods, this region is home to a wide array of plants and animals. Often called the driftless area, this portion of southeastern Minnesota was missed by the Wisconsin glaciation, the most recent glacial movement. As the last glacier retreated northward approximately 12,000 years ago, wind-blown soil was deposited here and melt waters carved the great Mississippi River Valley. Streams and rivers relentlessly cut their own valleys. Compared to the rest of Minnesota, which was scoured by glacial ice and littered with rock and ground debris, the southeast region's landscape remained relatively untouched.

A. B. Sheldon

Cope's gray treefrog

Plant and animal communities in this corner of the state represent an era long gone. Pleistocene snails, for example, can still be found on cool, north-facing bluff ridges.

Although European settlement and modern agriculture have greatly altered southeast Minnesota's diverse landscape, many plant communities remain relatively intact, though in smaller proportions. Floodplain forests still grow along the river bottoms. Oak woodlands and maple basswood forests cover steep uplands in the stream and river-cut valleys. Prairie remnants scatter across the south and west sides of many bluffs and road ditches. Cropland and pasture cover a good portion of the flatland today.

You can see the transition between plant communities as you travel from the region's east to west side. The blufflands give way to big woods and grasslands. Shallow lakes and wetlands appear among the extensive farm fields in Freeborn, Steele and Rice Counties. Small tracts of maple basswood forest add interest to this otherwise-groomed landscape.

The entire region has a greater number of amphibian and reptile species than any other portion of the state. Timber rattlesnakes, blue racers, hognose, smooth green and bull snakes are an integral part of the area. The 12 native species of frogs and toads fill the night air with ear-ringing choruses. Other wildlife species include white-tailed deer, wild turkeys, ruffed grouse and ring-necked pheasants. Bird species flock to southeast Minnesota. Wintering bald eagles have discovered the open water on the Mississippi River and congregate in large numbers along the water's edge. Both grassland and woodland songbirds have found their niche in the varied habitats of this region. Waterfowl rest along Mississippi Flyway and nest near this region's waters, from the Mississippi River to the western lakes.

If you plan to hike in the southeast region's blufflands, prepare for rough terrain by wearing ankle-supporting footgear. Stay on designated trails and be wary of the remote chance of encountering a timber rattlesnake. Watch where you place your hands and feet to avoid inadvertent encounters. Timber rattlesnakes are the most timid of North American rattlesnakes and their population is very low, so you're not likely to meet one, but it's still a good idea to be prepared. If you do encounter a rattlesnake, simply maneuver around the animal and continue on. Report any sightings to the local resource manager.

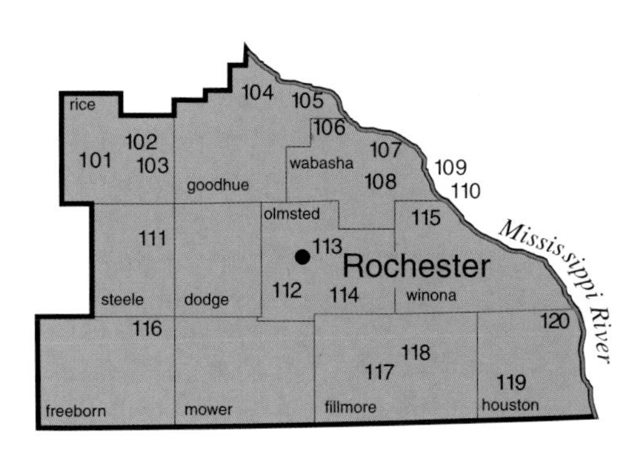

Sites

101. Boyd Sartell WMA
102. Cannon River Wilderness Area
103. Nerstrand Big Woods State Park
104. Colville Park
105. Frontenac State Park
106. Hok-Si-La City Park
107. Read's Landing
108. Zumbro Bottoms Forestry Unit
109. McCarthy Lake WMA/ Kellogg-Weaver Dunes SNA
110. Weaver Bottoms
111. Rice Lake State Park
112. Keller WMA
113. Silver Lake
114. Chester Woods County Park
115. Whitewater WMA/State Park
116. Geneva Lake WMA
117. Forestville State Park
118. Hvoslev WMA
119. Beaver Creek Valley State Park
120. Sheperd's Marsh

101–Boyd Sartell WMA

Best viewing time:

Why is this area special?

The brilliant golden bloom of marsh marigolds in April and May welcome you to the emergent marsh and maple-basswood forests of the Boyd Sartell WMA. Here you can watch migrating waterfowl in their mating plumage along the headwaters of the Cannon River and adjacent Shield's Lake. Mallards, blue-winged teal, wood ducks, hooded mergansers and green-winged teal join comical ruddy ducks on the water.

Watch the sedge meadows for a northern harrier trying to scare up one of the migrating shorebirds on the scattered mud flats. Stop here later in the breeding season and look for sandhill cranes lurking in the marsh. Boyd is an excellent place to sit and listen to calling sora and Virginia rails. Other species to watch for include Forster's terns, pied-billed grebes, red-winged blackbirds, semipalmated sandpipers, short-billed dowitchers, green herons, muskrats, beavers and softshell turtles.

 Hunting allowed. Call ahead for hunting season dates.

C. Henderson

Forster's tern

How do I get there?

Maps: MN Highway Coordinate: J-19
PRIM Area: Faribault
DeLorme MN Atlas Grid #: 33 D-6

Additional directions:

Take Highway 21 (Shieldsville Blvd.) north out of Faribault through Shieldsville, past Shields Lake to County Road 64 (Irwin Tr.) and turn southwest.

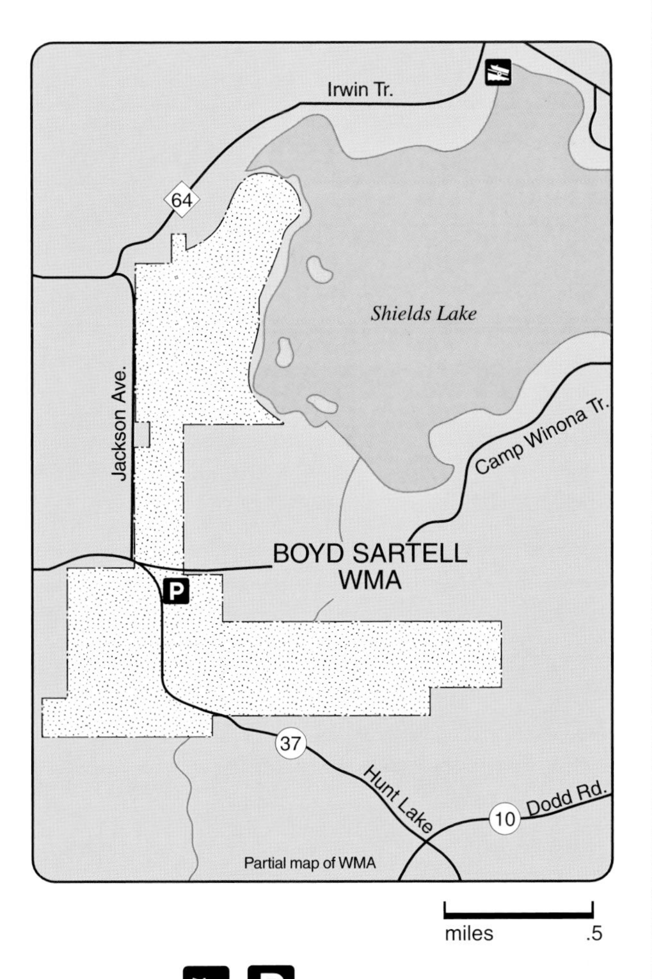

Facilities: P

Recreational Opportunities:

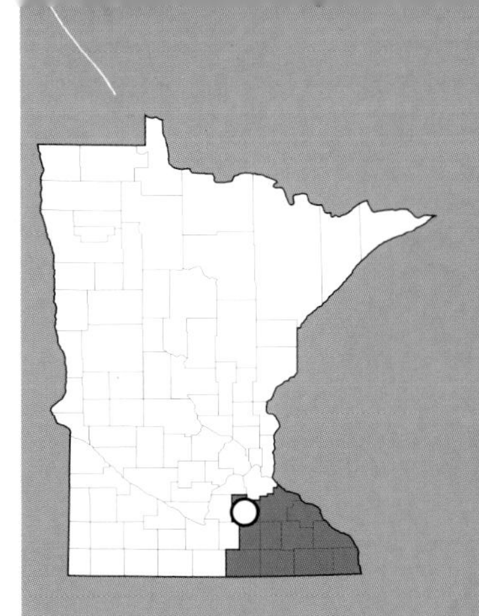

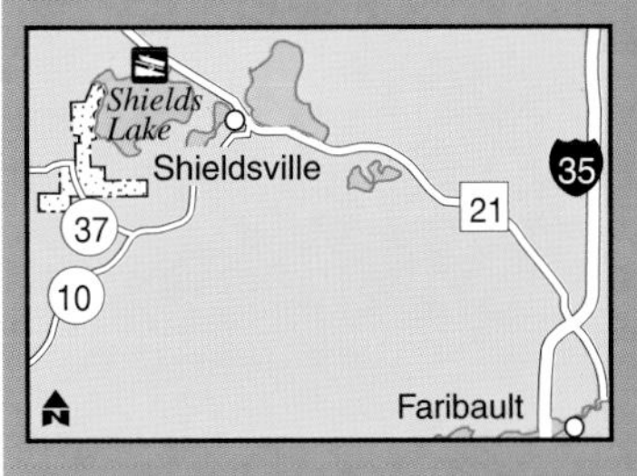

Contact:

DNR Area Wildlife Office
8485 Rose Street
Owatonna MN 55060
(507) 455-5841

102–Cannon River Wilderness Area

Why is this area special?

Escape from city life to the Cannon River Wilderness Area, where you'll find upland habitats including maple basswood forests, oak woodlands, savannas and prairies. Lowland habitats include floodplain forests, wet meadows, willow swamps and rare calcareous fens.

In early spring, fragile wildflowers carpet the forest. In the floodplain forest, look for elms ravaged by Dutch elm disease, a tragedy that has added another habitat to the area. Watch woodpeckers as they search the disease-stricken bark crevices for insects and nesting holes. Eastern bluebirds and wood ducks also make themselves at home in these tree cavities.

C. Henderson
Raccoon

You will find a variety of bird species here, including scarlet tanagers, turkey vultures, Cooper's hawks, spotted sandpipers, Canada geese, green herons, orchard orioles, red-bellied and pileated woodpeckers, yellow-bellied sapsuckers, great-horned and barred owls, wood and hermit thrushes, veeries, eastern bluebirds, wood ducks and prothonotary and Nashville warblers.

Watch also for other wildlife: opossums, deer mice, eastern cottontails, short-tailed weasels, eastern pipistrelle bats, common garter snakes, red-bellied snakes and Cope's gray tree frogs can all be found in the Cannon River area.

During the summer, the marshes, prairies and savannas burst into bloom, attracting a humming throng of dragonflies, butterflies, moths and birds.

C. Henderson
Mourning warbler

Best viewing time:

How do I get there?

Maps: MN Highway Coordinate: K-26
PRIM Area: Faribault
DeLorme MN Atlas Grid #: 33 D-8

Additional directions:

Go four miles north of Faribault on Highway 3. Turn onto access roads 145th St. E or 151st St. E.

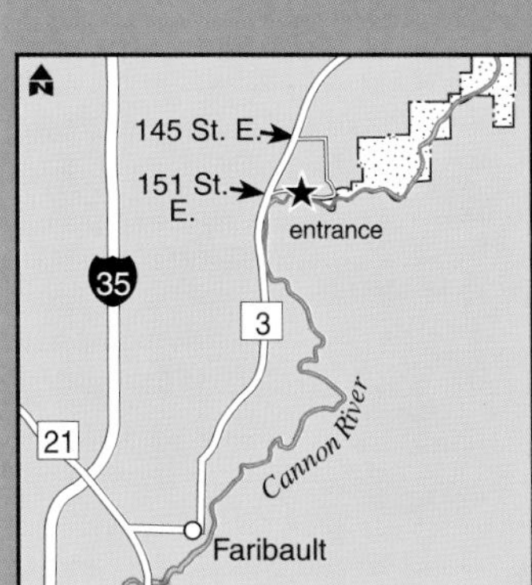

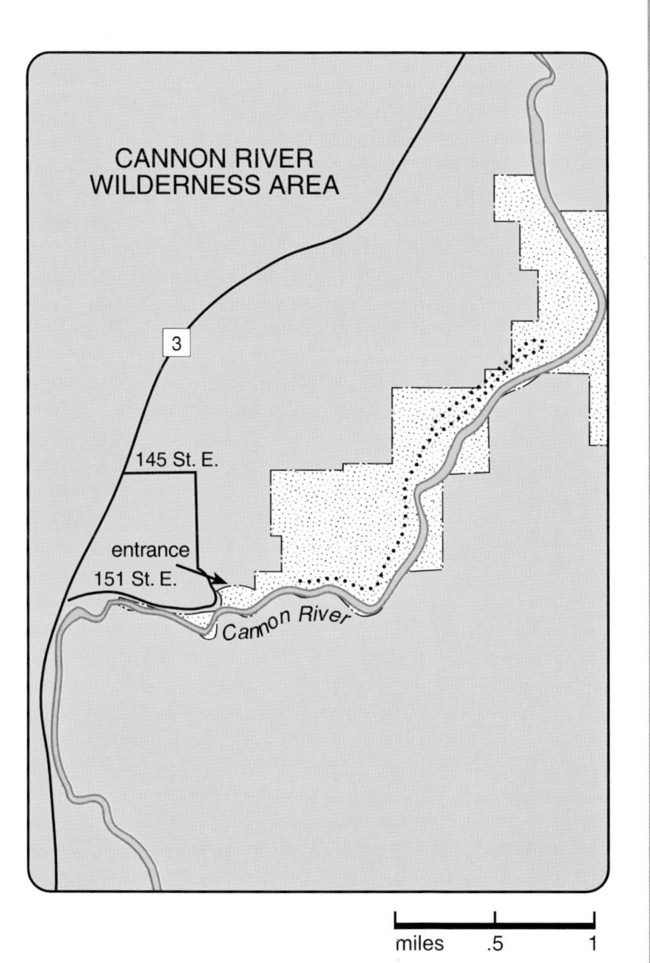

Facilities:

Recreational Opportunities:   

Contact:

Rice County Parks and Recreation
320 NW 20th Street
Faribault MN 55021
(507) 332-6112

103–Nerstrand Big Woods State Park

Why is this area special?

The Big Woods—or Bois Grand, as French explorers called this unique forested landscape—once covered over 3,400 square miles in Minnesota. Less than ten square miles of this sugar maple, basswood, American elm, green ash, ironwood and red oak hardwood forest remain.

Nerstrand Big Woods State Park is the largest remaining high-quality tract of this once-massive forest. Towering sugar maple and basswood trees shade a forest floor carpeted with spring wildflowers. Spring beauty, sharp-lobed hepatica, Dutchman's breeches and Minnesota's own rare dwarf trout lily are among more than 50 species gracing the forest floor. The trout lily is Minnesota's only endemic wildflower.

This relatively large tract of natural forest is a magnet for migrating and nesting forest birds. You'll find cerulean and chestnut-sided warblers, blue-gray gnatcatchers, wood thrushes, whip-poor-wills, ovenbirds, ruffed grouse and pileated and red-headed woodpeckers. You might also come across a white-tailed deer, gray squirrel, fox squirrel or mourning cloak butterfly. Be on the alert for the antics of resident woodchucks and raccoons.

Note:

Hike or ski along the 14 miles of trails of this park to increase your chances of seeing wildlife.

C. Henderson

Best viewing time:

How do I get there?

Maps: MN Highway Coordinate: K-19
PRIM Area: Faribault
DeLorme MN Atlas Grid #: 33 D-9

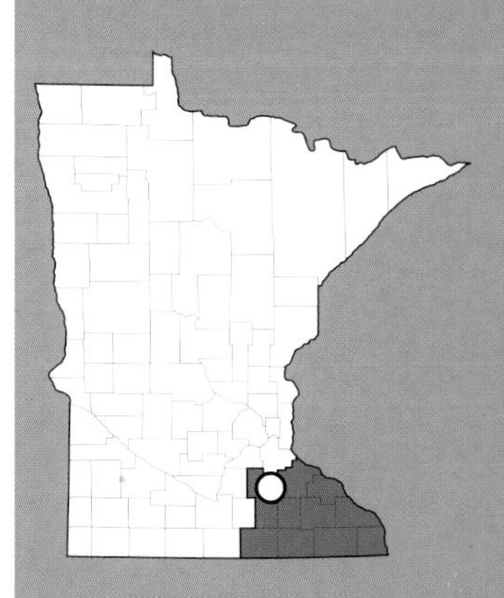

Additional directions:

This site is approximately 11 miles southeast of Northfield. From Highway 3 take Highway 246 southeast out of Northfield and follow the signs to the park. The park is 12 miles northeast of Faribault on County 27.

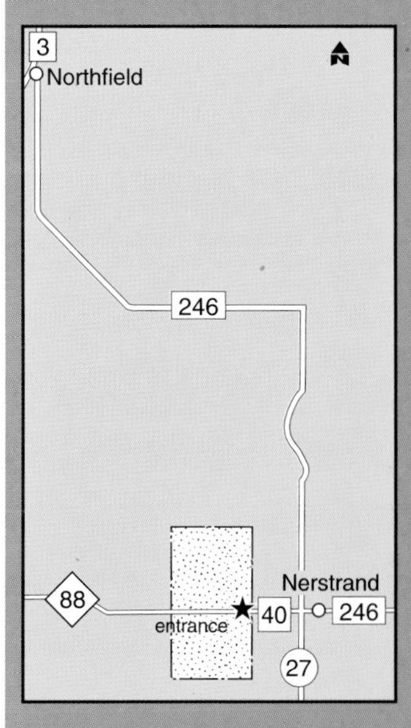

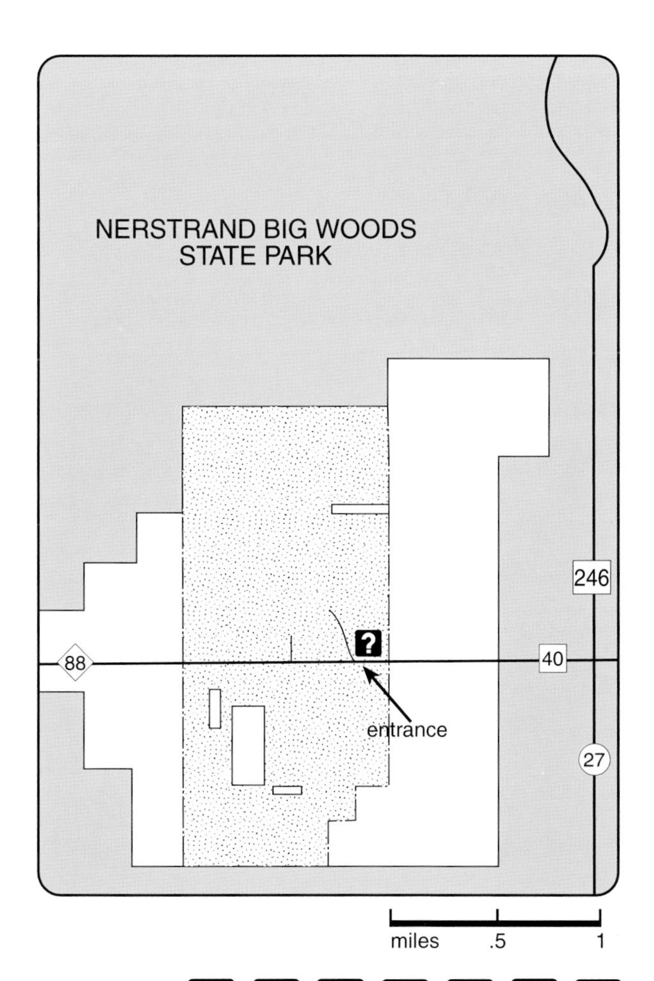

Facilities:

Recreational Opportunities:

Contact:

Nerstrand Big Woods
State Park
9700 170th Street E
Nerstrand MN 55053
(507) 334-8848

104–Colville Park

Why is this area special?

Situated on the southwest bank of the Mississippi River near Red Wing, the floodplain forest of Colville Park is one of the most popular spots in Minnesota to watch wintering bald eagles. Open water conditions persist all winter, providing the eagles with opportunities to fish. You will often see eagles perched along the wooded river banks waiting for their quarry to come within reach. In late winter you might catch a glimpse of the eagles' impressive aerial mating displays.

In the spring and fall you can see migrating ducks such as mallards, common mergansers and common goldeneyes feeding and loafing below the poised raptors. Look for an occasional great blue heron in the quiet bay off the main channel. You might also see downy, hairy and red-bellied woodpeckers, white-tailed deer, mink and gray squirrels.

Note:

Highway 61 is part of the Great River Road.

See the Featured Species section on page 16 for more information on eagles.

A. B. Sheldon

Bald eagles at Colville Park

Best viewing time:

How do I get there?

Maps: MN Highway Coordinate: L-18
PRIM Area: Metro South
DeLorme MN Atlas Grid #: 34 B-4

Additional directions:

Colville Park is south of Red Wing on the north side of Highway 61. Turn off Highway 61 onto frontage road by Days Inn Motel, follow signs to Colville by going under Highway 61.

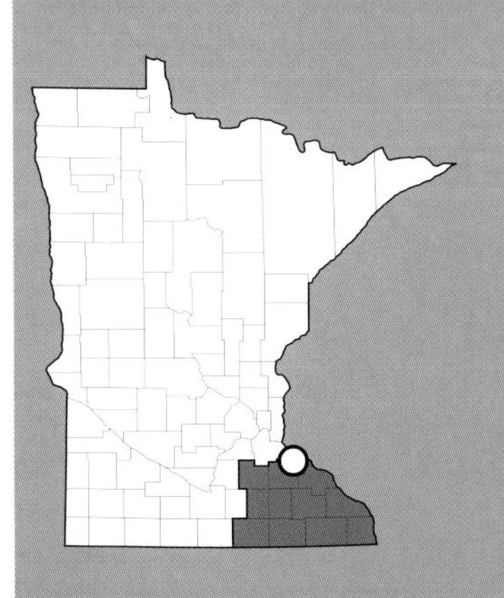

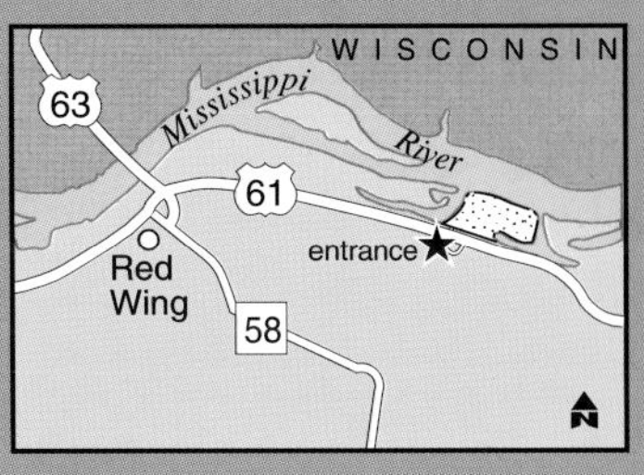

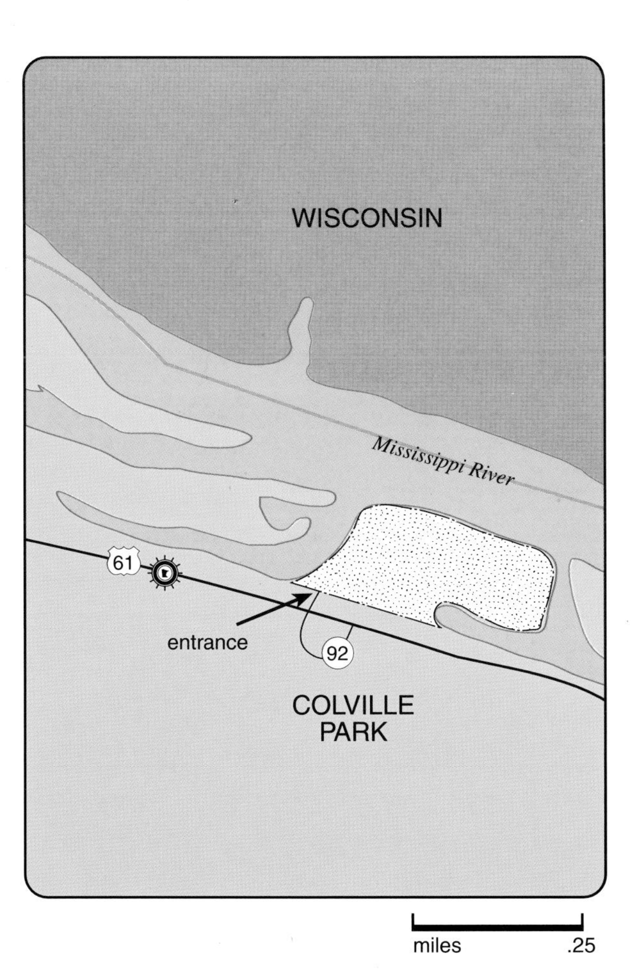

miles .25

Facilities:

Recreational Opportunities: 

Contact:

Red Wing Area
Chamber of Commerce
Box 133
Red Wing MN 55066
(800) 762-9516

105–Frontenac State Park

Why is this area special?

Frontenac State Park rises 450 feet above an expanse of the Mississippi River called Lake Pepin. A spectacular view of the river valley extends for miles in all directions. The park contains floodplain forest, maple-basswood forest, oak woodland, bluff prairie and grassland.

In autumn you can see migrating eagles, tundra swans, turkey vultures and broad-winged, red-tailed and sharp-shinned hawks as they soar above the blufftops. Prairie wildflowers and native grasses cling to the bluff prairies, where fox snakes sun themselves on rock outcrops.

C. Henderson

Wood duck ducklings

Contrast the blufftop experience with a hike through the silver maple and American elm in the floodplain forest. Birdwatchers flock to Frontenac to watch hundreds of warblers flitting in the floodplain forest canopy each spring. Take a spring evening excursion to the bottoms and be serenaded by choruses of frogs, toads and owls.

Other species to watch for at Frontenac include wild turkeys, rose-breasted grosbeaks, hermit thrushes, scarlet tanagers, blue-gray gnatcatchers, sanderlings, ruddy turnstones, white-tailed deer, red foxes and green, northern leopard, wood and tree frogs.

Note:

Check out the two and a half miles of self-guided trails in the park. Hiking or cross-country skiing often provides opportunities to see animals and birds not normally spotted while driving.

Some of the bluffside trails may be closed seasonally for visitors' protection.

Best viewing time:

How do I get there?

Maps: MN Highway Coordinate: M-18
PRIM Area: Metro South
DeLorme MN Atlas Grid #: 34 B-5

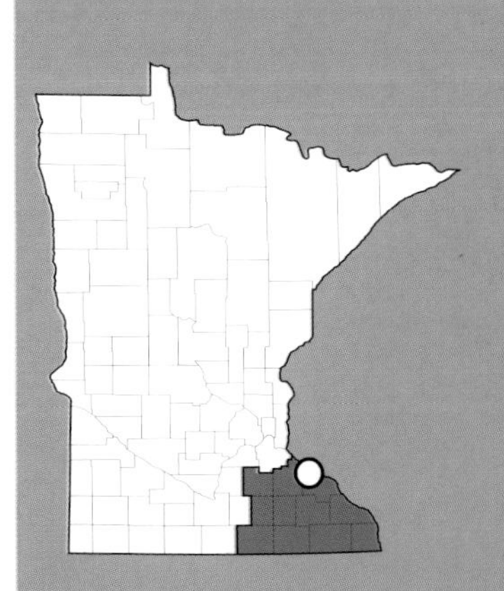

Additional directions:

Frontenac is located off Highway 61 ten miles southeast of Red Wing on the shore of Lake Pepin.

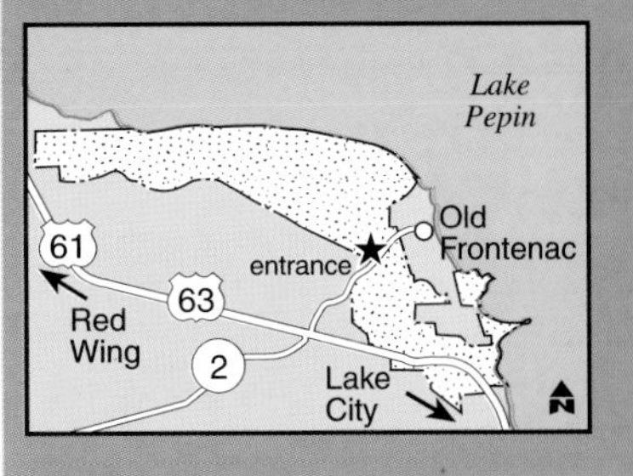

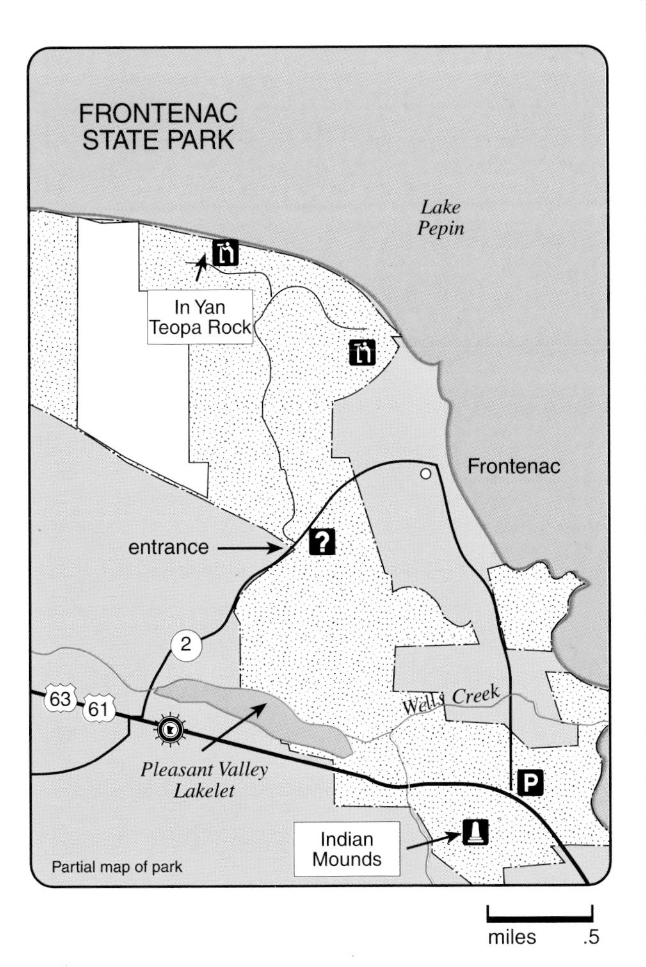

Facilities:

Recreational Opportunities:

Contact:

Frontenac State Park
29223 County 28 Boulevard
Lake City MN 55041
(612) 345-3401

106–Hok-Si-La City Park

Why is this area special?

The Hok-Si-La area is rich in history. The site of the Hotel Russel in the late 1800s, it has since been a silver fox farm, farmland, a Boy Scout camp and a city park. Despite its history, this floodplain forest hasn't changed much in the last 100 years.

The Mississippi River Valley is rich in biological diversity. Search for migrating shorebirds and warblers in the large oaks near the shore. You can find solitary, spotted and least sandpipers, ruddy turnstones and sanderlings here. Hok-Si-La is known to birders as a spring migration hot spot for warblers. Cape May, magnolia, bay-breasted, chestnut-sided and Nashville warblers all frequent the area.

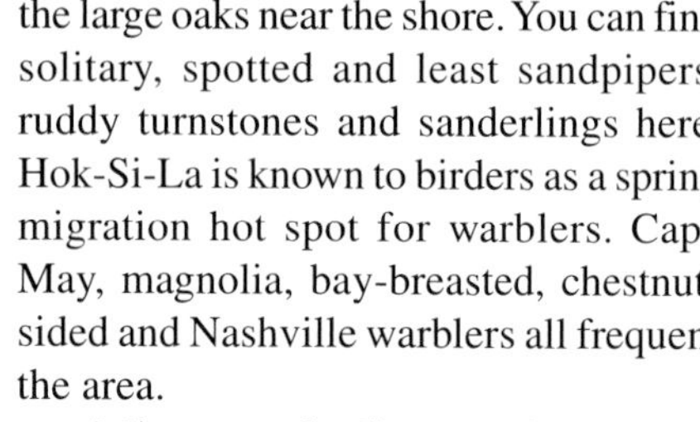

Bay-breasted warbler

Minnesota's first eagle nesting platform was erected in Hok-Si-La Park. Several bat houses also provide shelter for natural mosquito control. If you look hard, you might also run across an opossum, gray, fox or red squirrel, white-tailed deer, Cope's gray tree frog, American toad or smooth soft-shelled turtle.

Note:

See the Featured Species section on page 32 for more information on warblers.

Black-throated green warbler

Best viewing time:

How do I get there?

Maps: MN Highway Coordinate: M-18
PRIM Area: Rochester
DeLorme MN Atlas Grid #: 35 C-6

Additional directions:

Hok-Si-La Park is located on Highway 61 one mile north of Lake City on the shore of Lake Pepin.

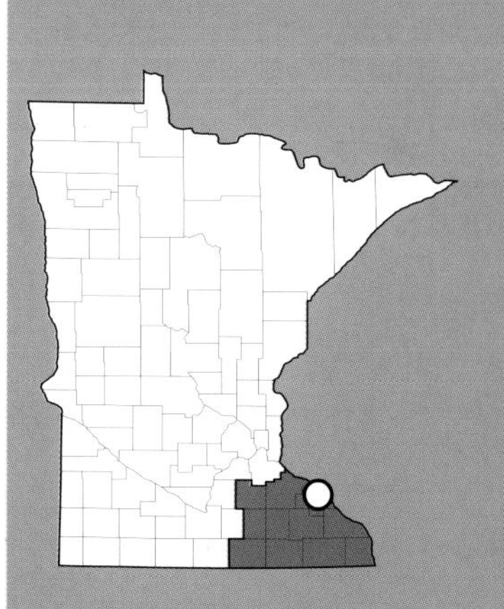

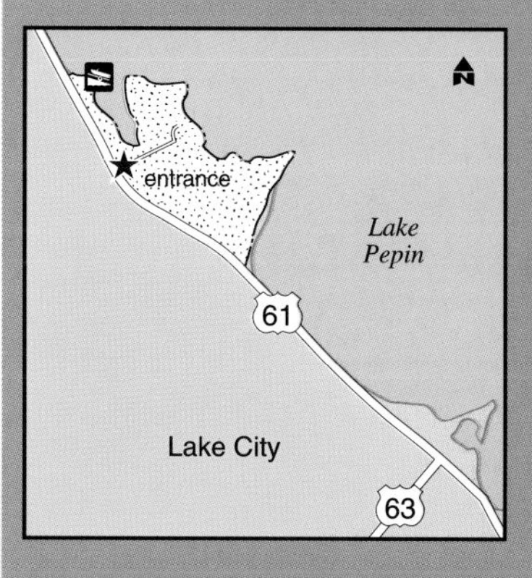

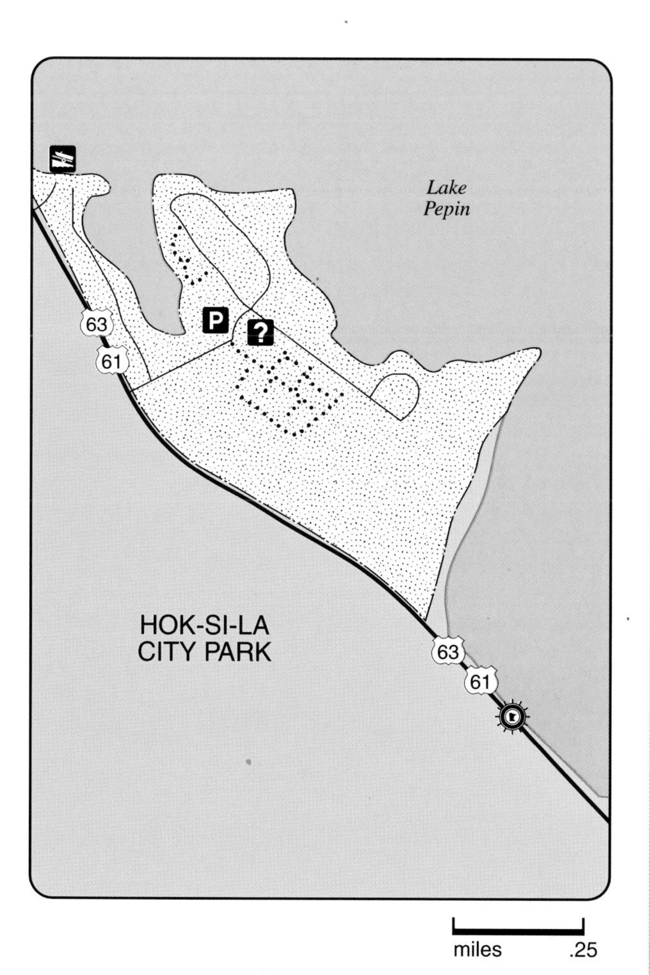

Facilities: 

Recreational Opportunities:

Contact:

Lake City Chamber of Commerce
212 South Washington Street
Lake City MN 55041-0151
(800) 369-4123

107–Read's Landing

Why is this area special?

On a summer day, you can watch bald eagles soar in the blue sky over Read's Landing and Camp Lacupolis. Watching bald eagles is also a fabulous winter activity at this site.

The flow of the Chippewa River emptying into the Mississippi keeps the water open in the winter. Here eagles use the ice-free spot near Read's Landing and Camp Lacupolis. They congregate in the open-water areas to feed on fish and waterfowl. Look for them along the edge of the ice and in trees along the shoreline.

Even though Benjamin Franklin hoped the wild turkey would be our national symbol, today we are proud of our bald eagles. You will get the thrill of seeing majestic bald eagles swooping low over the water or perched in a nearby tree.

A. B. Sheldon

Bald eagle

The Read's Landing floodplain forest is one of the best places to watch bald eagles in the Midwest. These eagles were once on the brink of extinction, and to see between 25 and 50 in a single day is a treat and a tribute to their comeback.

You could also see wintering rough-legged and red-tailed hawks, common mergansers and common goldeneyes at this site.

Note:

Use caution when you park along the town road and along Highway 61. There is a scenic overlook south of Camp Lacupolis that allows you to park off the highway. Keep a watchful eye on children near the fast-moving traffic. It's also a good idea to keep clear of the railroad tracks in Read's Landing, as trains come by often.

See the Featured Species section on page 16 for more information on bald eagles. A spotting scope is very useful at this site.

You'll notice large deposits of sand, known as "dredge spoils" across the shore. These deposits are a result of maintenance activities enabling barge traffic to travel up and down the river.

From December through March, continue south on Highway 61 to Wabasha to visit the Eaglewatch platform on the riverfront.

Best viewing time:

How do I get there?

Maps: MN Highway Coordinate: M-18
PRIM Area: Rochester
DeLorme MN Atlas Grid #: 35 D-8

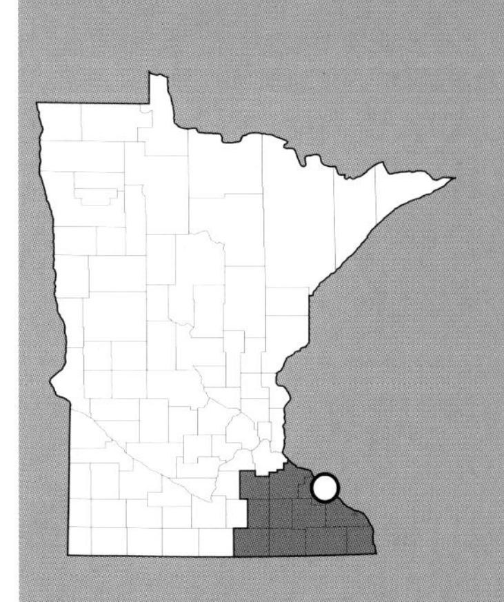

Additional directions:

The town of Read's Landing is 15 miles north of Wabasha on Highway 61. There are three MNDOT pulloffs north of Read's Landing on Highway 61 that offer scenic overlooks of Lake Pepin.

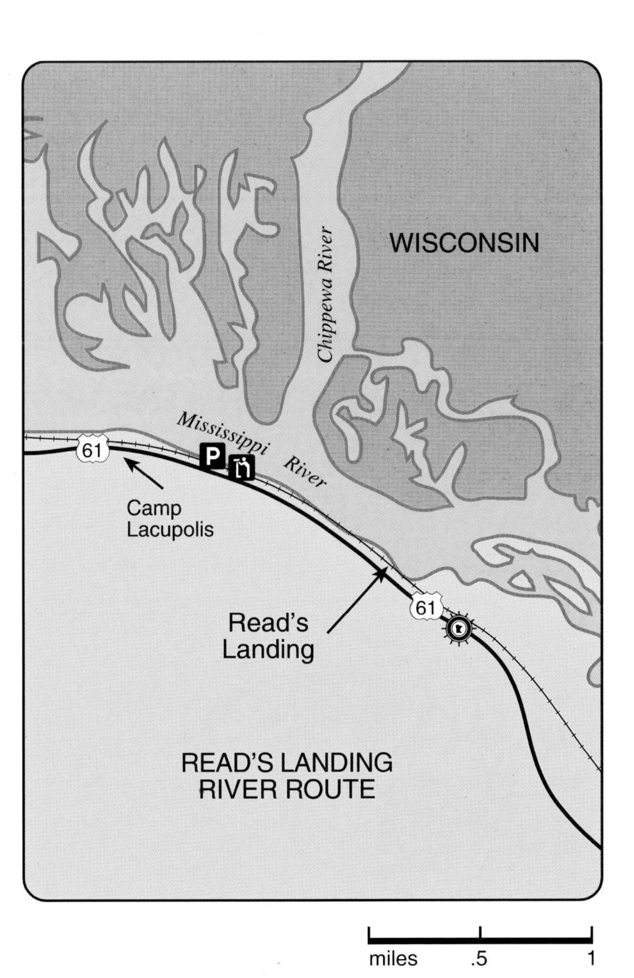

Facilities:

Recreational Opportunities:

Contact:

Wabasha Area Chamber of Commerce
PO Box 105 E
Wabasha MN 55981
(612) 565-4158
(800) 565-4158

108–Zumbro Bottoms Forestry Unit

Why is this area special?

The Zumbro River meanders along a flat floodplain below forested bluffs in the Zumbro Bottoms Unit. Walk along the river's edge to search for snapping, painted and map turtles. You might glimpse the threatened wood turtle in its preferred habitat, a narrow floodplain with both grassy and forested areas. Smooth and spiny soft-shelled turtles also make their homes here.

Clear-cuts and forest plantings of different ages add to the habitat variety in Zumbro Bottoms and increase the diversity of wildlife. White-tailed deer feed on the plentiful supply of acorns. Wild turkeys stand still when a bald eagle soars overhead. Red-shouldered hawks scan the floodplain forest for a meal of snake, frog or mouse. Keep an eye out for pileated woodpeckers, turkey vultures and scarlet tanagers.

Note:

The area is irregularly shaped and adjacent to private lands. Respect landowner rights; always ask permission before entering private land.

Follow the extensive trail system; you can hike all day and not see the same area twice.

Hunting allowed. Call ahead for hunting season dates.

Andrea Lee Lambrecht

Red-tailed hawk

Best viewing time:

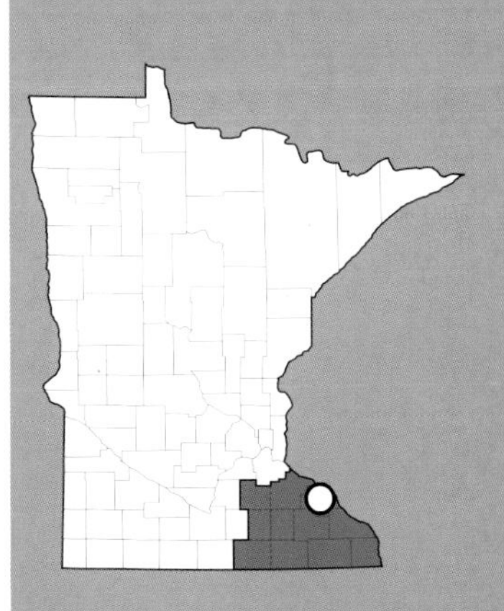

How do I get there?

Maps: MN Highway Coordinate: M-19
PRIM Area: Rochester
DeLorme MN Atlas Grid #: 35 D-8

Additional directions:

To reach this site from Wabasha, go south on Highway 61, turn west on Highway 60 for 6 miles. Zumbro Bottoms Forestry Unit is located south of Dumfries. You can enter the unit from the north on County Road 86, or from the south off of County Road 19.

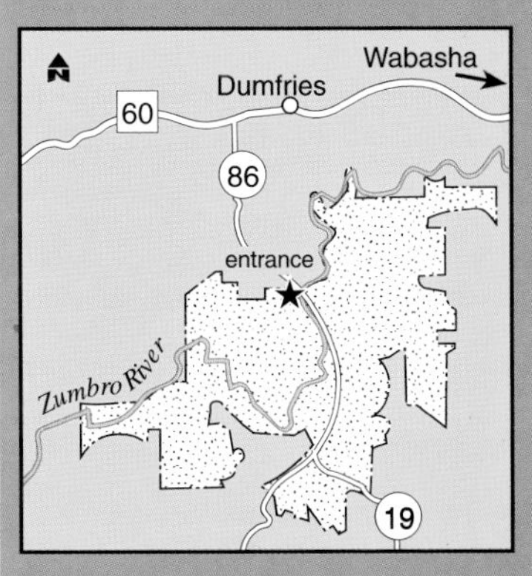

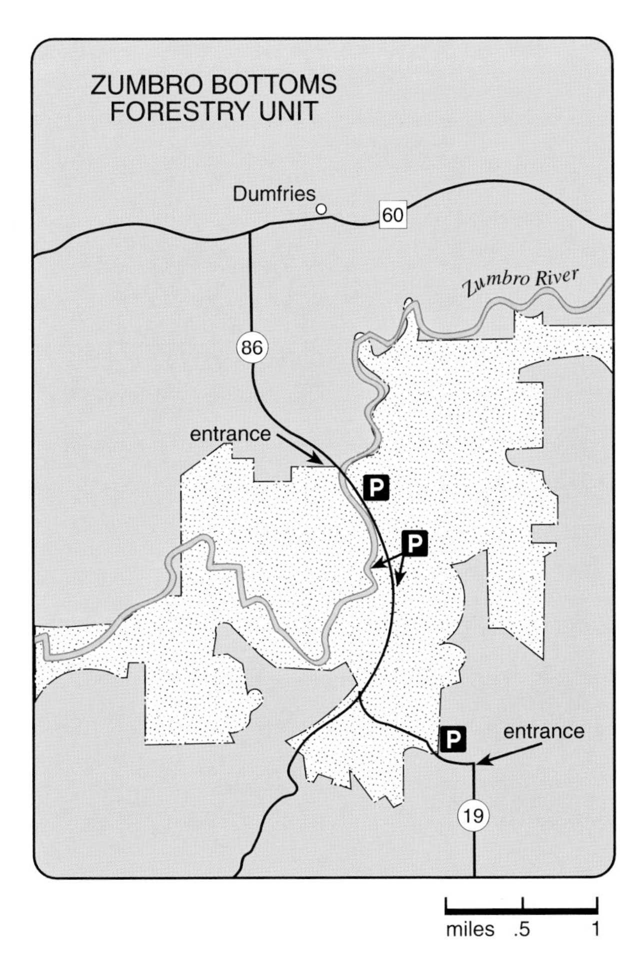

Facilities:

Recreational Opportunities:   

Contact:

DNR Area Forestry Office
1801 South Oak
Lake City MN 55041
(612) 345-3216

109–McCarthy Lake WMA/ Kellogg-Weaver Dunes SNA

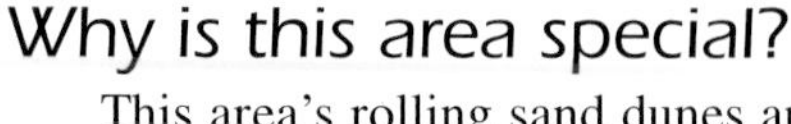

Why is this area special?

This area's rolling sand dunes and adjacent wetland and savanna support a wide array of plant species. On the sand prairies you'll find spiderwort, hoary puccoon, June grass, leadplant, silky aster, purple prairie clover and prairie larkspur. This habitat is also home to Minnesota's largest snake species, the bull snake.

Watch for turtle crossing signs on the highway separating the two state properties. State-threatened Blanding's turtles require grasslands like the ones found here for nesting and nearby marshes for feeding and wintering.

A. B. Sheldon

Northern spring peeper

Birders travel here to see nesting Bell's vireos, turkey vultures, willow flycatchers and orchard orioles. Look for lark and grasshopper sparrows and sandhill cranes on the prairies and grasslands. Other species you might see here include sedge wrens, dickcissels, American kestrels and upland sandpipers. Wild rice in the wetland attracts blue-winged teal, wood ducks and mallards.

Watch for beavers on the water and white-tailed deer, muskrats and mink along the shore.

Note:

In the spring or fall you may witness a prescribed burn, conducted to deter shrubs and to revitalize the prairie.

Hunting allowed. Call ahead for hunting season dates.

C. Henderson

Monarch caterpillar

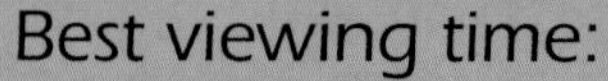

Best viewing time:

How do I get there?

Maps: MN Highway Coordinate: N-19
PRIM Area: Rochester
DeLorme MN Atlas Grid #: 35 D-9

Additional directions:

McCarthy Lake WMA is south of Kellogg. Turn east off of Highway 61 onto County Road 84. The WMA is on the west side of the road and the SNA is on the east side.

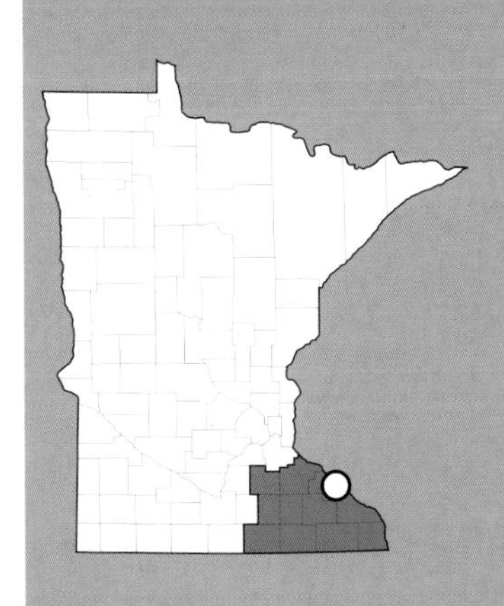

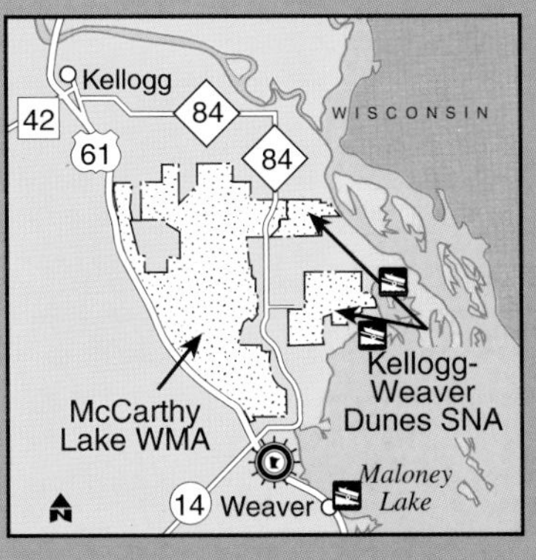

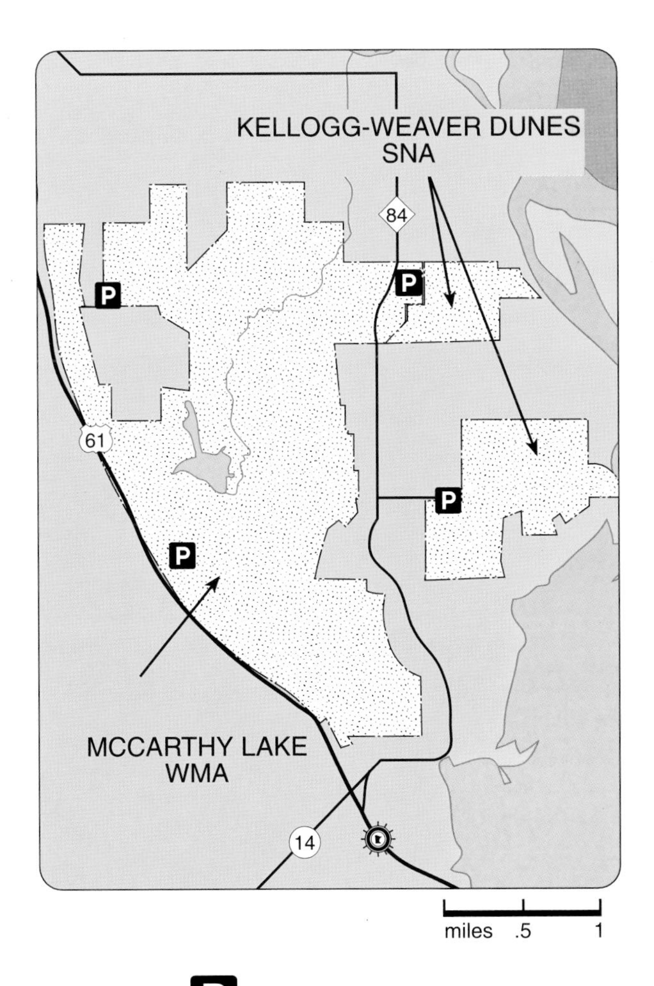

Facilities: P

Recreational Opportunities:

Contact:

DNR Area Wildlife Office
411 Exchange Building
Winona MN 55987
(507) 453-2950

110–Weaver Bottoms (Upper Miss. NWR)

Why is this area special?

One of the best-known waterfowl migration stopover sites in southeast Minnesota is at the Weaver Bottoms in the Upper Mississippi National Wild Life and Fish Refuge. Large concentrations of swans start arriving at Weaver Bottoms in mid-October and linger until late November.

The tundra swans begin their migration at nesting grounds on the Alaskan and Canadian coasts near the Arctic Circle. They cross the Canadian prairie provinces and North Dakota, where they turn east. They stop to rest along the Mississippi River before flying through the Great Lakes states and on to the Atlantic Coast.

A. B. Sheldon

Tundra swans

Swans stay in family groups during migration and they winter in flocks on shallow ponds, lakes and estuaries near Chesapeake Bay and the coasts of Virginia and North Carolina.

You can see thousands of swans on a late fall trip to Weaver Bottoms and the surrounding area. Make sure you check out both sides of the river, because swan feeding areas change rapidly. The plants that swans eat can be lost in lock and dam operations. When sedimentation increases and fills backwater marshes, vegetation doesn't get the occasional drying-out time that germinates its seeds, and swans must look elsewhere for food.

In the Mississippi area, swans feed mainly on the bulbous tubers of wild celery and duck potato roots. Watch the swans' feeding process; they use their feet to dislodge roots from the marsh bottom, then reach down with their long necks. See if you can find the one swan in the flock that stays upright, standing guard to warn the others of approaching danger.

An adult swan's all-white plumage is striking. Immature swans are pearly gray, a plumage they retain until they're fifteen months old. Sometimes adult swans' heads have a brown or orange stain, the result of feeding in ponds rich with iron.

Search for other waterfowl that feed in this area, such as Canada geese, northern shovelers, canvasbacks, gadwalls, northern pintails, mallards, American black ducks, blue-winged and green-winged teal, redheads, American wigeons, buffleheads, lesser scaup, wood ducks and snow geese. You might also see bald eagles.

See the Featured Species section on page 28 for more information on tundra swans.

Best viewing time:

How do I get there?

Maps: MN Highway Coordinate: N-19
PRIM Area: Rochester
DeLorme MN Atlas Grid #: 35 E-9

Additional directions:

Weaver Bottoms is located north of Winona and Lock and Dam #5 along Highway 61. You may be able to see waterfowl from the public access parking lot at Weaver, or travel 1.7 miles south from Weaver on Highway 61. Just before the cemetery, turn right and take a second right that goes up the hill to a roadside vantage point. For more details see the Tundra Swan featured species section on page 28.

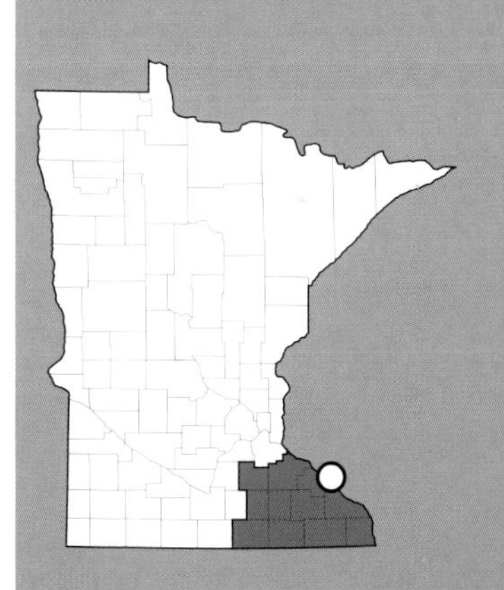

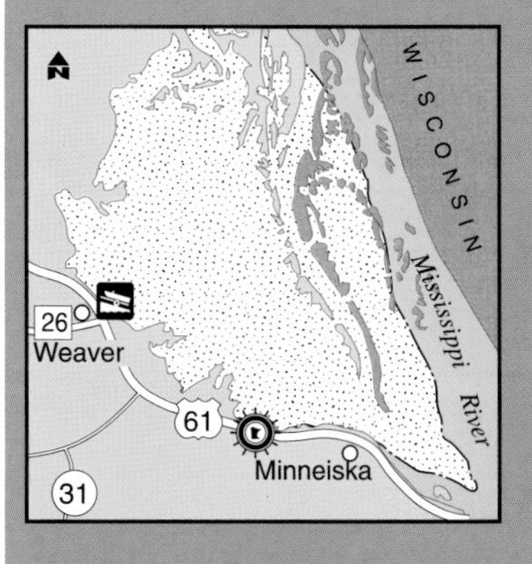

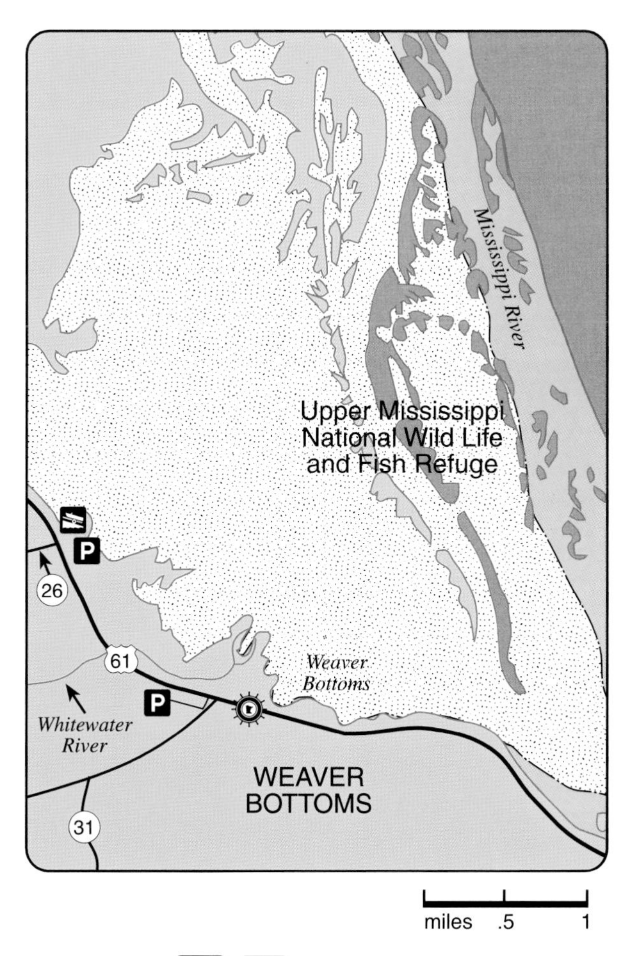

Facilities:

Recreational Opportunities:

Contact:

U.S. Fish and Wildlife Service
51 E 4th Street
Winona MN 55987
(507) 452-4232

Rieck's Lake Park Volunteers:
(608) 685-4249

111–Rice Lake State Park

Why is this area special?

Rice Lake State Park is a wildlife oasis in the middle of farm country. Rice Lake is an ice block "lake on a hill" between the Cannon and Zumbro River watersheds.

The shallow lake serves as a headwater source for the South Branch of the Middle Fork of the Zumbro River. During spring and fall, the lake surface shimmers with the movement of tundra swans and Canada geese. Flocks of diving and surface-feeding ducks visit the lake during migration. Look also for spotted sandpipers, marsh wrens, rails and great blue herons near the marshes.

On a summer day, you might see nesting western grebes or the area's largest colony of nesting black terns. You might also see muskrats feeding on aquatic plants. Other wildlife species to look for by the lake are western chorus, gray tree and northern leopard frogs, snapping turtles and painted turtles.

Follow the woodland trail and watch the park's indigo buntings, rose-breasted grosbeaks and its seven species of woodpeckers. Mammals to watch for in the forests are foxes, coyotes, fox squirrels and white-tailed deer. Wildflowers are also abundant in the spring.

Note:

Visit the waterfowl observation site in the picnic area for a view of the lake. Try hiking or skiing the trails in the park to see its resident and migratory wildlife.

C. Henderson

Sora

Best viewing time:

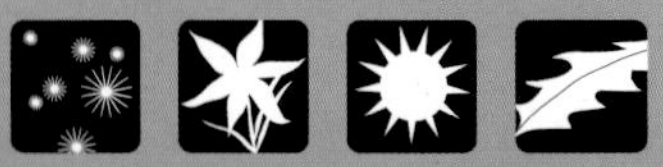

How do I get there?

Maps: MN Highway Coordinate: K-20
PRIM Area: Faribault
DeLorme MN Atlas Grid #: 24 A-4

Additional directions:

Rice Lake State Park is 7 miles east of Owatanna on Steele County Road 19 (East Rose Street). This road turns into Dodge County Road 20.

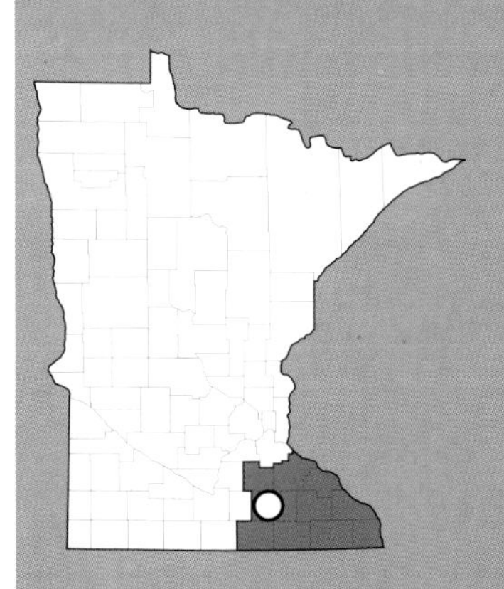

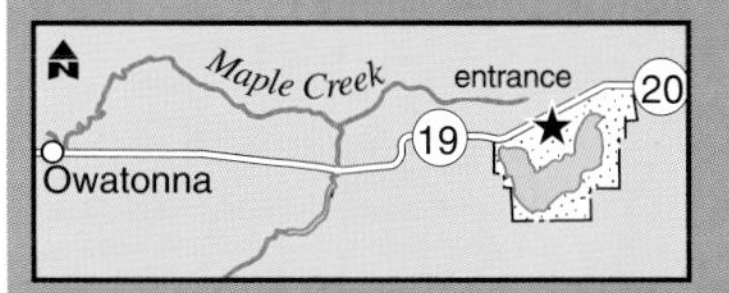

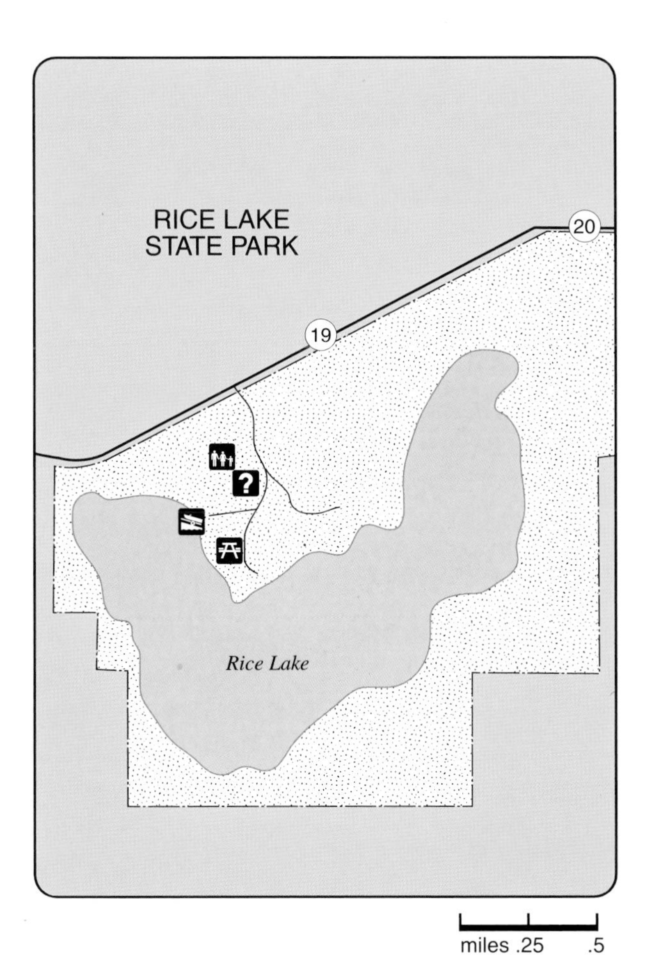

miles .25 .5

Facilities:

Recreational Opportunities:

Contact:

Rice Lake State Park
RR 3 Box 45
Owatanna MN 55060
(507) 455-5871

112–Keller WMA

Why is this area special?

Located near Rochester, this 207-acre wildlife management area is sure to become a popular destination. Grassland, brushland, hardwoods and stream corridor habitat all exist in this irregular tract of land.

As you hike through the grasslands or woodland trail, listen for the cheerful songs of eastern bluebirds and meadowlarks. Watch American kestrels and red-tailed hawks search the grasses for their next meal. You may also spot American goldfinches, wild turkeys, black-capped chickadees, downy and red-bellied woodpeckers, rose-breasted grosbeaks and Baltimore orioles.

W. L. Penning

Wild turkey

At the edge of the woods, look for tree swallows, northern cardinals and blue jays. They favor this transitional area between the grasslands and the forest. Blue jays are one of nature's best foresters, planting thousands of acorns every year.

You might also see coyotes and white-tailed deer in this transitional area. Watch for eastern chipmunks, red foxes, raccoons, fox squirrels and bull snakes too.

Note:

Prescribed burns for grasslands may be carried out during the spring or fall. Look for deer in winter near the corn food plot. There is a snowmobile trail that passes through the area.

 Hunting allowed. Call ahead for hunting season dates.

Best viewing time:

How do I get there?

Maps: MN Highway Coordinate: L-20
PRIM Area: Austin
DeLorme MN Atlas Grid #: 25 B-8

Additional directions:

Keller WMA is 8 miles southwest of Rochester. Take County Road 25 4 miles west and turn south on County Road 15 for 4 miles. Parking lot is on the east side of the road south of the junction of County Roads 126 and 15.

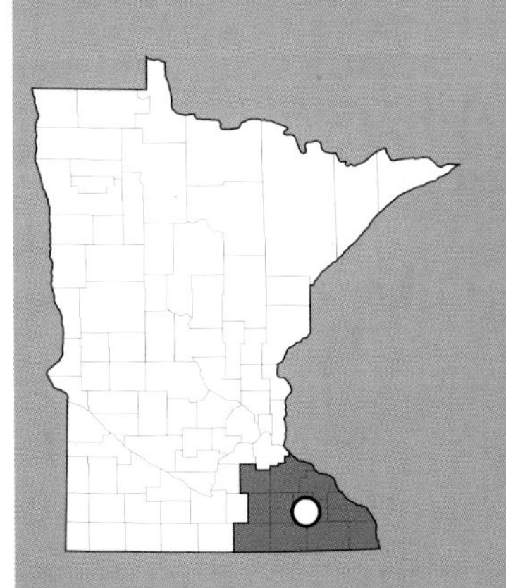

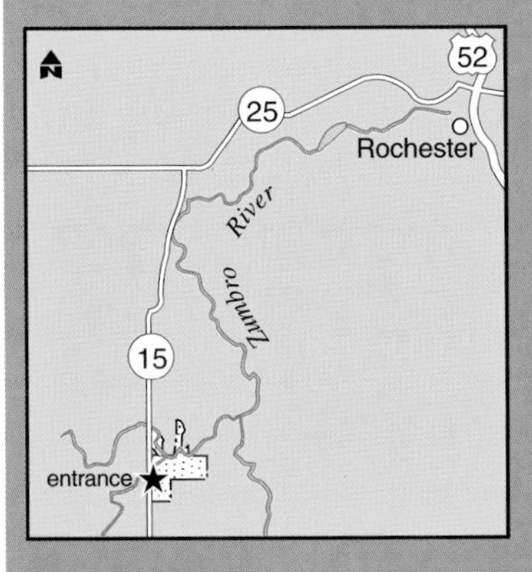

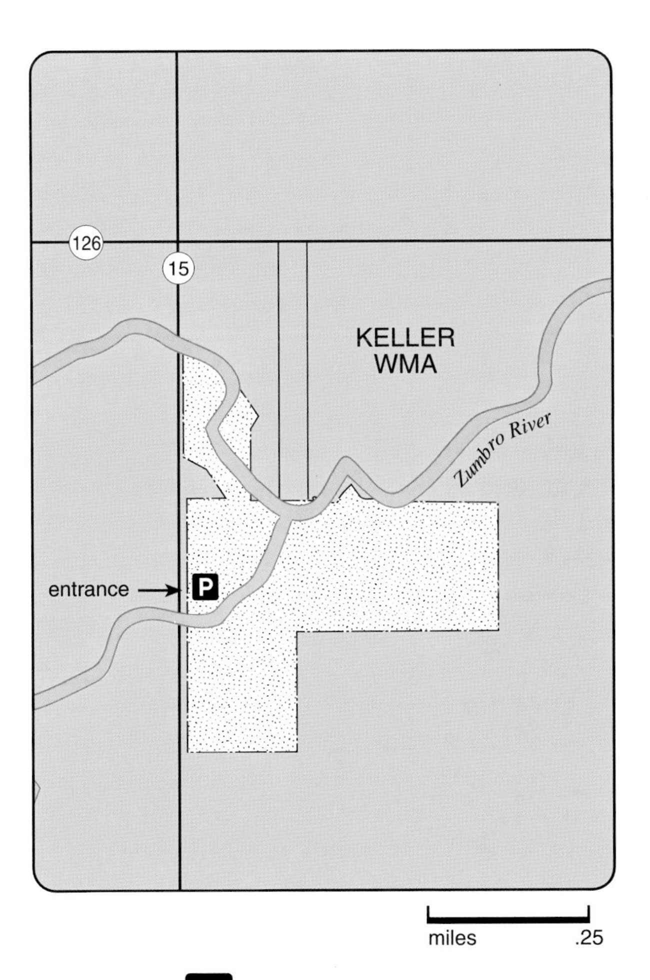

Facilities: P

Recreational Opportunities:   

Contact:

DNR Area Wildlife Office
2300 Silver Creek Road NE
Rochester MN 55906
(507) 280-5066

113–Silver Lake

Why is this area special?

Silver Lake, located in the center of Rochester, has become a gathering place for thousands of giant Canada geese. At one time, this race of Canada goose was thought to be on the verge of extinction. Now the throng at Silver Lake is an example of their impressive comeback.

This species is the first to migrate north in the spring and the last to leave in the fall. Migrating geese begin arriving at Silver Lake towards the end of September, with the bulk of the flock arriving between the last week of October and the third week of November. At the peak of migration, you can see between 25,000 and 30,000 geese in the area.

Visit the park in the evening to witness a sky full of geese returning from nearby corn fields and search the flocks for a lone snow goose, ruddy duck, tundra swan, great blue heron, a rare Ross' goose or other migrating waterfowl. You might also see common goldeneyes, buffleheads, American coots, ring-necked ducks, downy woodpeckers, or mammals such as gray and red squirrels along the shores of Silver Lake.

C. Henderson

Canada geese and mallards

Note:

There are two parks along the shoreline with biking and walking paths, benches and restrooms, as well as play and picnic areas. Opt for renting a canoe or paddleboat if you'd like to see things from the water.

Best viewing time:

How do I get there?

Maps: MN Highway Coordinate: L-20
PRIM Area: Rochester
DeLorme MN Atlas Grid #: 25 A-9

Additional directions:

Silver Lake is located in north-central Rochester. Turn east off Highway 63 onto 7th St. NE, then north on W. Silver Lake Dr. to parking area. The best viewing area is on the west side of the lake, from W. Silver Lake Dr. between 7th St. NE and 14th St. NW.

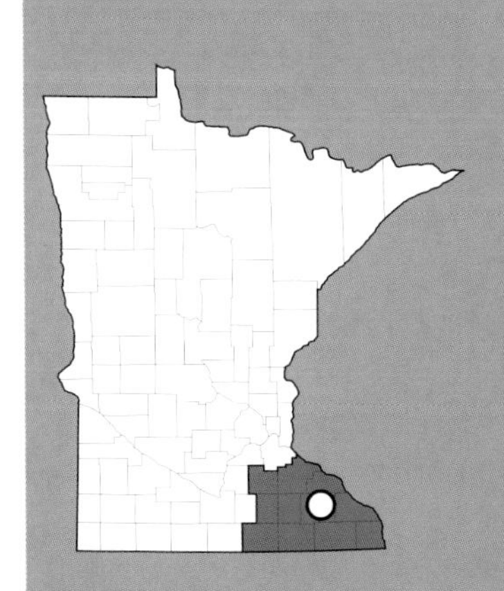

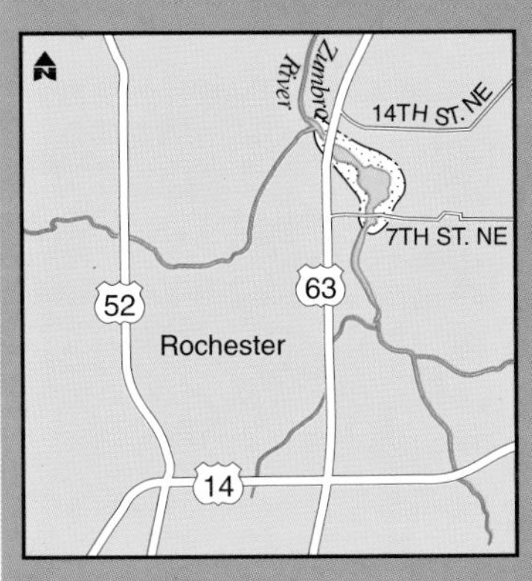

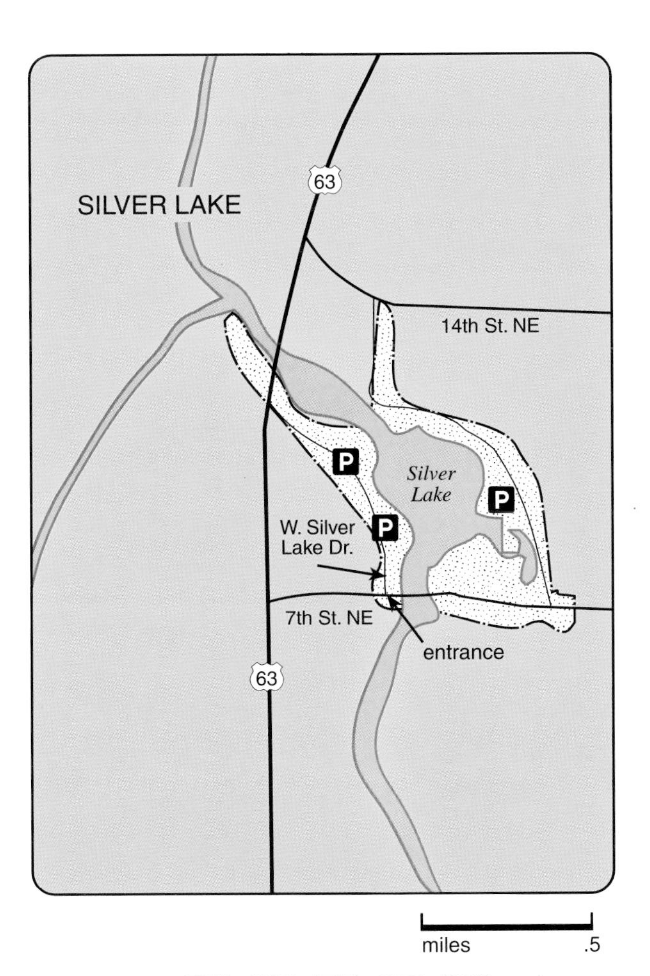

Facilities:

Recreational Opportunities:

Contact:

Rochester Convention and Visitors Bureau
150 South Broadway
Rochester MN 55904
(800) 634-8277

114–Chester Woods County Park

Why is this area special?

Chester Woods is a haven for wildlife and wildlife watchers. The reservoir forms a many-fingered lake which beckons to be explored by canoe. Wood ducks and hooded mergansers feed on the lake; watch for them as you paddle. Listen for the gung-gung of green frogs calling from the water's edge.

On land, roam the trail toward the dam overlook, across fields, through the oak woods, and break out onto the bluff prairie. Beaver Creek lies hidden in the valley below, covered by a thick forested canopy. Dry sand prairie and oak savanna hide in the distance where the valley opens up.

K. Haws

The park's prairies display an ever-changing palette of wildflowers, including prairie phlox, silver-leaf scurf-pea, coreopsis, purple prairie clover, compass plant and many asters. Prairies and grasslands are home to savanna and grasshopper sparrows and bobolinks.

During the winter, check the campground pine trees for roosting owls. Watch for wild turkeys roosting in wide-branching oak. Other bird species you might see here include wood thrushes, veeries, eastern bluebirds, eastern towhees, broad-winged and Cooper's hawks, long-eared and short-eared owls, American redstarts, red-eyed vireos and cedar waxwings. Keep your eyes open for other animals like white-tailed deer, bull snakes, fox snakes and painted turtles.

Note:

The fishing pier and paved trail are handicapped accessible.

Hunting allowed by special permit only. Call ahead for hunting season permit application details.

Best viewing time:

How do I get there?

Maps: MN Highway Coordinate: M-20
PRIM Area: Austin
DeLorme MN Atlas Grid #: 26 B-1

Additional directions:

Located 7 miles east of Rochester on Highway 14, the park is on the south side of the road.

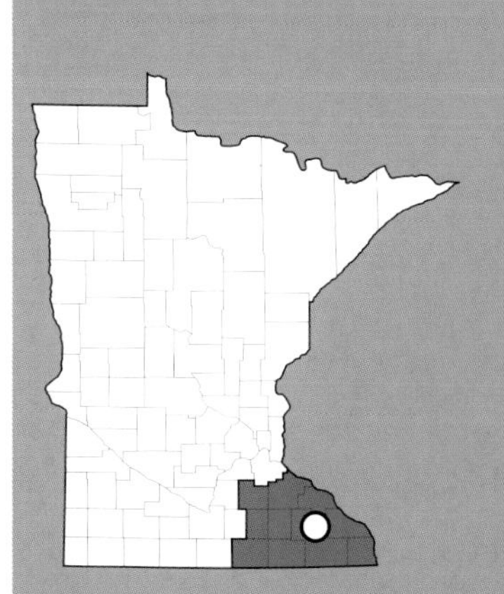

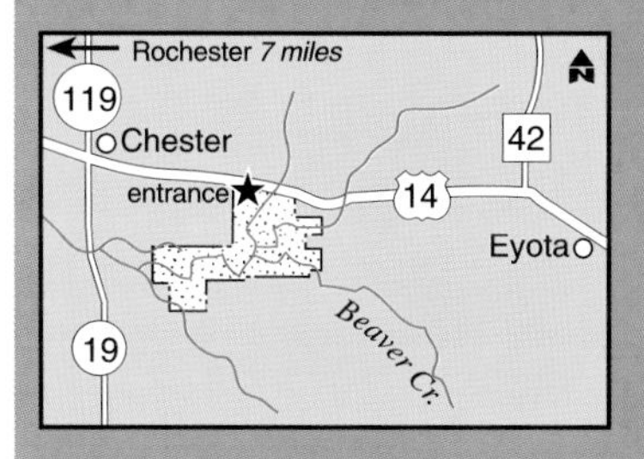

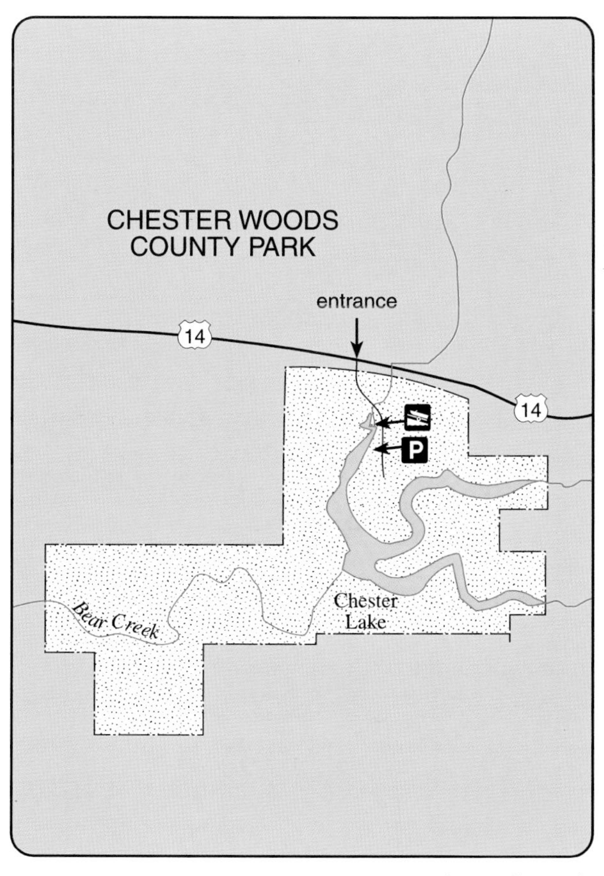

Facilities:     

Recreational Opportunities: 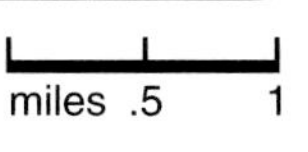

Contact:

Chester Woods Park
8378 Highway 14 E
Eyota MN 55934
(507) 285-7050

115– Whitewater WMA/State Park

Why is this area special?

The Whitewater WMA contains 27,000 acres of wildlife habitat. Three sparkling branches of the Whitewater River flow together in the Whitewater Valley, converging below dramatic river valley bluffs.

Wildflowers abound in the area's oak woodlands, savanna, wetlands and bluff prairies. Remnant stands of white pine and other plants usually found further north remain here from a time when the climate was colder and glaciers covered other parts of the state.

A. B. Sheldon

Karner blue

The wetlands along Highway 74 attract migrating and nesting waterfowl. Look for ospreys, great egrets, giant Canada geese and belted kingfishers. Stop by the wetlands just after dark on warm evenings in late April through May for a real treat: thousands of frogs join voices in a symphony of peeps, chorts, chuckles and moans. You might see chorus, leopard, pickerel and green frogs.

Another option is to explore from the north parking lot along Highway 74. Listen for the piercing call of red-shouldered hawks and keep an eye out for wild turkeys in the wooded valleys. Wild turkeys from Whitewater have been successfully introduced into other wildlife areas around the country.

Other bird species you can look for include cerulean, prothonotary and blue-winged warblers, ruffed grouse, sandhill cranes, rose-breasted grosbeaks and indigo buntings.

In the savanna where the oak woods are more open and prairie plants cover the ground, you may discover eastern bluebirds, endangered Karner blue butterflies and their host plant, wild lupine. If you hike or cross country ski in the valley, watch for wintering golden eagles. White-tailed deer frequent the meadows and birds chatter throughout the steep wooded slopes and stream corridors.

Note:

Whitewater State Park is a great place to enter this valley, and offers camping, easy access to excellent trout fishing and trails for all abilities. Watch for animals crossing the roads in the wildlife management area. The Whitewater WMA does not have camping.

Hunting allowed in the WMA. Call ahead for hunting season dates.

Best viewing time:

How do I get there?

Maps: MN Highway Coordinate: M-20
PRIM Area: Rochester
DeLorme MN Atlas Grid #: 26 A-3

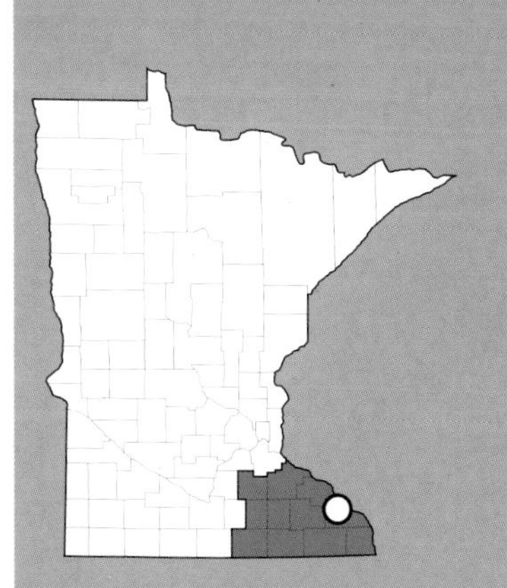

Additional directions:

The Whitewater State Park is located 3 miles south of Elba on Highway 74 and 10 miles north of St. Charles. The Whitewater WMA is located on Highway 74 between Weaver and Elba.

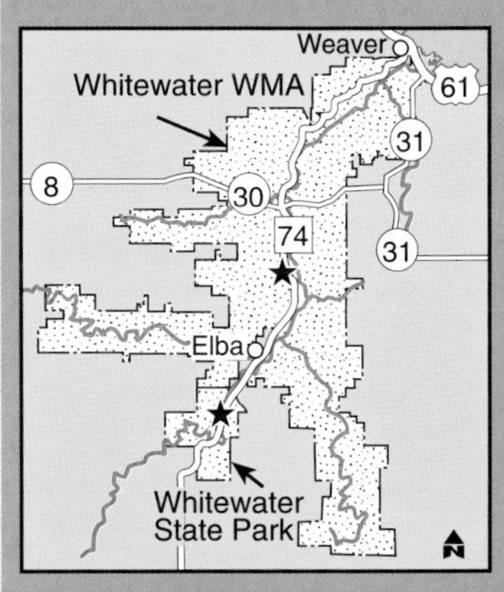

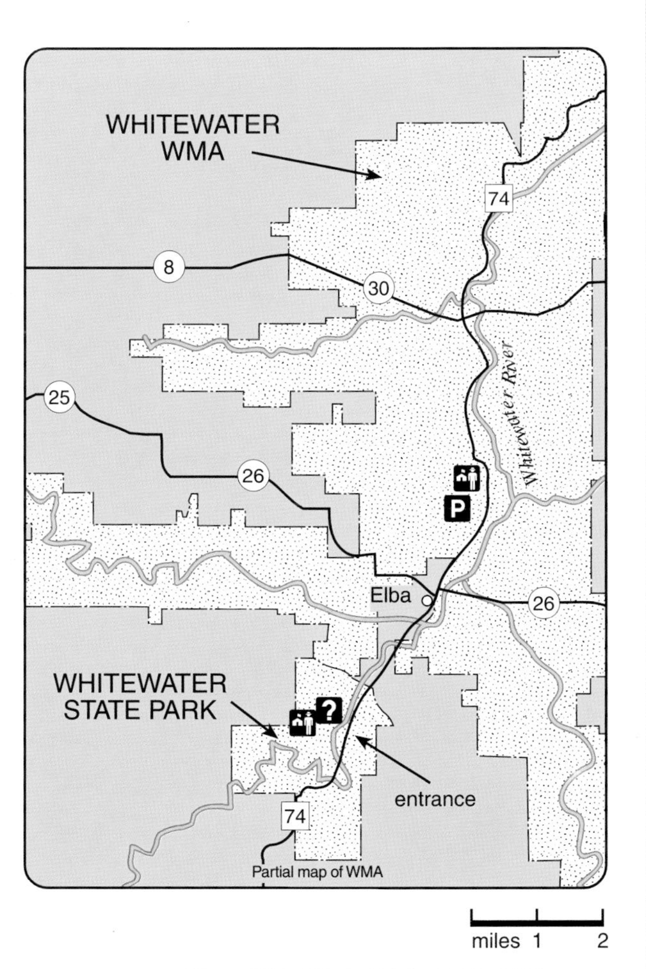

Facilities:

Recreational Opportunities:     

Contact:

DNR Wildlife Area Office
Whitewater WMA
RR 2 Box 333
Altura MN 55910
(507) 932-4133

Whitewater State Park
RR 1 Box 256
Altura MN 55910
(507) 932-3007

116–Geneva Lake WMA

Why is this area special?

Geneva Lake, located in Freeborn County, is a wetland wildlife oasis surrounded by farm country. During spring and fall migrations, large flocks of waterfowl mingle here.

Watch as an American white pelican flock feeds. The pelicans form a large circle on the water, which slowly decreases in size. Under the water, fish dart away from the pelicans' feet toward the center of the circle. After the fish are herded into the middle, the pelicans gulp below the water's surface with their large beaks, feasting on the harvest of rough fish.

C. Henderson

American white pelican

You should also look for two Geneva Lake nesting species: western grebes and yellow-headed blackbirds. Other species you might find include pied-billed grebes, black, Forster's and Caspian terns, marsh wrens, great egrets, American wigeons, gadwalls, wood ducks, northern shovelers, buffleheads, canvasbacks, redheads, ring-necked ducks, lesser scaups, hooded and red-breasted mergansers, belted kingfishers, muskrats, minks, chorus frogs, spring peepers and painted turtles.

Note:

It's easiest to get a good view of Geneva Lake by driving along the roads that follow the shoreline. There is very little traffic, but be cautious. You can also see the lake from the public water access.

Most of the lake shoreline is in private ownership, with the exception of the small WMA on the northwest corner of the lake. Respect landowners rights. Always ask permission before entering private land.

C. Henderson

Redhead

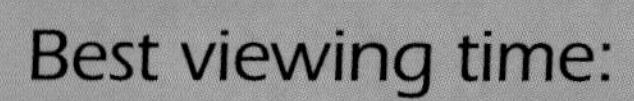

Best viewing time:

How do I get there?

Maps: MN Highway Coordinate: J-21
PRIM Area: Albert Lea
DeLorme MN Atlas Grid #: 24 C-2

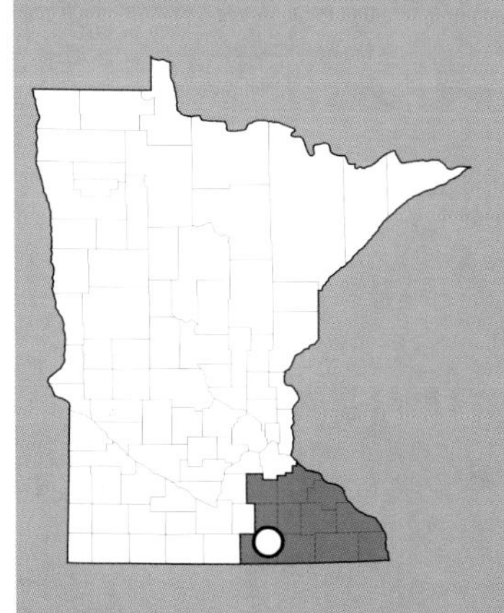

Additional directions:

The lake is south of Geneva and approximately 5 miles north of Albert Lea.

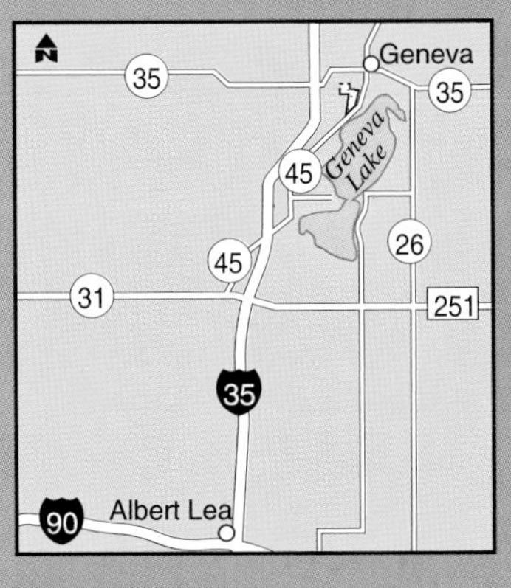

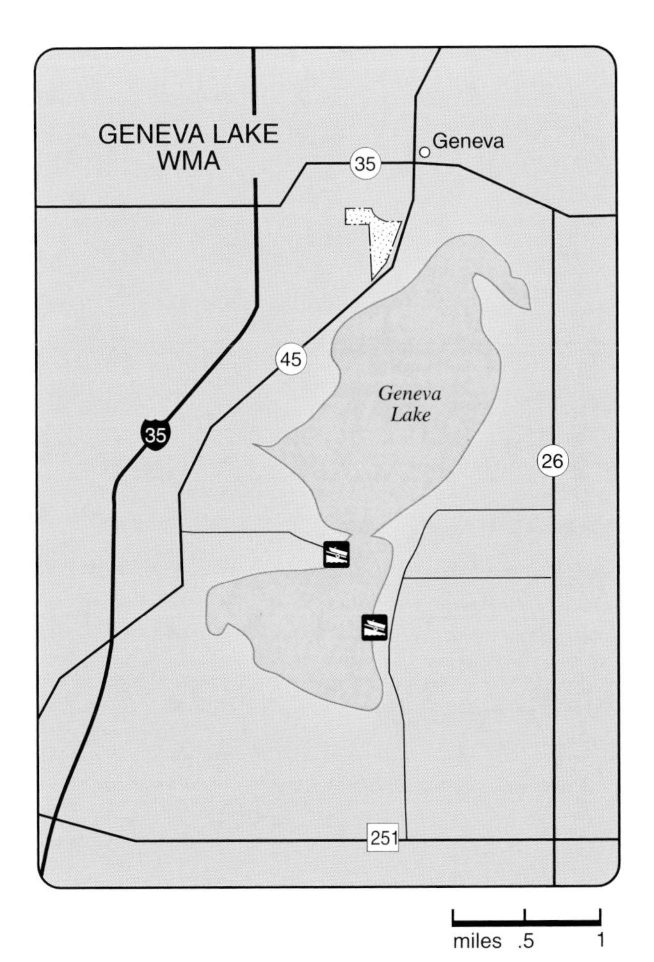

Facilities:

Recreational Opportunities: 

Contact:

DNR Area Wildlife Office
8485 Rose Street
Owatonna MN 55060
(507) 455-5841

117–Forestville State Park

Little brown bat

Why is this area special?

Due to its position at the western edge of the blufflands, the Forestville State Park area contains a variety of wildlife habitats: streams and floodplains, mature oak ridge forests, brushy south-facing slopes, moist maple-basswood forests, meadows and a few pockets of white pine and balsam fir.

One of the park's key features is historic Forestville, a Minnesota Historical Society-operated site. This pre-Civil War town site with its restored tallgrass prairie is a great place to watch red-tailed hawks and other raptors. You will find deer all year long, particularly in the morning and at sunset. Look for birds and squirrels around the town's Meighen Residence. The town's outbuildings are also an excellent place to see little brown myotis bats leaving their roosts to forage for insects at dusk during middle to late summer.

In 1988 the park acquired Mystery Cave, which is a winter home for about 2,000 bats. You can see them during early and late-season cave tours. A large raccoon population inhabits the park's many smaller caves and sinkholes.

Forestville's extensive closed-canopy forest, the largest expanse in Fillmore County, is great bird habitat. The park is home to more than 161 species of birds including red-shouldered hawks, cerulean warblers, blue jays, house wrens, cedar waxwings and American redstarts. Up to 25 different species of warblers and five species of vireos have been recorded here. If you camp at this site you might be awakened by barred owls.

Pileated woodpeckers are common and you can see them best during the winter. Bald eagles also visit this region's streams throughout the winter. In March, observe the woodcocks' courtship ritual in the meadows. Mature oak trees produce food for wild turkeys, whose gobbling is commonly heard in the spring.

Six different springs flow through the park, attracting aquatic birds and animals including herons, Blanding's turtles, spring peepers, northern water snakes and beavers. You'll certainly see an abundance of nongame fish in the Mystery Cave area. If you're an angler, you'll be excited to see brown trout as they spawn in the shallow riffles of park streams in late October.

Other animals you can look for include mink, red-bellied snakes, foxes, shrews, pocket gophers, woodchucks, muskrats, opossums, striped skunks, weasels, cottontails and red, gray and fox squirrels. During cold snaps, coyotes will use frozen streams as highways.

Best viewing time:

How do I get there?

Maps: MN Highway Coordinate: M-21
PRIM Area: Austin
DeLorme MN Atlas Grid #: 26 D-2

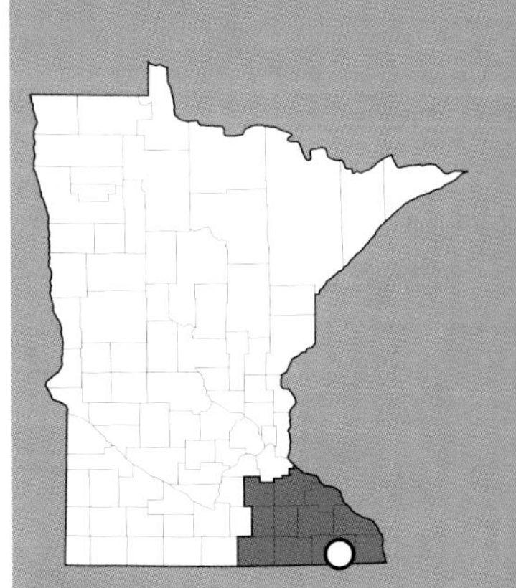

Additional directions:

This site is between Spring Valley and Preston. The entrance to the park is located 4 miles south of Highway 16 on Fillmore County Road 5 and 2 miles east on County 12.

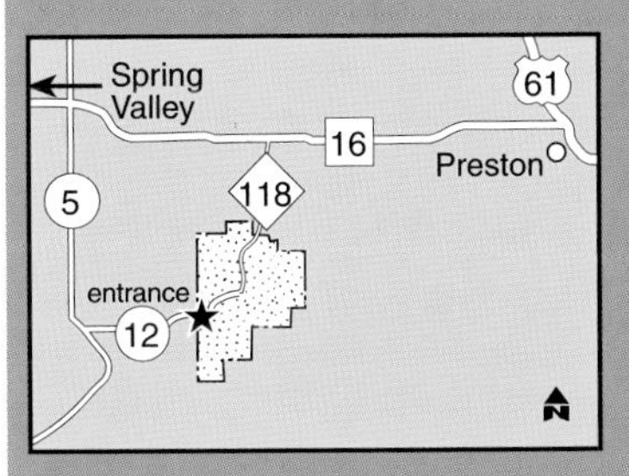

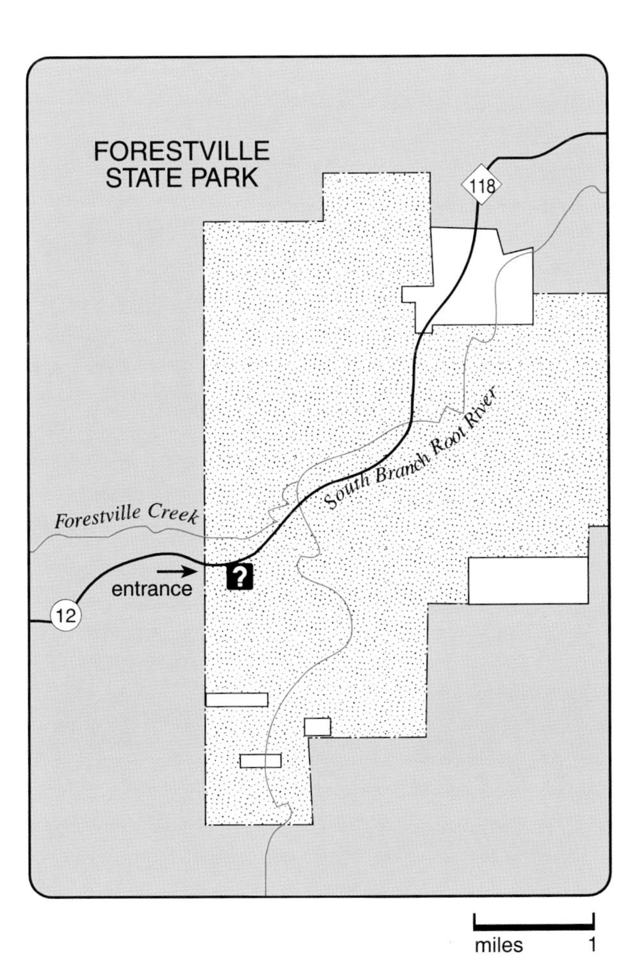

Facilities:    

Recreational Opportunities:

Contact:

Forestville State Park/
Mystery Cave
RR 2 Box 128
Preston MN 55965
Main park: (507) 352-5111
Mystery Cave: (507) 937-3251
Historic Forestville (MHS):
(507) 765-2785

118–Dr. Johann C. Hvoslef WMA

Why is this area special?

Wide open grasslands drop to a wooded valley, where the South Fork of the Root River hugs the curving limestone cliff. Tucked in the rolling farmland of southeast Minnesota, at the edge of the blufflands, lies this area designated for preserving nongame wildlife, primarily songbirds.

Follow the township road down into the filtered sunlight of the stream valley. Lively sounds surround you as black-capped chickadees flit anxiously above, red-bellied woodpeckers drum on old oaks, and in the background, Cedar Springs bubbles from the hillside. Footprints of white-tailed deer, raccoon and gray fox tell who recently passed by. Look for Louisiana waterthrush and belted kingfisher near the water's edge and watch for brown trout, minnows and tadpoles in the clear river. Winter wrens and migrating warblers may also be spotted in the woods.

C. Henderson

In spring and summer, wildflowers blanket the woodland floor. Scan for the threatened nodding wild onion along the north-facing cliff of the township road.

Butterflies, wildflowers of the air, flit over all the habitats. Search for red spotted purple, red admiral, pearl crescent, eastern tailed-blue and common woodnymph butterflies at flowers or on the wing.

Birds of prey circle over the upland fields, scanning for their next meal—watch for a broad-winged hawk or the large turkey vultures. Speaking of turkeys, don't be surprised if you come across wild ones in the woods or open areas. Listen too for the beautiful melody of the eastern meadowlark in the grasslands.

Note:

Dr. Johann C. Hvoslef lived and practiced medicine in the Lanesboro area from 1876 until his death in 1920. He was known as a meticulous observer of birds and thoroughly enjoyed each glorious detail of nature. Visitors to his namesake WMA will enjoy exploring the wide open fields and secluded nooks. This 205-acre area was donated by Dr. Kinsey Anderson to the Nongame Wildlife Program in 1996.

Best viewing time:

Hunting and trapping are permitted, but special regulations and a delayed seasonal start are in effect to accommodate fall birding. Check for dates and details.

How do I get there?

Maps: MN Highway Coordinate: N-21
PRIM Area: Caledonia
DeLorme MN Atlas Grid #: 26 E-4

Additional directions:

From Preston travel south on Highway 52 for two miles, turn left (east) on County Road 12 for six miles, south on County Road 23 for 2.5 miles and turn left (east) at Amherst onto a township road. The Hvoslef WMA sign is approximately one mile east on the right.

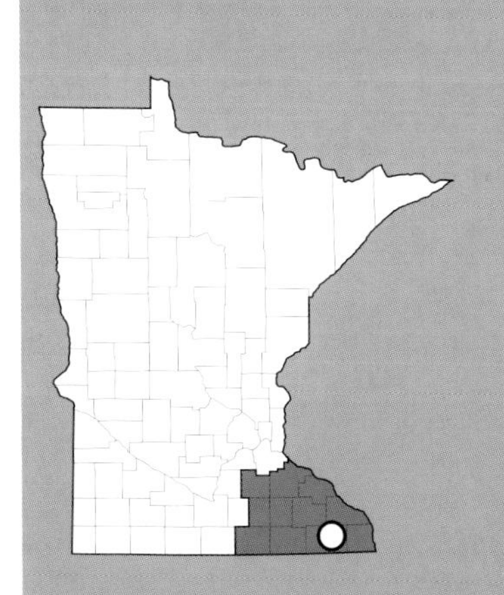

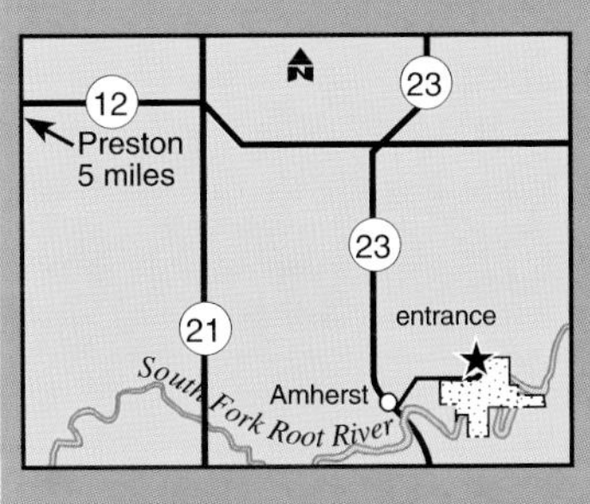

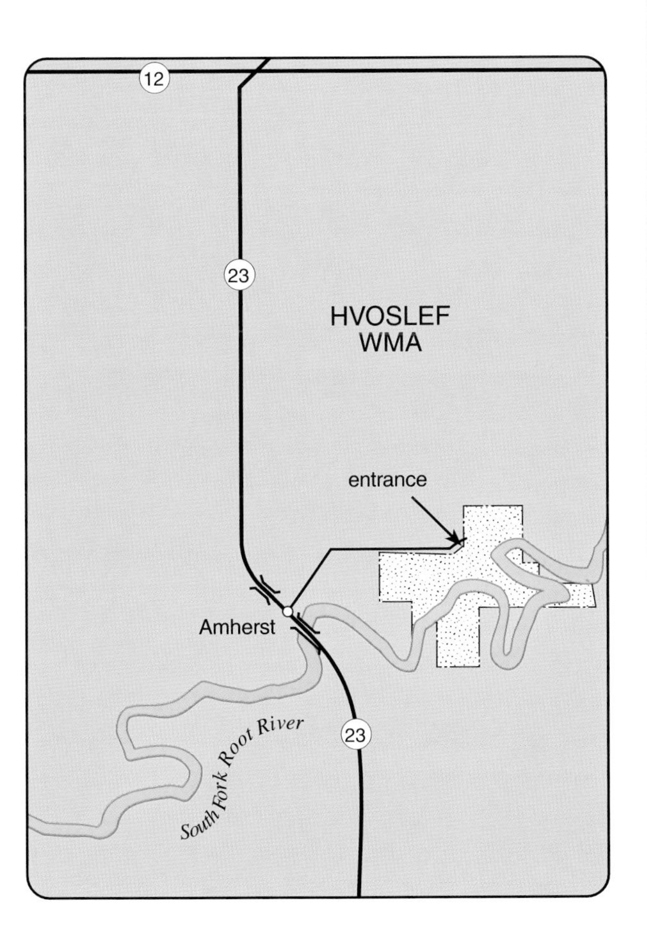

Facilities:

Recreational Opportunities:

Contact:

DNR Nongame Wildlife Office
2300 Silver Creek Rd. NE
Rochester MN 55904
(507) 280-5070

DNR Area Wildlife Office
411 Exchange Building,
Winona MN 55987
(507) 453-2950

119–Beaver Creek Valley State Park

Why is this area special?

Wooded valley walls rise 250 feet above spring-fed Beaver Creek, ushering it through this beautiful park. The view from the upland oak woods is dramatic. Watch for brown and brook trout in the cold, crystal-clear creek. Watercress, a vibrant green aquatic plant, grows in the creek all year long.

During the spring and summer, search the lowland hardwood forest and stream corridor for Louisiana waterthrushes, acadian flycatchers and cerulean warblers. These birds and their habitats are rarely found in other parts of Minnesota.

As you hike deeper into the forest, you may find scarlet tanagers flashing their brilliant colors through the dense green foliage. Other bird species you should look for at Beaver Creek include yellow warblers, least flycatchers, blue-gray gnatcatchers, American redstarts, ruffed grouse and wild turkeys.

Barney Oldfield

Five-lined skink

Keep your eyes open for white-tailed deer, beaver, gray and fox squirrels, woodchucks, raccoons, coyotes, chipmunks, pickerel frogs, spring peepers, American toads and timber rattlesnakes. You might even glimpse an elusive five-lined skink. These little striped lizards have been seen at small bluff prairie openings in the park.

Note:

There is a potential for flash flooding in the park, so be aware of the weather as you explore, especially if it involves heavy rains. Timber rattlesnakes in the park pose no threat if you leave them alone. All wildlife species, including snakes, are protected in state parks.

Best viewing time:

How do I get there?

Maps: MN Highway Coordinate: O-21
PRIM Area: Caledonia
DeLorme MN Atlas Grid #: 26 D-7

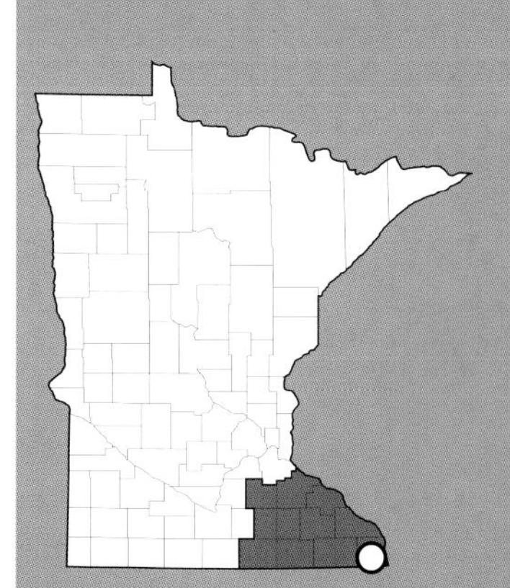

Additional directions:

This site is located 5 miles west of Caledonia on County Road 1 off Highway 76.

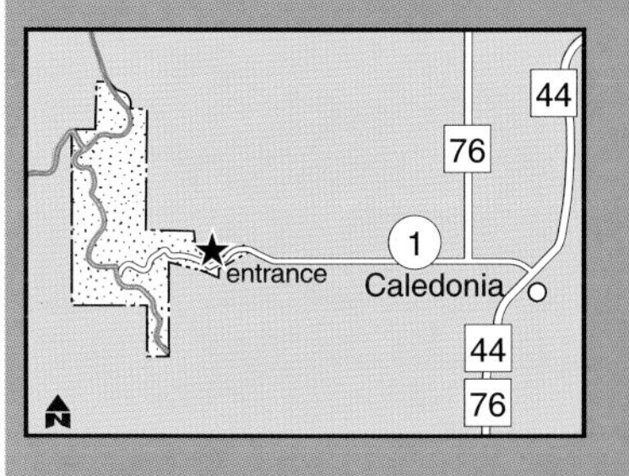

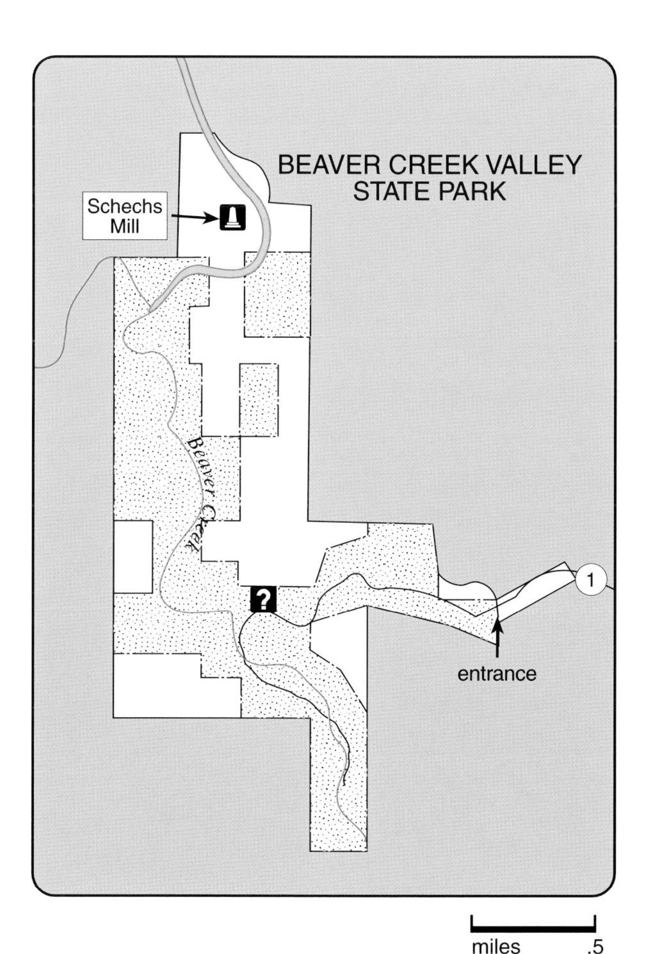

Facilities:

Recreational Opportunities:

Contact:

Beaver Creek Valley State Park
RR 2 Box 57
Caledonia MN 55921
(507) 724-2107

120–Sheperd's Marsh (Upper Miss. NWR)

C. Henderson

Red-winged blackbird

Why is this area special?

A serene Mississippi River backwater experience awaits you in Sheperd's Marsh near La Crescent. This stretch of the Upper Mississippi National Wild Life and Fish Refuge is a mix of floodplain forest and emergent marsh filled with white and yellow water lilies, lotus and pondweeds.

This area is also teeming with water birds, including wood ducks, mallards, blue-winged teal, great egrets, Virginia and sora rails, even an occasional black-crowned night heron or least bittern. Look for river otters, painted turtles and map turtles. You may happen upon a non-venomous water snake slithering through the water on its way to catch a leopard frog or a duckling. At night, listen to nature's symphony brought to you by frogs, toads and owls.

Other bird species to watch for at Sheperd's Marsh include bald eagles, great blue herons, Bell's vireos, common moorhens, black terns and prothonotary warblers.

Note:

The best access to the wetland is by canoe. You can put your canoe in along the shore or dike.

This is the southernmost wildlife watching site along the scenic Great River Road, which continues southward to the Mississippi's delta at New Orleans.

C. Henderson

Ouachita map turtle

Best viewing time:

How do I get there?

Maps: MN Highway Coordinate: O-21
PRIM Area: Caledonia
DeLorme MN Atlas Grid #: 27 C-9

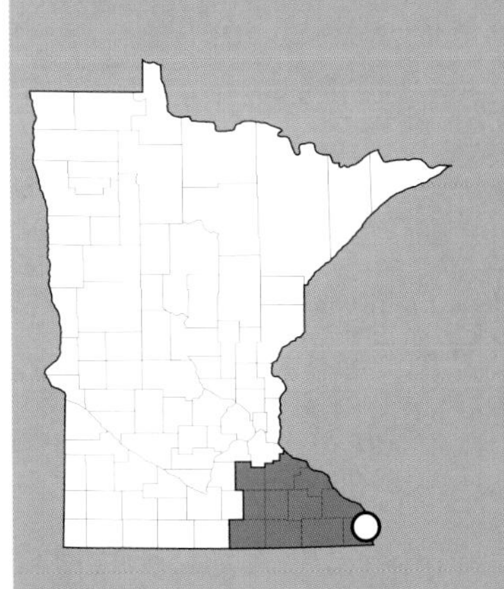

Additional directions:

In La Crescent, take the old highway (Main Street) along the east side of Highways 61/14. Turn east at the car wash, cross the tracks and through the gate to the marsh. If the gate is closed, hike the short distance to the marsh.

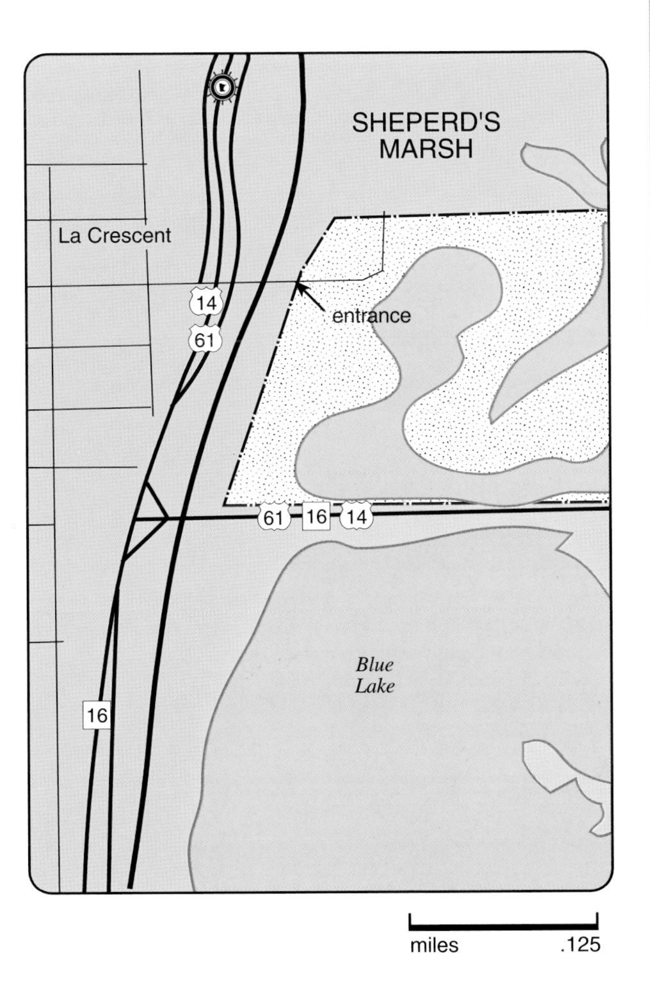

Facilities:

Recreational Opportunities:

Contact:

LaCrosse District 5
Upper Mississippi River
National Wild Life and
Fish Refuge
55 Lester Avenue
Onalaska WI 54650
(608) 783-8405

Alphabetical Site Listing

Site Name	Site #	County	Nearest Town
Afton State Park	99	Washington	Afton
Agassiz Dunes SNA/Prairie Smoke Dunes SNA/Agassiz ELC	9	Polk	Fertile
Agassiz NWR	6	Marshall	Thief River Falls
Banning State Park	49	Pine	Sandstone
Bass Brook WMA	32	Itasca	Grand Rapids
Battle Creek Regional Park	97	Ramsey	St. Paul
Beaver Bay to Grand Portage	29	Cook/Lake	Beaver Bay to Grand Rapids
Beaver Creek Valley State Park	119	Houston	Caledonia
Big Island Natural & Recreation Area	42	Crow Wing	Pequot Lakes
Big Stone NWR	62	Lac qui Parle	Ortonville
Blue Mounds State Park	77	Rock	Luverne
Boot Lake SNA	81	Anoka	Linwood
Boyd Sartell WMA	101	Rice	Faribault
Buffalo River State Park/ Bluestem Prairie SNA	15	Clay	Glyndon
Camden State Park/ Prairie Marshes WMA	69	Lyon	Marshall
Cannon River Wilderness Area	102	Rice	Northfield
Carlos Avery WMA	82	Anoka	Forest Lake
Carver Park Reserve	92	Hennepin	Victoria
Chengwatana State Forest	51	Pine	Pine City
Chester Woods County Park	114	Olmsted	Rochester
Colville Park	104	Goodhue	Red Wing
Crane Meadows NWR/Rice-Skunk & Crane Meadows WMAs	53	Morrison	Little Falls
Crosby Farm-Hidden Falls Parks	98	Ramsey	St. Paul
Crow-Hassan Park Reserve	84	Hennepin	Rogers
Deep Portage Conservation Reserve	17	Cass	Hackensack
Elm Creek Park Reserve	85	Hennepin	Osseo
Eloise Butler Wildflower Garden & Bird Sanctuary/The Quaking Bog	89	Hennepin	Minneapolis
Felton Prairie WMA/SNA	13	Clay	Felton
Flandrau State Park	71	Brown	New Ulm
Forestville State Park	117	Fillmore	Preston
Frontenac State Park	105	Goodhue	Frontenac
Geneva Lake WMA	116	Freeborn	Albert Lea
George Washington State Forest	23	Itasca	Grand Rapids
Glendalough State Park	19	Ottertail	Battle Lake
Gold Portage WMA	21	Koochiching	International Falls
Graham's Island in the Mississippi River	55	Benton	Sauk Rapids
Hawk Ridge Nature Reserve	36	St. Louis	Duluth
Heron Lake System	78	Jackson	Heron Lake

Site Name	Site #	County	Nearest Town
Hok-Si-La City Park	106	Goodhue	Lake City
Hole-in-the-Mountain WMA/ SNA/TNC/County Park	70	Lincoln	Lake Benton
Hvoslev WMA	118	Fillmore	Lanesboro
Inspiration Peak	20	Ottertail	Parkers Prairie
Itasca State Park	12	Clearwater	Park Rapids
Kasota Prairie SNA	74	LeSueur	Kasota
Keller WMA	112	Olmsted	Rochester
Kilen Woods State Park/ Prairie Bush Clover SNA	79	Jackson	Jackson
Lac qui Parle WMA/State Park	64	Lac qui Parle	Milan
Lake Bemidji State Park	10	Beltrami	Bemidji
Lakes Calhoun & Harriet	90	Hennepin	Minneapolis
Lake Maria State Park	57	Wright	Monticello
Lake of the Woods	3	Lk. of the Woods	Baudette
Lake Osakis	52	Todd	Osakis
Lake Vadnais-Sucker Lake	96	Ramsey	Vadnais Heights
Lebanon Hills Regional Park	95	Dakota	Apple Valley
Lost Valley Prairie SNA	100	Washington	Afton
Maplewood State Park	18	Ottertail	Pelican Rapids
McCarthy Lake WMA	109	Wabasha	Kellogg
Mille Lacs Lake-North Shore (Hwy 18)	45	Aitkin	Garrison to Malmo
Mille Lacs Lake Area & Kathio State Park	47	Mille Lacs	Onamia
Mille Lacs WMA	48	Mille Lacs	Onamia
Minnesota Landscape Arboretum	93	Hennepin	Chanhassen
Minnesota Valley NWR/ Black Dog Preserve SNA	91	Hennepin	Bloomington
Mississippi River	33	Itasca	Grand Rapids
Mississippi River/Cass Lake/ Lake Winnibigoshish	11	Beltrami/Itasca/ Cass	Cass Lake
Moose Lake State Park	40	Carlton	Moose Lake
Mud-Goose WMA	30	Cass	Remer
Murphy City/Stoney River Grade	35	Lake	Finland
Murphy Hanrehan Park Reserve	94	Scott	Lakeville
Nerstrand Big Woods State Park	103	Rice	Faribault
Northern Light Lake	26	Cook	Grand Marais
Northland Arboretum/ Paul Bunyan Jack Pine Savanna	44	Crow Wing	Brainerd
Park Point Recreation Area/ Minnesota Point Forest	38	St. Louis	Duluth
Peloquin WMA	24	Itasca	Side Lake
Pembina Trail Preserve SNA/ Environmental Learning Center	8	Polk	Crookston
Pigeon Lake Rookery	66	Meeker	Dassel
Pine Point Research Natural Area	16	Cass	Walker
Pipestone National Monument	75	Pipestone	Pipestone

Site Name	Site #	County	Nearest Town
Portage Brook Overlook	27	Cook	Hovland
Read's Landing	107	Wabasha	Wabasha
Red Lake Peatland SNA	7	Beltrami	Waskish
Red Lake WMA	4	Beltrami	Williams
Rice Lake NWR/Kimberly WMA/ McGregor Marsh SNA	46	Aitkin	McGregor
Rice Lake State Park	111	Steele	Owatonna
Roscoe Prairie SNA	54	Stearns	Roscoe
Roseau River WMA	1	Roseau	Roseau
Salt Lake WMA	63	Lac qui Parle	Marietta
Sand Dunes State Forest/Uncas Dunes SNA	59	Sherburne	Zimmerman
Sand Prairie WMA	56	Sherburne	St. Cloud
Sax-Zim Bog	34	St. Louis	Zim-Sax
Schaefer Prairie	67	McLeod	Glencoe
Seven Mile Creek County Park	73	Blue Earth	Mankato
Sharp-tailed Grouse Dancing Grounds	25	Carlton	Kettle River
Sharp-tailed Grouse Dancing Grounds	39	St. Louis	Cook
Sheperd's Marsh (Upper Miss. NWR)	120	Houston	LaCrescent
Sherburne NWR	58	Sherburne	Zimmerman
Sibley State Park	65	Kandiyohi	New London
Silver Lake	113	Olmsted	Rochester
Springbrook Nature Area	83	Anoka	Fridley
Snively and Magney City Parks	37	St. Louis	Duluth
St. Croix State Park	50	Pine	Hinckley
Suomi Hills Recreation Area	31	Itasca	Marcell
Swamp River WMA	28	Cook	Hovland
Swan Lake	72	Nicollet	Nicollet
Swede's Forest SNA	68	Redwood	Sacred Heart
Talcot Lake WMA	76	Cottonwood	Dundee
Tamarac NWR	15	Becker	Detroit Lakes
Thief Lake WMA	5	Marshall	Thief River Falls
Thielke Lake WMA	61	Big Stone	Ortonville
Twin Lakes WMA	2	Kittson	Karlstad
T.S. Roberts Bird Sanctuary	87	Hennepin	Minneapolis
Uppgaard WMA	43	Crow Wing	Crosslake
Vermilion Lake	22	St. Louis	Tower
Walnut Lake WMA	80	Faribault	Wells
Washburn Lake Solitude Area	41	Cass	Outing
Weaver Bottoms (Upper Miss. NWR)	110	Wabasha	Winona
Whitewater State Park/WMA	115	Winona	St. Charles
Wild River State Park	60	Chisago	Almelund
Wolsfeld Woods SNA	86	Hennepin	Long Lake
Wood Lake Nature Center	88	Hennepin	Richfield
Zumbro Bottoms Forestry Unit	108	Wabasha	Wabasha

Species List

Resident Breeding Birds

These are the bird species believed to breed in Minnesota. However, it does include species for which there is only a single nesting record, or records of some antiquity. The list does not include birds observed only during migration. Species are listed in the traditional taxonomic order that is used in most bird field guides.

Common Loon
Pied-billed Grebe
Horned Grebe (T)
Red-necked Grebe
Eared Grebe
Western Grebe
American White Pelican (SC)
Double-crested Cormorant
American Bittern
Least Bittern
Great Blue Heron
Great Egret
Green Heron
Black-crowned Night-Heron
Yellow-crowned Night-Heron
Trumpeter Swan (T)
Canada Goose
Wood Duck
Green-winged Teal
American Black Duck
Mallard
Northern Pintail
Blue-winged Teal
Cinnamon Teal
Northern Shoveler
Gadwall
American Wigeon
Canvasback
Ring-necked Duck
Lesser Scaup
Common Goldeneye
Bufflehead
Hooded Merganser
Common Merganser
Red-breasted Merganser
Ruddy Duck
Turkey Vulture
Osprey
Bald Eagle (SC, Fed. status: T)
Northern Harrier
Sharp-shinned Hawk
Cooper's Hawk
Northern Goshawk
Red-shouldered Hawk (SC)
Broad-winged Hawk
Swainson's Hawk
Red-tailed Hawk
American Kestrel
Merlin
Peregrine Falcon (T, Fed status: E)
Gray Partridge
Ring-necked Pheasant
Spruce Grouse
Ruffed Grouse
Greater Prairie-Chicken (SC)
Sharp-tailed Grouse
Wild Turkey
Northern Bobwhite
Yellow Rail (SC)
King Rail (E)
Virginia Rail
Sora
Common Moorhen (SC)
American Coot
Sandhill Crane
Piping Plover (E, Fed. status: T)
Killdeer
American Avocet
Solitary Sandpiper
Spotted Sandpiper
Upland Sandpiper
Marbled Godwit (SC)
Common Snipe
American Woodcock
Wilson's Phalarope (T)
Franklin's Gull (SC)
Ring-billed Gull
Herring Gull
Caspian Tern

Key: E-endangered T-threatened SC-special concern

Common Tern (T)
Forster's Tern (SC)
Black Tern
Rock Dove
Mourning Dove
Black-billed Cuckoo
Yellow-billed Cuckoo
Eastern Screech-owl
Great Horned Owl
Northern Hawk-owl
Burrowing Owl (E)
Barred Owl
Great Gray Owl
Long-eared Owl
Short-eared Owl (SC)
Boreal Owl
Northern Saw-whet Owl
Common Nighthawk
Whip-poor-will
Chimney Swift
Ruby-throated Hummingbird
Belted Kingfisher
Red-headed Woodpecker
Red-bellied Woodpecker
Yellow-bellied Sapsucker
Downy Woodpecker
Hairy Woodpecker
Three-toed Woodpecker
Black-backed Woodpecker
Northern Flicker
Pileated Woodpecker
Olive-sided Flycatcher
Eastern Wood-Pewee
Yellow-bellied Flycatcher
Acadian Flycatcher (SC)
Alder Flycatcher
Willow Flycatcher
Least Flycatcher
Eastern Phoebe
Great Crested Flycatcher
Western Kingbird
Eastern Kingbird
Horned Lark
Purple Martin
Tree Swallow
N. Rough-winged Swallow
Bank Swallow
Cliff Swallow
Barn Swallow

Gray Jay
Blue Jay
Black-billed Magpie
American Crow
Common Raven
Black-capped Chickadee
Boreal Chickadee
Tufted Titmouse
Red-breasted Nuthatch
White-breasted Nuthatch
Brown Creeper
House Wren
Winter Wren
Sedge Wren
Marsh Wren
Golden-crowned Kinglet
Ruby-crowned Kinglet
Blue-gray Gnatcatcher
Eastern Bluebird
Mountain Bluebird
Veery
Swainson's Thrush
Hermit Thrush
Wood Thrush
American Robin
Gray Catbird
Brown Thrasher
Sprague's Pipit (E)
Cedar Waxwing
Loggerhead Shrike (T)
European Starling
White-eyed Vireo
Bell's Vireo
Solitary Vireo
Yellow-throated Vireo
Warbling Vireo
Philadelphia Vireo
Red-eyed Vireo
Blue-winged Warbler
Golden-winged Warbler
Tennessee Warbler
Orange-crowned Warbler
Nashville Warbler
Northern Parula
Yellow Warbler
Chestnut-sided Warbler
Magnolia Warbler
Cape May Warbler
Black-throated Blue Warbler

Key: E-endangered T-threatened SC-special concern

Yellow-rumped Warbler
Black-throated Green Warbler
Blackburnian Warbler
Pine Warbler
Palm Warbler
Bay-breasted Warbler
Cerulean Warbler (SC)
Black-and-white Warbler
American Redstart
Prothonotary Warbler
Ovenbird
Northern Waterthrush
Louisiana Waterthrush (SC)
Kentucky Warbler
Connecticut Warbler
Mourning Warbler
Common Yellowthroat
Hooded Warbler (SC)
Wilson's Warbler
Canada Warbler
Yellow-breasted Chat
Scarlet Tanager
Northern Cardinal
Rose-breasted Grosbeak
Blue Grosbeak
Indigo Bunting
Dickcissel
Rufous-sided Towhee
Chipping Sparrow
Clay-colored Sparrow
Field Sparrow
Vesper Sparrow
Lark Sparrow
Savannah Sparrow
Baird's Sparrow (E)
Grasshopper Sparrow
Henslow's Sparrow (E)
Le Conte's Sparrow
Nelson's Sharp-tailed Sparrow (SC)
Song Sparrow
Lincoln's Sparrow
Swamp Sparrow
White-throated Sparrow
Dark-eyed Junco
Chestnut-collared Longspur (E)
Bobolink
Red-winged Blackbird
Eastern Meadowlark
Western Meadowlark
Yellow-headed Blackbird
Rusty Blackbird
Brewer's Blackbird
Common Grackle
Brown-headed Cowbird
Orchard Oriole
Baltimore Oriole
Purple Finch
House Finch
Red Crossbill
White-winged Crossbill
Pine Siskin
American Goldfinch
Evening Grosbeak
House Sparrow

Mammals

Virginia opossum
Arctic shrew
Masked shrew
Smokey shrew (SC)
Hayden's shrew
Pygmy shrew
Water shrew
Northern short-tailed shrew
Least shrew (SC)
Eastern mole
Star-nosed mole
Little brown myotis
Northern myotis (SC)
Eastern red bat
Hoary bat
Silver-haired bat
Eastern pipistrelle (SC)
Big brown bat
Eastern cottontail
Snowshoe hare
White-tailed jackrabbit
Least chipmunk
Eastern chipmunk
Woodchuck
Franklin's ground squirrel
Richardson's ground squirrel
Thirteen-lined ground squirrel
Gray squirrel
Fox squirrel
Red squirrel
Northern flying squirrel
Southern flying squirrel

Key: E-endangered T-threatened SC-special concern

Northern pocket gopher (SC)
Plains pocket gopher
Plains pocket mouse (SC)
American beaver
Western harvest mouse
White-footed mouse
Deer mouse
Northern grasshopper mouse
Southern red-backed vole
Heather vole (SC)
Rock vole
Prairie vole (SC)
Meadow vole
Woodland vole (SC)
Common muskrat
Northern bog lemming (SC)
Southern bog lemming
Norway rat
House mouse
Meadow jumping mouse
Woodland jumping mouse
Common porcupine
Coyote
Gray (timber) wolf (SC, Fed. status: T)
Red fox
Gray fox
Black bear
Common raccoon
American pine marten
Fisher
Ermine
Long-tailed weasel
Least weasel (SC)
Mink
American badger
Eastern spotted skunk (T)
Striped skunk
Northern river otter
Mountain lion (SC)
Lynx
Bobcat
Elk (SC)
White-tailed deer
Moose

Reptiles

Snapping turtle (SC)
Common musk turtle
Wood turtle (T)
Common map turtle
False map turtle
Ouachita map turtle
Painted turtle
Blanding's turtle (T)
Smooth softshell (SC)
Spiny softshell
Six-lined racerunner
Five-lined skink (SC)
Prairie skink
Northern water snake
Brown snake
Redbelly snake
Plains garter snake
Common garter snake
Lined snake (SC)
Western hognose snake (SC)
Eastern hognose snake
Ringneck snake
Blue Racer (SC)
Smooth green snake
Rat snake (SC)
Fox snake
Gopher snake (SC)
Milk snake
Massasauga (E)
Timber rattlesnake (T)

Amphibians

Mudpuppy
Blue-spotted salamander
Tiger salamander
Eastern newt
Redback salamander
Four-toed salamander (SC)
American toad
Great Plains toad
Canadian toad
Northern cricket frog (E)
Cope's gray treefrog
Gray treefrog
Spring peeper
Chorus frog
Bullfrog
Green frog
Pickerel frog
Northern leopard frog
Mink frog
Wood frog

Key: E-endangered T-threatened SC-special concern

References & Resources

Maps

Official Minnesota Highway Map
Travel Information Center
250 Skyway Level
375 Jackson Street
St. Paul MN 55101
(612) 296-5029 (Twin Cities Metro Area)
(800) 657-3700 (U.S.)
(800) 766-8687 (Canada)

Map, travel and tourism information may be obtained at other Minnesota Travel Information Centers (TIC), as well as at many chamber of commerce offices throughout the state. Free.

PRIM (Public Recreation Information Maps)
MN Department of Natural Resources
500 Lafayette Road
St. Paul MN 55155-4040
(612) 296-6157 (Twin Cities Metro Area)
(800) 766-6000 (Outstate Minnesota)
Hearing impaired (612) 296-5484
(800) 657-3929 (Outstate)

PRIM maps, which divide the state into 51 Areas, give a comprehensive overview of governmental recreation facilities and opportunities. They are available through the DNR Gift Shop (612-228-9165), some map stores and larger sporting goods retailers. Cost at press time $4.95/each area.

DeLorme Minnesota Atlas & Gazetteer
DeLorme Mapping
P. O. Box 298
Freeport ME 04032
(207) 865-4171
The *DeLorme Atlas*, which divides the state into 95 grid blocks, provides detail down to the forest trail level. It is available at many bookstores nationwide. Cost at press time $16.95.

Minnesota Atlas—A Complete Guide to Public Lands & Water Accesses
John M. Hanson, 1990,
Adventure Publications
Cambridge MN 55008
Cost at press time $19.95.

Twin Cities Birding Map
1995, Little Transport Maps
P.O. Box 8123
Minneapolis MN 55408
Cost at press time $7.95.

Bird Checklists

Field Check List of Minnesota Birds
Minnesota Ornithologists' Union
J.F. Bell Museum of Natural History
University of Minnesota
10 Church Street S.E.
Minneapolis MN 55455-0104

Minnesota Books & Field Guides

Amphibians & Reptiles Native to Minnesota
Barney Oldfield & John J. Moriarty, 1994, U of Minnesota Press

A Birder's Guide to Minnesota
Kim R. Eckert, 1994,
Williams Publication

Birding Minnesota
Jay Michael Strangis, 1996,
Falcon Press

Birds in Minnesota
Bob Janssen, 1987,
U of Minnesota Press

Fishes of the Minnesota Region
Gary L. Phillips, Wm. Schmid, James Underhill, 1982, U of Minnesota Press

A Guide to Minnesota's Scientific & Natural Areas
1995, MN DNR Section of Wildlife, SNA Program MN Natural Heritage

Mammals of Minnesota
Evan B. Hazard, 1982,
U of Minnesota Press

Minnesota's Endangered Flora & Fauna
Ed. Barbara Coffin & Lee Pfannmuller, 1988, U of Minnesota Press

Minnesota's Geology
Richard W. Ojakangas & Charles L. Matsch, 1982, U of Minnesota Press

Minnesota Weatherguide Calendar
Tom Cousins, Freshwater Foundation

Minnesota's Natural Heritage-An Ecological Perspective
John R. Tester, 1995, U of Minnesota Press

The Nature Conservancy Preserve Guide
1994, TNC Minnesota Chapter

Northland Wildflowers-A Guide for the Minnesota Region
John B. & Evelyn W. Moyle, 1977, U of Minnesota Press

Orchids of Minnesota
Welby Smith, 1993, U of Minnesota Press

Parks & Wildlands-A Guide to 170 Special Places In & Around the Twin Cities
Kai Hagen, 1989, Nodin Press

Magazines, Newsletters, etc.

The Loon
Minnesota Ornithologists' Union
J.F. Bell Museum of Natural History
University of Minnesota
10 Church Street S.E.
Minneapolis MN 55455-0104

The Minnesota Volunteer
MN Department of Natural Resources
500 Lafayette Road
St. Paul MN 55155-4035

Better View Desired Newsletter
P.O. Box 162
Rehoboth NM 87322

"Binocular & Spotting Scope Buying Guide"
National Camera Exchange & Video
9300 Olson Memorial Highway
Golden Valley MN 55427

"A Visitor's Guide to the Fall Migration"
Hawk Ridge Nature Reserve
c/o Biology Department
University of Minnesota
Duluth MN 55812

The Computer Connection

Minnesota Birding Network
e-mail: MnBird@vax2.Winona.MSUS.edu
Web site: http://www.skypoint.com/members/dac/mnbird.html

Minnesota Ornithologists' Union (MOU)
e-mail: mou@biosci.cbs.umn.edu
Web site: http://biosci.cbs.umn.edu/~mou/

The Raptor Center
e-mail: raptor@umn.edu
Web site: http://www.raptor.cvm.umn.edu

MOU Birding Hotlines

Minnesota Statewide/Twin Cities Hotline
(612) 780-8890

Duluth & North Shore Hotline
(218) 525-5952

Organizations

National Audubon Society
(Minnesota Audubon Council)
26 E. Exchange Street-Suite 207
St. Paul MN 55101

Bird Clubs:
- Agassiz Audubon Society (Thief River Falls)
- Albert Lea Audubon Society
- Austin Audubon Society
- Bee-Nay-She Bird Club (Crow Wing County)
- Central Minnesota Audubon Society (St. Cloud)
- Cottonwood County Bird Club

- Duluth Audubon Society
- Fargo-Moorhead Audubon Society
- Grand Forks (ND) Audubon Society
- Hiawatha Valley Bird Club (Winona)
- Jackson County Bird Club
- La Crosse (WI) Audubon Society
- Lakes Area Bird Club (Detroit Lakes)
- LeSueur Valley Bird Club
- Mankato Bird Club
- Minneapolis Audubon Society
- Audubon Chapter of Minneapolis
- Minnesota River Valley Audubon Club (Bloomington)
- Mississippi Headwaters Audubon (Bemidji)
- Owatonna Audubon Society
- Rice County Bird Club
- Roseville Bird Club
- St. Paul Audubon Society
- Upper Hiawatha Valley Audubon (Red Wing)
- White Pines Audubon (Pine County)
- Wilderness Heritage Audubon (Grand Rapids)
- Wild River Audubon Society (Chisago County)
- Zumbro Valley Audubon Society (Rochester)

Hawk Ridge Nature Reserve
Duluth Audubon Society
c/o Biology Department
University of Minnesota
Duluth MN 55812

Minnesota Herpetological Society
J.F. Bell Museum of Natural History
University of Minnesota
10 Church Street S.E.
Minneapolis MN 55455-0104

Minnesota Ornithologists' Union (MOU)
J.F. Bell Museum of Natural History
University of Minnesota
10 Church Street S.E.
Minneapolis MN 55455-0104

The Nature Conservancy-MN Chapter
1313 5th Street S.E.-Suite 320
Minneapolis MN 55414

Nongame Wildlife Program
Department of Natural Resources
Box 7
500 Lafayette Road
St. Paul MN 55155

Other Places to See Minnesota Wildlife

In addition to the many nature centers and governmental parks, forests, wildlife management areas (WMAs) and scientific & natural areas (SNAs):

Bell Museum of Natural History
University of Minnesota
10 Church Street S.E.
Minneapolis MN 55455-0104

Como Zoo
Midway Parkway & Kaufman Drive
St. Paul MN 55103

International Wolf Center
1396 Highway 169
Ely MN 55731-8129

Minnesota Zoo
13000 Zoo Boulevard
Apple Valley MN 55124

The Raptor Center
University of Minnesota
1920 Fitch Avenue
St. Paul MN 55108

Wildlife Science Center
5463 W. Broadway
Forest Lake MN 55025

Lake Superior Zoo
7210 Fremont Street (off Grand Avenue)
Duluth MN 55807

Index of Selected Species

Birds	Sites
Wilson's Phalarope	3, 7, 8
Franklin's Gull	3, 5, 6, 78
Caspian Tern	42, 45, 47, 52, 116
Common Tern	3, 16, 38, 45, 47
Forster's Tern	3, 5, 6, 15, 52, 61, 64, 72, 78, 88, 101, 116
Black Tern	2, 3, 5, 6, 16, 30, 46, 47, 56, 61, 72, 78, 88, 111, 120
Northern Hawk-owl	1, 34, 46
Burrowing Owl	77
Great Gray Owl	1, 4, 7, 29, 34, 35
Snowy Owl	29, 34
Short-eared Owl	3, 7, 45, 53, 56, 62, 114
Boreal Owl	4, 29
Black-backed Woodpecker	4, 10, 12, 16, 34
Gray Jay	1, 7, 12, 23, 27, 28, 34, 35
Black-billed Magpie	1, 6
Common Raven	3, 28, 29
Boreal Chickadee	1, 4, 27, 28, 34, 35
Sprague's Pipit	13
Loggerhead Shrike	13, 14, 62–64, 68, 74
Blue-winged Warbler	94, 115
Black-throated Blue Warbler	29
Cerulean Warbler	73, 103, 115, 117, 119
Prothonotary Warbler	98, 115, 120
Hooded Warbler	94
Scarlet Tanager	3, 10, 12, 15, 17–19, 31, 41, 51, 57, 58, 60, 94, 99, 102, 105, 108, 119
Blue Grosbeak	77
Dickcissel	14, 69, 70, 75, 109
Lark Sparrow	6, 7, 109
Baird's Sparrow	13
Henslow's Sparrow	14, 42
LeConte's Sparrow	6–8, 13
Nelson's Sharp-tailed Sparrow	4, 6, 7, 46
Lincoln's Sparrow	11
Chestnut-collared Longspur	13
Bobolink	7–9, 13, 14, 20, 46, 54, 56, 62, 65, 67, 69, 70, 75–77, 84, 92, 114

MAMMALS	SITES
Richardson's Ground Squirrel	69
Timber Wolf	1–4, 11, 12, 15, 23, 24, 31, 34, 35, 41, 50
Black Bear	1–4, 10–12, 16, 17, 21–24, 29–31, 33, 34, 44–50, 58, 60, 82
Pine Marten	23, 29, 34
Fisher	4, 7, 10, 15, 16, 23, 24, 30
American Badger	8, 60
Northern River Otter	2, 3, 6, 11, 12, 15, 21, 23, 24, 26, 28, 30–32, 44, 46, 48, 50, 53, 60, 62, 64, 82, 85, 120
Moose	1, 2, 4, 5 ,6, 8, 9, 21, 22, 26–28, 35, 41
American Bison	77
Elk	5

REPTILES	
Wood Turtle	108
Blanding's Turtle	50, 53, 56–59, 70, 81, 84, 109, 117
Five-lined Skink	68, 119
Blue Racer	74
Lined Snake	77

The Minnesota Birding Network

MNBird is an unmoderated discussion group of those interested in Minnesota birds. Minnesota was the third state to have a computer network of birders. The group began in 1993 and currently has about 450 birders on-line, who are mostly from our state.

How the Birding Network is Used

If someone on the network writes a message about a recent birding excursion, the message lists birds seen and exact directions to the locations of anything unusual. The message is then sent to all of us within seconds.

Meet Other Birders

What a wonderful way to meet other birders-there are more than 450 of us, and growing. By its nature, birding is often a solitary pastime. But using your computer to share the passion with others is fun (especially in winter, or on rainy days).

Activities

We keep annual and seasonal lists of all the birds reported via the network. During the summer months, we collect nesting data. We have an ongoing feature called "Looking for...", in which experienced birders share ID tips as well as information on where and when in Minnesota to look for specific species. We have a membership list which includes e-mail address, home county, address and phone numbers of each participant. We are an affiliate club of Minnesota Ornithologists' Union (MOU).

Join Us Today!

To participate in MnBird, just send an e-mail message to:
MnBird-REQUEST@linux.winona.msus.edu
In the body (not the subject) of the message,
put the single-line command: subscribe

If you are an AOL or Compuserve subscriber, you may not be able to subscribe easily because you need to have something in the subject line. So you need to "fool" the subject line. Do this by hitting the space bar several times when you are on the subject line.

To Send Mail to the Group:

MnBird@linux.Winona.msus.edu
Note: Request is not in the address
Please sign your message giving your name,
e-mail address, and city/county/location.

Internet Web Site:

http://www.skypoint.com/members/dac/mnbird.html

Minnesota Office of Tourism

Minnesota Travel Information Centers (TIC)

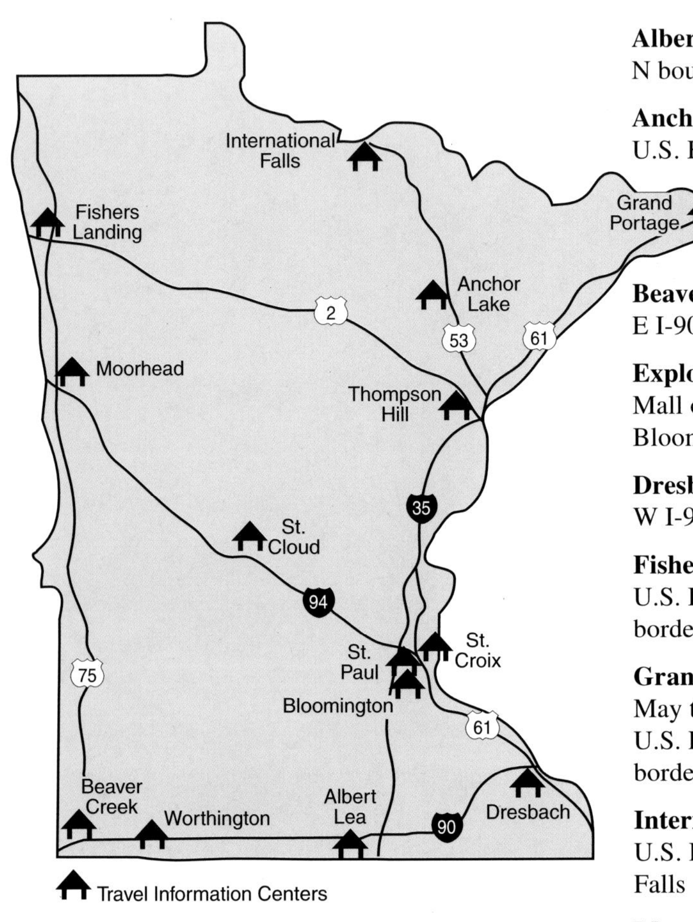

For Travel Information Call

(800) 657-3700 toll free

(612) 296-5029 Twin Cities

(800) 627-3529 V/TTY Relay Service for the Deaf

Fax: (612) 296-2800

Visit Our Internet Web Site

www.exploreminnesota.com

E-mail Address

explore@state.mn.us

Albert Lea TIC
N bound 1-35 at Iowa border

Anchor Lake TIC
U.S. Hwy 53 S of Eveleth

Beaver Creek TIC
E I-90 at SD border-Sioux Falls

Explore Minnesota USA Store
Mall of America
Bloomington

Dresbach TIC
W I-90 & Hwy 61 at WI border

Fisher's Landing TIC
U.S. Hwy 2, 10 mi E of ND border

Grand Portage TIC
May through October
U.S. Hwy 61, S of Canada border

International Falls TIC
U.S. Hwy 53 downtown Int'l Falls

Moorhead TIC
E bound I-94 at ND border

St. Cloud TIC
On U.S. Hwy 10, 3 mi SE of Jct. Hwy 23

St. Croix TIC
W bound I-94 at WI border

Thompson Hill TIC
I-35 at Jct. U.S. Hwy 2 Duluth

Worthington TIC
U.S. Hwy 59 & 60, 5 mi S of Worthington

Wild Bird Food Conservation Program

Look for this logo when you buy wild bird food in Minnesota!

This logo identifies wild bird food products from companies that are members of the Minnesota Wild Bird Food Conservation Program. These companies make regular donations to the Program based on their sales in Minnesota. These funds are used by the State of Minnesota to help preserve wild birds and their habitats-not just birds at feeders, but also the wild birds of forests, prairies and wetlands that do not visit bird feeders.

The Minnesota Wild Bird Food Conservation Program received $6100 in donations from 16 participating wild bird food manufacturers in 1996. These donations were matched by donations from private citizens and conservation groups up to a total of $60,000! This money was used to fund 13 wild bird conservation projects the following year. A total of $50,000 in private matching funds has already been received for 1998. If you wish to offer a matching donation to help the birds, call (612) 296-0700.

Teaming With Wildlife

Teaming with Wildlife is a national effort to create a funding source that will help preserve the nation's wildlife. It is based on helping wildlife—specifically the unhunted species referred to as nongame—in the same manner that hunters and anglers raise funds for the conservation of game species. Funds for game management are derived from a user fee/excise tax on the sale of equipment used by those persons to enjoy their sports.

Game fish and wildlife populations, for example, benefit from excise taxes on the sale of hunting and fishing equipment. Teaming with Wildlife is based on expanding this concept to equipment and supplies used for the enjoyment of wildlife, like binoculars, spotting scopes, field guides, bird food and feeders and related outdoor equipment.

This proposal is supported by a national coalition of over 2400 businesses and conservation groups that represent over 50 million Americans. In Minnesota, over 150 businesses and conservation groups have united to support this proposal because it will help preserve wildlife at a time that state or federal general fund taxes are no longer available to protect wildlife, and it will be good for tourism and businesses that depend on healthy wildlife populations for the sale and use of their products and services.

For more information on how you can help wildlife through this effort, contact the International Association of Fish and Wildlife Agencies, 444 North Capitol St. NW, Suite 544, Washington, D.C. 20001, or the Nongame Wildlife Program, DNR, 500 Lafayette Road, St. Paul, MN 55155.

Minnesota's Nongame Wildlife Program

The Minnesota Department of Natural Resources created the Nongame Wildlife Program in 1977 to manage and protect the state's wildlife species that are not traditionally hunted or harvested. Examples of nongame wildlife species are loons, bald eagles, trumpeter swans, eastern bluebirds, butterflies, mussels, frogs, toads, turtles, bats and songbirds. There are over 800 nongame species in Minnesota, compared to 110 game species.

NONGAME WILDLIFE PROGRAM • MINNESOTA DEPARTMENT OF NATURAL RESOURCES •

Since its creation 20 years ago, more than 600 conservation projects have been carried out, including acquisition of important nesting and migratory habitats for birds, regular surveys of hundreds of bald eagle nests and heron colonies, development of management guidelines for protection of sensitive woodland wildlife, protection and management of prairies and wetlands, restoration of peregrine falcons and trumpeter swans, educational efforts like Project Wild, publication of five books on how to help and enjoy wildlife, research on the life history and habitat requirements of rare species like Blanding's turtles and boreal owls, and management of the state's threatened and endangered wildlife like the bald eagle.

Among species that have received special efforts during the past 20 years are the bald eagle, trumpeter swan, peregrine falcon, piping plover, eastern bluebird, common tern, sandhill crane, great blue heron, common loon, Blanding's turtle, wood turtle, five-lined skink, great gray owl, boreal owl, prairie butterflies, bats, mussels and loggerhead shrikes.

Over 95 percent of the money that supports the Nongame Wildlife Program comes from the voluntary donations to the "Nongame Wildlife Checkoff" on state tax forms. These donations are extremely important to the survival of the state's wildlife because most other sources of general tax revenue and conservation funding are not available to help nongame wildlife. Only about one person in 25 remembers to help wildlife at tax time. Donations to the checkoff have been in decline since 1988, so your help is needed more than ever to help the wildlife that contributes so much to our enjoyment of Minnesota's outdoors.

Minnesota's Nongame Wildlife Program is considered to be one of the best in the nation. It has many achievements to show for the past twenty years, but continues to improve and adapt as threats to our wildlife change with time. With continuing public support, there can be many more wildlife success stories to share in the future.

Look for the Loon on your Minnesota tax forms, and give generously to help our state's wildlife!